Global Exchanges

GLOBAL EXCHANGES

Scholarships and Transnational Circulations in the Modern World

Edited by Ludovic Tournès and Giles Scott-Smith

berghahn
NEW YORK · OXFORD
www.berghahnbooks.com

First published in 2018 by
Berghahn Books
www.berghahnbooks.com

© 2018, 2023 Ludovic Tournès and Giles Scott-Smith
First paperback edition published in 2023

All rights reserved. Except for the quotation of short passages
for the purposes of criticism and review, no part of this book
may be reproduced in any form or by any means, electronic or
mechanical, including photocopying, recording, or any information
storage and retrieval system now known or to be invented,
without written permission of the publisher.

Library of Congress Cataloging-in-Publication Data
Names: Tournès, Ludovic, editor. | Scott-Smith, Giles, 1968- editor.
Title: Global exchanges: scholarships and transnational circulations in
   the modern world / edited by Ludovic Tournès and Giles Scott-Smith.
Description: New York, NY : Berghahn Books, 2018. | Includes bibliographical
   references and index.
Identifiers: LCCN 2017037366 (print) | LCCN 2017046094 (ebook) | ISBN
   9781785337031 (ebook) | ISBN 9781785337024 (hardback : alk. paper)
Subjects: LCSH: Educational exchanges--History--19th century. | Educational
   exchanges--History--20th century. | Scholarships--History--19th century. |
   Scholarships--History--20th century. | International
   education--History--19th century. | International education--History--20th
   century. | Higher education and state--History--19th century. | Higher
   education and state--History--20th century.
Classification: LCC LB2375 (ebook) | LCC LB2375 .E84 2018 (print) | DDC
   370.116/2--dc23
LC record available at https://lccn.loc.gov/2017037366

British Library Cataloguing in Publication Data
A catalogue record for this book is available from the British Library

ISBN 978-1-78533-702-4 hardback
ISBN 978-1-80073-919-2 paperback
ISBN 978-1-78533-703-1 ebook

https://doi.org/10.3167/9781785337024

Contents

List of Figures and Tables — viii
Acknowledgments — ix
List of Abbreviations — x

Introduction A World of Exchanges: Conceptualizing the History of International Scholarship Programs (Nineteenth to Twenty-First Centuries) — 1
Ludovic Tournès and Giles Scott-Smith

Part I. National and Imperial Power Politics

Chapter 1 The Politics of Scholarly Exchange: Taking the Long View on the Rhodes Scholarships — 33
Tamson Pietsch and Meng-Hsuan Chou
Appendix: Derek John de Sa — 46

Chapter 2 The Defeat of University Autonomy: French Academic Diplomacy, Mobility Scholarships and Exchange Programs (1880s–1930s) — 50
Guillaume Tronchet
Appendix: The French-Serbian Academic Exchange Agreement of 1916 — 60

Chapter 3 The Commonwealth University Interchange Scheme: Promoting Exchanges in a Changing World (1948–60) — 65
Alice Byrne
Appendix: Sir Hector Hetherington (1888–1965) — 75

Chapter 4 Students as Ambassadors: German–American Exchange Diplomacy during the 1980s — 79
Jacob S. Eder
Appendix: Hildegard Hamm-Brücher (1921–2016) — 89

Part II. International Understanding and World Peace

Chapter 5 Muscular Christian Exchanges: Asian Sports Experts and the International YMCA Training School (1910s–1930s)   97
Stefan Hübner
Appendix: Dong Shouyi (1895–1978)   108

Chapter 6 Managing Scientific Exchange in Interwar Germany: August Wilhelm Fehling and Rockefeller Foundation Fellowships   113
Judith Syga-Dubois
Appendix: Eva Flügge   122

Chapter 7 Wedges and Webs: Rockefeller Nursing Fellowships (1920–40)   127
Pierre-Yves Saunier
Appendix: Katarina Stipetic   137

Chapter 8 Fellowship Programs for Public Health Development: The Rockefeller Foundation, UNRRA and the WHO (1920s–1970s)   140
Yi-Tang Lin, Thomas David and Davide Rodogno

Chapter 9 New Missionaries for Social Development: The ILO Internship Program (1950–63)   156
Véronique Plata-Stenger
Appendix: Fresia Carballo de Mendoza   166

Part III. The Cold War: A Golden Age of Scholarship Programs

Chapter 10 The Fulbright Program and the Philosophy and Geography of US Exchange Programs since World War II   173
Lonnie R. Johnson
Appendix: The Long-Term Impact of the Fulbright Program. An Assessment by Bronislaw Marciniak   183

Chapter 11 Grassroots Diplomacy: Fighting the Cold War on the Family Farm with the International Farm Youth Exchange   188
Peter Simons
Appendix: Preparing for Farm Life Abroad   197

Chapter 12	Third World Students at Soviet Universities in the Brezhnev Period *Julie Hessler*	202
Chapter 13	US Exchange Programs with Africa during the Civil Rights Era *Hannah Higgin*	216
Chapter 14	Working on/Working with the Soviet Bloc: IREX, Scholarly Exchanges and Détente *Justine Faure* Appendix: Allen H. Kassof 241	231

Part IV. The Globalization Moment: New Geography and New Challenges

Chapter 15	American Foundations and the Challenge of Funding International Fellowship and Exchange Programs since 1970 *Patricia L. Rosenfield*	247
Chapter 16	Global Networks, Soft Power and the US Military *Carol Atkinson* Appendix: Kristin Lund 273	262
Chapter 17	American Fulbrighters in China (1979–2014) *Guangqiu Xu*	276
Chapter 18	Importing Barbarian Knowledge: The JET Program and the Development of Cultural Internationalism in Japan (1987–2014) *Jesse Sargent* Appendix: The JET Alumni Association 300	290
Chapter 19	New Actors of the Post-Cold War World (Europe, China, India): Toward a Genuine Globalization of Scholarship Programs *Ludovic Tournès*	305
Conclusion	150 Years of Scholarship Programs: Old Trends and New Prospects in the Global Landscape *Giles Scott-Smith and Ludovic Tournès*	322

Selected Bibliography	329
Web Resources	338
Index	341

Figures and Tables

Figure 1.1	Election constituencies of all Rhodes Scholars, 1902–2012	39
Figure 1.2	Female Rhodes Scholars, 1977–2012 (%)	42
Figure 1.3	Geographic mobility of Rhodes Scholars, 1913–83 (%)	43
Figure 1.4	Geographic mobility of US versus non-US Rhodes Scholars (%)	44
Figure 8.1	Number of fellowships in public health granted by the RF, 1915–45, and the WHO, 1947–73	148
Table 2.1	Serbian students in French universities, 1914–21	61
Tables 5.1–5.4	The BPE curriculum of 1920: Freshman, Sophomore, Junior and Senior	106–7

Acknowledgments

The editors wish to express their gratitude to the institutions that have supported this project since the contributors first shared their work with one another at the Global Studies Institute of the University of Geneva in December 2014: the Department of History, the Faculty of Letters, the Global Studies Institute, the Swiss National Fund, the Rectorate of Geneva and the Maison de l'histoire. They would also like to thank their colleagues and students who participated in 2014, especially Matthias Schulz (University of Geneva) and Davide Rodogno (IHEID, Geneva), who oversaw two presentation sessions. Finally, they would like to thank Laetitia Corbière (teaching assistant in history, University of Geneva) for having taken care of the event's material and technical organization.

 Abbreviations

ACLS	American Council of Learned Societies
AEGEE	Association des Etats Généraux des Etudiants de l'Europe
ASPAU	African Scholarship Program of American Universities
AUBC	Association of Universities of the British Commonwealth
BFS	Board of Foreign Scholarships
BGU	Belorussian State University
BPI	Belorussian Polytechnical Institute
CBYX	Congress-Bundestag Youth Exchange Program
CCNY	Carnegie Corporation of New York
CGSC	Command and General Staff College
CIES	Council for International Exchange of Scholars
CLAIR	Council of Local Authorities for International Relations
CPSU	Communist Party of the Soviet Union
CRO	Commonwealth Relations Office
CSFP	Commonwealth Scholarship and Fellowship Plan
CU	Bureau of Educational and Cultural Exchange
CUIS	Commonwealth University Interchange Scheme
EPTA	Expanded Program of Technical Assistance
FAFP	Foreign Area Fellowship Program
FAO	Food and Agriculture Organization
FDP	Freie Demokratische Partei
FF	Ford Foundation
FLP	Foreign Leader Program
GDR	German Democratic Republic
IECE	Institute of East-Central Europe
IFYE	International Farm Youth Exchange
IHB	International Health Board
IHD	International Health Division
IIE	Institute of International Education
IILS	International Institute for Labor Studies
ILC	International Labor Conference
ILO	International Labor Organization
IMET	International Military Education and Training

IOC	International Olympic Committee
IREX	International Research and Exchanges Board
IRS	Internal Revenue Service
IUCTG	Inter-University Committee on Travel Grants
IVLP	International Visitor Leadership Program
IVP	International Visitor Program
JET	Japan Teaching and Exchange Program
JETAA	Japan Teaching and Exchange Program Alumni Association
LLP	Lifelong Learning Program
LNHO	League of Nations Health Organization
LoN	League of Nations
LSRM	Laura Spelman Rockefeller Memorial
NATO	North Atlantic Treaty Organization
NDU	National Defense University
NEH	National Endowment for the Humanities
OEEC	Organisation for European Economic Cooperation
OFAC	Office of Foreign Asset Control
ONUEF	Office National des Universités et Ecoles Françaises
OPEC	Organization of Petroleum Exporting Countries
OSF	Open Society Foundation
PRC	People's Republic of China
PUMC	Peking Union Medical College
RF	Rockefeller Foundation
ROC	Republic of China
SFIO	Section Française de l'Internationale Ouvrière
SSRC	Social Science Research Council
UN	United Nations
UND	University of Notre Dame
UNESCO	United Nations Educational, Scientific and Cultural Organization
UNFICYP	United Nations Peacekeeping Force in Cyprus
UNICEF	United Nations International Children's Emergency Fund
UNRRA	United Nations Relief and Rehabilitation Administration
USIA	United States Information Agency
USICA	United States Information and Communications Agency
WHO	World Health Organization
YMCA	Young Men's Christian Association

Introduction

A WORLD OF EXCHANGES
Conceptualizing the History of International Scholarship Programs (Nineteenth to Twenty-First Centuries)

Ludovic Tournès and Giles Scott-Smith

In 1986, Robert Marjolin, a former militant at the Section Française de l'Internationale Ouvrière (SFIO) in the early 1930s, and later Secretary General of the Organisation for European Economic Cooperation (OEEC) and Vice-President of the European Commission, stated in his autobiography the importance of the year he spent in the United States in 1932–1933 at Yale University under a scholarship granted by the Rockefeller Foundation:

> What can be said of the effect of this American stay upon me? It was above all a liberation. Less than two years before, I was an ordinary employee in a stockbroker in Paris, locked up in a narrow frame, without any perspective. Suddenly I was thrown into an environment over which reigned great professors whom I venerated and who treated me as an equal. Above all, I was learning something new every day. I had an impression of being continuously enriched ... When I made contact with the United States, it was not, at first, without a certain reservation ... This reservations soon vanished ... My ideas, not only about America, but about the world in general, were shaped during this stay ... Though they were not coherent yet, they had something in common: a deep admiration for the United States, which accompanied me for the rest of my life, and is still part of me today. It is one of the most intimate components of my thought, which, I am sure, will never disappear.[1]

This text tells us a lot about the role played by scholarships of any kind in the formative years and professional itineraries of generations of students, teachers, researchers, businessmen, politicians, journalists and many other professions all around the world. However, the study of scholarships and their historical development has hardly been addressed by historians. The purpose of this book is to redress that gap.

The State of the Art

In the contemporary world, social circulation via scholarship programs is so common that one does not realize how novel they were at the time of their introduction in the second half of the nineteenth century. The diversity of scholarships makes an all-inclusive definition almost impossible, and so for the purposes of this book they refer to official initiatives by individuals and/or institutions for organizing and structuring regular transnational circulations over a period of time, with some form of learning as the principal goal. This encompasses everything that would also normally be referred to under exchanges and fellowships. Scholarships of one kind or another, especially in the academic world, have existed since the Middle Ages, yet their institutionalization only began just over a century ago. Since then, the number of programs has expanded throughout the world, the most well-known being the Rhodes Scholarships, Erasmus, Fulbright and, more recently, Confucius. These represent a vast circulation of people and knowledge, yet, despite their obvious relevance for international relations, the field has so far not received the historical attention it deserves. Scholarship programs have rarely been taken as a topic worthy of investigation. Whereas the social sciences (in particular, psychology, sociology, communication research, business administration and pedagogy) have produced a wealth of data on utility, transfer, impact and best practices, it is only with the increasing popularity of transnational and global history that historical studies have come into vogue.

Until recently, results from historical research were somewhat superficial, hagiographic and Western-centric. First, they were superficial because historians have often only mentioned exchanges in passing and with little analytical depth. The topic falls between different fields of enquiry: international relations, history of science, cultural history, history of higher education, history of philanthropy and migration history. For a long time, none of these fields considered scholarship programs as a topic of serious study in their own right. The history of international relations has generated important work on (predominantly US) cultural diplomacy, and there is a wealth of scholarship on international education, but there is little on the actual history and practice of exchanges themselves.[2] The recent Cold War anthologies from Oxford and Cambridge do not address them in any detail.

The *Global Interdependence* anthology refers to "official exchange programs" only in passing. The *Palgrave Dictionary of Transnational History* refers to scholarships in half a page under the heading of "Temporary Migrations."[3] Public diplomacy studies often follow Nicholas Cull's typology, which sets scholarships apart as a separate field of study, but rarely does public diplomacy research actually devote them sufficient attention.[4] The history of philanthropic organizations (the most important funders of scholarship programs) has been well-covered, but this has tended to concentrate on the institutional development and strategic outlook of the large American foundations, with little attention for the intricacies and microhistories of their scholarship and fellowship programs.[5] The history of science has mostly concentrated on the institutionalization of disciplines and the construction of national scientific policies.[6] Migration history has mostly focused on mass movements of people and the social and economic causes and consequences of this, whereas scholarship programs, with their temporary character and comparatively small numbers, have remained outside its scope, with a few exceptions.[7] In the field of cultural and intellectual history, important contributions have focused on transnational networks of academics and experts, especially in the first half of the twentieth century,[8] but they have not specifically addressed the contribution of scholarship programs.

Second, previous historical research have tended to be hagiographic, because many studies have been written by actors involved in exchanges celebrating the history and impact of their respective programs. This is particularly clear as regards those works covering the Fulbright Program, where archive-based (critical) studies are only now emerging.[9] "Success" has often been measured in terms of the great careers of former grantees, the Nobel Prizes won, and the numbers of heads of state or university professors who participated. The list is indeed impressive: J. William Fulbright, Dean Rusk and Walt W. Rostow were Rhodes scholars; Swedish economist Gunnar Myrdal and French biologist Jacques Monod were Rockefeller fellows; American composer Philip Glass and Spanish politician Javier Solana were Fulbright scholars; British Prime Ministers Margaret Thatcher and Tony Blair, and French journalist Jean-Jacques Servan-Schreiber were Foreign Leader Program grantees. Yet how did these programs contribute to their success, if at all? How far can we generalize from these high-profile cases that all participants on these programs benefit from career-enhancing outcomes?

Third and finally, previous historical research has largely been Western-centric, with many of the studies so far produced concentrating on programs run by European and North American actors, whereas significant examples also exist elsewhere. India's Technical and Economic Cooperation Programme, which has been active since 1964, is one such model of South–South cooperation in this field. Circulations within the communist world were also extensive, including countries like Mongolia and North Korea.[10] Yet research on these areas remains scarce. More recently, universities and sites of religious learning in the Arab world, and particularly Saudi Arabia, have drawn a significant number of participants, and studies of this intellectual migration (and the patronage that encourages and supports it) are necessary for the future.[11] In this sense, this book does not claim to be comprehensive. There are plenty of official exchanges and circulations that still need to be investigated. Instead, it provides a template for understanding the first century of official scholarship by covering the principal conduits of circulation and their organizational nodes. These stemmed predominantly from European imperial networks and, later, their variants as practiced by the United States, China and the European Union (EU). In doing so, the global scale of knowledge circulation via scholarships and exchanges can be brought into focus as the central hubs of this circulation shift over time, from European imperial metropolises to superpower capitals to new centers of power in the twenty-first century.

A New Framework of Analysis

In this context, there is valuable scope for rethinking the history of scholarships as a unique subject area that opens up access to dense networks of knowledge and cultural transfer between regions over many decades, some of which have never been brought into focus before.[12] Until recently, most studies of scholarships have been constructed around two different epistemological perspectives. First (and mostly composed of the hagiographic works mentioned above), the programs are studied through an institutional perspective and seen as success stories. Second, programs are considered as instruments of (especially American) soft power. Yet neither of these perspectives has caught the complex nature of scholarships, because they both tend to interpret them in terms of simple success or failure, using famous grantees and statistics per country or area as unique indicators.

A broader and deeper perspective is therefore required to consider scholarship programs as a specific object of interest linked to technical, political, social, cultural and economic developments. For this, the actors involved—both as administrators and participants—are the prime targets of investigation. As Patricia Clavin has rightly stated, "transnationalism, despite its early identification with the transfer or movement of money and goods, is first and foremost about people: the social space that they inhabit, the networks they form and the ideas they exchange."[13] It is exactly the human dimension and the human connections that this book wants to bring more into focus. Many of the chapters devote attention to personal itineraries and experiences, and significant examples of scholars, program administrators and alumni associations have been highlighted.

Historians now have the possibility to elaborate a holistic, multifaceted analysis of scholarship programs, combining insights on individual itineraries with the developing interests of institutions, in the context of changing local, national and global trends. Transnational history now offers many examples of the structural role of circulations in shaping knowledge, practice and politics on a global scale.[14] The trajectory of scientific, social scientific and humanities disciplines through the twentieth century are now well-documented.[15] Theoretical frameworks for analyzing the conditions of production, legitimation and circulation of knowledge exist.[16] The recent historiography of philanthropic foundations has dissected the modus operandi of these major actors of scholarship programs in coproducing and circulating knowledge and practices together with local actors, thanks to a policy combining worldwide strategy and on-the-spot action.[17] Cultural history has for a long time been investigating the coproduction and appropriation of knowledge and practices.[18] Anthropological and sociological studies have shown how contemporary cultures were forged through complex articulations between the global and the local, and how they have continued to be "open spaces" in permanent reconfiguration through transnational circulations.[19]

The goal is therefore to analyze how scholarships shaped career paths, disciplines, institutions and national cultures, and how they have in turn been shaped by them, combining a top-down approach centered on institutions with a bottom-up approach centered on actors. This will insert scholarship programs into the construction and circulation of knowledge through the twentieth century, which up till now has been a significant lacuna. It highlights the global circulation of individuals as bearers of knowledge on a large scale as a distinctly twentieth-century phenomenon, their experience testing our frameworks and categories of understanding "progress" and change.[20] According to this framework, historical studies on scholarship should focus on four main dimensions.

How Scholarship Programs Function

The first is the technical and administrative dimension, in order to address the diversity of scholarship programs. The first field of activity that comes to mind is academic networks, forming as they do the mainstay of scholarship programs since the late nineteenth century. But this is only part of the picture; many other institutions have been involved. Governmental bureaucracies, the military, international organizations and private institutions, each with their own specific goals, have contributed to the scholarship landscape, and several examples are covered in the following chapters. In theory, there seems to be a clear division between privately and publicly funded programs, but in practice they tend to overlap. Funding for both often comes from diverse sources, and both public and private institutions actually organize the programs and host the grantees. Claiming to distinguish between "public" and "private" programs is therefore not always a pertinent basis for analysis, since the public and private have merged and diverged depending on the local, national and international circumstances.

Scholarship programs are also diverse as regards their structure, goals and geographic scale. Some programs award scholarships to send students for study abroad, but do not organize a return of foreign students. Others are bilateral and organized according to an equal exchange, involving the institutionalization of the principle of reciprocity between two countries or two institutions. Then there are the multilateral programs that organize the transfer of grantees on a global scale. The age of scholars also differs from one program to another, with some catering for secondary school students, others for undergraduates, graduates, young or senior researchers or professionals. Gender is another important criterion, as some chapters in this book demonstrate, since some programs are exclusively for men or women, while others are mixed. As to their duration, programs can vary from one or two weeks to several months or years, in which case grantees can be considered as temporary migrants who go to another country for a set period of time. Finally, some programs focus on a specific field of activity such as health, labor or the armed forces, while others are more diverse in their coverage. This diversity makes it compulsory to have a precise knowledge about the organization, structure and day-to-day functioning of the programs, in order to appreciate their underlying "philosophy." A sufficient number of case studies is also required in order to draw appropriate conclusions on scholarships as a whole.

Scholarships and Politics

Second, there is the political dimension of scholarship programs. The creation and development of these programs is deeply embedded in transformations within global politics. The late nineteenth century saw the construction and affirmation of nation-states on the international scene, competing not only for political, military and imperial supremacy, but also for leadership in education, scientific research and economic development. Scholarship programs became part of this competition, with the international flow of students being from this moment onward a matter of actual political importance. Scholarships were a central part of cultural diplomacy, a new way for nation-states to reinforce their prestige by exporting the products of their national cultures and by attracting as many producers of knowledge as possible. This two-way process continued after World War I, when governments initiated national science policies in order to be prepared for a future war. It reached unprecedented dimensions during World War II, when the mobilization of scientific assets became central for ensuring victory. During the Cold War, the relevance of science and culture in international politics remained high in the context of the ideological struggle between the superpowers. Cultural diplomacy also became important for post-imperial powers looking to counterbalance a decline in international influence, and emerging powers aiming to assert themselves on the global stage. Post-Cold War scholarships have both (re)integrated intellectual pools on a trans-European or transatlantic scale and have seen the growth of alternative circuits centered on rising powers.

Scholarships are also implicated in global politics through the arrival of international organizations. From the 1920s onward, several organizations created and developed scholarship programs that differed in outlook from those run by nation-states, since they aimed at elaborating universal norms and fostering among their participants a sense of membership as part of a universal community. While the interwar period was the founding moment in this process, the intent continued through the Cold War and remains on the agenda of many agencies in the United Nations (UN) system. This has especially been the case in terms of UN activities in the Global South. This leads to important considerations concerning the extent to which they have succeeded in going beyond national interests and whether they have actually brought about new connections, practices or belief systems based on a "post-national" worldview.

A Long-Term Perspective

The third dimension of the study of scholarship programs is the analysis of grantees. The social, intellectual and institutional itineraries of the actors need to be engaged with over the longer term. So far, beyond the names of well-known grantees, what do we know about the many others who participated but never achieved fame? Where did they come from? What were their social and educational backgrounds? In what period of their lives did they benefit from the scholarship? Where did they go and what did they do? What influence did these travels have on their subsequent careers? Can we evaluate the influence of programs based on the itineraries of individuals or groups (academics, journalists, politicians, physicians or social scientists)? These questions are of fundamental importance if one wants to evaluate the in-depth and lasting impact, and move beyond vague generalizations or abstract statistics. Groundbreaking analysis along these lines has begun and can now be taken further.[21] This necessarily follows the grantees before, during and after their interactions with the scholarship experience.

(1) Before: tracing the historical significance of scholarships requires a knowledge of the background of grantees and an analysis of the selection process. Selection is a crucial aspect of all scholarships, and deserves particular attention, not only for who was selected but also for who was rejected because they did not meet the program criteria. Archives do not always hold information on rejected applications, but this issue is important to break the traditional narrative of institutions that focus on the winners (the famous grantees). Moreover, studying what happened prior to the selection is a way to avoid overestimating the role of the scholarship as the founding moment of a personal career. Programs tend to claim that they have provided the "added value" that shapes the profile of a successful grantee, but this bypasses the fact that the selection process already chooses profiles that fit with their goals.

(2) During: what grantees do during the time of their scholarship is of course of major importance. The influence of the host nation, the institution(s) they attend and the cultural exchange that takes place there can all be formative experiences. Scholarships can be a powerful factor for creating transnational networks and constructing and transferring knowledge. Yet what occurs during the scholarship often only appears in the memoirs of former scholars, in anecdotal form. The actual time of the scholarship itself is, paradoxically, often a blindspot in the history of scholarship programs.

(3) After: impact is probably the most difficult question, especially because it is often visible only ten, twenty or thirty years later, for the

career of the grantees, the institutions they visited, their home institution and the academic field in which they worked. What are the consequences of the grant on research tracks and career development? To what extent did scholarship programs contribute to the construction of transnational research networks? How did these networks develop and evolve over the longer term? How did this contribute to shaping particular disciplines or fields of study? In many cases, the relationship between the grantees and their host institutions does not end after the grant. Some benefit from several grants from the same institution, and former grantees are also frequently brought back as advisors. Sometimes they create alumni associations. There are multiple forms of long-term connections that provide clues for identifying the scale and scope of transnational networks. Such questions have so far mostly been neglected by sociological and political science studies on networks, which have tended to overlook their historical development to focus on structural aspects. Instead, historical studies of their origins, development and termination or transformation are needed.

Scholarships are also about Money

Lastly, scholarship programs are more than the circulation of culture, knowledge and ideas. Their history is also about economics, not only because they cost money to run (and so need to be justified in budgetary terms), but also because attracting students and researchers is considered a way to strengthen the national economy. Grantees spend money in their host countries. At the beginning of the twenty-first century, the sum injected by international students into the US economy was estimated at US$24 billion annually.[22] In her chapter, Carol Atkinson also reminds us that foreign governments spent more than US$447 million to send their personnel to US military schools in 2013. Scholarship programs are thus a good deal for host countries, because a significant part of the investment they make in awarding a scholarship is recouped, not to mention the added value of the grantees' expertise and input into host institutions as a whole.

The circulation of scholars can also lead to the opening of foreign markets. It is significant that in the early years of the Fulbright Program, grantees coming to the United States were provided with a small budget for purchasing material goods (clothes, books, music, etc.) in order to partake in the "American way of life," thus sowing the seeds of material desire for American products when returning home. During the Cold War, when the United States and the USSR competed in proselytizing their political and economic models, their economic assistance programs to postcolonial countries were always underpinned by the idea of converting the recipients to liberal or state-run economies. The productivity missions of the Marshall Plan that brought more than 25,000 European engineers and managers to the United States between 1948 and 1955 were explicitly organized to transplant American methods to Europe in order to develop commerce between the two continents.[23]

Knowledge itself can also be considered to hold an economic value. Academia has always been a form of market, and the term "knowledge-based economy" has gained a growing relevance in policy-making circles.[24] Countries compete in order to attract students and researchers. These economic impulses were already present when scholarships were established on a large scale in the late nineteenth century. The structure of the academic market was much more Eurocentric at that time, but no less competitive, as is noted in Guillaume Tronchet's chapter. Nowadays, academic rankings have become very important for university marketing. The Academic Ranking of World Universities (also known as the Shanghai Ranking) was created in 2003, the Times Higher Education World University Ranking in 2004, the Global University Ranking (a Russian system) in 2009 and so on. In 2014 the European Union launched its own program, U-Multirank, in accordance with the ambition formulated in 2000 by the Lisbon strategy to develop a "knowledge-based" economy.

Historical Epochs in Scholarship History

In addition to adopting a new framework of analysis, historical studies on scholarship programs should also deepen their reflections about periodization. Since the nineteenth century, four major historical trends have provided the context and impetus for scholarships to be developed.

National and Imperial Power Politics

The first trend occurred in the second half of the nineteenth century. As stated above, scholarships were created in the context of a strong affirmation of and rivalry between national/imperial powers. Organizing the mobility of elites for scientific and economic gain became an instrument of foreign policy. From the late nineteenth century onward, scholarship programs of various types, from natural sciences to military training to nursing education, were implemented by great powers in order to gain intellectual prestige and scientific strength. The importance of knowledge in international relations became evident from the World War I onward, not only because of the role of science in the elaboration of new weapons, but also because of the role of experts in determining the conditions of peace. From the Hague Conferences to today, experts have entered and shaped the political arena.[25]

The programs organized within the British Empire are a case in point. From the 1860s to the beginning of the twentieth century, a wide range of scholarships were established between Dominion universities in order to reinforce their connections with Great Britain. This created an "empire of scholars" that attracted the best colonial students to Britain and laid the framework for a global web of exchanges centered on British universities.[26] The Rhodes program (see the chapter by Tamson Pietsch and Meng-Hsuan Chou) is the most famous and perhaps most influential as a model, but it was neither the only nor the first one. Largely conceived as a one-way process to bring Dominion elites to the British metropole, this movement of intellectual talent from the imperial periphery to the center also contributed to the modernization of the university system in Britain.[27]

The other European great powers also created scholarship programs and organized academic mobility during the same period. Germany's prestigious academic system attracted students from all over Europe and the United States. France, following its defeat by Germany in 1870, initiated an ambitious form of "academic diplomacy," which, by the beginning of the 1920s, had propelled the country into a dominant position in the international academic market. In 1931, out of around 80,000 students studying abroad throughout the world, 17,000 went to France (see Guillaume Tronchet's chapter). This movement was organized by both public and private bodies (universities, Alliances françaises and local entrepreneurs) before the government began to coordinate through the Office National des Universités et des Écoles Françaises. Created in 1910, this bureau positioned scholarships as a matter of national policy.

The case of the United States is also interesting, since it demonstrates the importance of World War I in the evolution of scholarship geography. The United States was already sending and receiving students in the late nineteenth century, but it was not before the 1920s that it became a major player in the academic market. After World War I, a number of important scholarship programs were organized by universities and foundations (the Rockefeller Foundation and the Carnegie Corporation in particular), and new institutions such as the Institute of International Education and the Social Science Research Council were created to monitor and encourage these transactions. The foundations played a crucial role by both running their own programs and funding the institutions that oversaw them. US scholarship programs were both global in scope and run on a massive scale. Already by 1923, the United States was the second most popular destination in the world for foreign students, with 8,357 at American universities, second only in number to France. This rose to 10,000 by 1930, with 5,000 American students going abroad in that year.[28] By 1931, there were 457 university programs open to all categories of foreign students and researchers, mostly funded by private individuals, philanthropic organizations and/or businesses, while 320 programs were actively sending American students abroad.[29] In less than ten years, the United States had become one of the most important protagonists on the international academic scene.

After 1945, the growing imbalance between the US and European powers became more evident.[30] Scholarship programs were now more than ever instruments for strengthening national influence, but it was more difficult for European powers to successfully develop them. As Alice Byrne demonstrates in her chapter, British efforts to maintain ties with the former colonies did not succeed due to their reluctance to occupy a subservient position and their interest in developing their own policies. Byrne points out that the Commonwealth University Interchange Scheme was conceived during the interwar period, but was only launched in 1948, which led its hierarchical form of organization, with Britain at the center, to be totally out of sync with the conditions of the post-World War II period.[31] For France, the destruction of the war and the consequent difficult economic situation prevented the country from regaining its leading position in the scholarship geography before the late 1950s. (West) Germany was a defeated nation and its educational system as a whole was discredited by the Nazi experience. But Germany did not give up on its ambitions, as demonstrated by the revival of the Humboldt Stiftung in 1953 and the global scope of its scholarship program.[32] The Congress-Bundestag Youth Exchange Program (see the chapter by Jacob S. Eder) is further evidence of the return of Germany to a significant place in scholarship networks, with its particular focus on building ties for the future.

Scholarship Programs, International Understanding and World Peace

A second major trend in the history of scholarship programs can be identified as the wave of internationalism. Indeed, from the 1910s onward, scholarship programs started to be used not only as instruments of national politics, but were also considered as a means for developing international cooperation and understanding. Internationalists considered the mobility of people and ideas as a way to promote peace through the emergence of an "international mind" resulting from repeated contacts between people of different countries and cultures.[33] The notion of international (or intercultural) understanding emerged during this period. This idea developed on both sides of the Atlantic. In France, French banker and philanthropist Albert Kahn created the Autour du Monde Scholarship Program in 1898, which sent French students and professors abroad to represent French culture and (with not a little chauvinism) to promote the "culture of mankind" as a whole.[34] Similar rhetoric was also employed by US philanthropic foundations such as the Carnegie Endowment for International Peace, which organized its first fellowship program in 1917 and promoted the norms of international law for resolving disputes, and the Rockefeller Foundation, whose officers were ardent promoters of internationalism.[35] The Rockefeller Foundation began its first scholarships in 1914 and expanded its influence in the 1920s with the Fellowship Program, which would generate more than 10,000 fellows up to 1970. In all these cases, internationalism and nationalism effectively merged, but nevertheless the tone of internationalism is a definite characteristic of the 1910s–1920s period.[36]

The internationalist credo was also used by organizations focused on youth. The Young Men's Christian Association (1844) and the Student Volunteer Movement (1886) promoted the mobility of young people throughout the world as a way to evangelize non-Christians. In order to achieve this goal, they created worldwide organizations such as the World Alliance of YMCAs, with multiple local sections through which the circulation of grantees could be organized. The scout movement was structured on the same pattern, and by the 1920s, Rotary International and the Lions Club were also organizing youth mobility, a trend that has continued until today. As Stefan Hübner's chapter shows, students awarded a YMCA scholarship were trained at Springfield College on the condition that they would spread the Association's philosophy following their return to their home country. This ensured that the YMCA would spread its model abroad, but it also allowed national sections to construct their own methods under their own leadership that did not simply replicate the American version. This method had several advantages: it reduced costs with fewer YMCA officers sent abroad; it spread influence through US-trained ambassadors who possessed more local credibility; and it was a way to avoid accusations of imperialism by anticolonial movements that were increasingly active in the countries where the YMCA was present.

The Rockefeller Foundation Fellowship Program best exemplifies the internationalist credo (and the notion of scholarships as a form of global circulation). Based on the Rhodes Scholarships, it was extended to the whole world, and although the United States was the central node of the program, it was not the only destination for grantees. The chapters by Judith Syga-Dubois and Pierre-Yves Saunier demonstrate how the foundation adopted specific selection criteria and stayed in contact with the fellows in order to keep updated on the realities they faced on the ground. The program also promoted connections between present, future and former fellows in order to encourage multigenerational transnational networks over time.

From the 1920s onward, a new type of actor entered the field of global mobility: international organizations (IOs). The League of Nations is paramount here. Soon after its creation, the League established programs to overcome national boundaries and rivalries, and to create the mutual understanding that was considered indispensable for maintaining world peace. There was also the motivation to encourage the standardization of international norms in various domains such as economic statistics, healthcare and disease control, and bibliographical methods. The Hygiene section of the League, in cooperation with the Rockefeller Foundation, organized multinational group study tours for public health officials from 1922 to 1937 for the exchange of ideas and methods.[37] Scholarships were from the beginning essential instruments of IO policy, developing approaches that are still in use by UN agencies today: individual scholarships; collective study tours; "problem-solving" conferences between grantees; training courses; and technical assistance missions. In 1943 the newly created United Nations Relief and Rehabilitation Administration (UNRRA) organized a fellowship program for public health officers in order to assist the reconstruction of war-devastated countries. This was continued by the World Health Organization (WHO) Fellowship Program after World War II (see the chapter by Yi-Tang Lin, Thomas David and Davide Rodogno). From 1948 to 2014, the WHO awarded grants to over 1,000 fellows per year, with the total number reaching 120,000 for that period. Other UN agencies have also created scholarship programs, such as UNESCO and the International Labor Organization (see the chapter by Véronique Plata-Stenger). Scholarships are therefore an important chapter in the history of international organizations, not only because of the numbers involved, but also because the organized global mobility of people and ideas has always been a founding principle of these organizations.

One other important characteristic of the internationalist moment is the notion of exchange as reciprocity. The early programs were not conceived to exchange students, but to demonstrate national prowess and strength. The notion of reciprocity appeared during and immediately after World War I (see the chapter by Guillaume Tronchet) and following the war, many bilateral exchanges were created. In the case of the United States, the Institute of International Education (IIE) created bilateral programs with France (1921), Czechoslovakia (1922), Germany (1924), Hungary (1925), Switzerland (1926), Austria and Italy (1929), Spain (1930) and Argentina (1931). These bilateral programs were administered either by universities, the IIE or binational foundations, as was the case with the Commission for the Relief in Belgium Educational Foundation (1919) and the China Foundation for the Promotion of Education and Culture, created in 1925 by the Chinese government with the remaining funds from the indemnity due to the United States after the Boxer Rebellion.[38]

The Cold War: A "Golden Age" of Scholarship Programs

The third moment in the history of scholarship programs is the Cold War, which can be considered a golden age due to the large-scale American and Soviet programs used to promote their socioeconomic and political models across the globe. More than ever, scholarship programs were instruments of national power politics, but the novelty of the Cold War moment is that they were part of polarized strategies developed on a global scale by two superpowers fighting to impose their respective models. Both tried (and partly succeeded) to organize, control and benefit from the flow of scholarship program laureates to an unprecedented degree. In a sense, this was a form of ultra-politicization of scholarship programs. The US programs are better known than their Soviet counterparts, with the Fulbright and Foreign Leader Programs among the most important examples of US cultural diplomacy on a global scale.[39] Knowledge for, of and as global power became central to superpower status.[40] Between 1948 and 1975, 39,000 US Fulbright grantees went abroad and 78,000 from 110 countries went to the United States.[41] These American programs had two key goals: first, to strengthen the ties between the United States and its allies by developing a sense of community through the circulation of people and ideas; second, to use these channels to internationalize American opinion and promote understanding among American citizens of their place in the world (see the chapters by Lonnie R. Johnson and Peter Simons). From the late 1950s onward, various scholarship channels were used to establish ties with the communist world. From 1973, the Fulbright Program was also extended to the Soviet Union, which opened up the possibility of introducing liberal ideas into Soviet society. Between 1966 and 1991, the Fondation pour une Entraide Intellectuelle Européenne, funded by the Ford Foundation, awarded 2,536 fellowships to East European artists, writers, academics, translators, journalists and intellectuals to enable them to undertake short periods of study, research and conference attendance in the West. The grantees were often Polish, Romanian and Hungarian, and came predominantly to France, West Germany and Britain.[42] The IREX program (see the chapter by Justine Faure) also contributed to the formation of transnational networks that crossed the East–West divide. As Cold War historians are increasingly demonstrating, that divide was permeable, and the complexity of these two-way relationships ensures that simplistic notions of democratic ideas flowing eastwards are mistaken. On the Soviet side (see the chapter by Julie Hessler), major investments were also made to use scholarships for the purpose of fostering socialist unity, particularly with the postcolonial world. The Lumumba University in Moscow became an international hub for those from the Global South seeking alternative paths to development based on equality.[43]

However, it would be simplistic to consider that the Cold War programs were merely a product of the political and ideological superpower struggle. As we have seen, the genealogy of these programs can be traced back to the interwar years and the rise of the United States (and the Soviet Union) as "beacons of progress" in the global arena. This allows us to use scholarships and their networks as a way to view the Cold War differently. The Fulbright Program may have been launched in 1946, at the prime moment of US dominance, but it drew heavily on the interwar experience. It was based on the principle of reciprocity and thus on prewar internationalist culture, and its administrative organization (and financial formula) was based on that of the binational foundations from the aftermath of World War I. As with the Commission for the Relief in Belgium Educational Foundation, the creation of the Fulbright Program was a pragmatic way to use US assets located abroad without losing money in the process of repatriation and exchange. The Fulbright was also geared toward training local leaders, an approach practiced and perfected in the interwar years by the Rockefeller Foundation Fellowship Program and the YMCA. Finally, the Fulbright Program was partly based on the concept of technical assistance. Rockefeller fellowships had already pioneered this with the aim to assist in the reform and modernization of public health and medical education around the world,[44] and the same mentality was adopted by UNRRA fellowships from 1943 to 1947, before the first generation of US Fulbright grantees went abroad to teach agronomics, public health, city planning and tropical medicine. In the Philippines, following independence in 1946, American grantees were also invited to act as technical advisors in order to help restructure the local education system at the secondary, tertiary and vocational levels.[45] The Fulbright Program was therefore a synthesis of different models of scholarship programs practiced before World War II. Its bilateral administrative organization made it very adaptable to different national contexts, another reason for its success beyond the attractiveness of US higher education and the money it had at its disposal.[46]

The Globalization Moment: New Geography and New Challenges

From the 1970s onward, the Cold War framework of scholarship programs has undergone a gradual transformation and the geography of transnational circulations has entered a new phase. To begin with, there has been a transformation in American policy, even before the collapse of the Communist Bloc. From the 1970s to the beginning of the twenty-first century, there has been a relative retreat of the United States from the landscape of scholarship programs. There are several reasons for this. Lonnie R. Johnson's chapter emphasizes the impact of President Nixon and the considerable decrease of federal funding for the Fulbright Program; this coincided with growing international criticism of the war in Vietnam and the relative decline of US soft power during the 1970s as a whole. But the weakness of scholarship programs was also a consequence of US domestic controversies: Patricia L. Rosenfield's chapter explains the causes and consequences of the 1969 Tax Reform Act, which led to the decline of some existing scholarship programs and certainly prevented a number of foundations from creating new ones, and how the new rules passed after 11 September 2001 have considerably increased the administrative burden for foundations managing scholarship programs. Additionally, new approaches to evaluation have tended to emphasize short-term results, in contrast to the long-term philosophy that was the cornerstone of foundation policy since the interwar period. Finally, the evolution of the geopolitical context undermined the argument for scholarship programs. The end of the Soviet threat weakened the perceived need to justify a strong cultural diplomacy, especially with a critical Republican-controlled Congress after 1994. However, the attack on the World Trade Center on 11 September 2001 led to another reorientation and the co-optation of all forms of public diplomacy under a counterterrorism imperative. Funding was increased, but so were concerns about openness and reciprocity. In contrast, national security interests have seen the United

States consolidate its role in military programs (see the chapter by Carol Atkinson).[47] While this does not mean that the United States has replaced academic scholarships with military programs, the growth of the latter has demonstrated how this country now concentrates more on security matters than on intellectual cross-fertilization with the rest of the world.

The next transformational development in the contemporary world has been the emergence of new actors on the scene. China is a case in point: following the isolationist radicalism of the Cultural Revolution and Mao Zedong's death, the rise to power of Deng Xiaoping saw China turn positively toward international exchange. The US–China Fulbright Program was revived in 1979, thirty years after its cancellation following the communist takeover, and it contributed greatly to the influx of Western ideas and educational methods during the 1980s. As the chapter by Guangqiu Xu argues, this fed into the rising desire for democratic reforms, and ultimately the tragic events of Tiananmen Square in 1989. More recently, in 2004, China's affirmation as a global power has seen the creation of the Confucius Institutes, a global network of language and cultural centers that use scholarships to expand Chinese influence abroad.

Likewise, other actors have emerged as major scholarship providers, as shown in the chapter by Ludovic Tournès. This is the case with the EU. Partly propelled by the end of the Cold War and the opening up of the European continent, the EU has pursued an ambitious but discreet cultural diplomacy campaign since the 1980s. In contrast to the elitism and professional focus of early twentieth-century scholarships, the Erasmus Program operates on a massive scale to generate, if not European citizens, at least a sense of community among the younger generations. In the context of global competition, it also seeks to enhance the intellectual influence of Europe. The case of the Erasmus Program is another sign that the history of scholarship programs entered a new phase before the end of the Cold War in 1989–91. Primarily an outgrowth of the Single European Act (1986) and launched in 1987, it grew spectacularly in the post-Cold War period, partly through the integration of the former communist countries in 1990, 1995, 2004 and 2007 (which brought both new candidates and new destinations), and also partly due to factors that accelerated the circulation of people in Europe, such as the deregulation of air traffic in 1997 and the growth of low-cost transport. With three million students and 350,000 professors and administrators having taken part between 1987 and 2013, the Erasmus Program has imposed itself as the most important scholarship program in history. Its goal is not only to strengthen the relationship between EU members in order to pave the way for a European identity, but also to improve competition with the United States and other new powers such as China in the so-called "knowledge-based economy" sectors. As Jose Manuel Barroso once said in a 2007 press conference, Europe is in a sense "the first non-imperial empire," pooling sovereignty and working toward the creation of a single socioeconomic and political Eurosphere. Erasmus has contributed greatly to that goal.[48]

There are many other examples of new actors in the scholarship scene. Japan is one of them, and Jesse Sargent's chapter confirms how scholarship programs are still today a way to strengthen national position in the international arena. India is another particularly interesting example (see the chapter by Ludovic Tournès), since this country's long tradition of creating scholarship programs only became visible in the international arena from the 1990s onward. One of the main reasons for the absence of this country in the existing literature on scholarship programs lies in the fact that most Indian programs are oriented toward the Asian world. But India, with its huge academic system, its ambitious scholarship policy and its rapid economic development, might become during the course of the twenty-first century one of the main destinations of scholars in the world.

The mushrooming of newcomers in the landscape of scholarship programs suggests that the story is not coming to an end. In 2000, 1.8 million students were studying in a country other than their own[49] (compared with the figure of 70,000 in the 1920s), and there are many reasons to think that this movement will continue in the following years. Scholarships and the networks they create are now a vast, global phenomenon. Whereas Western countries, especially the United States and Europe, have long dominated the field and will continue to hold considerable leverage in terms of quality and prestige, there is no doubt that the geography of scholarships has changed, and so have the circuits of exchange (see the Conclusion). It is striking to note that the technological revolution of the 1990s, and in particular the development of the Internet, has not stopped this expansive trend. Whereas many disgruntled commentators warned of the terrifying prospect of a world obsessed with forms of digital and virtual communication, in fact the circulation of people through scholarship programs has only increased. It remains to be seen how geopolitical developments in the 2000s, in particular the instability in the Middle East, the return of nationalist tensions and xenophobia to the Eurasian space, and the rise of China will influence this trend toward another period of growth of exchanges or, conversely, a cycle of "deglobalization."[50]

Ludovic Tournès is a professor of international history at the University of Geneva (Department of History and Global Studies Institute). His publications include *New Orleans sur Seine. Histoire du jazz en France* (Fayard, 1999), *L'argent de l'influence: Les fondations américaines et leurs réseaux européens* (Autrement, 2010), *Sciences de l'homme et politique: Les fondations philanthropiques américaines en France au XXe siècle* (Garnier, 2011, new ed. 2013) and *Les Etats-Unis et la Société des Nations (1914–1946): le système international face à l'émergence d'une superpuissance* (Peter Lang, 2015). He is also a member of the editorial board of *Monde(s): Histoire, espaces, relations*.

Giles Scott-Smith is Ernst van der Beugel Chair in the Diplomatic History of Transatlantic Relations since World War II at Leiden University, and Academic Director of the Roosevelt Institute for American Studies. From 2013 to 2016, he was Chair of the Transatlantic Studies Association. His publications include *Western Anti-Communism and the Interdoc Network: Cold War Internationale* (Palgrave Macmillan, 2012), *Networks of Empire: The US State Department's Foreign Leader Program in the Netherlands, France, and Britain 1950–70* (Peter Lang, 2008) and *The Politics of Apolitical Culture: The Congress for Cultural Freedom, the CIA, and Post-war American Hegemony* (Routledge, 2002).

Notes

1. Robert Marjolin, *Le travail d'une vie: Mémoires. 1911–1986* (Paris: Robert Laffont, 1986), 41–45.
2. Kenneth Osgood's excellent study of the Eisenhower years, *Total Cold War: Eisenhower's Secret Propaganda Battle at Home and Abroad* (Lawrence, KS: University Press of Kansas, 2006), only refers to the People-to-People program. Nicholas Cull's extensive history of the United States Information Agency (USIA) deliberately excludes specific attention for exchanges, despite mentioning them as a central element in US public diplomacy; see *The Cold War and the United States Information Agency: American Propaganda and Public Diplomacy, 1945–1989* (Cambridge: Cambridge University Press, 2009). Justin Hart's re-examination of the World War II foundations of US cultural diplomacy does not address the relevance of exchanges; see *Empire of Ideas: The Origins of Public Diplomacy and the Transformation of US Foreign Policy* (Oxford: Oxford University Press, 2013). For an attempt to link exchanges with international relations (IR) theory, see Giles Scott-Smith, "Mapping the Undefinable: Some Thoughts on the Relevance of Exchange Programs within International Relations Theory," *Annals of the American Academy of Political and Social Science* 616 (2008): 173–195.

3. See Akira Iriye and Pierre-Yves Saunier (eds), *The Palgrave Dictionary of Transnational History* (Basingstoke: Palgrave Macmillan, 2009); Melvin Leffler and Odd Arne Westad (eds), *The Cambridge History of the Cold War*, 3 vols (Cambridge: Cambridge University Press, 2012); Richard Immerman and Petra Goedde (eds), *The Oxford Handbook of the Cold War* (Oxford: Oxford University Press, 2013); Akira Iriye (ed.), *Global Interdependence* (Cambridge, MA: Belknap Press, 2014).
4. Notable exceptions are Giles Scott-Smith, *Networks of Empire: The US State Department's Foreign Leader Program in the Netherlands, France and Britain, 1950–1970* (Brussels: Peter Lang, 2008); Andreas Akerlund, *Public Diplomacy and Academic Mobility in Sweden: The Swedish Institute and Scholarship Programs for Foreign Academics, 1938–2010* (Lund: Nordic Academic Press, 2016).
5. A few authors have delved into the specifics of intellectual exchange via national case studies: see Ludovic Tournès, "Le réseau des boursiers Rockefeller et la recomposition des savoirs biomédicaux en France (1920–1970)," *French Historical Studies* 29(1) (2006): 77–107; Ludovic Tournès, *Sciences de l'homme et politique. Les fondations philanthropiques américaines en France au XXe siècle* (Paris: Editions des classiques Garnier, 2011); Inderjeet Parmar, *Foundations of the American Century: The Ford, Carnegie and Rockefeller Foundations in the Rise of American Power* (New York: Columbia University Press, 2012).
6. For an attempt to merge the two, see Giles Scott-Smith, "The Fulbright Program in the Netherlands: An Example of Science Diplomacy," in Jeroen van Dongen (ed.), *Cold War Science and the Transatlantic Circulation of Knowledge* (Leiden: Brill, 2015), 136–61.
7. See, for example, Vassiliki Papatsiba, "Student Mobility in Europe: An Academic, Cultural and Mental Journey? Some Conceptual Reflections and Empirical Findings," *International Perspectives on Higher Education Research* 3 (2005): 29–65.
8. Daniel Laqua (ed.), *Internationalism Reconfigured: Transnational Ideas and Movements between the World Wars* (London: I.B. Tauris, 2011); Heather Ellis and Simone M. Müller, "Educational Networks, Educational Identities: Connecting National and Global Perspectives," *Journal of Global History* 11(3) (2016): 313–19; Tomás Irish, "Scholarly Identities in War and Peace: The Paris Peace Conference and the Mobilization of Intellect," *Journal of Global History* 11(3) (2016): 365–86; Charlotte Lerg, "'We are No Teutomanics...' Cultural Diplomacy, the Study of German and the Germanic Museum at Harvard before the First World War," *Germanistik in Irland* 3 (2013): 43–54; Emily Levine, "Baltimore Teaches, Göttingen Learns: Cooperation, Competition and the Research University," *American Historical Review* 121(3) (2016): 780–823; Thomas Weber, *Our Friend "The Enemy": Elite Education in Britain and Germany before World War I* (Stanford, CA: Stanford University Press, 2008).
9. Work on the Fulbright Program has largely been institutional or anecdotal, but various detailed country studies are now available: Sachidananda Mohanty, *In Search of Wonder: Understanding Cultural Exchange: Fulbright*

Program in India (New Delhi: Vision Books, 1997); Frank Salamone (ed.), *The Fulbright Experience in Benin* (Williamsburg, VA: College of William and Mary, 1994); Jan C.C. Rupp, "The Fulbright Program, or the Surplus Value of Officially Organized Academic Exchange," *Journal of Studies in International Education* 3 (1999): 59–82; Guangqiu Xu, "The Ideological and Political Impact of US Fulbrighters on Chinese Students: 1979–1989," *Asian Affairs* 26(3) (1999): 139-57; Thomas König, "Das Fulbright in Wien: Wissenschaftspolitik und Sozialwissenschaften am 'versunkenen Kontinent,'" Ph.D. dissertation (Vienna: University of Vienna, 2008); Lorenzo Delgado Gomez-Escalonilla, *Westerly Wind: The Fulbright Program in Spain* (Madrid: LID Editorial Empresarial-AECID, 2009); Matt Loayza, "A Curative and Creative Force: The Exchange of Persons Program and Eisenhower's Inter-American Policies 1953–1961," *Diplomatic History* 37 (2013): 946–70; Alice Garner and Diane Kirby, "'Never a Machine for Propaganda?' The Australian-American Fulbright Program and Australia's Cold War," *Australian Historical Studies* 44 (2013): 117–33; Scott-Smith, "The Fulbright Program in the Netherlands."

10. Rachel Applebaum, "The Friendship Project: Socialist Internationalism in the Soviet Union and Czechoslovakia in the 1950s and 1960s," *Slavic Review* 74 (2015): 484–507.
11. Gilles Keppel, *Beyond Terror and Martyrdom: The Future of the Middle East* (Cambridge, MA: Belknap Press, 2008).
12. See Sarah Holloway and Heike Jöns, "Geographies of Education and Learning," *Transactions of the Institute of British Geographers* 37 (2012): 482–88.
13. Patricia Clavin, "Defining Transnationalism," *Contemporary European History* 14 (2005): 422.
14. See, for example, Daniel T. Rodgers, *Atlantic Crossings: Social Politics in a Progressive Age* (Cambridge, MA: Harvard University Press, 1998); Ian Tyrrell, *Reforming the World: The Creation of America's Moral Empire* (Princeton, NJ: Princeton University Press, 2010).
15. Dominique Pestre and John Krige (eds), *Science in the Twentieth Century* (Amsterdam: Harwood Academic Publisher, 1997); Michèle Lamont, Charles Camic and Neill Gros (eds), *Social Knowledge in the Making* (Chicago: University of Chicago Press, 2011).
16. See, for example, Pierre Bourdieu, "Le champ scientifique," *Actes de la Recherche en Sciences Sociales* 2–3 (1976): 88–104; Bruno Latour, *Science in Action: How to Follow Scientists and Engineers through Society* (Cambridge, MA: Harvard University Press, 1987).
17. Tournès, *Sciences de l'homme et politique*; Nicolas Guilhot (ed.), *The Invention of International Relations Theory: Realism, the Rockefeller Foundation and the 1954 Conference on Theory* (New York: Columbia University Press, 2011).
18. See, among others, Roger Chartier, *The Cultural Uses of Print in Early Modern France* (Princeton, NJ: Princeton University Press, 1987, trans. from French); Michel Espagne and Michael Werner (eds), *Transferts: Les relations interculturelles dans l'espace franco-allemand* (xviiie–xixe siècles) (Paris: Éditions Recherche sur les Civilisations, 1988).

19. Arjun Appadurai, *Modernity at Large: Cultural Dimensions of Globalization* (Minneapolis, MN: University of Minnesota Press, 1996); Roland Robertson, "Glocalisation: Time-Space and Homogeneity-Heterogeneity," in Mike Featherstone, Scott Lash and Roland Robertson (eds), *Global Modernities* (London: Sage, 1995), 26–44; Paul Gilroy, *The Black Atlantic: Modernity and Double Consciousness* (Cambridge, MA: Harvard University Press, 1993); Serge Gruzinski, *La pensée métisse* (Paris: Fayard, 1999); Serge Gruzinski, *Les quatre parties du monde: Histoire d'une mondialisation* (Paris: La martinière, 2004).
20. The itinerary of Albert O. Hirschman (former Rockefeller fellow) is a case in point; see Jeremy I. Adelman, *Worldly Philosopher: The Odyssey of Albert O. Hirshman* (Princeton, NJ: Princeton University Press, 2013).
21. See Heike Jöns, Elizabeth Mavroudi and Michael Heffernan, "Mobilising the Elective Diaspora: US-German Academic Exchanges since 1945," *Transactions: Institute of British Geographers* 40 (2015): 113–27.
22. Tara Sonenshine, "A Fulbright is Not a Political Football," *Huffington Post*, 26 September 2014, retrieved 22 March 2017 from http://www.huffingtonpost.com/tara-sonenshine/a-fulbright-is-not-a-poli_b_5890702.html?utm_hp_ref=impact&ir=Impact.
23. See Richard Kuisel, "L'American Way of Life et les missions françaises de productivité," *Vingtième siècle: Revue d'histoire* 17 (1988): 21–38; Jonathan Zeitlin and Gary Herrigel, *Americanization and its Limits: Reworking US Technology and Management in Postwar Europe and Japan* (Oxford: Oxford University Press, 2004).
24. For its origins, see "The Knowledge-Based Economy," OECD Report ODCE GD(96)102 (Paris, 1996), retrieved 22 March 2017 from https://www.oecd.org/sti/sci-tech/1913021.pdf.
25. Peter M. Haas, "Introduction: Epistemic Communities and International Policy Coordination," *International Organization* 46 (1992): 1–35.
26. Tamson Pietsch, *Empire of Scholars: Universities, Networks and the British Academic World 1850–1939* (Manchester: Manchester University Press, 2013).
27. Christopher Bayly, *The Birth of the Modern World: Global Connections and Comparisons 1780–1914* (New York: Wiley Blackwell, 2004).
28. George F. Zook, *Bulletin of the Bureau of Education* (Department of the Interior) 18 (1922); *Institute of International Education Bulletin* 11(2) (1930).
29. "Fellowships and Scholarships Open to Foreign Students to Study in the United States," *Institute of International Education Bulletin* 12 (1931); "Fellowships and Scholarships Open to American Students for Study in Foreign Countries', *Institute of International Education Bulletin* 13 (1932).
30. See Paul Kramer, "Is the World Our Campus? International Students and US Global Power in the Long Twentieth Century," *Diplomatic History* 33 (2009): 775–806.
31. For an interesting critique of assumptions that lie behind national interests and the introduction of scholarships, see Iain Wilson, "Ends Changed, Means Retained: Scholarship Programs, Political Influence, and Drifting Goals," *British Journal of Politics and International Relations* 17 (2015): 130–51.

32. See Heike Jöns, "Brain Circulation and Transnational Knowledge Networks: Studying Long-Term Effects of Academic Mobility to Germany, 1954–2000," *Global Networks* 9 (2009): 315–38.
33. See Jessica Reinisch, "Agents of Internationalism," and the articles collected in the special issue of *Contemporary European History* 25(2) (2016).
34. Whitney Walton, *Internationalism, National Identities, and Study Abroad: France and the United States, 1890–1970* (Stanford, CA: Stanford University Press, 2010).
35. Patricia L. Rosenfield, *A World of Giving: Carnegie Corporation of New York and a Century of International Philanthropy* (New York: Public Affairs, 2014); Giles Scott-Smith, "Attempting to Secure an 'Orderly Evolution': American Foundations, the Hague Academy of International Law, and the Third World," *Journal of American Studies* 41 (2007): 509–32; Ludovic Tournès, "La fondation Rockefeller et la naissance de l'universalisme philanthropique américain," *Critique Internationale* 35 (2007): 173–97.
36. See Glenda Sluga, *Internationalism in the Age of Nationalism* (Philadelphia, PA: University of Pennsylvania Press, 2013).
37. Ludovic Tournès, *Les États-Unis et la Société des Nations (1914–1946): Le système international face à l'émergence d'une superpuissance* (Berne: Peter Lang, 2015).
38. Kenneth Bertrams, "De l'action humanitaire à la recherche scientifique: Belgique, 1914–1930," in Ludovic Tournès (ed.), *L'argent de l'influence: Les fondations américaines et leurs réseaux européens* (Paris: Autrement, 2010), 45–63; *Rockefeller Foundation Annual Report* (1926), 311.
39. Robert Elder, *The Foreign Leader Program: Operations in the United States* (Westport, CT: Greenwood, 1961); Nancy Jachec, "Transatlantic Cultural Politics in the Late 1950s: The Leaders and Specialists Grant Program," *Art History* 26 (2003): 533–55; Scott-Smith, *Networks of Empire*.
40. David Engermann, "American Knowledge and Global Power," *Diplomatic History* 31 (2007): 599–622.
41. Reinhold Wagnleitner, *Coca-colonization and the Cold War: The Cultural Mission of the United States in Austria after the Second World War* (Chapel Hill, NC: University of North Carolina Press, 1994), 157–58.
42. Ioana Popa, "Discreet Intermediaries: Transnational Activities of the Fondation pour une entraide intellectuelle européenne 1966–1991," in Simo Mikkonen and Pia Koivunen (eds), *Beyond the Divide: Entangled Histories of the Cold War Era Europe* (New York: Berghahn Books, 2015), 151–73; Nicolas Guilhot, *The Democracy Makers: Human Rights and the Politics of Global Order* (New York: Columbia University Press, 2005).
43. The classic study is Frederick Barghoorn, *The Soviet Cultural Offensive: The Role of Cultural Diplomacy in Soviet Foreign Policy* (Westport, CT: Greenwood Press, 1976). For more recent analysis, see Nigel Gould-Davies, "The Logic of Soviet Cultural Diplomacy," *Diplomatic History* 27(2) (2003): 193–214; Simon Godard, "Construire le bloc de l'Est par l'économie? La délicate émergence d'une solidarité internationale socialiste au sein du Conseil d'aide économique mutuelle," *Vingtième Siècle: Revue d'histoire* 109 (2011): 45–58.

44. See the French case in Tournès, *Sciences de l'homme*.
45. Isabel Avila Ward, "The Fulbright Act," *Far Eastern Survey* 16 (1947): 198–200; Isabel Avila Maurer, "The Fulbright Act in Operation," *Far Eastern Survey*, 18 (1949): 104–7.
46. For a recent study of the intellectual and institutional impulses that lay behind the Fulbright Program, see Sam Lebovic, "From War Junk to Educational Exchange: The World War II Origins of the Fulbright Program and the Origins of American Cultural Globalism 1945–1950," *Diplomatic History* 37 (2013): 280–312.
47. See Carol Atkinson, *Military Soft Power: Public Diplomacy through Military Educational Exchanges* (Lanham, MD: Rowman & Littlefield, 2014).
48. See Honor Mahony, "Barroso Says EU is an Empire," *EU Observer*, 11 July 2007, retrieved 22 March 2017 from https://euobserver.com/institutional/24458. On the Eurosphere concept, see Jan Zielonka, *Europe as Empire* (Oxford: Oxford University Press, 2006).
49. Amanda J. Daly and Michele C. Barker, "Australian and New Zealand University Students' Participation in International Exchange Programs," *Journal of Studies in International Education* 9 (2005): 26–41.
50. Frederick Cooper, "What is the Concept of Globalization Good for? An African Historian's Perspective," *African Affairs* 100 (2001): 206.

References

Adelman, Jeremy I. *Worldly Philosopher: The Odyssey of Albert O. Hirshman* (Princeton, NJ: Princeton University Press, 2013).

Akerlund, Andreas. *Public Diplomacy and Academic Mobility in Sweden: The Swedish Institute and Scholarship Programs for Foreign Academics, 1938–2010* (Lund: Nordic Academic Press, 2016).

Appadurai, Arjun. *Modernity at Large: Cultural Dimensions of Globalization* (Minneapolis, MN: University of Minnesota Press, 1996).

Applebaum, Rachel. "The Friendship Project: Socialist Internationalism in the Soviet Union and Czechoslovakia in the 1950s and 1960s," *Slavic Review* 74 (2015): 484–507.

Atkinson, Carol. *Military Soft Power: Public Diplomacy through Military Educational Exchanges* (Lanham, MD: Rowman & Littlefield, 2014).

Barghoorn, Frederick. *The Soviet Cultural Offensive: The Role of Cultural Diplomacy in Soviet Foreign Policy* (Westport, CT: Greenwood Press, 1976).

Bayly, Christopher. *The Birth of the Modern World: Global Connections and Comparisons 1780–1914* (New York: Wiley Blackwell, 2004).

Bertrams, Kenneth. "De l'action humanitaire à la recherche scientifique: Belgique, 1914–1930," in Ludovic Tournès (ed.), *L'argent de l'influence: Les fondations américaines et leurs réseaux européens* (Paris: Autrement, 2010), 45–63.

Bourdieu, Pierre. "Le champ scientifique," *Actes de la Recherche en Sciences Sociales* 2–3 (1976): 88–104.

Chartier, Roger. *The Cultural Uses of Print in Early Modern France* (Princeton, NJ: Princeton University Press, 1987, trans. from French).
Clavin, Patricia. "Defining Transnationalism," *Contemporary European History* 14 (2005): 421–439.
Cull, Nicholas J. *The Cold War and the United States Information Agency: American Propaganda and Public Diplomacy, 1945–1989* (Cambridge: Cambridge University Press, 2009).
Cooper, Frederick. "What is the Concept of Globalization Good for? An African Historian's Perspective," *African Affairs* 100 (2001): 189–213.
Daly, Amanda J., and Michele C. Barker, "Australian and New Zealand University Students' Participation in International Exchange Programs," *Journal of Studies in International Education* 9 (2005): 26–41.
Elder, Robert. *The Foreign Leader Program: Operations in the United States* (Westport, CT: Greenwood, 1961).
Ellis, Heather and Simone M. Müller. "Educational Networks, Educational Identities: Connecting National and Global Perspectives," *Journal of Global History* 11(3) (2016): 313–19.
Engermann, David. "American Knowledge and Global Power," *Diplomatic History* 31 (2007): 599–622.
Espagne, Michel, and Michael Werner (eds). *Transferts: Les relations interculturelles dans l'espace franco-allemand (xviiie–xixe siècles)* (Paris: Éditions Recherche sur les Civilisations, 1988).
Garner, Alice, and Diane Kirby. "'Never a Machine for Propaganda?' The Australian-American Fulbright Program and Australia's Cold War," *Australian Historical Studies* 44 (2013): 117–33.
Gilroy, Paul. *The Black Atlantic: Modernity and Double Consciousness* (Cambridge, MA: Harvard University Press, 1993).
Godard, Simon. "Construire le bloc de l'Est par l'économie? La délicate émergence d'une solidarité internationale socialiste au sein du Conseil d'aide économique mutuelle," *Vingtième Siècle: Revue d'histoire* 109 (2011): 45–58.
Gomez-Escalonilla, Lorenzo Delgado. *Westerly Wind: The Fulbright Program in Spain* (Madrid: LID Editorial Empresarial-AECID, 2009).
Gould-Davies, Nigel. "The Logic of Soviet Cultural Diplomacy," *Diplomatic History* 27(2) (2003): 193–214.
Gruzinski, Serge. *La pensée métisse* (Paris: Fayard, 1999).
———. *Les quatre parties du monde: Histoire d'une mondialisation* (Paris: La martinière, 2004).
Guilhot, Nicolas. *The Democracy Makers: Human Rights and the Politics of Global Order* (New York: Columbia University Press, 2005).
Guilhot, Nicolas (ed.). *The Invention of International Relations Theory: Realism, the Rockefeller Foundation and the 1954 Conference on Theory* (New York: Columbia University Press, 2011).
Haas, Peter M. "Introduction: Epistemic Communities and International Policy Coordination," *International Organization* 46 (1992): 1–35.
Hart, Justin. *Empire of Ideas: The Origins of Public Diplomacy and the Transformation of US Foreign Policy* (Oxford: Oxford University Press, 2013).

Holloway, Sarah, and Heike Jöns. "Geographies of Education and Learning," *Transactions of the Institute of British Geographers* 37 (2012): 482–88.
Immerman, Richard, and Petra Goedde (eds). *The Oxford Handbook of the Cold War* (Oxford: Oxford University Press, 2013).
Irish, Tomás. "Scholarly Identities in War and Peace: The Paris Peace Conference and the Mobilization of Intellect," *Journal of Global History* 11(3) (2016): 365–86.
Iriye, Akira, and Pierre-Yves Saunier (eds). *The Palgrave Dictionary of Transnational History* (Basingstoke: Palgrave Macmillan, 2009).
Iriye, Akira (ed.). *Global Interdependence* (Cambridge, MA: Belknap Press, 2014).
Jachec, Nancy. "Transatlantic Cultural Politics in the Late 1950s: The Leaders and Specialists Grant Program," *Art History* 26 (2003): 533–55.
Jöns, Heike. "Brain Circulation and Transnational Knowledge Networks: Studying Long-Term Effects of Academic Mobility to Germany, 1954–2000," *Global Networks* 9 (2009): 315–38.
Jöns, Heike, Elizabeth Mavroudi, and Michael Hefferman, "Mobilising the Elective Diaspora: US-German Academic Exchanges since 1945," *Transactions: Institute of British Geographers* 40 (2015): 113–27.
Keppel, Gilles. *Beyond Terror and Martyrdom: The Future of the Middle East* (Cambridge, MA: Belknap Press, 2008).
König, Thomas. "Das Fulbright in Wien: Wissenschaftspolitik und Sozialwissenschaften am 'versunkenen Kontinent,'" Ph.D. dissertation (Vienna: University of Vienna, 2008).
Kramer, Paul. "Is the World Our Campus? International Students and US Global Power in the Long Twentieth Century," *Diplomatic History* 33 (2009): 775–806.
Kuisel, Richard. "L'American Way of Life et les missions françaises de productivité," *Vingtième siècle: Revue d'histoire* 17 (1988): 21–38.
Laqua, Daniel (ed.). *Internationalism Reconfigured: Transnational Ideas and Movements between the World Wars* (London: I.B. Tauris, 2011).
Lamont, Michèle, Charles Camic, and Neill Gros (eds). *Social Knowledge in the Making* (Chicago, IL: University of Chicago Press, 2011).
Latour, Bruno. *Science in Action: How to Follow Scientists and Engineers through Society* (Cambridge, IL, MA: Harvard University Press, 1987).
Lebovic, Sam. "From War Junk to Educational Exchange: The World War II Origins of the Fulbright Program and the Origins of American Cultural Globalism 1945–1950," *Diplomatic History* 37 (2013): 280–312.
Leffler, Melvin, and Odd Arne Westad (eds). *The Cambridge History of the Cold War*, 3 vols (Cambridge: Cambridge University Press, 2012).
Lerg, Charlotte. "'We are No Teutomanics…' Cultural Diplomacy, the Study of German and the Germanic Museum at Harvard before the First World War," *Germanistik in Irland* 3 (2013): 43–54.
Levine, Emily. "Baltimore Teaches, Göttingen Learns: Cooperation, Competition and the Research University," *American Historical Review* 121(3) (2016): 780–823.

Loayza, Matt. "A Curative and Creative Force: The Exchange of Persons Program and Eisenhower's Inter-American Policies 1953–1961," *Diplomatic History* 37 (2013): 946–70.

Marjolin, Robert. *Le travail d'une vie: Mémoires. 1911–1986* (Paris: Robert Laffont, 1986).

Mohanty, Sachidananda. *In Search of Wonder: Understanding Cultural Exchange: Fulbright Program in India* (New Delhi: Vision Books, 1997).

Osgood, Kenneth. *Total Cold War: Eisenhower's Secret Propaganda Battle at Home and Abroad* (Lawrence, KS: University Press of Kansas, 2006).

Papatsiba, Vassiliki. "Student Mobility in Europe: An Academic, Cultural and Mental Journey? Some Conceptual Reflections and Empirical Findings," *International Perspectives on Higher Education Research* 3 (2005): 29–65.

Parmar, Inderjeet. *Foundations of the American Century: The Ford, Carnegie and Rockefeller Foundations in the Rise of American Power* (New York: Columbia University Press, 2012).

Popa, Ioana. "Discreet Intermediaries: Transnational Activities of the Fondation pour une entraide intellectuelle européenne 1966–1991," in Simo Mikkonen and Pia Koivunen (eds), *Beyond the Divide: Entangled Histories of the Cold War Era Europe* (New York: Berghahn Books, 2015), 151–73.

Rodgers, Daniel T. *Atlantic Crossings: Social Politics in a Progressive Age* (Cambridge, MA: Harvard University Press, 1998).

Pestre, Dominique, and John Krige (eds). *Science in the Twentieth Century* (Amsterdam: Harwood Academic Publisher, 1997).

Pietsch, Tamson. *Empire of Scholars: Universities, Networks and the British Academic World 1850–1939* (Manchester: Manchester University Press, 2013).

Reinisch, Jessica. "Agents of Internationalism," *Contemporary European History* 25(2) (2016): 195–205.

Robertson, Roland. "Glocalisation: Time-Space and Homogeneity-Heterogeneity," in Mike Featherstone, Scott Lash and Roland Robertson (eds), *Global Modernities* (London: Sage, 1995), 26–44.

Rosenfield, Patricia L. *A World of Giving: Carnegie Corporation of New York and a Century of International Philanthropy* (New York: Public Affairs, 2014).

Rupp, Jan C.C. "The Fulbright Program, or the Surplus Value of Officially Organized Academic Exchange," *Journal of Studies in International Education* 3 (1999): 59–82.

Salamone, Frank (ed.). *The Fulbright Experience in Benin* (Williamsburg, VA: College of William and Mary, 1994).

Scott-Smith, Giles. "Mapping the Undefinable: Some Thoughts on the Relevance of Exchange Programs within International Relations Theory," *Annals of the American Academy of Political and Social Science* 616 (2008): 173–195.

———. *Networks of Empire: The US State Department's Foreign Leader Program in the Netherlands, France and Britain, 1950–1970* (Brussels: Peter Lang, 2008).

———. "Attempting to Secure an 'Orderly Evolution': American Foundations, the Hague Academy of International Law, and the Third World," *Journal of American Studies* 41 (2007): 509–32.

———. "The Fulbright Program in the Netherlands: An Example of Science Diplomacy," in Jeroen van Dongen (ed.), *Cold War Science and the Transatlantic Circulation of Knowledge* (Leiden: Brill, 2015), 136–61.
Sluga, Glenda. *Internationalism in the Age of Nationalism* (Philadelphia, PA: University of Pennsylvania Press, 2013).
Tournès, Ludovic. "Le réseau des boursiers Rockefeller et la recomposition des savoirs biomédicaux en France (1920–1970)," *French Historical Studies* 29(1) (2006): 77–107.
———. "La fondation Rockefeller et la naissance de l'universalisme philanthropique américain," *Critique Internationale* 35 (2007): 173–97.
———. *Sciences de l'homme et politique: Les fondations philanthropiques américaines en France au XXe siècle* (Paris: Editions des classiques Garnier, 2011).
———. *Les États-Unis et la Société des Nations (1914–1946): Le système international face à l'émergence d'une superpuissance* (Berne: Peter Lang, 2015).
Tyrrell, Ian. *Reforming the World: The Creation of America's Moral Empire* (Princeton, NJ: Princeton University Press, 2010).
Wagnleitner, Reinhold. *Coca-colonization and the Cold War: The Cultural Mission of the United States in Austria after the Second World War* (Chapel Hill, NC: University of North Carolina Press, 1994).
Walton, Whitney. *Internationalism, National Identities, and Study Abroad: France and the United States, 1890–1970* (Stanford, CA: Stanford University Press, 2010).
Weber, Thomas. *Our Friend "The Enemy": Elite Education in Britain and Germany before World War I* (Stanford, CA: Stanford University Press, 2008).
Wilson, Iain. "Ends Changed, Means Retained: Scholarship Programs, Political Influence, and Drifting Goals," *British Journal of Politics and International Relations* 17 (2015): 130–51.
Xu, Guangqiu. "The Ideological and Political Impact of US Fulbrighters on Chinese Students: 1979–1989," *Asian Affairs* 26(3) (1999): 139-57.
Zeitlin, Jonathan, and Gary Herrigel. *Americanization and its Limits: Reworking US Technology and Management in Postwar Europe and Japan* (Oxford: Oxford University Press, 2004).
Zielonka, Jan. *Europe as Empire* (Oxford: Oxford University Press, 2006).

PART I

NATIONAL AND IMPERIAL POWER POLITICS

1

THE POLITICS OF SCHOLARLY EXCHANGE
Taking the Long View on the Rhodes Scholarships
Tamson Pietsch and Meng-Hsuan Chou

Introduction

Founded in 1901, the Rhodes scholarship scheme is one of the longest-running programs of scholarly exchange still in existence. It has been the model for many schemes that have since emerged. As such, it offers an ideal context for examining as well as raising new questions about the organization and overall efficacy of scholarly exchange across the twentieth century.

This chapter is the first attempt at a general historical analysis of the way in which the scholarship shaped the lives of those who received it. It takes a dual approach to the long view on scholarly exchange. Not only does it track the scholarship through the twentieth century, it also looks back to the 1890s and to the ideas and precedents that informed Cecil John Rhodes and his executors. Beginning by placing the foundation of the Rhodes scholarships in their historical context, the chapter then goes on to examine three basic issues that underpin most international exchange programs: first, the geographic distribution of award; second, gender parity in award; and, third, the long-term geographic mobility of scholars. By bringing together historical and quantitative methods, it points to identifiable patterns of continuity, change, and regional diversity in the management and effect of the scheme.

Rhodes Scholarships: History and Origins

In 1901, the Cape Town politician and mining magnate, Cecil Rhodes, left his considerable fortune to the establishment of a scheme of traveling scholarships. Bringing the most promising young men from across the English-speaking world to Oxford, Rhodes hoped to "instil into their minds the advantage to the Colonies as well as to the United Kingdom of the retention of the Unity of the Empire" and affect "the union of the English-speaking peoples throughout the world." At the heart of Rhodes' scheme was his belief that the experience of living and studying together in a residential university would "broaden [the] views" of his scholars, "instruct them in life and manners" and in the process foster ties of mutual understanding that would serve to "render war impossible." It was, Rhodes believed, "educational relations [that] make the strongest tie."[1] Interpersonal relationships and informal forms of association, rather than the explicit content of educational programs, were therefore at the core of Rhodes' idea.

In attempting to define the type of scholar he sought, Rhodes stipulated four selection criteria: (1) literary and scholastic attainment; (2) energy to use one's talents to the full, as exemplified by fondness for and success in sports; (3) qualities of truth, courage, devotion to duty, sympathy for the protection of the weak, kindliness, unselfishness and fellowship; and (4) the exhibition of moral force of character and of instincts to lead that will guide one to esteem the performance of public duty as the highest aim. He explicitly sought scholars who would be "not merely bookworms," but rather "capable leaders of men": a global elite who, through influence and public office, would work for future world order. This was a notion of leadership that extended beyond disciplinary proficiency and intellectual capacity. It emphasized the physical and charismatic qualities of leaders, and placed as much stress on character and personality as it did on their academic attainments.

Targeted initially at the British colonies of white settlement (Canada, Australia, Southern Africa and New Zealand) and also the United States, Germany, Bermuda and Jamaica, the program expanded over the course of the twentieth century to also include African states, India and Pakistan, and for a time also Malaysia, Singapore and Hong Kong.[2] From 2015, a further expansion has extended the scholarships to China.[3]

Across this period, the meaning and representation of the scholarship has also changed. It was initially embraced by liberal imperialist politicians, who saw it as a way of creating common sentiments across borders, but received a lukewarm reception from Oxford academics, who thought that selection on the basis of well-roundedness would lower academic standards of the whole institution. From the 1930s on, Rhodes' vision of imperial citizenship came under further criticism, not least from Rhodes scholars themselves, who began to champion national sentiments. The emphasis and popular understanding of the scheme shifted again after World War II, when in the 1950s its remit was expanded to include the countries of what was newly styled as the multiracial British Commonwealth of Nations—moving from a discourse that emphasized race and the English-speaking peoples to one that rather invoked internationalism. It was at this time too that the Rhodes program was taken up as a model for the Fulbright scholarships and since then it has been frequently cited as the inspiration of many newer schemes. Throughout this period, a key message from the Rhodes Trust was the informal moral obligation upon scholars to return and contribute to their countries of selection. At the start of the twenty-first century, the emphasis has shifted again. Reflecting changing political and economic governance patterns, "rather than imperial or national, it is increasingly now good global citizens that Cecil Rhodes' traveling scholarships are thought to create."[4] The Trust itself has begun to highlight the contributions of Rhodes scholars in various fields, including as Nobel laureates, Olympians and heads of state.[5]

How are we to examine the effects of the Rhodes program when not only its geographic distribution but also its stated aims, self presentation and context have changed radically across the twentieth century? High-profile individuals such as Bill Clinton, Bob Hawke, Wasim Sajjad, John Turner and Norman Manley have done much to shape the public image and maintain the program's prestige. But—although they form an important subset of alumni—most scholars have not gone on to careers as political representatives.[6] Despite publicly available information on eligibility, internal analyses of more recent cohorts, sectional studies (e.g. The Rhodes Project on female Rhodes scholars) and the Trust's promotional materials, a consolidated, longitudinal assessment of the Rhodes program is still needed. In this chapter we analyze the publicly accessible data on Rhodes scholars as published in the *Register of Rhodes Scholars* to reveal their mobility patterns over the course of the twentieth century.[7]

The Rhodes Foundation in Context

This volume emphasizes the need to take the long view on scholarly exchange programs—to move away from a hagiographic focus on a small cohort of prominent "familiar suspects" and instead to examine the program's impact on the later careers of all grantees. This is an important and necessary endeavor, but in focusing on the after-effects of exchange programs, there is a danger of reifying their moment of foundation—an event that is frequently given mythic status by the programs themselves and their institutional histories. This is particularly true in the case of the Rhodes scholarships which are frequently celebrated as the personal creation of Cecil Rhodes and abstracted from the wider context out of which they grew. Until very recently, it was traditional for scholars to raise a toast to "The Founder" at formal events of the Rhodes Trust.

In his 1998 biography of Cecil Rhodes, Robert Rotberg does acknowledge that Rhodes "almost certainly derived his ideas" from two men who, in the 1890s, were already planning a scholarship scheme for colonial students.[8] In the July of 1891, J. Astley Cooper, editor of the London weekly publication *Greater Britain*, had published his proposal for a "periodical gathering of representatives of the [English] race in a festival and contest of industry, athletics, and culture."[9] Cooper argued that such an event would foster imperial goodwill while also strengthening "family bonds" with the United States. He first proposed the idea of university scholarships as part of this festival in an article a few months later, adding in parentheses "(there are none in existence yet)."[10]

A year later, Professor Thomas Hudson Beare, an engineer from South Australia who held chairs at University College London and the University of Edinburgh, developed Cooper's plans further, suggesting they should be called the "Britannic scholarships" and outlining the details of a scheme that shares distinct similarities with that later proposed by Rhodes.[11] A hundred scholars were to travel to Britain from each of the principal (white settler) colonies, while postgraduate awards were to enable British students to pursue research in the empire. "On his return to his Colony," concluded Beare, "each student would form a nucleus around which would gather all that was best, and each would form another of those invisible ties, stronger than any which can be devised by the cunning of law makers, which will keep together, for good or ill, the Anglo-Saxon race." According to Rotberg, Rhodes "doubtless learned" of these ideas through his and Cooper's close associate, the journalist and imperialist William Thomas Stead, and throughout the 1890s Rhodes gave more and more attention to his educational "big idea."[12] With their emphasis on fostering informal ties through friendship among students from the white settler colonies, and with their connection to sport and physical activity, Cooper and Beare's

"Britannic Scholarships" point clearly to the connections that Rhodes' contemporaries were making between imperial federation, sociability and education.

At the time of Cooper's 1891 claim, there in fact already existed an empire-wide scheme of traveling scholarships. These were the 1851 Exhibition scholarships, established in 1899 by the Commissioners of the 1851 Great Exhibition and awarded to "the most promising students" from the universities of the settler colonies, Ireland and the provincial cities of Britain so that they might "complete their studies either in those colleges or in the larger institutions of the metropolis." Given the publicity accorded to the 1851 Exhibition scholarships in scientific circles, it is likely that Beare knew them well. With a focus on "extending the influence of science and art upon productive industry," they differed from the scheme of Cooper and Beare in two main respects: first, the 1851 Exhibition scholarships placed an explicit emphasis upon the content of studies; and, second, they placed the universities in the colonies alongside those in the provincial centers of Britain, seeing both as key to "national" development.[13]

Unlike Cooper and Beare, and later Rhodes, the 1851 commissioners did not principally see their scholarships as a mechanism for fostering imperial loyalty, but rather as a means of building national scientific and industrial capacity.[14] In this, the 1851 Exhibition scholarships were by no means unique. By the 1890s, a host of universities across the colonies of the British empire had established scholarships that were designed to take their most promising graduates on to further study in Britain.[15] In fact, Thomas Hudson Beare was himself a recipient of one of them—the South Australian scholarship. And when in the 1890s Rhodes was thinking about the form his own program might take, there were already eight "traveling scholarships" taking graduates from the Cape of Good Hope University to the United Kingdom. Such scholarships were focused on academic attainment and saw study in the ancient universities of Scotland and England as the apex of local educational structures.

The tension between these two hopes for scholarly exchange—as a means of fostering identity and goodwill on the one hand, and intellectual and technical capacity on the other—sit at the heart not just of the Rhodes program, but also of similar exchange schemes throughout the twentieth century. From Fulbright to Erasmus, it is a tension that has rarely been resolved.

Election Constituencies: Changing with the (Political and Economic) Times

In his will of 1901, Rhodes stipulated the constituencies to which he wanted scholarships to go. Rhodesia was to receive three a year, South Africa five, Australia six, New Zealand one, Canada three, and Bermuda and Jamaica one each. A further thirty-two were allotted on a more complex formula to the United States. In a codicil written in 1901, Rhodes also noted that the German Emperor had "made instruction in English compulsory in German schools," and on the basis of this he left five yearly scholarships to students of German birth, the object being "that an understanding between the three great powers [Britain, the United States and Germany] will render war impossible [as] educational relations make the strongest tie."[16]

The original footprint of the scholarship thus reflected the racial and imperial philosophy at the heart of Rhodes' scheme. It was not just friendship between the leading powers of the day that he sought to foster, but particularly friendship between the "Anglo-Saxon peoples" of Britain, the United States and Germany. As indicated above, this geographic distribution has changed significantly over time, to such an extent that the Rhodes scholarships are now sometimes claimed as the first that sought to fashion and attract the "human capital" of a global knowledge economy.[17] Just how "global" they are, however, is less clear. In order to track the changing patterns of regional allocation of the scholarship over the twentieth century, we used the data published by the Rhodes Trust to calculate the number of scholarships awarded by country per year.[18]

As Figure 1.1 shows, the number of scholarships awarded annually has varied considerably, from a low of one (in 1943) to a high of ninety-eight (in 1911), but averaging at sixty-seven per year across the whole 110-year period. Throughout this period, the Trustees have added (but also subsequently discontinued) approximately forty additional scholarships. Notably, the first decade of the scheme's operation points to the regional nature of this variation, with the American arm of the program displaying an episodic pattern of award. Immediately evident is the variation of award in some constituencies (such as Germany and East Africa) and the continuity of award in others (South Africa, the United States, Australia, New Zealand and Canada).

This long view on the changing geographic distribution of award points to the close relationship between it and the wider contemporary global political and economic forces. The shifting politics of the

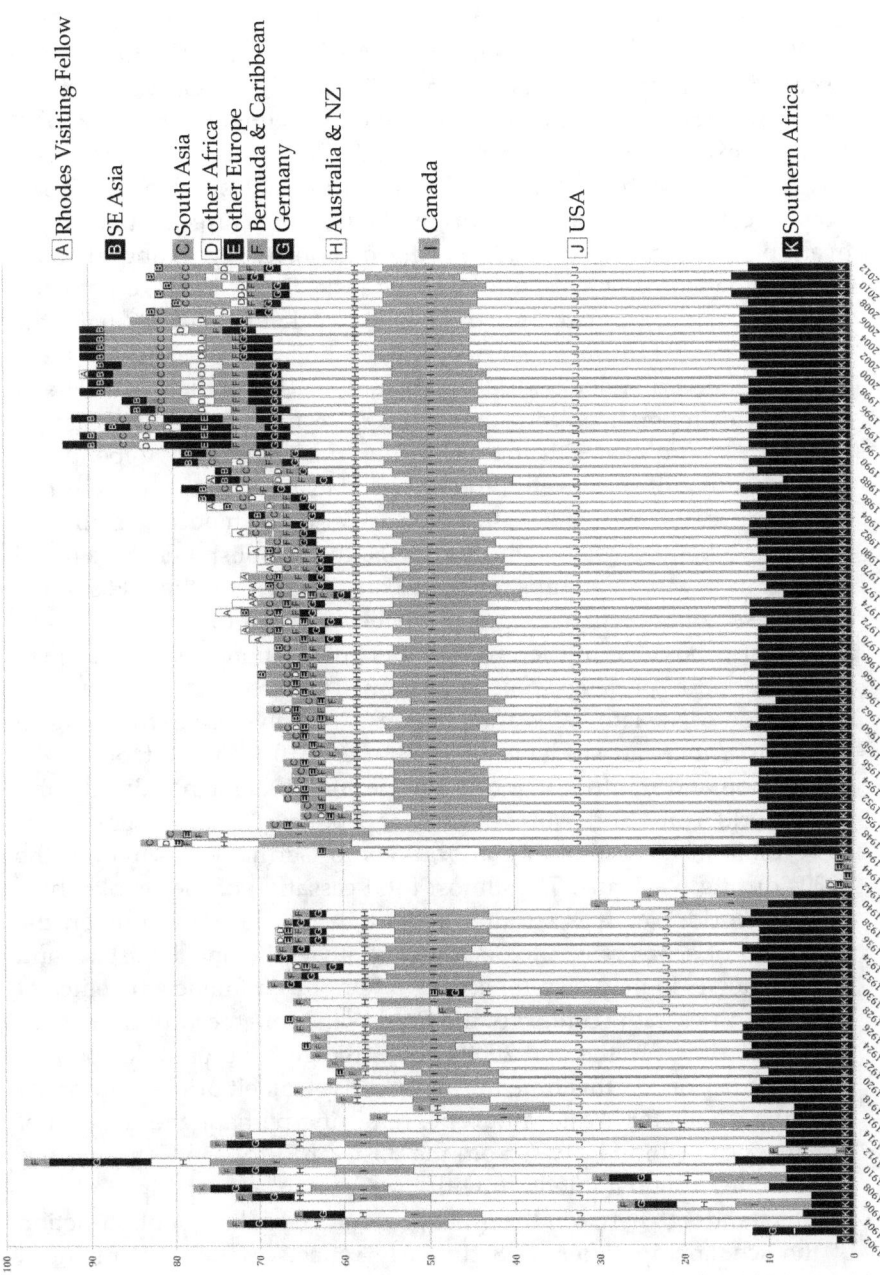

Figure 1.1 Election constituencies of all Rhodes Scholars, 1902–2012

Note: For a list of all scholars, please see http://www.rhodeshouse.ox.ac.uk/about/rhodes-scholars/rhodes-scholars-complete-list

British empire is clearly reflected in this data. The regions initially identified by Rhodes in his will reflect the concern at the turn of the twentieth century in British imperial politics with the "settler colonies" and moves toward what was called at the time "imperial federation."[19] With the exception of Germany (on which see below), since 1902 there has continued to be a stability of award in these core constituencies. This reflects a stipulation in the original will, which directed that, in the event of insufficient income, the order of priority regulating the payment of the scholarships should be: Rhodesia, South Africa, other colonial scholarships (Canada, Australia, New Zealand etc.) and finally the United States.[20] But the expansion of the scholarships to include India and Pakistan, Sri Lanka and Malaysia in the 1940s to the 1970s reflects changes to imperial politics that took place in this period. From an approach before the 1930s that bifurcated the settler and "dependent" colonies, it manifests the shift to a more inclusive focus on the "British Commonwealth" of nations after World War II. With decolonization in Africa and South East Asia in the 1970s, the establishment of a small number of new scholarships for these constituencies in the 1980s traces both these political changes and ambivalence about them.

It is also possible to identify broader international politics at play in the variation of geographic allocation. The effects of the economic depression of the late 1920s and early 1930s are evident in the reduced award to American students in 1928 and 1930. Most notable is the suspension and reintroduction of the German scholarship during and after World War I and World War II, and policies of appeasement are discernible in the continuing allocations to Germany throughout the 1930s during Nazi rule. The almost total cessation of the scholarships during World War II is striking. Although not large in number, the extension of scholarships to Asia (especially India and Pakistan) and Africa after 1945 may also reflect the attempt to influence the elites of these countries in the context of the Cold War. More recently, the expansion of the 1990s to the mid 2000s tracks the global economic boom of the same period. At this time the Trust chose—albeit briefly—to create new allocations for Western Europe, reflecting perhaps the creation of the European Union in 1993 from the postwar European Communities and Rhodes' original intention with the German scholarships to foster "understanding" between the great powers. The subsequent retraction of the scholarships after 2008 similarly reflects the "global financial crisis" of the period and the Trust's attendant financial difficulties.[21] A notable exception is the Hong Kong scholarship, which was abolished in 1997 following its withdrawal from the Commonwealth, but was reintroduced in the same year with a benefaction from the Lee Hysan

Foundation. The recent expansion to include China similarly reflects the changing geopolitics of the early twenty-first century.

Two factors are evident in this overview: first, the long-term path dependencies that have ensured consistency of award to the original election constituencies; and, second, the Trust's sensitivity to changing global contexts. Although guided by the terms laid out in Rhodes' will, the Trust has not been insulated from wider political and economic forces, and has taken an active role in directing awards accordingly.

Gender Selection: Slowly Moving toward Parity

At its inception, the Rhodes scheme was open only to men. Women were expressly prevented from applying by the terms and language of Rhodes' will. After sustained pressure from scholars and universities, particularly from North America, in the early 1970s the Rhodes Trustees petitioned the (British) Home Secretary to request that a provision be included in the antidiscrimination legislation then proceeding through the Houses of Parliament to allow educational charities to amend their trusts to include women. With the successful passage of this bill, the Rhodes Trustees then asked the Secretary of State for Education and Science to pass an Act of Parliament (passed in 1976) to amend the terms of the original bequest, making women eligible to apply. The first women Rhodes scholars arrived in Oxford in 1977.[22] Prior to this legislative change, from 1970 until the early 1980s, Rhodes Visiting Fellowships allowed a small number of women to take up residence in Oxford's women's colleges.

To track the relative selection of women since eligibility in 1977, we calculated the number of women scholars selected as a percentage of the total number of scholars for each year.

As Figure 1.2 shows, the percentage of women scholars selected has varied since 1977 in a consistent "ripple pattern" (peak follow by dips, then peak again). Although there is a general trend toward parity, the numbers have only reached fifty percent and above at two points in this thirty-five year period: in 1999 and 2012. This data makes clear the extent to which men, more so than women since their eligibility in 1977, have dominated the total numbers of recipients of Rhodes scholarships. While this may not be surprising, the "ripple pattern" of women Rhodes scholars is curious to note and requires further analysis.

Earlier we highlighted the emphasis that Rhodes placed on informal association and character in the selection and cultivation of his scholars. As Tamson Pietsch has shown more broadly for academic appointments

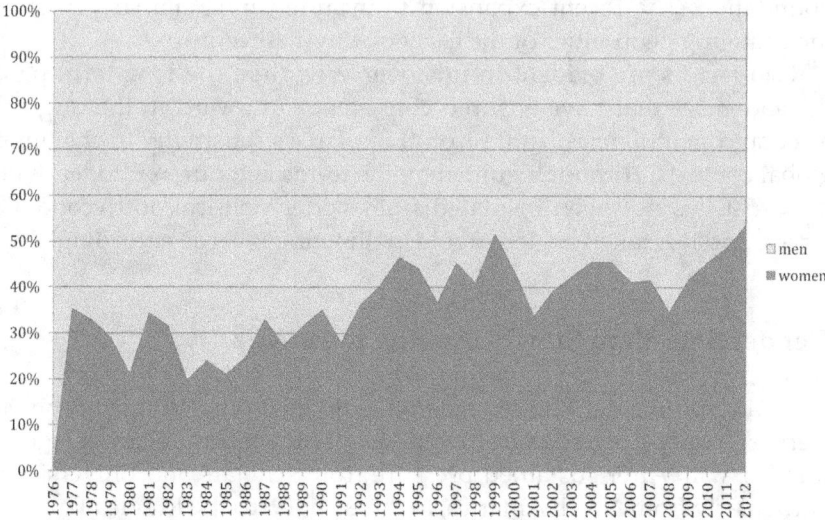

Figure 1.2 Female Rhodes Scholars, 1977–2012 (%)

in the period to 1939, the centrality of gendered and raced academic cultures of sociability to selection created highly uneven opportunities for access.[23] Although racial and religious minority groups were in theory accepted as scholars from the very beginning, in practice opportunities for them were severely limited by the policies of the countries and institutions from which they came. We also note that analyzing the outcomes of higher education programs is inherently problematic, because the attainment of scholarships at the tertiary level is built on access to and performance at primary and secondary-stage schooling that is itself heavily influenced by a range of socioeconomic factors.

Geographic Mobility: Return to Countries of Election

Geographic mobility is at the heart of contemporary debate concerning knowledge exchange and generation. The assumption is that mobility enables scholars to make new contacts and acquire different knowledge that could lead to the acquisition of cultural and social capital, and opportunities for new collaboration and possible innovation. Hence, states encourage the mobility of scientists, scholars and students via funding support and through the reduction of administrative barriers to entry. The Rhodes scheme has traditionally brought selected participants to Oxford, envisioning that they would likely return to

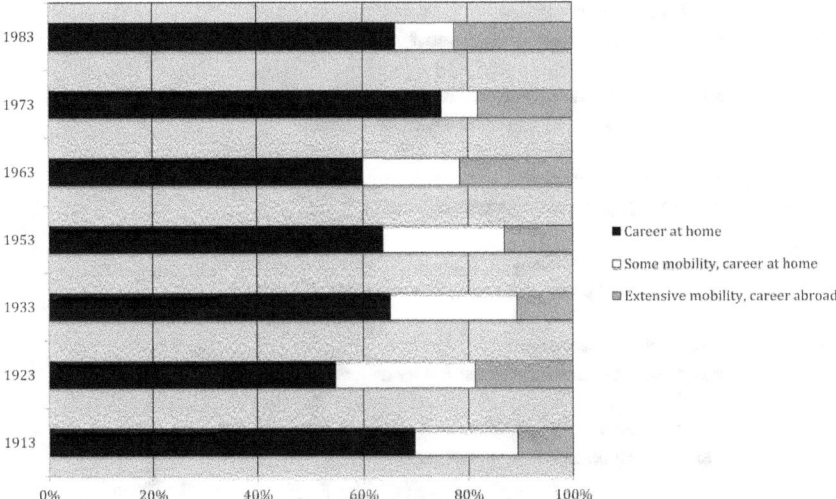

Figure 1.3 Geographic mobility of Rhodes Scholars, 1913–1983 (%)

their countries of election and take up public positions of leadership. However, how far this has actually been the pattern for scholars has not been systematically examined. In order to track the geographic mobility of Rhodes scholars across the twentieth century, we therefore developed three indicators: (a) those who made their careers at home; (b) those who made their careers both at home and abroad; and (c) those who principally made their careers outside their country of election.

As Figure 1.3 shows, the majority of scholars elected in the years analyzed established their careers in their countries of election, with limited mobility to some mobility (more than seventy-five percent of all cohorts for all coded years). Scholars with extensive mobility, who established their careers outside of their countries of election, have generally remained in the minority (around twenty to twenty-five percent of their cohorts). However, since 1913, it is evident that the percentage of scholars in this category has been steadily increasing. We believe that it is likely that more recent cohorts, especially those from the late 1990s onward, may have still greater geographic mobility patterns than earlier cohorts.[24]

One of the difficulties of this data is that it collapses the particular local and cultural contexts that shape patterns of behavior in different countries. To provide more fine-grained differentiation between the election constituencies, we have therefore disaggregated the geographic mobility patterns of Rhodes scholars who have been elected

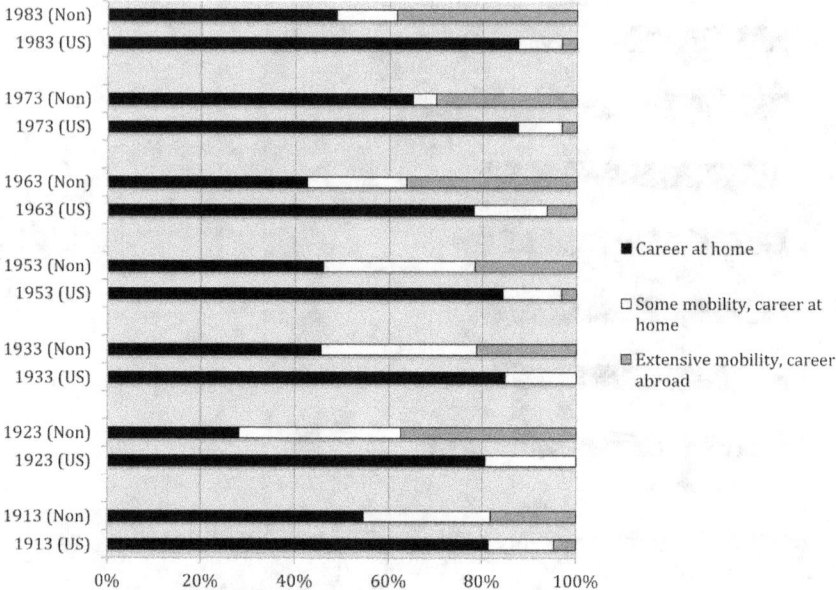

Figure 1.4 Geographic mobility of US versus non-US Rhodes Scholars (%)

from the United States (a dominant cohort for most years) in comparison to those who were from other election regions.

Figure 1.4 reveals several striking patterns. First, Rhodes scholars from the United States have been more likely (about twice as likely) to spend part of their careers at home than their counterparts from other election regions. Second, while very few US scholars established their professional careers abroad, many more non-US scholars pursued this option (between twenty-two percent in 1913 and sixty-two percent in 1983). Third, the relatively high mobility (compared to other decades) of non-US scholars elected in 1923 points to the danger of telling a linear story of increasing mobility across the century. The opportunities and constraints of the interwar and World War II years, the period in which this cohort developed their careers, meant that more non-US scholars built their lives abroad than did so in later decades. This data clearly shows that awardees from different constituencies have used the Rhodes experience differently in the establishment and consolidation of their professional careers: while US scholars have utilized it as a platform to pursue a variety of careers principally at home, non-US scholars have employed the Rhodes program as a springboard to careers outside of their countries of election.

We caution, however, against making assumptions between these patterns and the notion of "brain drain." As several recent studies in other contexts have shown, the notion of brain drain is likely to oversimplify the relationship that Rhodes scholars have had with their countries of election.[25] Work by Tamson Pietsch suggests that Rhodes scholars who were academics maintained strong ties with their home countries, supervising the next generation of leaders and scholars from their countries of origin by hosting their stay abroad.[26] The importance of such intergenerational networks might also be considered in other professional contexts, notably medicine or management consulting. In these instances, rather than acting as the source of brain drain, Rhodes scholars who have made their careers outside their countries of origin have nonetheless still contributed to knowledge mobility and circulation—factors that are usually considered to sit at the heart of national innovation.

Conclusion

Taking the long view on the Rhodes scholarships highlights both the gravitational weight exerted by the terms and context of their foundation, and their protean and plural nature. The centrality of the original constituencies, the continuity of the Trust's broad conception of leadership, its continuing belief in informal relations between scholars and the slowness of progress on questions of gender equity substantiate one of the central claims of historical institutionalism, which proposes that institutions, once created, are "sticky" and may be resistant to change.[27]

But a long view on the Rhodes scholarships also shows that although exchange programs such as the Rhodes scholarships play a significant role in shaping elites through providing opportunity and connection, they are never insulated from broader historical and political forces affecting social and economic development. Such schemes sit in relation to the political imperatives that animated the era of their foundation, are guided by the changing objectives of those who manage them, are reshaped by future benefactions and are influenced by the exposure of their endowments to market and political forces. They will always be utilized for a variety of purposes by scholars, some of which will be contrary to the original aims of their foundation. It is in this deft political and social mutability that we perhaps find much deeper forces of continuity. As scholars of internationalism are increasingly showing, the United States first competed with and then assumed the mantle of British liberal imperialism. Culture was one of its key methods. And culture is one of the key methods being utilized by a wider variety of state and institutional actors as nations, corporations, foundations and individuals alike seek to adjust to the emerging geopolitical order of the twenty-first century.

Tamson Pietsch (DPhil, University of Oxford) is Senior Lecturer in Social and Political Sciences and Australian Research Council DECRA Fellow at the University of Technology Sydney. Her research focuses on the history of universities, knowledge, empire and international politics in the nineteenth and twentieth centuries. She is the author of *Empire of Scholars: Universities, Networks and the British Academic World, 1850–1939* (Manchester, 2013) and, with Meng-Hsuan Chou and Isaac Kamola, the editor of *The Transnational Politics of Higher Education: Contesting the Global/Transforming the Local* (Routledge, 2016). Tamson was awarded an Australia-at-Large Rhodes Scholarship in 2003.

Meng-Hsuan Chou (Ph.D., University of Cambridge) is Nanyang Assistant Professor in Public Policy and Global Affairs at Nanyang Technological University, Singapore. Her research interests lie at the intersection of public policy, regionalism and international relations. She has published in the *Journal of European Public Policy*, *PS: Political Science and Politics* and the *Journal of Contemporary European Research*, and is the co-editor of *Building the Knowledge Economy in Europe: New Constellations in European Research and Higher Education Governance* (with Åse Gornitzka, Edward Elgar, 2014) and *The Transnational Politics of Higher Education: Contesting the Global /Transforming the Local* (with Isaac Kamola and Tamson Pietsch, Routledge, 2016).

Appendix: Derek John de Sa

Derek John de Sa, was one of two students awarded the Rhodes scholarship for India in 1963. He was born in Lahore in 1939 and was educated at Sherwood College and the Christian Medical College in Ludhiana, graduating with a Bachelor of Medicine and Bachelor of Science in 1962. At Oxford he was a member of Jesus College and undertook a doctoral degree in Pathology. Graduating in 1967, he stayed on in Oxford to work in the Radcliffe Infirmary and as Lecturer and Assistant and Honorary Consultant. In 1973 he accepted a post as Associate Professor of Pathology at McMaster University in Ontario, Canada, where he also served as staff pathologist at St Joseph's Hospital and Chedoke

Hospital. In 1982 he was appointed Professor of Pathology and Head of Paediatric Pathology at the University of Manitoba and Pathologist-in-Chief at the Children's Hospital of Winnipeg. He returned to McMaster University as Professor of Pathology in 1986 and in 1996 was made Professor of Pathology at the University of British Columbia. Derek de Sa. He is a Fellow of the Royal College of Pathologists, served on the Council of the Society of Paediatric Pathology and was chairman of its publication committee. He was a consultant for the US Center of Disease Control, the National Institutes of Health and the Ontario Health Ministry. In 2013 he returned to Oxford to attend the 110th Anniversary of the Rhodes scholarships.

Notes

1. Philip Zeigler, *Legacy: Cecil Rhodes, the Rhodes Trust, and the Rhodes Scholarships* (New Haven, CT: Yale University Press, 2008), Appendix 1.
2. "Rhodes Scholars: complete list, 1903–2014," Rhodes Trust, retrieved 20 March 2017 from http://www.rhodeshouse.ox.ac.uk/about/rhodes-scholars/rhodes-scholars-complete-list.
3. "The Rhodes Scholarships for China," Rhodes Trust, retrieved 20 March 2017 from http://www.rhodeshouse.ox.ac.uk/china.
4. Tamson Pietsch, "Many Rhodes: Travelling Scholarships and Imperial Citizenship in the British Academic World, 1880–1940," *History of Education* 40(6) (2011): 723–39 (724).
5. "Rhodes Trust Infographics," Rhodes Trust, retrieved 20 March 2017 from http://www.rhodeshouse.ox.ac.uk/infographic.
6. Thomas J. Schaeper and Kathleen Schaeper, *Cowboys into Gentlemen: Rhodes Scholars, Oxford, and the Creation of the American Elite* (Berghahn Books, 1998), pp. 277–79.
7. Ralph Evans (ed.), *Register of Rhodes Scholars, 1903–1998*, 1988 and 1996 edns (Oxford: Rhodes Trust, 1988 and 1996).
8. Robert I. Rotberg and Miles F. Shore, *The Founder: Cecil Rhodes and the Pursuit of Power* (Oxford: Oxford University Press, 1988), p. 664.
9. J. Astley Cooper, "Many Lands—One People: A Criticism and a Suggestion," *Greater Britain*, 15 July 1891.
10. J. Astley Cooper, "The Proposed Periodic Britannic Contest and All-English Speaking Festival," *Greater Britain*, 15 November 1891.
11. Thomas Hudson Beare, "Britannic Scholarships," *Greater Britain*, 15 October 1892.
12. Rotberg and Shore, *Founder*, 665.
13. Pietsch, "Many Rhodes," pp. 729–30.
14. Katrina Dean, "Inscribing Settler Science: Ernest Rutherford, Thomas Laby and the Making of Careers in Physics," *History of Science* 41 (2003): 217–40 (222).

15. Pietsch, "Many Rhodes," 734.
16. "Will and Codicils of the Rt. Hon. Cecil John Rhodes," Rhodes Trust, retrieved 20 March 2017 from http://files.rhodesscholarshiptrust.com/governancedocs/WillandCodicils.pdf, 15.
17. Ben Wildavsky, "The Great Brain Race: Rise of the Global Education Marketplace," lecture at the London School of Economics, 21 October 2010, retrieved 20 March 2017 from http://itunes.apple.com/podcast/london-school-economics-public/id279428154.
18. "Rhodes Scholars: Complete List, 1903–2014."
19. Pietsch, "Many Rhodes," p. 729.
20. "Will and Codicils," p. 11.
21. *Annual Report and Financial Statements for the Year Ended 30 June 2010* (Oxford: Rhodes Trust, 2010), p. 6.
22. William J. Barber, "A Footnote to the Social History of the 1970s: The Opening of the Rhodes Scholarships to Women," *American Oxonian* 87(2) (2000): 135–46.
23. Tamson Pietsch, *Empire of Scholars: Universities, Networks and the British Academic World, 1850–1939* (Manchester: Manchester University Press, 2013), pp. 61–89.
24. "Rhodes Scholars: Complete List, 1903–2014."
25. Akram Al Ariss and Jawad Syed, "Capital Mobilization of Skilled Migrants: A Relational Perspective," *British Journal of Management* 22 (2011): 286–304; Stuart C. Carr, Kerr Inkson and Kaye Thorn, "From Global Careers to Talent Flow: Reinterpreting 'Brain Drain,'" *Journal of World Businesses* 40 (2005): 386–98; Heike Jöns, "'Brain Circulation' and Transnational Knowledge Networks: Studying Long-Term Effects of Academic Mobility to Germany, 1954–2000," *Global Networks* 9(3) (2009): 315–38.
26. Pietsch, *Empire*.
27. Kathleen Thelen and Sven Steinmo, "Historical Institutionalism in Comparative Politics," in Sven Steinmo, Kathleen Thelen and Frank Longstreth (eds), *Structuring Politics: Historical Institutionalism in Comparative Analysis* (Cambridge: Cambridge University Press, 1992), pp. 1–32; James Mahoney and Kathleen Thelen (eds), *Explaining Institutional Change: Ambiguity, Agency, and Power* (Cambridge: Cambridge University Press, 2010).

References

Al Ariss, Akram, and Jawad Syed. "Capital Mobilization of Skilled Migrants: A Relational Perspective," *British Journal of Management* 22 (2011): 286–304.
Barber, William J. "A Footnote to the Social History of the 1970s: The Opening of the Rhodes Scholarships to Women," *American Oxonian* 87(2) (2000): 135–46.
Carr, Stuart C. Kerr Inkson, and Kaye Thorn, "From Global Careers to Talent Flow: Reinterpreting 'Brain Drain,'" *Journal of World Businesses* 40 (2005): 386–98.

Dean, Katrina. "Inscribing Settler Science: Ernest Rutherford, Thomas Laby and the Making of Careers in Physics," *History of Science* 41 (2003): 217–40.

Evans, Ralph (ed.). *Register of Rhodes Scholars, 1903–1998*, 1988 and 1996 edns (Oxford: Rhodes Trust, 1988 and 1996).

Jöns, Heike. "'Brain Circulation' and Transnational Knowledge Networks: Studying Long-Term Effects of Academic Mobility to Germany, 1954–2000," *Global Networks* 9(3) (2009): 315–38.

Mahoney, James, and Kathleen Thelen (eds). *Explaining Institutional Change: Ambiguity, Agency, and Power* (Cambridge: Cambridge University Press, 2010).

Pietsch, Tamson. "Many Rhodes: Travelling Scholarships and Imperial Citizenship in the British Academic World, 1880–1940," *History of Education* 40(6) (2011): 723–39.

———. *Empire of Scholars: Universities, Networks and the British Academic World, 1850–1939* (Manchester: Manchester University Press, 2013).

Rotberg, Robert I., and Miles F. Shore. *The Founder: Cecil Rhodes and the Pursuit of Power* (Oxford: Oxford University Press, 1988).

Schaeper, Thomas J., and Kathleen Schaeper. *Cowboys into Gentlemen: Rhodes Scholars, Oxford, and the Creation of the American Elite* (New York: Berghahn Books, 1998).

Thelen, Kathleen, and Sven Steinmo. "Historical Institutionalism in Comparative Politics," in Sven Steinmo, Kathleen Thelen, and Frank Longstreth (eds), *Structuring Politics: Historical Institutionalism in Comparative Analysis* (Cambridge: Cambridge University Press, 1992), 1–32.

Zeigler, Philip. *Legacy: Cecil Rhodes, the Rhodes Trust, and the Rhodes Scholarships* (New Haven, CT: Yale University Press, 2008).

 2

THE DEFEAT OF UNIVERSITY AUTONOMY
French Academic Diplomacy, Mobility Scholarships and Exchange Programs (1880s–1930s)
Guillaume Tronchet

Introduction

From the late nineteenth century to the 1930s, an increasing number of international students chose to study in France. They were only 500 in 1868. From 6,000 regularly enrolled students before World War I, their number reached to more than 17,000 in the interwar period, making the French university market one of the most attractive in the world. At the same time, the French Third Republic created a high-level academic network with around twenty institutes abroad, several hundred teachers of French language, and university chairs all over the world.

It is generally accepted that this development was a key part of French cultural diplomacy, in a sense a compensatory mechanism for restoring national prestige after the Franco-Prussian War of 1870. But international competition between states does not explain everything, and the concept of "cultural diplomacy" may be a trap for historians in understanding the richness and complexity of international higher education history. The international life of universities involved multiple transnational connections (mainly between institutions, academics, etc.) regardless of governments. Moreover, we must never forget that the concept of "cultural diplomacy," before being a useful category of analysis, was a category of practice, which foreign ministries used to incorporate under their administrative control all international activities distinct from military, economic or political considerations.[1] Under the French Third Republic, international higher education was a social space for struggles between different actors in order to dominate the field. Using the concept of "cultural diplomacy" therefore abides by the views of the winners, at the expense of studying specific social dynamics and actors forgotten by history.[2]

For these reasons, it is better to use the concept of "academic diplomacy," meaning the international and transnational actions developed in higher education, whether by state or nonstate actors, provided that such actions bear witness to the autonomy of academia from diplomacy. This chapter attempts to sketch out the rise of French academic diplomacy and the changing landscape of international academic policies throughout the French Third Republic, at the end of which the monopoly of the academic field declined in favor of the diplomatic field and its cultural diplomacy. This chapter will especially focus on mobility scholarships and exchange programs launched during this period, not just as useful examples to reveal what happened, but also to consider them as factors in the progressively weakening of university autonomy in international relations.

A Multilevel Approach

The beginning of the French Third Republic was a key moment for the emergence of international higher education in France and thinking on academic questions in a global context. This process resulted from interactions occurring on different scales (local, national and international), within which new scholarships and exchange programs were founded for the benefit of a small French elite.

National Trends

On a national scale, two trends of internationalization can be identified. The first one resulted from the fact that republicans who were involved in the reform of the French higher education system (members of the French government, senior members of the Ministry of Public Instruction and academics close to the government) looked beyond the French borders to learn from foreign models—particularly Germany—in order to upgrade the training of French elites[3] and strengthen the spread of French language and culture, in accordance with the imperialism of the Third Republic. In this context, in 1873 the Ministry of Public Instruction created the first national scholarships for mobility abroad, mainly to go to German universities. Six French students were selected annually for this award.[4] The same process was related to the foundation, in 1882, of a government office (Service des échanges universitaires) dedicated to the exchange of academic dissertations and scientific publications between French and thirty-nine foreign universities, mostly in Germany (about 45,000 copies were send abroad and 100,000 copies were received in France before 1914).[5]

The second national trend of internationalization was supported by academics (mainly in modern languages, history and archeology) who were interested in the creation of international mobility scholarships (between 1883 and 1914, about twenty young teachers in modern languages received a government-funded scholarship to study abroad each year)[6] or in the foundation of new French schools abroad, in order to develop their own fields of teaching and research (like the Ecole française de Rome, which was founded in 1873 to train a new generation of historians and archeologists).

By the 1880s, these proponents of internationalization met together to share ideas and projects within national and extraparliamentary fora (Alliance française, Société de l'enseignement supérieur, Société pour la propagation des langues étrangères, etc.). These formed a "reformist nebula"[7] in which certain norms of internationalization emerged or stabilized in the 1880–1890s. The "intellectual expansion" of France abroad was not a new theme,[8] but higher education now occupied a central role.

International Trends

At the same time, this internationalization process was also supported by social dynamics on a global scale. First, as Victor Karady has argued, rising levels of international migration in the 1890s led to the development of French courses being offered to foreigners, in order to meet the growing demand coming from national elites who lacked a higher education system, or people forced into academic exile because they had lost the right of access to higher education in their home country.[9] Among the forty nationalities represented in French universities before World War I, 51 percent of the international students came from the Russian Empire (including many Jewish refugees), while a majority of others came from Eastern Europe and the Ottoman Empire. At the time, there were no French scholarships for these international students.

In addition, the process was strengthened by the fact that French reformers and academics established new international standards that circulated via the 'global academic web' woven by the back-and-forth movement of actors and ideas in the worldwide higher education community.[10] Through organizing and attending international congresses and events in higher education, French participants benefited from discussions with their peers and ministry officials on topics ranging from the equivalence of degrees between different countries, the reception of international students and the general organization of higher education systems.[11]

Local trends

Local initiatives were also crucial in the rise of French academic diplomacy and mobility scholarships. With new standards for international development circulating within the global academic web and the French government keen to reform the university system, French universities launched initiatives to promote themselves on a global scale and thereby increase their number of students. They were assisted by local actors (mayors, lawyers, doctors and merchants) who wanted to develop their social capital, international networks, tourism and other economic opportunities for their cities. The national competition among French universities, especially between Paris and the rest and also between provincial universities themselves, was here a key factor in this international scramble. From the 1890s, academics and philanthropic citizens founded "committees of patronage for foreign students" in a dozen French university towns, such as Paris (1890), Lyon (1891), Nancy (1893) and Grenoble (1896), in order to raise funds, welcome international students and finance international activities. These committees provided information for foreign students on living facilities and finding accommodation in hotels or private homes in university towns. French universities did not have a campus[12] and student housing was therefore a key area for helping international students when they arrived in France. "The goal of these committees is to make the student's stay in France agreeable as well as profitable," said one observer.[13] Above all, holiday courses (or summer schools) for international students were created, particularly under the influence of the Oxford Summer Meetings, launched in 1888, and the German *Ferienkurse*, created in 1889. Prior to World War I, French universities took the leading position in organizing such events.[14]

These initiatives were significant for university budgets, contributed toward developing university course catalogs and stimulated the creation of new local academic degrees highly valued by international students.[15] To promote these developments, universities also drew up marketing campaigns with the financial support of the committees of patronage, which customized marketing materials (handbooks, posters and advertisements in the international press in many languages). In order to study in France, international students still had to rely on their own funding because the field of scholarships was still limited to

French mobility abroad only. Some of the French universities accepted private donations for funding two or three mobility scholarships a year (like the Albert Kahn Around-the-World Scholarships funded by the University of Paris in 1898),[16] while other universities invested in building branch campuses abroad at the beginning of the 1900s in order to mobilize transnational networks of municipal communities. In this way, the University of Lyon was very active in the Middle East with the foundation of a Law School in Beirut in 1913 (where some local students could learn French law), while Grenoble turned to Italy, Bordeaux and Toulouse to Spain, and Lille to Great Britain. The first French institutes of Florence, Madrid and London were also created in the early twentieth century.[17]

Toward a State Public Policy

The 1910s represented a turning point in the history of international academic relations for France. For the first time, and with different names—"foreign policy of universities" and "university expansion"— French academic diplomacy no longer depended only on uncoordinated local initiatives, intellectual debates and public authorities, but became a state public policy, conceptualized as a whole, and openly debated in Parliament and the national press. The beginning of the first exchange programs of students and professors launched or controlled by the government introduced a new framework for the landscape of scholarships.

The Nationalization of French Academic Diplomacy

This nationalization process saw a new generation of actors, often born in the 1870s, who thought that international higher education policies could serve their own careers, such as newly elected members of Parliament seeking a national cause to distinguish themselves in the political sphere or academics interested in going into senior public service. In 1910, all these actors teamed together in the Office national des universités et écoles françaises (ONUEF), an interest group that obtained investment credits from the Parliament for French academic diplomacy. A new budget line was introduced in 1912 via the Ministry of Public Instruction to support international academic activities. The ONUEF itself received subsidies to advise on the organization of French academic diplomacy and to propose reforms. Up to 1914, its director, Professor Jules Coulet, was very active. Social rights for French teachers who wanted to teach abroad were obtained in 1913 (their years abroad being recognized as part of their career progression); job offers for teachers of French were methodically listed by the ONUEF; the creation of French studies departments in foreign universities was encouraged (the University of Reykjavik in 1911, the universities of London and Amsterdam in 1912, the universities of Copenhagen, Helsinki and Oslo in 1913, and the universities of Kansas and Minnesota in 1914); a French handbook of higher education was published in 1914; and more equal terms for international students were introduced (equivalence of degrees and equal tuition fees for French and foreign students). The first exchange programs between French and US universities were negotiated and managed at a national level by the ONUEF. In 1911 an agreement was made between Harvard and the Sorbonne for an annual exchange of two professors (the first exchange professors were William M. Davis, Professor of Geology at Harvard, and Charles Diehl, Professor of Byzantine History at the Sorbonne), and in 1912 a similar arrangement was made for a young French professor to reside at Columbia in New York.

Government administration therefore became more present in the process, but the lack of centralized and dedicated offices for international academic affairs caused the organization of French academic diplomacy to develop as a federal apparatus. Provincial university initiatives, which sometimes tried to group themselves together for international activities without governmental agreement, were frozen. This nationalization process was not peculiar to France: national regulation of international academic affairs also took place in Germany, Spain (with the creation in 1907 of the Junta para Ampliacion de estudios e investigaciones scientificas) and Britain (with the creation in 1912 of the Universities Bureau of the British Empire). Far from narrowing the field of possibilities, these new national strata elevated existing initiatives, but did not replace them, instead shaping the opportunities for new repertoires of action. Ultimately, interstate cooperation would be improved by World War I.

World War I and Interstate Cooperation

The outbreak of war obviously impacted the international academic arena.[18] Some projects were brought to a standstill, like those for the development of student exchange. By 1915, French universities had lost 70 percent of their international students. Conversely, other sectors were boosted, like the sending of books and academic speakers abroad for French propaganda. In 1915 the ONUEF was charged by the government to send hundreds of thousands of copies of the *Manifesto by French Universities to the Universities of Neutral Countries*, published in November 1914, all over Europe.

But the main change was the reorganization of French academic relationships with foreign universities according to the diplomatic position of their country vis-à-vis France (allied, neutral or enemy). The war severed connections with German higher education, while it strengthened those with Allied nations. This situation disrupted the transnational dynamics of cooperation between academics and institutions, and led French academic diplomacy into interstate cooperation. The first step of this process was the arrival of thousands of Serb refugees, including students, and the conclusion of an academic exchange agreement between the two countries in November 1916, which provided the first French government scholarships for foreign students. The second step concerned the presence of US demobilized soldier-students in France, which led in 1919–20 to the organization by the ONUEF of an academic program for 5,000–6,000 American students in French universities.[19] These two episodes pushed all actors involved to take into account the increasing need for reciprocity in international higher education standards, building a bridge between the French imperialism of the nineteenth century and the intellectual cooperation that would shape international academic affairs in the 1920s. The decision to allow universities the right to confer honorary degrees on international figures—the Sorbonne conferred the first French degree of Doctor *Honoris causa* on President Woodrow Wilson in December 1918—was one of the symbols of this new state of affairs.

At the same time, French decision-making in international academic affairs increasingly followed a top-down process. With the general increase of the government's power during the war[20] and the ONUEF gradually becoming a pro-internationalization official higher education agency, universities were no longer able to stay at the forefront of international innovation. Gone were the days when back and forth was the norm between actors operating on different levels (local, national and global). At the end of the war, the Ministry of Public Instruction clearly set the tone. At the beginning of the 1920s, it concluded a dozen academic and scientific agreements between France and other countries, mainly for the exchange of professors: with Italy and Romania (1919), Yugoslavia (1920), Belgium (1921), Poland (1922) and Czechoslovakia (1923).

From Academic Diplomacy to Cultural Diplomacy

After World War I, the development of international academic relations benefited from the rise of "Geneva internationalism."[21] In 1933 an observer noted that "the number of agents—national and international, private and official—devoting all or part of their time to promoting understanding among nations through schools and universities [was] legion."[22] Only four national university offices, like the ONUEF, had been created before the war: in Germany, Britain, France and Spain. A dozen similar organizations were established afterwards, like the Institute of International Education in the United States (1919) and the Romanian University Office (1923), to promote their national education systems and launch academic exchange programs. Numerous international organizations were interested in international educational relations as well, such as the International Institute of Intellectual Cooperation, created in Paris in 1924.[23] As a result, the international mobility of students and professors increased. About 80,000 students were studying outside their country at the end of the 1920s.[24]

France quickly took the leading position in the international student market: 17,000 students came to France in 1931, about 20–25 percent of the number of those studying abroad at that time, while only 9,000 international students went to the United States, about 7,000 to Germany and 5,000 to Britain. In some provincial universities this rate even reached 80 percent, such as at the Rouen Faculty of Sciences in 1930. Beyond the intellectual influence of France after World War I, this leading position was due to the increasing investment of the government in the field of international higher education, which pursued a very liberal policy until the mid 1930s.[25] But academia no longer enjoyed the autonomy it had possessed in the 1900s for its international activities. The universities and the Ministry of Public Instruction were of course still involved in academic diplomacy, especially through the ONUEF, but the main change in the field of international academic affairs concerned the French Ministry of Foreign Affairs developing its own cultural diplomacy to compete with other nations, especially the fascist countries. In 1920, the Service des œuvres françaises à l'étranger was created to reorganize academic mobility abroad, to stimulate the foundation of French cultural institutes in strategic countries and to manage grants for international students in France. It was a turning point for academic exchanges, which not only became part of an imperial policy of academic *grandeur*, but were also progressively integrated into French foreign policy, under the control of diplomats. At the beginning of the twentieth century, academic exchange programs had not been based on diplomatic efforts to isolate Germany, like the Franco-Russian Alliance or the Entente Cordiale. Following World War I, academic activities at the international level were openly in line with the new goals of French foreign policy, mainly toward Central and Eastern Europe.

For example, new French Institutes were founded in Prague (1920), Zagreb (1922), Sofia (1922), Damascus (1922), Bucharest (1924), Warsaw (1925), Berlin (1930) and Vienna (1930). The directors, often academics, were not appointed by universities or the Ministry of Public Instruction, as was the case for French institutes in the 1910s, but by the Ministry of Foreign Affairs. At the same time, many government scholarships, based on the model established by French–Serbian cooperation during World War I, were created as part of a new state strategy to dominate the market of student elites coming from Eastern and Central Europe. Each year, about 800 international students (approximately 5 percent of the total number of students who came to France) benefited from fee reductions and government scholarships created by the Ministry of Public Instruction. The Russians were the most numerous (about 300 students), followed by the Yugoslavs (about 200) and Romanians (about 100). The Ministry of Foreign Affairs also created its own scholarships for about 100 international students selected each year by French embassies and consulates, with a focus on Czechs (fifteen to twenty scholarships per year), Yugoslavs (about fifteen scholarships), Poles (about fifteen scholarships), Hungarians (between eight and ten scholarships) and Bulgarians (between six and nine scholarships).[26]

To ensure that the accommodation conformed to new hygiene and healthcare standards, the French government was also involved in building new campuses. The first and the largest was the Cité universitaire de Paris, created in 1921 with the help of the University of Paris, the municipality of Paris and the wealthy and philanthropic industrialist Emile Deutsch de la Meurthe. In south Paris, near the Parc Montsouris, thirty-five hectares were taken for nineteen student houses built between 1921 and 1939, with financial support from leading figures of transnational philanthropy (such as Murry Guggenheim, John D. Rockefeller, Jr. and David David-Weill).[27] Before World War II, up to 2,500 French and international students lived each year in the Cité universitaire. With this as a model several other *cités universitaires* were created in France during the 1930s, contributing to the attractiveness of provincial universities. To confirm the government's dominant position, in 1938 the ONUEF and the Cité universitaire de Paris were themselves contracted by the Ministry of Foreign Affairs for the housing of scholarship students.

As there were frequent conflicts within the French government between actors related either to the Ministry of Public Instruction or to the Ministry of Foreign Affairs,[28] the academic diplomats tried to preserve their autonomy throughout the 1930s, but without success. The international academic policy of France gradually came under the control of governmental cultural diplomacy. In 1932, when Paul-Henri Siriex, a student in political sciences, benefited from the first scholarship provided by Oxford University to a French student (under a general agreement negotiated by the ONUEF with the universities of Oxford and London to exchange five French and five British students), he clearly received instructions to spy on the British student aristocracy, as well as the activities of German students on the campus, and his reports were duly sent by the ONUEF to the Ministry of Foreign Affairs.[29]

This instrumental political reaction was part of a growing global trend. At the end of the interwar period, international higher education was certainly not just an arena reserved for academics or pacifists. Specialists in comparative education were under no illusions. In 1933, in a critical review of a book on intellectual relations, an observer pointed out this ambiguity: "many will be inclined to wonder what meaning is to be attached to the phrase 'international understanding' when the funds expended by the French Government in bringing students from Yugoslavia to Paris are cited as evidence of its pursuit in the section dealing with International Student Exchange."[30] In the middle of the 1930s, international understanding or peace was clearly not a French priority in relation to organizing academic exchanges.

Conclusion

The economic crisis and the rise of nationalisms in the 1930s, in shrinking the access to national academic markets, generated a contraction in the internationalization of higher education and an increasing role for governments in academic affairs, both of which induced a decline in university autonomy. In this context, reciprocity was less an academic ideal than a political tool, and scholarships and exchange programs founded after World War I were under the control of diplomatic imperatives, even when programs were still managed by universities or the Ministry of Public Instruction. This "diplomatization" process was not temporary either. World War II and the postwar context would not fundamentally change the new dynamics of international educational exchange.

Guillaume Tronchet is professeur agrégé d'histoire, research associate at the Institut d'histoire moderne et contemporaine (ENS, University of Paris 1 Panthéon-Sorbonne, CNRS) and special adviser to the director of the Ecole normale supérieure. He holds a Ph.D. from the University of Paris 1 Pantheon-Sorbonne and specializes in international history of higher education. He has coedited a book on the history of the Cité internationale universitaire de Paris with Dzovinar Kévonian: *La Babel étudiante. La Cité internationale universitaire de Paris* (Presses universitaires de Rennes, 2013). He is preparing a single-authored monograph on the internationalization of French Higher Education in the nineteenth and twentieth centuries.

Appendix: The French-Serbian Academic Exchange Agreement of 1916

From the beginning of World War I, France took several academic initiatives to support her Serbian ally: a "Serbian Day" was launched in March 1915 by the Ministry of Public Instruction to raise funds for Serbian school children; conferences on Serbia were organized in universities; and propaganda books were published. In the autumn of 1915, the retreat of the Serbian army caused a wave of refugees. French academic diplomacy was mobilized and the Ministry of Public Instruction founded a committee in December 1915 to coordinate the reception of Serbian refugees in the French education system. The ONUEF led the operations for the reception of hundreds of Serbian students in universities. In order to strengthen cooperation, France and Serbia signed a convention in Corfu, on 9 November 1916, and another one in Paris, on 27 November 1917. These agreements provided scholarships for Serbian students who wanted to study in France (400 were created by the Serbian Government and 100 by the French government each year); courses in Serbian for students in French universities (a chair of Serbian language and literature was created at the Ecole nationale des langues orientales); and conferences on Serbia for French students. This was the first academic agreement concluded between two states on such a large scale (in 1918, 44 percent of international students in French universities were Serbs) and based on reciprocity. It became a model for all of the academic agreements concluded in the 1920s by France with other countries.

Table 2.1 Serbian students in French universities, 1914–21

	1914	1915	1916	1917	1918	1919	1920	1921
Serbian students	103	15	125	586	1,416	1,546	1,437	1,179
Percentage of Serbians among foreign students	1.6	0.8	6.4	24.4	44.2	25.6	28.3	18.2
French scholarships for Serbian students	–	–	–	84	112	105	107	106

Source: *Annuaire statistique de la France*, 1916–18, 1919–20

Notes

1. Pierre Bourdieu, *Esquisse d'une théorie de la pratique* (Paris: Droz, 1972).
2. Guillaume Tronchet, "Savoirs en diplomatie: Une histoire sociale et transnationale de la politique universitaire internationale de la France, années 1870–années 1930," Ph.D. dissertation (Paris: University of Paris 1 Panthéon-Sorbonne, 2014).
3. George Weisz, *The Emergence of Modern Universities in France, 1863–1914* (Princeton, NJ: Princeton University Press, 1983); Christophe Charle, *La République des universitaires, 1870–1940* (Paris: Le Seuil, 1994); Christine Musselin, *The Long March of French Universities* (London: Routledge, 2004).
4. We have practically no information on these scholarships, which were founded by the Ministry of Public Instruction Jules Simon. The few existing documents in the archives of the Ministry suggest that the system was not formalized.
5. Tronchet, "Savoirs en diplomatie," 110–24.
6. Tronchet, "Savoirs en diplomatie," 81–85.
7. Christian Topalov (ed.), *Laboratoires du nouveau siècle: La nébuleuse réformatrice et ses réseaux en France, 1880–1914* (Paris: Editions de l'EHESS, 1999).
8. Rahul Markovits, *Civiliser l'Europe. Politique du théâtre français au XVIIIe siècle* (Paris: Fayard, 2014).
9. Victor Karady, "La République des lettres des temps modernes. L'internationalisation des marchés universitaires occidentaux avant la Grande Guerre," *Actes de la recherche en sciences sociales* 121–22 (1998): 92–103; "La migration internationale d'étudiants en Europe (1890–1940)," *Actes de la recherche en sciences sociales* 145 (2002): 47–60.
10. This idea is inspired by Pierre-Yves Saunier's work about the "municipal web": "La toile municipale aux 19e–20e siècles: un panorama transnational vu d'Europe," *Revue d'histoire urbaine* 24(2) (2006): 163–76.
11. Tronchet, "Savoirs en diplomatie," 101–66.
12. Tronchet, "Savoirs en diplomatie," 214–18; Pierre Moulinier, *Les étudiants étrangers à Paris au XIXe siècle* (Rennes: Presses universitaires de Rennes, 2011).

13. "The Reception of Foreign Students in French Universities and Schools," *Science*, March 27, 1896, 467.
14. Tronchet, "Savoirs en diplomatie," 195–201.
15. Between 1898 and 1914, French universities created about 190 academic degrees (Ph.D. degrees, certificates of French studies, etc.).
16. Guillaume Tronchet, "Les bourses de voyage 'Autour du Monde' de la Fondation Albert Kahn (1898–1930): les débuts de l'internationalisation universitaire, 1860–1914," in Christophe Charle and Laurent Jeanpierre (eds), *La vie intellectuelle en France, XIXe–XXe s.* (Paris: Le Seuil, 2016), 618–20; Whitney Walton, "Cultural Internationalism in the Albert Kahn Around-the-World Boursiers's Report on France and the United States (1898–1930)," in Anne Dulphy, Robert Frank, Marie-Anne Matard-Bonucci and Pascal Ory (eds), *Les relations culturelles internationales au XXe siècle: De la diplomatie culturelle à l'acculturation* (Brussels: Peter Lang, 2010), 471–82.
17. For an updated bibliography on these institutions, see Tronchet, "Savoirs en diplomatie," 575–76.
18. Tomás Irish, *The University at War, 1914–25: Britain, France, and the United States* (New York: Palgrave Macmillan, 2015).
19. Tronchet, "Savoirs en diplomatie," 353–69; Caroline Barrera, "Les étudiants-soldats américains en France au sortir de la Première Guerre mondiale," *Histoire de l'éducation* 125 (2010): 27–47.
20. Nicolas Roussellier, *La force de gouverner: Le pouvoir exécutif en France, XIXe–XXe siècles* (Paris: Gallimard, 2015).
21. Hans de Wit, *Internationalization of Higher Education in the United States of America and Europe: A Historical, Comparative and Conceptual Analysis* (Westport, CT: Greenwood Publishing Group, 2002).
22. Spencer Stoker, *The Schools and International Understanding* (Chapel Hill, NC: University of North Carolina Press, 1933), 3.
23. Founded in 1924, this Institute was distinct from the International Committee on Intellectual Cooperation of the League of Nations, but worked closely with it. See Jean-Jacques Renoliet, *L'Unesco oubliée: La Société des nations et la coopération intellectuelle, 1919–1946* (Paris: Publications de la Sorbonne, 1999).
24. Herbert Scurla, *Umfang und Richtung des Ausländerstudiums* (Dresden: Studentenwerk, 1929).
25. Patrick Weil, *How to Be French: Nationality in the Making since 1789* (Durham, NC: Duke University Press, 2008).
26. Tronchet, "Savoirs en diplomatie," 455–58.
27. Dzovinar Kévonian and Guillaume Tronchet (eds), *La Babel étudiante: La Cité internationale universitaire de Paris, 1920–1950* (Rennes: Presses universitaires de Rennes, 2013); Guillaume Tronchet, "La Cité universitaire: une *joint-venture* transnationale dans le Paris des années 1920 et 1930. Note de recherche," in Serge Jaumain and Pierre Van den Dungen (eds), *Biermans-Lapôtre: Histoire d'un mécène et de sa fondation* (Paris: Roche, 2013), 85–100.
28. For a concrete example, see also Guillaume Tronchet, "'Un bluff perpétuel' : Les dessous de la présence française dans l'Université turque (années 1930)," in Gunes Isiksel and Emmanuel Szurek (eds), *Turcs et Français:*

Une histoire culturelle, 1860–1960 (Rennes: Presses universitaires de Rennes, 2014), 285–305.
29. Paul-Henri Siriex, Souvenirs en vérité, 1930–1980: Oxford, Londres 1940, Afrique, Madagascar, Djibouti, Inde, URSS, Sibérie (Paris: Editions des écrivains, 1998).
30. International Affairs (Royal Institute of International Affairs 1931–1939) 12(6) (1933): 790–91.

References

Barrera, Caroline. "Les étudiants-soldats américains en France au sortir de la Première Guerre mondiale," Histoire de l'éducation 125 (2010): 27–47.
Bourdieu, Pierre. Esquisse d'une théorie de la pratique (Paris: Droz, 1972).
Charle, Christophe. La République des universitaires, 1870–1940 (Paris: Seuil, 1994).
De Wit, Hans. Internationalization of Higher Education in the United States of America and Europe: A Historical, Comparative and Conceptual Analysis (Westport, CT: Greenwood Publishing Group, 2002).
Irish, Tomás. The University at War, 1914–25: Britain, France, and the United States (New York: Palgrave Macmillan, 2015).
Karady, Victor. "La migration internationale d'étudiants en Europe (1890–1940)," Actes de la recherche en sciences sociales 145 (2002): 47–60.
——. "La République des lettres des temps modernes: L'internationalisation des marchés universitaires occidentaux avant la Grande Guerre," Actes de la recherche en sciences sociales 121–22 (1998): 92–103.
Kevonian, Dzovinar, and Guillaume Tronchet (eds). La Babel étudiante: La Cité internationale universitaire de Paris, 1920–1950 (Rennes: Presses universitaires de Rennes, 2013).
Moulinier, Pierre. Les étudiants étrangers à Paris au XIXe siècle (Rennes: Presses universitaires de Rennes, 2011).
Musselin, Christine. The Long March of French Universities (London: Routledge, 2004).
Renoliet, Jean-Jacques. L'Unesco oubliée: La Société des nations et la coopération intellectuelle, 1919–1946 (Paris: Publications de la Sorbonne, 1999).
Roussellier, Nicolas. La force de gouverner: Le pouvoir exécutif en France, XIXe–XXe siècles (Paris: Gallimard, 2015).
Saunier, Pierre-Yves. "La toile municipale aux 19e–20e siècles: un panorama transnational vu d'Europe," Revue d'histoire urbaine XXIV(2) (2006): 163–76.
Topalov, Christian (ed.). Laboratoires du nouveau siècle: La nébuleuse réformatrice et ses réseaux en France, 1880–1914 (Paris: Editions de l'EHESS, 1999).
Tronchet, Guillaume. "La Cité universitaire: une joint-venture transnationale dans le Paris des années 1920 et 1930. Note de recherche," in Serge Jaumain and Pierre Van den Dungen (eds), Biermans-Lapôtre. Histoire d'un mécène et de sa fondation (Paris: Roche, 2013), 85–100.
——. "'Un bluff perpétuel': Les dessous de la présence française dans l'Université turque (années 1930)," in Gunes Isiksel and Emmanuel Szurek

(eds), *Turcs et Français: Une histoire culturelle, 1860–1960* (Rennes: Presses universitaires de Rennes, 2014), 285–305.

———. "Savoirs en diplomatie: Une histoire sociale et transnationale de la politique universitaire internationale de la France, années 1870–années 1930," Ph.D. dissertation. Paris: University of Paris 1 Panthéon-Sorbonne, 2014.

———. "Les bourses de voyage 'Autour du Monde' de la Fondation Albert Kahn (1898–1930): les débuts de l'internationalisation universitaire," in Christophe Charle and Laurent Jeanpierre (eds), *La vie intellectuelle en France (XIXe–XXe s.)* (Paris: Seuil, 2016), 618–20.

Walton, Whitney. "Cultural Internationalism in the Albert Kahn Around-the-World Boursiers's Report on France and the United States (1898–1930)," in Anne Dulphy, Robert Frank, Marie-Anne Matard-Bonucci and Pascal Ory (eds), *Les relations culturelles internationales au XXe siècle: De la diplomatie culturelle à l'acculturation* (Brussels: Peter Lang, 2010), 471–82.

Weil, Patrick. *How to Be French: Nationality in the Making since 1789* (Durham, NC: Duke University Press, 2008).

Weisz, George. *The Emergence of Modern Universities in France, 1863–1914* (Princeton, NJ: Princeton University Press, 1983).

 3

THE COMMONWEALTH UNIVERSITY INTERCHANGE SCHEME
Promoting Exchanges in a Changing World (1948–60)

Alice Byrne

Introduction

When Eric Ashby published his informal portrait of the Association of Universities of the British Commonwealth (AUBC) in 1963, he noted that the interchange and secondment of staff between Commonwealth universities had long been one of its perennial topics of discussion. He commented: "It is extraordinary how frequently this last topic is talked about and approved and yet how difficult it is to turn pious resolutions into fruitful action."[1]

This chapter is concerned with the AUBC's first concerted attempt to do just this through the establishment of the Commonwealth University Interchange Scheme (CUIS) in 1948. It explores both the "pious resolutions" on which the scheme was founded and the reasons why it proved so difficult to turn them into "fruitful action." In particular, the scheme's administrators would grapple with the profound changes that were redefining the Commonwealth and their implications for academic exchange. Their story is one of failure: although the CUIS ran until 1980, within a decade of its launch it had already been largely superseded by the Commonwealth Scholarship and Fellowship Plan (CSFP). But this is also a story that reveals the tensions inherent in using an international framework to promote a transnational academic community whose members belonged to universities that were themselves guided by national imperatives.

As Ashby pointed out, the interchange of staff had been regularly discussed at meetings of the AUBC's predecessor, the Bureau of Empire Universities, since the beginning of the twentieth century. Tamson

Pietsch has described the interwar consensus as to the importance of individual academics moving within the network of empire universities as a means of consolidating this "expansive British community."[2] Yet the first comprehensive program of exchanges aimed exclusively at the universities of the Commonwealth did not come into existence until after World War II, by which time the "bonds of empire" that it was arguably intended to hold in place were already unraveling.[3] As we shall see, the CUIS failed to evolve into the large-scale program that its originators had imagined, largely because it did not match the pattern of development of academic communities in the "old" Dominions. At the same time, the establishment of the CUIS coincided with Indian independence and the subsequent mutation of the British Commonwealth into the Commonwealth.

At a basic level, the CUIS offered travel grants to encourage greater academic mobility between the countries of the Commonwealth. However, it was also an ambitious attempt to create a centralized, independent, university-led Commonwealth body, which would collect funds contributed by the governments of all the member states and use them to give concrete expression to the somewhat nebulous ties of the Commonwealth. Although the scheme was mainly funded by the UK government, and its committee met in London, it cannot be defined as a solely British enterprise. Nor did the project emanate from the UK government with clear foreign policy objectives in mind. The scheme sprang instead from the overlapping interests of different agencies, which did not necessarily agree as to its ideal form and purpose. This chapter deals first with the origins of the scheme, in an attempt to identify its objectives. It then focuses on its unsuccessful expansion, illustrating the tensions at work in the field of Commonwealth exchange. At heart, the different parties involved did not share the same visions of the Commonwealth, nor did they seek the same benefits from the scheme.

Establishing the CUIS

Aims and Objectives

The conception of the scheme may be ascribed to Sir Hector Hetherington, the Principal of Glasgow University and Chairman of the British Committee of Vice-Chancellors and Principals. Hetherington was the driving force behind the 1948 Congress, which revived the Bureau of Empire Universities, enabling its transformation into the Association of Universities of the British Commonwealth (significantly, the qualifying "British" was not dropped until 1963). The CUIS was thus part of a wider attempt to consolidate longstanding university connections within the Commonwealth after the disruption of war. Furthermore, Sir Hector had his finger in a multitude of cultural and educational pies at an international level. He worked with the Foreign Office in re-establishing exchange with West German universities, participated in a committee on cultural relations with India and was also involved in the Fulbright Program.[4] He was therefore particularly well-placed to judge how the refashioning of international relations would impact both the British universities and the wider British academic world. It seems reasonable to assume that he was concerned with making sure that British universities would be able to compete with their US counterparts by encouraging the circulation of academics within the Commonwealth. Certainly the comparison with the Fulbright Program and the need to provide similar opportunities within the Commonwealth for the interchange of scholars was brought out explicitly in a 1953 report on the scheme.[5]

One of the most obvious obstacles to establishing a formal exchange program was financial. Although some universities already ran bilateral exchanges with Commonwealth partners, a more ambitious scheme would inevitably require substantial funding. Hetherington's position at the heart of a wide network of educational and political relations enabled him to lay the groundwork for the scheme by obtaining an informal commitment from Patrick Gordon-Walker, the parliamentary Under-Secretary of State at the Commonwealth Relations Office (CRO), to provide £15,000 a year, channeled through the British Council.[6] The scheme offered obvious political advantages to the United Kingdom. The Empire and Commonwealth remained the cornerstone of the United Kingdom's claim to great power status and yet by the late 1940s, it had become an empire of "influence and identity" rather than one characterized by commercial and military power.[7] Reinforcing a sense of community among its increasingly independent members through cultural and educational links would serve to bolster UK foreign policy.

With the assurance that some support would be forthcoming from the UK government, Hetherington was able to invite delegates at the 1948 Congress of Empire Universities to seek funding from the official bodies of their respective countries in order to "enable teaching staffs on leave to travel within the Commonwealth, and to facilitate visits of distinguished scholars of one part of the Commonwealth to another."[8] Attendance at the Congress was in itself proof of his audience's commitment to the Commonwealth. Nevertheless, he sought to persuade them of the importance of extending opportunities for academics to circulate within the Commonwealth by arguing:

> We are very different from one another. Each of us is bent on going his own way, yet in some genuine spiritual sense we belong together. We share in a great political and social experiment and our very diversity means that interchange between us is an experience which enlarges the resources of all of us.[9]

Hetherington's introductory remarks carefully avoided any suggestion of British predominance within the proposed scheme, while reasserting the profound sense of community that held the Commonwealth together.

Structure and Key Players

A resolution in favor of establishing an interchange scheme was easily carried by the 1948 Congress. With Hetherington in the chair, a committee was formed that rapidly drew up a plan to offer travel grants to three different types of visitors: university teachers and officers on paid study leave who would spend at least six months in another Commonwealth country (category A); distinguished scholars invited by universities for shorter visits (category B); and, finally, postgraduate researchers, who were given the lowest priority (category C). The scheme thus sought to encourage the circulation of established scholars rather than students or future leaders. It was intended to maintain the long-established links between the universities of the Commonwealth, to bind them in a unit within which academics could pursue their careers, and to spread knowledge and good practice throughout the Commonwealth.

The CUIS committee was made up of representatives of the AUBC, the Committee of Vice-Chancellors and Principals of Universities in the United Kingdom and of the Universities Advisory Committee of the British Council. In practice, membership of the three bodies overlapped: Hetherington, for example, was active in all three and was largely responsible for the composition of the latter. There was an inevitable British bias and although three of the seven members were in fact Australian, they did not specifically represent Australian interests. Furthermore, the committee was comprised of university officials rather than representatives of public bodies, the only exception being the secretary who was provided by the British Council. Despite this, the Council would come to play an essential role in running the program.

The British Council was an arm's-length organization through which the UK government pursued its international cultural and educational policies. In 1934, the Council had been assigned the task of making "the life and thought of the British peoples more widely-known abroad" and many of its senior executives had defined this task in imperial terms. Its postwar policy was to encourage the countries of the Commonwealth to set up their own "sister" councils, with the British Council playing the role of the elder sibling.[10] The British Council envisaged the CUIS fitting into a comprehensive program of Commonwealth cultural relations, managed by this network of national councils.[11]

The Council naturally accepted the CRO's invitation to provide the secretariat for the CUIS and to administer the funds it provided. Unfortunately, the Treasury initially refused to sanction the necessary increase in the CRO's grant to the British Council and, despite the 1948 resolution, none of the universities took any steps toward obtaining funds from private or public bodies elsewhere in the Commonwealth.[12] The first round of awards was therefore funded out of the Council's budget by reducing the number of the Council's own dominion scholarships, to the consternation of some of its staff.[13] When CRO funding was finally established the following year, it was half the sum that had originally been promised.[14]

In these circumstances, it is not surprising that there was a certain amount of confusion as to where responsibility for the interchange scheme lay. In theory the scheme was to be run in the interests of the Commonwealth universities, not of UK foreign policy, but given the involvement of different partners, the selection process inevitably proved problematic. The CUIS committee insisted that candidates should be selected according to their academic merit, whereas the Council tended to take other criteria into consideration. As the Council Representative in Australia put it: "from the point of view of the Council some candidates are good ambassadors and other of the recluse type are less good."[15] In practice, some Council representatives pressed to be given a say in the choice of candidates and their confidential comments were communicated discreetly to the CUIS committee.[16] The Council also on rare occasions did contribute directly to the scheme's budget to ensure funding for particular candidates and/or countries. The Council's role therefore went beyond simple administrative duties.

Extending the Scheme

Obstacles to Expansion

Despite the CUIS committee's insistence on academic criteria, the political implications of the scheme were clearly drawn out in a report submitted to the AUBC's 1953 Congress. It stressed the role that university teachers played in training future elites and the importance of contact between universities as a means of ensuring the "mutual understanding of the differences of outlook" on which the Commonwealth depended.[17] This section was deliberately aimed at Commonwealth governments in the hope that they would fund the scheme. In particular, it wished to counter the belief that the Dominions basically shared the same outlook because of their "common origin."[18] Even the UK government, the only one to actually fund the scheme, was skeptical of the need to support such programs with other "British" nations. As a result, the CUIS and the British Council's Commonwealth policy were both badly affected by postwar austerity budget cuts in the late 1940s and early 1950s, culminating in the closure of the Council's offices in Australia and New Zealand in 1954. The easing of spending restrictions in the mid 1950s coincided with a shift in the UK government's policy, which, following its acceptance of the Drogheda Report (1954), directed the Council to give priority to developing countries. The Hill Report, commissioned in the wake of the Suez Crisis, recommended boosting public spending on educational work in developing countries as a way to restore the United Kingdom's much-damaged prestige. Thus, in the late 1950s, new funding became available for the developing parts of the Commonwealth and the Empire, including money earmarked for scholarships.[19] The future development of the CUIS would therefore be determined by the political priorities of Commonwealth governments, none of which considered the maintenance of a peculiarly British academic community a prime concern.

Lack of funds meant that in its first years, the CUIS remained little more than a pilot scheme. In April 1951, the CUIS committee noted with pleasure the Massey Report's recommendations in favor of widening Canada's international academic contact through scholarships, the Australian government's decision to create the Australian National University and the moves being made in India toward establishing a University Grants Committee.[20] All of this progress seemed to augur well for the CUIS. However, in fact, as the countries of the Commonwealth set up their own institutions, the appeal of a centralized Commonwealth interchange scheme diminished. Investment in these projects tended to detract funding from Commonwealth plans while endowing these countries with sufficient national capacity as to make foreign travel less important.²¹ When the CUIS committee tried to win more committed support for the scheme at the AUBC's Seventh Congress in Cambridge in 1953, it found itself running up against political and constitutional issues.

One possibility explored by the CUIS committee was that of following the model of foreign university interchange administered by the British Council. In this system participating countries negotiated bilateral agreements. This was rejected almost outright, partly on the grounds that the United Kingdom would struggle to find enough candidates to send abroad.²² The implication here was that, despite the rhetoric of the Commonwealth family, exchanges with European universities were more symmetrical. The committee also felt that decentralization was incompatible with a "unified Commonwealth project" and would not allow the whole Commonwealth to benefit from the larger contribution that the United Kingdom could be expected to make, "in view of its special position."²³ It was taken as axiomatic that the United Kingdom would continue to play a dominant role. Although the committee was willing to admit new members if and when other Commonwealth bodies provided funding, the location of its meetings and the predominantly British nature of its composition were never called into question.

Commonwealth Reactions to the Committee's Plans

The committee's determination to maintain a centralized system faced opposition at the meeting of the heads of universities held immediately before the 1953 AUBC Congress.²⁴ The resolution placed before the Congress referred, with deliberate ambiguity, to a "co-operatively administered fund" and was passed without receiving the votes of the delegates from Montreal.²⁵ The 1951 Massey Report, which had called for a new federal commitment to Canadian education and culture, had stoked French Canadian opposition to federal interference in higher education, which was constitutionally the preserve of provincial government. The St Laurent government then started an "intergovernmental tug-of-war" by offering universities federal grants that Quebec instructed its institutions to refuse.²⁶ In such circumstances, the Quebecois universities were unlikely to seek federal funding for a scholarship scheme administered from London.²⁷ The National Conference of Canadian Universities subsequently informed the CUIS committee that it would not approach the federal government with a request for extra funds for the scheme because it was already trying to persuade it to establish federal scholarships.[28] According to Granatstein, until the Canada Council was set up in 1957, funding scholarships had simply not formed part of the "Canadian tradition."[29] Given the political sensitivity of this issue, it is no surprise that the Canada Council later refused to pay into the centralized Commonwealth fund, even though it did offer awards to candidates recommended by the CUIS committee.[30]

The universities of New Zealand and Ceylon (Sri Lanka) also declined to approach their governments: the first argued that it was not an "opportune" moment, while the second cited university and government policy as well as emphasizing financial constraints.[31] Requesting central government funding was also problematic for the South African universities. Although the introduction of apartheid in 1948 does not appear to have affected the position of the South African universities within the AUBC, the 1953 Congress proceedings indicated attempts by their government to make university grants conditional on the strict implementation of racial segregation among students.[32] The South African universities nevertheless made a request to the National Party government, which had been returned to power in the 1953 elections. As a Afrikaner nationalist party with, at best, an ambivalent attitude to the United Kingdom and the Commonwealth, it was unlikely to be sympathetic to the CUIS.[33] The South African request was refused.[34]

Of all the Commonwealth countries, Australia was the most involved in the CUIS: it received the highest number of awards and the largest slice of the scheme's budget, as well as being better represented on the committee.[35] The Australian universities proved more supportive, but opted to fund the scheme directly rather than approach the central government.[36] As in Canada, funding was a contentious issue as universities like Melbourne were seeking a commitment from all levels of government to finance their expansion. Their willingness to contribute to the CUIS depended on its perceived usefulness within the framework of the national development of higher education. The Australian grant averaged £ 2,000 per annum, but was not matched by any other Commonwealth country and the committee's budget remained insufficient for the proposed expansion.[37]

The CUIS committee had been hopeful that India would also provide a significant contribution to its funds, on a par with the £ 5,000 mooted for Canada and Australia.[38] No such contribution was forthcoming, though the CUIS archives do not provide an explanation. Indian and Pakistani delegates at the 1953 AUBC Congress had nevertheless spoken in favor of the scheme, inasmuch as it could work in the interests of their scientific, technological and economic development and contribute to the expansion of their universities. Dr Bashir Ahmad, Vice-Chancellor of the University of the Panjab, warmly welcomed the proposed expansion of the scheme in 1953, whilst reminding delegates of the importance of supporting the development of certain parts of the Commonwealth as "real unity and solidarity can develop only between equal partners."[39] In the same discussion, Sir C.P. Ramaswami Aiyar of Annamalai University, India highlighted the importance of ensuring a two-way exchange of teachers as a means to encouraging "deep ideological comprehension."[40] The latter speaker wished to see more distinguished Indian scholars being sent abroad as a means of educating fellow members of the Commonwealth in Indian culture, serving also to enhance Indian prestige. The most recent members of the Commonwealth supported the CUIS as a way of furthering their national interests rather than consolidating a transnational academic community.

The CUIS and the "New" Commonwealth

The universities of the Indian subcontinent were clearly not integrated into the British academic world in the way that those of the "old" Commonwealth were. The CUIS committee's lack of knowledge of these institutions and of contacts with their executives made it more difficult for it to assess their candidates.[41] This partly explains why comments from British Council representatives were unofficially welcome in relation to Indian and Pakistani applicants.[42] The secretary of the interchange scheme was aware of the danger of "making invidious distinctions between the older and newer countries of the Commonwealth." Yet distinctions were made, albeit off the record.[43] The fact that the awards only covered travel costs in itself indicates that the scheme was not devised with the needs of Indian and Pakistani candidates in mind. University teachers' salaries were much lower in these countries; even on fully paid leave, they struggled to meet the costs of living in Britain, especially if they had families to support back home.[44] This reinforced the asymmetrical nature of exchanges with the Indian subcontinent that Ramaswami Aiyar touched on. It also explains why the CUIS committee struggled at times to find sufficient candidates to take up travel grants in the late 1950s when more funds were made available for these countries.[45]

This lack of attention to the needs of scholars from these countries is perhaps surprising given that, from the point of view of both the British Council and the UK government, university exchanges with the newer members of the Commonwealth were of far greater political importance than the longer-established patterns of mobility between the United Kingdom and the Dominions. Cultural and educational relations were seen as a way of maintaining a degree of UK influence over the new states, particularly when it enabled British academics to hold positions of authority in institutes of higher education and research where they might mold future leaders.[46] The universities were defined as the most important target for British Council activities in India, not least because they were seen as "breeding grounds" for communism.[47] Keeping Indian higher education within a British sphere of influence became a Cold War objective, though resisting US influence was considered equally important.[48] The interchange scheme could contribute to this objective by facilitating the circulation of academics between the United Kingdom and India. This was a concrete way of responding to a 1954 memorandum by the UK High Commission in India, which urged strengthening and encouraging what it termed the "healthier elements" in Indian universities, i.e. pro-British professors and students.[49]

Cold War imperatives and the shift to a developmental agenda meant that when pressure to limit public spending began to ease in the United Kingdom, priority would be given to increasing the number of CUIS travel grants to candidates from the Indian subcontinent. This coincided with the decision to extend the scheme to university institutes in the colonies, for which the committee had obtained approval from both the 1953 AUBC Congress and the Colonial Office. When the CUIS budget began to rise in the second half of the 1950s, this was largely thanks to an annual £ 2,000 grant from the Colonial Development and Welfare Fund and, in 1959, an additional £ 6,000 per year from the CRO destined for India and Pakistan.[50] At the February meeting of the committee in 1958, four category A awards were made to India; in the same month two years later, thirteen such awards were made, four of them financing travel to Australia. Indeed, thanks to the Australian and Colonial contributions, a limited number of awards were finally being used to promote travel between Commonwealth countries other than the United Kingdom.[51] However, sending colonial students to India elicited concern about communist indoctrination.[52]

Conclusion

The CUIS as it was drawn up in 1948 had represented the belated application of the ideas of the interwar period. As the 1950s gave way to the 1960s, Commonwealth interchange could no longer be defined in terms of traditional patterns of mobility between the United Kingdom as "mother country" and the Dominions. The failure to attract significant contributions from the "old" Commonwealth, combined with the UK government's new policy, led to a repositioning of the CUIS. The Commonwealth ceased to be conceived as a diverse but organic whole. Facilitating exchanges between the developed and developing countries of the Commonwealth came to the fore, arguably placing the CUIS in a better position to ease the transition to a vastly expanded multiracial Commonwealth. However, the success of the Canadian proposal for a Commonwealth Scholarship and Fellowship Plan (CSFP) in 1958 indicated that the future of Commonwealth exchanges lay in a looser, decentralized program.[53] The academics who had sought the British Council's support ten years earlier were quick to press the AUBC's case as the UK government's agent in administering the new fund. The British Council was assigned a secondary role. Above all, it was the CSFP that would attempt to give body to the new academic community of the Commonwealth which resulted from the expansion of universities in both its older member states and in the countries that were acceding to independence. The CUIS lived on as effectively a British rather than a Commonwealth program.

Alice Byrne lectures in British Studies at Aix Marseille Université and is a member of the LERMA research group. Her research explores different facets of British cultural diplomacy in the twentieth century, ranging from cultural propaganda in World War II and the early Cold War to the development of educational and cultural exchanges within the Commonwealth.

Appendix: Sir Hector Hetherington (1888–1965)

Sir Hector Hetherington began his career as a lecturer in philosophy and later held chairs in that discipline at Cardiff, Exeter and Glasgow. However, it was primarily in the field of university administration that he made his mark, first at Exeter and Liverpool before returning to Glasgow. During his time as Principal of the University of Glasgow (1936–61), he also served as chairman of the Committee of Vice-Chancellors and Principals. Outside of academia, he contributed to a large number of royal commissions, public bodies and private trusts, particularly those dealing with social and economic issues. He was a committee man par excellence, occupying important positions in over fifty educational and charitable organizations.

Hetherington's commitment to public service was international in scope, starting with his involvement in the League of Nations Labour Conference (1919). He was particularly active in pursuing university interests within the Commonwealth, gaining him recognition as the "doyen" of its Vice-Chancellors. In addition to his work for the AUBC and the British Council, he acted as chairman of the Colonial Universities Grants Committee from 1942 to 1948, and subsequently provided advice on university affairs in both India and Malta. He also possessed a broad network of personal and professional contacts among North American universities, many of which awarded him honorary degrees. In addition to his Commonwealth activities, he maintained regular correspondence with the US Educational Commission in the UK and chaired the Commonwealth (Harkness) Fellowships Committee from 1951 to 1956.

Notes

1. Eric Ashby, *Community of Universities* (Cambridge: Cambridge University Press, 1963), 49.
2. Tamson Pietsch, *Empire of Scholars: Universities, Networks and the British Academic World, 1850–1939* (Manchester: Manchester University Press, 2013), 162. I would like to thank Tamson Pietsch and Hilary Perraton for their helpful comments on an earlier draft of this chapter.
3. Tamson Pietsch, "Many Rhodes: Travelling Scholarships and Imperial Citizenship in the British Academic World, 1880–1940," *History of Education* 40(6) (2011): 723–39.
4. Hetherington papers, University of Glasgow Library.
5. Draft attached to minutes of the CUIS committee, February 26, 1953, the National Archives, London (hereafter TNA): BW 118/1.
6. Correspondence between Symonds, Shreeve (British Council) and Hope (CRO) June–November 1949, TNA: BW 1/59.
7. John Darwin, *The Empire Project: The Rise and Fall of the British World-System 1830–1970* (Cambridge: Cambridge University Press, 2009), 579.
8. *Proceedings of the Sixth Congress of the Universities of the British Commonwealth, 1948* (London: AUBC, 1951), 67.
9. Ibid., 69.
10. Alice Byrne, "The British Council and the British World 1934–1954," GRAAT Online 13 (March 2013), http://www.graat.fr.
11. Dr A.E. Morgan, British Council Education Division, *Proceedings of the Sixth Congress*, p. 83.
12. CUIS, draft report on the period October 1948–May 1949, TNA: BW 1/59. Minutes of the CUIS committee, October 15, 1948, TNA BW 118/1
13. Deputy Director-General, British Council, to Hope, CRO, August 4, 1949, TNA: BW 1/59. Minute by Searls, British Council Education Division, 14 July 1949, TNA: BW 1/59.

14. Report for the two years ending March 1951, TNA: BW 118/1. GHS July 12, 1949, TNA: BW 1/59.
15. Minute by Searls, 14 July 1949, TNA: BW 1/59.
16. Searls to Dundas, British Council Representative India (Confidential), 14 October 1953, TNA: BW 1/276.
17. Report attached to minutes of the CUIS committee, 25 September 1952, TNA: BW 118/1.
18. Minutes of the CUIS committee, 25 September 1952, TNA: BW 118/1.
19. Frances Donaldson, *The British Council: The First Fifty Years* (London: Jonathan Cape, 1984), 183–207.
20. Minutes of the CUIS committee, 24 April 1951, TNA: BW 118/1.
21. Pietsch, *Empire of Scholars*, 191.
22. Searls to Foster, December 6, 1951, TNA: BW 1/276.
23. *Proceedings of the Seventh Congress of the Universities of the British Commonwealth, 1953* (London: AUBC, 1954), 284.
24. Foster to Searls, July 10, 1953, TNA: BW 1/276.
25. *Proceedings of the Seventh Congress*, 100, 104–6, 112–14.
26. David M. Cameron, "The Federal Perspective," in Glen A. Jones (ed.), *Higher Education in Canada, Different Systems, Different Perspectives* (New York: Garland, 1997), 11–12.
27. Minutes of the CUIS committee, 13 November 1953, TNA: BW 118/1.
28. Ledds to Morris, June 17, 1953, TNA: BW 118/1.
29. J.L. Granatstein, *Canada 1957–1967: The Years of Uncertainty and Innovation* (Toronto: McClelland & Stewart, 1986), 162.
30. Trueman to Morris, 13 March 1958, TNA: BW 1/276.
31. I.F. McKenzie, Registrar University of New Zealand to AUBC, 14 September 1954, TNA: BW 1/276; Jennings, V.C. University of Ceylon to Foster, 7 April 1954, TNA: BW 1/276.
32. *Proceedings of the Seventh Congress*, 40–42.
33. Lindie Koorts, "An Ageing Anachronism: D.F. Malan as Prime Minister, 1948–1954," *Kronos* 36 (2010): 108–35.
34. Minutes of the CUIS committee, 17 March 1955, TNA: BW 118/1.
35. Searls to Morris, 2 July 1954, TNA: BW 1/276. Between 1949 and 1956, Australia received ninety-seven awards, followed by the United Kingdom with sixty-seven. Canada, in comparison, received only thirty-two.
36. Rowe to Morris, 14 April 1954, TNA: BW 118/1.
37. Minutes of the CUIS committee, 1955–60, TNA: BW 118/1 and BW 118/2.
38. Searls to Morris, 2 July 1954, TNA: BW 1/276.
39. *Proceedings of the Seventh Congress*, 90.
40. Ibid., 103.
41. Minutes of the CUIS committee, 20 May 1949, TNA: BW 118/1.
42. Searls to Dundas, 14 October 1953, TNA: BW 1/276.
43. Symonds to Owain-Jones, British Council Representative Pakistan (Confidential), 19 October 1951, TNA: BW 1/276.
44. Minutes of the CUIS committee, 21 February 1952, TNA: BW 118/1.
45. Ibid., 28 May 1959, TNA: BW 118/2.
46. British Council India, Annual Report 1948/49, TNA: BW 38/18.

47. L.R. Philips, British Council Representative India, memorandum "Political Atmosphere in the Mofussil," 15 December 1950. TNA: BW 38/17; V.C. Martin, UK High Commission, Memorandum "The Indian Universities," January 1954, TNA: DO 35/5373.
48. Alice Byrne, "The British Council in India, 1945–1955: Preserving 'Old Relationships under New Forms,'" in Laurent Dornel and Michael Parsons (eds), *Fins d'Empires* (Pau: Presses de l'Université de Pau, 2016).
49. Acting UK High Commissioner in India to Secretary of State for CRO, 15 January 1954, TNA: DO 35/5373.
50. Minutes of the CUIS committee, 28 May 1959, TNA: BW 118/2.
51. Ibid., February 1958–February 1960, TNA: BW 118/2.
52. Ormerod to West, 31 December 1954, TNA: DO 35/5373.
53. Hilary Perraton, *Learning Abroad: A History of the Commonwealth Scholarship and Fellowship Plan* (Newcastle: Cambridge Scholars Publishing, 2009).

References

Ashby, Eric. *Community of Universities* (Cambridge: Cambridge University Press, 1963).
Byrne Alice. "The British Council and the British World 1934–1954," GRAAT Online 13 (March 2013), http://www.graat.fr.
———. "The British Council in India, 1945–1955: Preserving 'Old Relationships under New Forms,'" in Laurent Dornel and Michael Parsons (eds), *Fins d'Empires* (Pau: Presses de l'Université de Pau, 2016), 119–35.
Cameron, David M. "The Federal Perspective," in Glen A. Jones (ed.), *Higher Education in Canada, Different Systems, Different Perspectives* (New York: Garland, 1997), 9–29.
Darwin, John. *The Empire Project: The Rise and Fall of the British World-System 1830–1970* (Cambridge: Cambridge University Press, 2009).
Donaldson, Frances. *The British Council: The First Fifty Years* (London: Jonathan Cape, 1984).
Granatstein, J.L. *Canada 1957–1967: The Years of Uncertainty and Innovation* (Toronto: McClelland & Stewart, 1986).
Koorts, Lindie. "An Ageing Anachronism: D.F. Malan as Prime Minister, 1948–1954," *Kronos* 36 (2010): 108–35.
Perraton, Hilary. *Learning Abroad: A History of the Commonwealth Scholarship and Fellowship Plan* (Newcastle: Cambridge Scholars Publishing, 2009).
Pietsch, Tamson. "Many Rhodes: Travelling Scholarships and Imperial Citizenship in the British Academic World, 1880–1940," *History of Education* 40(6) (2011): 723–39.
———. *Empire of Scholars: Universities, Networks and the British Academic World, 1850–1939* (Manchester: Manchester University Press, 2013).
Proceedings of the Sixth Congress of the Universities of the British Commonwealth, 1948 (London: AUBC, 1951).
Proceedings of the Seventh Congress of the Universities of the British Commonwealth, 1953 (London: AUBC, 1954).

 4

STUDENTS AS AMBASSADORS
German–American Exchange Diplomacy during the 1980s
Jacob S. Eder

Introduction

Exchange programs played a crucial role in the formation of social connections between the United States and West Germany after World War II. Since the late 1940s, the United States had heavily invested in the military alliance and the Federal Republic's economic recovery, as well as in building ties between Americans and Germans. "Exchange diplomacy"[1] emerged as a significant component of US public diplomacy.[2] After 1945, it served as a way to strengthen the alliance with the former enemy nation and to extend, as well as sustain, the United States' informal empire. Constituting a key element of US re-education/reorientation policies vis-à-vis West Germany, exchange diplomacy soon reached an unprecedented scale. During the first half of the 1950s, more than 14,000 Americans visited Germany and more than 12,000 Germans visited the United States.[3] According to American policy planning, "exchange programs should contribute to the democratization of German society."[4] Specifically, they focused on young generations of Germans in order to train them "as democrats through exchange sojourns in the United States."[5] Of course, the basic concept of such programs implied the reciprocal exchange of people across borders, but they were at the core an American enterprise, aiming at the one-way transmission of values and ideals. Until 1962, these efforts were exclusively US-funded, but had already gradually been in decline since 1955 with the end of military occupation in West Germany. In the eyes of its initiators, these programs were extraordinarily successful in the transformation of West German society, its embracing of democracy and Western values, as well as in laying the foundations for the close Cold War alliance.

Several decades later, however, top-level observers from the United States increasingly began to express concerns about the long-term social foundation of the Western alliance. Ronald Reagan succinctly stated in an address to the National Press Club in 1981 that "a new generation is emerging on both sides of the Atlantic. Its members were not present at the creation of the North Atlantic Alliance. Many of them do not fully understand its roots in defending freedom and rebuilding a war-torn continent."[6] The President's statement resonated a central motif of an evolving transatlantic discourse among politicians and social scientists about the so-called successor generation. Not only in the United States, but also in a number of Western European countries, politicians, government officials and social scientists began to ponder the dedication of future generations to the alliance in its confrontation with the Eastern Bloc. This applied particularly to West Germany, which was situated at the frontline of the Cold War.[7] In a detailed examination of West German political generations and their attitudes toward collective security, the Western alliance and the superpowers, Stephen F. Szabo, a professor in National Security Studies at the National War College, came to a more nuanced assessment than Reagan in the early 1980s. Nevertheless, he shared the premises of the latter's observations: "most of the postwar generations grew up under detente [sic] rather than Cold War, and matured in a period when the United States represented Vietnam and Watergate. This sharp break in historical experience has led to a growing concern that the next generation of German leaders will be less supportive of NATO and ties to the United States."[8]

It is not surprising that the leading Western superpower saw changes in attitude toward the United States with concern. Yet how did its European allies—the Federal Republic of Germany in particular—position themselves in this debate? This chapter takes the creation in 1983 of a state-sponsored exchange program for high school students and young professionals between the United States and West Germany—the Congress-Bundestag Youth Exchange Program (CBYX) or Parlamentarisches Patenschafts-Programm (PPP)—as a starting point to explore West German perspectives on this debate, as well as the country's policies and goals. How did West German policymakers perceive the political and social dynamics of German–American relations since the late 1970s? Which significance did they attribute to exchange diplomacy for the matured alliance between the United States and West Germany? And what role did the selection and preparation of the adolescent exchangees play? After all, they were—as informal ambassadors—supposed to reinforce the alliance between the two countries and contribute to sustaining "the West" as a community of values.[9]

Beyond an examination of a new initiative during the 1980s, the "golden age of Cold War American public diplomacy,"[10] this chapter aims to make a contribution to the vast literature on transatlantic transfers and exchanges. A large number of scholars has studied American public and cultural diplomacy abroad, American soft power, and the processes connected to "Americanization" before, during and after the Cold War.[11] However, looking at the role of West Germany's political and diplomatic establishment in this context opens up a perspective much less frequently taken: to examine the junior partner in this relationship.[12]

The Framework of the Second Cold War

In the 1970s and 1980s, to observers on both sides of the Atlantic, the achievements of the "founding generation" of German–American friendship in the 1950s seemed to be eroding, while its "successor generation" exhibited less commitment to the alliance.[13] While Americans worried about the reliability of their West German allies, their German counterparts saw a declining interest of young Americans—illustrated, for example, by decreasing enrollments in existing exchange programs—in the language, culture and history of Germany as particularly alarming. Such concerns were exacerbated by top-level political tensions between the Federal Republic and the United States, but also by new tensions between the Cold War blocs.[14] Often referred to as the "second" Cold War, they were epitomized, for instance, by the Soviet Union's invasion of Afghanistan and the highly controversial NATO double-track decision.[15]

In the context of the discourse about the "successor generation" and its alleged lack of commitment to the alliance, officials identified a knowledge deficit as a central political challenge.[16] From the West German perspective, the country's reputation abroad was at stake, and the Foreign Office assumed that large parts of American society held "a negative attitude" toward West Germany in the early 1980s.[17] Chancellor Helmut Schmidt was mindful of these tensions, even though he considered diplomatic relations with the United States under Reagan "excellent."[18] Nevertheless, the German government as well as the US government appointed new officials in charge of sustaining and reviving the alliance. In Germany, this task fell to the state minister in the Foreign Office, Hildegard Hamm-Brücher (FDP), a long-term champion of an invigoration of German–American relations. As the first "Coordinator for German–American Cooperation," she advocated exchange diplomacy, specifically targeting future leaders of the successor generations, as well as a number of other new public diplomacy initiatives.[19] In the United States, the career diplomat Lawrence Eagleburger took up the position as coordinator.

Even though these initiatives were geared toward the future relations between West Germans and Americans, German officials also began to fix their gaze on the role of the German past in this context. Since the mid 1970s, the crimes of the Third Reich, particularly the Holocaust, experienced a significant increase in public attention in the United States. New courses in high schools and universities, the establishment of museums and the very successful NBC-miniseries *Holocaust* (1978) confronted Americans in an unprecedented way with the mass crimes committed by Germans during the Third Reich.[20] From the West German perspective, this "Americanization of the Holocaust" had the potential to shadow the achievements of postwar German democracy.[21]

West German diplomats stationed in the United States expressed their worries of how this development would affect young Americans. For example, the German Consul General in New York Werner Ungerer was convinced that American teenagers knew hardly anything about present-day Germany, but were exposed to openly "anti-German" television programs instead.[22] Such exposure would not only reinforce clichés and prejudices, but would also undermine social ties between the United States and the Federal Republic in the long run. In fact, such fears evolved as a key concern of policymaking under Helmut Kohl, who became Chancellor in late 1982. Here, two central policy goals of the Kohl government overlapped: to revive the German–American alliance as well as—in the words of historian Wulf Kansteiner—to "reinvent the memory of Nazism and lay to rest the burden of collective symbolic guilt."[23]

Reviving German–American Friendship

During the 1980s, West German as well as American officials therefore set out to strengthen German–American friendship. In addition to the appointment of coordinators for German–American cooperation, the early 1980s also saw a number of high-profile public events, such as the celebration of the Tricentennial of German immigration to North America in 1983. New public diplomacy initiatives also included efforts to revise history textbooks for American high schools, the founding of academic institutions, plans to establish a German international television broadcaster for an American audience and negotiations with American Holocaust museums. The CBYX must be seen in this context. The Bundestag later summarized its purpose: "the exchange program aims at relating to the young generation in both countries the significance of amicable cooperation, which is based on shared political and cultural ethical values and moral concepts."[24] Against the backdrop of the debates outlined above, government officials and foreign policy experts on both sides of the Atlantic thus came to consider adolescents a most promising vehicle to improve and shape relations between both societies in the long run.[25] However, to equip adolescents with the necessary knowledge and thus enable them to act as informal ambassadors for German–American exchange diplomacy posed a number of significant challenges.

In contrast to already-existing exchange programs, the CBYX was supposed to become a reciprocal, highly prestigious enterprise, which would not only enable several hundred students to spend a year abroad with almost all expenses paid, but would also improve relations between the members and staffers of the Bundestag and Congress.[26] Students between the age of sixteen and nineteen and young professionals up to twenty-one (some up to twenty-four) were invited to apply to participate in the program, and members of the Bundestag and Congress acted as their sponsors. At the Tricentennial celebrations in Philadelphia in October 1983, West German President Karl Carstens and Ronald Reagan officially announced the creation of the program, underscoring its symbolic and political significance: "this program calls upon the successor generation to safeguard the values of freedom and democracy as our common heritage and to reaffirm the bonds of friendship between our two peoples."[27] The German government provided about five million deutschmarks per year for the CBYX, while the Americans contributed about half that amount.[28] In 1984, the first group of 334 young Germans and 248 young Americans traveled abroad; in 1985, these numbers almost doubled, but decreased to around 700 during the following years.[29] In the long run, both sides aimed for a total of 1,000 participants per year.[30] The actual organization, such as planning travels and finding host families, was delegated to private organizations. The Bundestag's Council of Elders oversaw the implementation of the CBYX in the Federal Republic.

Creating a German–American exchange program, ultimately modeled after the very successful Franco-German youth exchange, was already a highly symbolic act in and of itself. The exchange between

France and Germany was a successful contribution to end the "hereditary enmity" between the two nations; by the mid 1990s, over five million students had participated in this program.[31] The question of how to politicize such an initiative for adolescents was, however, a rather delicate one. Maintaining the credibility of an exchange program that aims to improve mutual understanding, friendship or partnership between two countries rendered it difficult and even problematic for governments to give the participants concrete mandates or even instructions.[32] Of course, the specific challenges of adolescence itself, but also adjusting to life in a foreign country, living with a host family, speaking a foreign language and struggling with "culture shock" more generally, needed to be taken into consideration. German officials were well-aware of these factors, but nevertheless aimed to achieve a number of concrete political goals with regard to the strengthening of the Cold War alliance.

On a very basic level, German teenagers were supposed to get to know the United States, its people, politics and culture, and recognize the shared values and significance of the Cold War alliance. It is safe to assume that the American side shared and supported these political goals. In fact, those in charge of the CBYX in the United States expressed "a high degree of concern" about the German successor generation, especially about those youths who had opposed the NATO double-track decision.[33] Then again, American teenagers were supposed to experience an open, modern and democratic West Germany, distinctly different from the country they knew from television series or movies about the Third Reich and the Holocaust.[34] Members of the Bundestag acted as "godparents"—the literal translation of the German word *Pate*—and introduced their American visitors to their constituents and arranged visits to government institutions in Bonn. American teenagers also participated in seminars on the history and culture of the Federal Republic. An important component, for example, was a workshop that took place in the areas immediately adjacent to the Communist German Democratic Republic. As such, the visitors received an intimate knowledge of the country, the culture, and above all the people who would be directly affected if the Cold War ever became a "hot" war.

The key, however, to increase the value of the CBYX for West German cultural diplomacy lay in the selection as well as the preparation of the German participants. Officials knew that the success of the entire program depended on the "quality of the scholarship holders."[35] Even though the Bundestag mandated private exchange organizations with the application process, it provided the guidelines for the selection of the participants. The private organizations prepared a list of suitable candidates, who were officially nominated by the members of the Bundestag. While the 1983 guidelines only expected the participants to be "willing to contribute to a better understanding between young Germans and Americans," the selection criteria were soon defined more precisely.[36] Already in 1985, the Bundestag's Council of Elders demanded that future participants be made aware that they did not participate in the program to learn a language or to increase their chances for a successful professional career,[37] but rather "first and foremost to achieve goals of public diplomacy."[38]

Thus, the preparation of the participants came to play a key role in the success of the program. Taking part in an eight-day-long seminar in Germany was a prerequisite for all participants, be they high school students or young professionals.[39] This seminar above all aimed to "enable the participants to represent as knowledgeable and active young Germans the Federal Republic of Germany in the United States." They were not only supposed to be open-minded and well-aware of political and cultural differences, but were also expected to "explain" and make a case in favor of the "historical, political, and legal dimensions of the question of German unity." Moreover, they had to be in a position to "explain" and "represent" the "democratic and social traditions of their home country."[40]

More specifically, this survey course on German history, the "German question" and German–American relations provided the participants with a historical narrative that emphasized the positive achievements of German history since 1800, but also the political implications of the Cold War for the Federal Republic, the significance of American support in this context and the contributions of German immigrants to American society, academia and culture.[41] The history of the Third Reich received only marginal attention in this seminar, addressed in a session titled "National Socialism and the German Resistance Movement." This should not come as a surprise, as the adolescent ambassadors were to convey a positive image of Germany in the United States, which included the history of Germans as resisters to or victims of National Socialism. The segment on the German Democratic Republic on the other hand, equipped them with much more detailed information on the deficiencies and criminal actions of the Communist regime in East Germany.

In 1987, however, an internal evaluation of the seminars stated that the participants felt overwhelmed by the intensity of the preparation and the amount of information provided to them; as a result, the segment on pre-1945 German history was to be reduced. In 1988, the

Bundestag's Council of Elders also acknowledged in an internal assessment that the exchangees did not enjoy participating in the seminars. The Council also criticized the fact that the private exchange organizations had begun to ignore the guidelines provided to them by the Bundestag. It maintained that participating in the seminar on German history and culture needed to remain an essential part of the CBYX.[42]

Evaluating Exchange Diplomacy

In the Federal Republic, the CBYX was a multipartisan effort, administered by the Bundestag, which points to a broad consensus among political parties about the goals to be achieved by the exchange program. Even though this constellation allowed individual members of parliament to leave their mark on the program, there were only limited possibilities of direct governmental steering or interference. Nevertheless, the West German coordinators for German–American cooperation played an important role in this context. They had no executive mandate, but officially reported to the German foreign minister and acted as an important hinge between the various government agencies and private organizations involved in German–American relations.[43] In fact, there was a close overlap between the development of the CBYX and the political priorities of the person specifically responsible for German–American relations for the respective German governments. The first coordinator, Hildegard Hamm-Brücher,[44] had played a key role in the establishment of the CBYX and her successors, especially Werner Weidenfeld,[45] were also closely involved in the further development of the exchange program.

In the second half of the 1980s, the Bundestag evaluated the CBYX thoroughly and came to the conclusion that it was extraordinarily successful.[46] Even though there had been some administrative problems, the number of applicants had steadily increased and the number of those who did not complete the program had remained very low. The most significant challenge had been to find adequate internships or programs in community colleges for young German apprentices without a college degree, as the functioning of vocational training differed significantly between the two countries.

A different point of complaint concerned the behavior of West Germany's adolescent ambassadors in the United States. In conversations with American officials, both sides realized that the "integration of Congress-Bundestag students into the regular programs of participating organizations while maintaining the 'specialness' of the program" proved difficult.⁴⁷ Participants in the CBYX often either did not appreciate the honor bestowed upon them or appeared arrogant and refused to integrate, to the point that "a segregation ... between them and regular students" occurred. In conversation with American host families and their German exchange students in the United States, German Bundestag members later also realized that often neither one of them was aware of the political goals behind the CBYX. Host families in particular complained that German students were not motivated to succeed in high school, which had a demoralizing effect on their American host brothers or sisters.⁴⁸ The German exchangees were, in any case, on the whole very content with their stays abroad.

Despite such challenges, the Bundestag extended the CBYX beyond its initial probation period.⁴⁹ In 1986, Kohl and Reagan had also established the German–American Youth Exchange Council to provide advice and suggestions to both governments on how to expand and increase exchange programs beyond the CBYX. Absent from the discussions and evaluations, however, was the issue that had been very important to the initiators of the program: the transfer of knowledge about the Federal Republic as a modern, democratic and Western country to the United States. The questions of whether West Germany's adolescent ambassadors had contributed to a better understanding between the two countries and what they had achieved in shaping Americans' perceptions of West Germany remained unanswered.

Conclusion

While the long-term political effects of exchange diplomacy are indeed difficult to assess, the founding history of the CBYX illuminates the dynamics of political and social relations between West Germany and the United States during the last decade of the Cold War.⁵⁰ It shows that in the 1970s, the Federal Republic no longer saw itself only on the "receiving end" of American public diplomacy.⁵¹ While there was a significant overlap between the long-term aims of both sides, the Federal Republic pursued its own political agenda and had a clear set of goals to be accomplished in the United States. Despite the challenges of turning teenagers into adolescent ambassadors, the preparation for their stay in the United States aimed to equip them with expertise about German history and the alliance, and also reflected the larger societal discourses about German history and identity since the 1970s. Simultaneously, West Germany's political elites actively sought for ways to escape the long shadow of the Nazi past, especially in the

Federal Republic's foreign policy handling. The deliberate category of the "successor generation" not only served in this context as a tool to facilitate a conversation about the future of the Cold War alliance, but also helped to create and justify new public diplomacy initiatives that put people at the center of policy planning. In the end, however, the positive experiences of those who—retrospectively—saw themselves as the founding generation of German–American friendship, such as Hildegard Hamm-Brücher, may have led to unrealistic expectations with regard to the possibilities of exchange diplomacy against the backdrop of a relationship that had significantly matured since the end of World War II.

In recent years, politicians and lawmakers in the United States have repeatedly called the continuing necessity of the CBYX into question. A change in political priorities and a shift in attention away from Europe and to the Middle East or China led to a significant reduction of US public diplomacy efforts in Europe. For the German side, however, the value and the symbolic significance of the CBYX and the pay-off of exchange diplomacy have remained uncontested. In response to US plans to cut funding for the CBYX, German Chancellor Angela Merkel responded in 2015: "especially now, 25 years after German reunification, we want to continue this program. Therefore, the German Bundestag has said: we stand behind this program. We hope that it is not a sign that it [the CBYX] is not seen as important anymore. I at least will use the opportunity when I speak with Representatives and Senators to point out that we place special significance on this partnership agreement."[52] Close political relations and the continuing formation of new social ties between both societies have thus remained a top priority of post-Cold War Germany. It seems as if the "receiving end" of post-1945 German–American exchange diplomacy has now become the "driving end."

Jacob S. Eder holds a Ph.D. from the University of Pennsylvania and is currently a research associate and lecturer at the Friedrich-Schiller-University Jena; his publications include *Holocaust Angst: The Federal Republic of Germany and American Holocaust Memory since the 1970s* (Oxford University Press, 2016) and *Holocaust Memory in a Globalizing World* (co-edited with Philipp Gassert and Alan E. Steinweis, Wallstein, 2017). He has received numerous research grants, fellowships and awards, including a Fulbright Fellowship, a Mellon Foundation Fellowship at the Elliott School of International Affairs, a research grant from the Robert Bosch Foundation and the Fraenkel Prize of the Wiener Library.

Appendix: Hildegard Hamm-Brücher (1921–2016)

Calling for a new public diplomacy for the Federal Republic and furthering cultural exchange since the late 1970s, Hamm-Brücher argued for domestic as well as foreign policy goals. The Federal Republic not only needed to improve its self-representation abroad, but exposure to foreign cultures could also help its citizens escape insecurity about their own culture. According to Hamm-Brücher, the "economic giant" West Germany should no longer act as a "midget" in the field of culture abroad.[53] But her advocacy for a new public diplomacy and the creation of exchange programs also had autobiographical reasons. She was a member of the "founding generation" of German–American friendship after World War II: born in 1921 and holding a doctorate in chemistry from the University of Munich, she had worked from 1945 onward as a science journalist for the American re-education newspaper *Neue Zeitung* in Munich and had studied political science at Harvard University in 1949/50 before launching a long career in German politics as a member of the Freie Demokratische Partei (FDP), which she joined in 1948. She specialized particularly in educational questions and in 1969 was appointed Staatssekretär of the Bundesministerium für Bildung und Wissenschaft (Federal Ministry of Education and Research), and, between 1977 and 1982, Staatsministerin of the Auswärtiges Amt (Federal Foreign Office), where she was in charge of the coordination of the CBYX.

Notes

1. Giles Scott-Smith, "Networks of Influence: US Exchange Programs and Western Europe in the 1980s," in Kenneth A. Osgood and Brian C. Etheridge (eds), *The United States and Public Diplomacy: New Directions in Cultural and International History* (Leiden: Martinus Nijhoff Publishers, 2010), 345–69; Nicholas J. Cull, "Public Diplomacy: Taxonomies and Histories," *Annals of the American Academy of Political and Social Science* 616(1) (2008): 33 f.; Nancy Snow, "International Exchanges and the US Image," *Annals of the American Academy of Political and Social Science* 616(1) (2008): 198–220. The research for this chapter was supported by the Robert Bosch Foundation.
2. Reinhild Kreis, *Orte für Amerika: Deutsch-Amerikanische Institute und Amerikahäuser in der Bundesrepublik seit den 1960er Jahren* (Stuttgart: Franz Steiner Verlag, 2012); Hermann-Josef Rupieper, *Die Wurzeln der westdeutschen Nachkriegsdemokratie: Der amerikanische Beitrag 1945–1952* (Opladen: Westdeutscher Verlag, 1993).

3. Karl-Heinz Füssl, "Between Elitism and Educational Reform: German-American Exchange Programs, 1945–1970," in Detlef Junker (ed.), *The United States and Germany in the Era of the Cold War, 1945–1990: A Handbook, vol. 1: 1945–1968* (Cambridge: Cambridge University Press, 2004), 409–16.
4. Ibid., 410.
5. Ibid., 411.
6. As quoted in Stephen F. Szabo, "Introduction," in Stephen F. Szabo (ed.), *The Successor Generation: International Perspectives of Postwar Europeans* (London: Butterworths, 1983), 1.
7. Reinhild Kreis, "Bündnis ohne Nachwuchs? Die 'Nachfolgegeneration' und die deutsch-amerikanischen Beziehungen in den 1980er Jahren," *Archiv für Sozialgeschichte* 52 (2012): 607–31.
8. Stephen F. Szabo, "West Germany: Generations and Changing Security Perspectives," in Szabo (ed.), *Successor Generation*, 44.
9. Michael Hochgeschwender, "Was ist der Westen? Zur Ideengeschichte eines Politischen Konstrukts," *Historisch-Politische Mitteilungen* 11 (2004): 1–30.
10. Carnes Lord, "The Past and Future of Public Diplomacy," *Orbis* 42(1) (1998): 50.
11. Victoria De Grazia, *Irresistible Empire: America's Advance through Twentieth-Century Europe* (Cambridge, MA: Belknap Press of Harvard University Press, 2005); Rob Kroes: *If You've Seen One, You've Seen the Mall: Europeans and American Mass Culture* (Urbana, IL: University of Illinois Press, 1996).
12. Manuela Aguilar, *Cultural Diplomacy and Foreign Policy: German-American Relations, 1955–1968* (New York: Peter Lang, 1996); Frank Trommler, *Kulturmacht ohne Kompass: Deutsche auswärtige Kulturbeziehungen im 20. Jahrhundert* (Cologne: Böhlau, 2014).
13. Giles Scott-Smith, "Reviving the Transatlantic Community? The Successor Generation Concept in US Foreign Affairs, 1960s–1980s," in Kiran Klaus Patel and Kenneth Weisbrode (eds), *European Integration and the Atlantic Community in the 1980s* (New York: Cambridge University Press, 2013), 201–25.
14. Klaus Wiegrefe, *Das Zerwürfnis: Helmut Schmidt, Jimmy Carter und die Krise der deutsch-amerikanischen Beziehungen* (Berlin: Propyläen, 2005); Rolf Steininger, *Deutschland und die USA: Vom Zweiten Weltkrieg bis zur Gegenwart* (Reinbeck: Lau-Verlag, 2014), 563–641.
15. Philipp Gassert, Tim Geiger and Hermann Wentker (eds), *Zweiter Kalter Krieg und Friedensbewegung: Der NATO- Doppelbeschluss in deutsch-deutscher und internationaler Perspektive* (Munich: Oldenbourg Verlag, 2011).
16. William R. Smyser, *Deutsch-amerikanische Beziehungen* (Bonn: Europa Union Verlag, 1980), 63–70.
17. Bundesarchiv (hereinafter BArch) B 136/17552, Seitz to Genscher, 25 February, 1982. All translations from German sources into English by the author.
18. BArch B 136/17552, Chancellery, "Sprechzettel," meeting with group of German-American parliamentarians on 11 February, 1982, n.d.
19. BArch 136/17557, Chancellery, Gablentz to Schmidt, 31 August 1981 and 25 September 1981; BArch B 136/17557, Foreign Office, Ad hoc measures for 1982/1983, n.d.

20. E.g. Peter Novick, *The Holocaust in American Life* (Boston, MA: Houghton Mifflin 1999).
21. Jacob S. Eder, *Holocaust Angst: The Federal Republic of Germany and American Holocaust Memory since the 1970s* (New York: Oxford University Press, 2016).
22. Politisches Archiv des Auswärtigen Amts, AV Neues Amt, Bd. 16.850, Ungerer to West German Embassy Washington, 29 November, 1977.
23. Wulf Kansteiner, *In Pursuit of German Memory: History, Television, and Politics after Auschwitz* (Athens, OH: Ohio University Press, 2006), 315; see also Andreas Wirsching, *Abschied vom Provisorium: 1982–1990* (Munich: Deutsche Verlags-Anstalt, 2006), 470–81 and 563–72.
24. Archiv des Instituts für Zeitgeschichte München, ED 379, Bd. 247, Informationen über das Parlamentarische Patenschafts-Programm, 21 April 1988.
25. Parlamentsarchiv des Deutschen Bundestages (hereinafter PA DBT), Schriftwechsel zum Deutsch-Amerikanischen Jugendaustausch (hereinafter Schriftwechsel), 48/98, 20, Auswärtiges Amt, Ergebnisvermerk 5. Sitzung des Arbeitskreises USA, 4 May 1984.
26. PA DBT, Schriftwechsel, 48/98, 17, James R. Huntley, Bericht, 12 November 1985; PA DBT, Schriftwechsel, 10/90, 2, Mitarbeiteraustausch, Deutschlandbesuch, 12–31 May 1984. See also Kreis, "Bündnis," 623–28.
27. PA DBT, Schriftwechsel, 48/98, 42, Urkunde für das Tricentennial (Entwurf), 12 September, 1983.
28. PA DBT, Schriftwechsel, 10/90, 2, Beitrag zum Haushaltsvoranschlag, 1985.
29. PA DBT, Schriftwechsel, 10/90, 2, Knuth to Winter, 19 April 1984; PA DBT, Schriftwechsel, Bericht zum deutsch-amerikanischen Jugendaustausch, 13 October 1986.
30. PA DBT, Schriftwechsel, 48/98, 17, James R. Huntley, Bericht, 12 November 1985, 6.
31. Wulf Köpke, "The Third Pillar of Foreign Policy: West German Cultural Policy in the United States," in Detlef Junker (ed.), *The United States and Germany in the Era of the Cold War, 1945–1990: A Handbook, vol 2: 1968–1990* (Cambridge: Cambridge University Press, 2004), 280–86; Cull, "Public Diplomacy," 40–42.
32. Giles Scott-Smith, "Exchange Programs and Public Diplomacy," in Nancy Snow and Philip M. Taylor (eds), *Routledge Handbook of Public Diplomacy* (New York: Routledge, 2009), 50 f.
33. PA DBT, Schriftwechsel, 48/98, 17, James R. Huntley, Bericht, 12 November 1985, 13.
34. PA DBT, Schriftwechsel, 48/98, 20, Klaus Allerbeck, Vorstudie zum Deutsch-Amerikanischen Jugendaustausch, 31 January 1986, 41.
35. PA DBT, Schriftwechsel, 10/90, 1, Ziel und Inhalt des PPP, 28 October 1983.
36. PA DBT, Schriftwechsel, 10/90, 1, Richtlinien zum PPP, 10 October 1983.
37. PA DBT, Schriftwechsel, 10/90, 2, Knuth to Winter, 19 April 1984.
38. PA DBT, Schriftwechsel, 48/98, 22, USA-Reise einer Delegation der Ältestenratskommission für den Deutsch-Amerikanischen Jugendaustausch, 26 February 1985.

39. PA DBT, Schriftwechsel, 10/90, 1, Entwurf für Faltblatt zum Austausch, n.d.
40. PA DBT, Schriftwechsel, 10/90, 1, Sitzung der Kommission des Ältesten-Rates für den dt.-amerik. Jugenaustausch, 19 January 1984.
41. Ibid. See also PA DBT, Schriftwechsel, 10/90, 2, Bericht: Vorbereitungsseminar Carl Duisberg Gesellschaft, 25 May 1984; PA DBT, Schriftwechsel, 48/98, 29, Entwurf zur Programmgestaltung des 2. Workshops, 4 November 1987.
42. PA DBT, Schriftwechsel, 48/98, 60, Kurzprotokoll 5. Sitzung Kommission des Ältestenrates für den Deutsch-Amerikanischen Jugendaustausch, 3 March 1988.
43. Kreis, "Bündnis," 623.
44. Jacob S. Eder, "Liberale Flügelkämpfe: Hildegard Hamm-Brücher im Diskurs über den Liberalismus in der frühen Bundesrepublik," *Vierteljahrshefte für Zeitgeschichte* 64 (2016): 291–325.
45. "Rede von Professor Dr. Werner Weidenfeld anläßlich seiner Amtseinführung als Koordinator für die deutsch-amerikanische Zusammenarbeit," in Auswärtiges Amt (ed.), *Brücken über den Atlantik 1988* (Bonn: Auswärtiges Amt, n.d.), 38.
46. PA DBT, Schriftwechsel, Bericht zum deutsch-amerikanischen Jugendaustausch, 13 October 1986; PA DBT, Schriftwechsel, 48/98, 17, James R. Huntley, Bericht, 12 November 1985; PA DBT, Schriftwechsel, 48/98, 20, Allerbeck, Vorstudie, 1986.
47. PA DBT, Schriftwechsel, 48/98, 1, Workshop zum PPP vom 2.-6.12.86 in Hardtberg, 5 May 1987.
48. PA DBT, Schriftwechsel, 48/98, 23, Delegationsreise in die USA, 5 May–2 June 1987.
49. PA DBT, Schriftwechsel, 48/98, 43, Beschluss der Kommission des Ältestenrats für den Deutsch-Amerikanischen Jugendaustausch, 30 October 1986.
50. PA DBT, Schriftwechsel, 48/98, 20, Allerbeck, Vorstudie, 42 f.
51. Cf. Rob Kroes, "American Empire and Cultural Imperialism: A View from the Receiving End," *Diplomatic History* 23(3) (1999): 437–61.
52. Transcript of Video-Podcast with Chancellor Merkel #05/2015, 7 February 2015, retrieved 22 March 2017 from http://savecbyx.org/wp-content/uploads/2015/02/Chancellor-Merkel-CBYX-Interview-02-07-2015.pdf.
53. Angela Nacken, "Der Wirtschaftsriese ist ein Kulturzwerg," *Frankfurter Allgemeine Zeitung*, 22 August 1979.

References

Aguilar, Manuela. *Cultural Diplomacy and Foreign Policy: German-American Relations, 1955–1968* (New York: Peter Lang, 1996).
Cull, Nicholas J. "Public Diplomacy: Taxonomies and Histories," *Annals of the American Academy of Political and Social Science* 616(1) (2008): 33–56.
De Grazia, Victoria. *Irresistible Empire: America's Advance through Twentieth-Century Europe* (Cambridge, MA: Belknap Press of Harvard University Press, 2005).

Eder, Jacob S. *Holocaust Angst: The Federal Republic of Germany and American Holocaust Memory since the 1970s* (New York: Oxford University Press, 2016).
——. "Liberale Flügelkämpfe: Hildegard Hamm-Brücher im Diskurs über den Liberalismus in der frühen Bundesrepublik," *Vierteljahrshefte für Zeitgeschichte* 64 (2016): 291–325.
Füssl, Karl-Heinz. "Between Elitism and Educational Reform: German-American Exchange Programs, 1945–1970," in Detlef Junker (ed.), *The United States and Germany in the Era of the Cold War, 1945–1990: A Handbook, vol. 1: 1945–1968* (Cambridge: Cambridge University Press, 2004), 409–16.
Gassert, Philipp, Tim Geiger and Hermann Wentker (eds). *Zweiter Kalter Krieg und Friedensbewegung: Der NATO- Doppelbeschluss in deutsch-deutscher und internationaler Perspektive* (Munich: Oldenbourg Verlag, 2011).
Hochgeschwender, Michael. "Was ist der Westen? Zur Ideengeschichte eines Politischen Konstrukts," *Historisch-Politische Mitteilungen* 11 (2004): 1–30.
Kansteiner, Wulf. *In Pursuit of German Memory: History, Television, and Politics after Auschwitz* (Athens, OH: Ohio University Press, 2006).
Köpke, Wulf. "The Third Pillar of Foreign Policy: West German Cultural Policy in the United States," in Detlef Junker (ed.), *The United States and Germany in the Era of the Cold War, 1945–1990: A Handbook, vol 2: 1968–1990* (Cambridge: Cambridge University Press, 2004), 280–86.
Kreis, Reinhild. *Orte für Amerika: Deutsch-Amerikanische Institute und Amerikahäuser in der Bundesrepublik seit den 1960er Jahren* (Stuttgart: Franz Steiner Verlag, 2012).
——. "Bündnis ohne Nachwuchs? Die Nachfolgegeneration und die deutsch-amerikanischen Beziehungen in den 1980er Jahren," *Archiv für Sozialgeschichte* 52 (2012): 607–31.
Kroes, Rob. *If You've Seen One, You've Seen the Mall: Europeans and American Mass Culture* (Urbana, IL: University of Illinois Press, 1996).
——. "American Empire and Cultural Imperialism: A View from the Receiving End," *Diplomatic History* 23(3) (1999): 437–61.
Lord, Carnes. "The Past and Future of Public Diplomacy," *Orbis* 42(1) (1998): 49–72.
Novick, Peter. *The Holocaust in American Life* (Boston, MA: Houghton Mifflin 1999).
Rupieper, Hermann-Josef. *Die Wurzeln der westdeutschen Nachkriegsdemokratie: Der amerikanische Beitrag 1945–1952* (Opladen: Westdeutscher Verlag, 1993).
Scott-Smith, Giles. "Exchange Programs and Public Diplomacy," in Nancy Snow and Philip M. Taylor (eds), *Routledge Handbook of Public Diplomacy* (New York: Routledge, 2009), 50–52.
——. "Networks of Influence: US Exchange Programs and Western Europe in the 1980s," in Kenneth A. Osgood and Brian C. Etheridge (eds), *The United States and Public Diplomacy: New Directions in Cultural and International History* (Leiden: Martinus Nijhoff Publishers, 2010), 345–69.
——. "Reviving the Transatlantic Community? The Successor Generation Concept in US Foreign Affairs, 1960s–1980s," in Kiran Klaus Patel and Kenneth Weisbrode (eds), *European Integration and the Atlantic Community in the 1980s* (New York: Cambridge University Press, 2013), 201–25.

Smyser, William R. *Deutsch-amerikanische Beziehungen* (Bonn: Europa Union Verlag, 1980).
Snow, Nancy. "International Exchanges and the US Image," *Annals of the American Academy of Political and Social Science* 616(1) (2008): 198–220.
Steininger, Rolf. *Deutschland und die USA: Vom Zweiten Weltkrieg bis zur Gegenwart* (Reinbeck: Lau-Verlag, 2014).
Szabo, Stephen F. "Introduction," in Stephen F. Szabo (ed.), *The Successor Generation: International Perspectives of Postwar Europeans* (London: Butterworths, 1983), 1–3.
——. "West Germany: Generations and Changing Security Perspectives," in Stephen F. Szabo (ed.), *The Successor Generation: International Perspectives of Postwar Europeans* (London: Butterworths, 1983), 43–75.
Trommler, Frank. *Kulturmacht ohne Kompass: Deutsche auswärtige Kulturbeziehungen im 20. Jahrhundert* (Cologne: Böhlau, 2014).
Wiegrefe, Klaus, *Das Zerwürfnis: Helmut Schmidt, Jimmy Carter und die Krise der deutsch-amerikanischen Beziehungen* (Berlin: Propyläen, 2005).
Wirsching, Andreas. *Abschied vom Provisorium: 1982–1990* (Munich: Deutsche Verlags-Anstalt, 2006).

PART II

INTERNATIONAL UNDERSTANDING AND WORLD PEACE

 5

Muscular Christian Exchanges
Asian Sports Experts and the International YMCA Training School (1910s–1930s)
Stefan Hübner

Introduction

In his autobiography published in 1943, Laurence L. Doggett informed his readers about the growing importance of academic exchanges within the transnational network created by the North American branch of the Young Men's Christian Association (YMCA) since the Christian revival of the 1880s. According to Doggett, former president of the International YMCA College in Springfield, MA, instead of going abroad as a missionary himself, he had contributed to the circulation of knowledge and personnel by educating foreign students in the United States:

> Along with others, I took the pledge that, if the way should be opened, I would become a foreign missionary. This pledge has had a definite influence upon my lifework. I offered myself both to the American Board [of Commissioners for Foreign Missions] and also to the YMCA, but chiefly because of obligations to my parents I was advised not to press the matter. This pledge to go as a foreign missionary was largely responsible for my activity in promoting the training of students from other countries at Springfield College, of whom three hundred and fifty have served in foreign lands.[1]

As Doggett told his readers, educating foreign students—350 until 1943—for leadership positions in the YMCA had increasingly gained in prominence during the early twentieth century.

The International YMCA College was not the only place—a second YMCA training school was located in Chicago—but it was the chief place for training YMCA staff for work in different YMCA-related offices. Such offices included managing associations, working with boys, and supervising physical education at gyms and sports events. This chapter focuses on the last topic, professional physical education, and particularly on Asians trained in Springfield between the 1910s and 1930s. This group of students was of eminent importance because they formed a major part of the first generation of Asians trained in modern Western scientific approaches to physical education. After their studies in the United States, most of them took up YMCA leadership positions in their countries of origin. Even more significant was their role as social engineering experts in modernization processes, which included activities such as serving as advisors to colonial and national governments or later joining them as civil servants. In such roles, they addressed public health issues, created or administered fitness and physical education programs for public schools and universities, and (not necessarily always) assisted in transforming their societies toward a Protestant-Evangelical interpretation of *democracy* and *capitalism*. Mass-based physical education and especially amateur sport thus contributed to shaping fitter and more efficient Asian bodies. At the same time, sportive citizenship training and character building—or muscular Christianity—served to transfer to Asia a set of Protestant American norms and values, such as fair play (discouraging corruption), competition-based belief in personal effort as the way to success (instead of a belief in luck or fate, as in many forms of gambling), individual equality and practical efficiency (by choosing athletes for the team based on their competence and not on their skin color or social background), team spirit (cooperation for a common goal), obedience of duly constituted authority (meaning duty and civic virtue), and especially self-control to decrease interhuman violence (encouraging a state monopoly on violence).[2]

This chapter argues that Springfield College played a *central role* in bringing about a leadership transfer from US to Asian physical educators during a period characterized by strongly growing anti-colonial nationalisms (1920s–1930s) in Asian countries such as the Philippines, China, and India. I therefore focus on an exchange program that was not based on reciprocity. Instead, Asian students were sent by the YMCA to the US to receive higher education, while American YMCA officials, normally having received higher education in the United States, were sent to Asia to educate the locals. However, the Asian graduates' Western education meant that knowledge-based unequal power relations between Westerners and Asians slowly eroded, resulting in Asian self-government in sport and physical education-related areas. Asian physical educators thus became part of a transnational epistemic community interested in topics such as fitness, public health, hygiene and medicine. Similar things can be said concerning the involvement of Asians in international organizations such as the International Olympic Committee (IOC). However, this does not mean that the YMCA's aim of controlling further developments by convincing its former Asian pupils of which path they must proceed along was ultimately achieved in every single case.

Following a short historical overview of the YMCA and its training school in Springfield, I outline the school's role in the YMCA's overseas activities, such as training students and establishing further schools, and conclude with very brief biographical data on some of its most prominent Asian graduates. I thus address the questions of why the YMCA decided to train Asians instead of keeping American officials abroad, and how the organization, duration and content of the study program were meant to shape long-term efforts in physical education.

The US YMCA and Springfield College

The YMCA was founded in Britain in 1844 as a Protestant lay organization to encourage young men to engage in Bible studies. Within a few years, the British YMCA turned into a transnational organization that spread to Continental Europe and North America, then expanded into other regions and by 1905 featured about 5,000 associations in twenty-four countries.[3] During the American Progressive Era (1890s–1920s), the results of industrialization and urbanization strongly contributed to the YMCA's growth as a highly important religious and social welfare organization. As its triangular symbol proclaimed, the YMCA's interpretation of Christian (meaning Protestant) citizenship training included mind, body and spirit: all three were to be trained through amateur sports to resist the negative impacts of industrialization and urbanization. Compared to rural life, anonymous city life made vices such as alcohol, drugs, prostitution and promiscuity more accessible. Moreover, a shift from outdoor physical farm labor to office work resulted in fears of deteriorating public health due to the "degeneration" of the white Anglo-Saxon Protestant body and stress-related problems such as neurasthenia. Rising numbers of physically fit Catholic immigrants contributed to these fears. Many Protestants also believed a more "masculine" religion that appealed to boys and young men was necessary to counteract "female" Victorian Protestantism. As a consequence, physical education and sport were increasingly accepted among "progressive" Protestants.[4]

Muscular Christianity and YMCA citizenship training targeted not only Protestant upper-class and middle-class boys and young men. Assimilating immigrants, ethnic minorities and the lower classes into Protestant society was also part of the YMCA's purpose. Certain parts of Asia also became part of what Ian Tyrrell has termed the American "moral empire," a product of the overseas activities of US missionaries inspired by the Christian revival of the 1880s.[5] The Spanish-American War (1898) and the following annexation of the Philippines (1899) further contributed to the construction of a transnational YMCA network in Asia, initiated and initially supervised by Americans, and aimed at moral reform and social transformation.

During the Progressive Era, changes in US philanthropy also affected the YMCA's social work.[6] A growing focus of donors, both large foundations and individuals, on *efficient, rational* and *scientific* solutions to social problems resulted in an academic boom in medicine, the social sciences and disciplines like physical education. Training *professional* YMCA staff in Springfield and engaging in physical education-related research corresponded to "progressive" tendencies of regulating public health, fitness and character building.

The International YMCA College was founded in 1885 as a department of the School for Christian Workers, which in 1890 was separated into four independent institutions.[7] The College became responsible for training YMCA personnel to be employed in a growing number of YMCA offices. Benevolent but often unprofessional and thus inefficient volunteers were increasingly substituted with professionals who had received an academic education in their later field of work. The need for them was immense, since already between 1866 and 1885, the number of professional YMCA staff rose from three to 400.[8] In 1886, the College added a gymnasium, which was supervised by Luther H. Gulick. Gulick later became a central person in spreading scientific approaches to physical education, fitness and public health. For instance, in Springfield he wrote a well-known anthropometric handbook, *Physical Measurements and How They are Used* (1889). His students included James Naismith and William G. Morgan, the former of whom invented basketball and the latter volleyball.[9] These and other activities related to sports medicine and sport pedagogy were deemed useful for encouraging public health and character building through mass sport.

Also in 1886, the word "International" was added to the College's name to illustrate its acceptance of foreign students. In 1891, the College moved to its current site near Lake Massasoit as a result of the need for additional space.[10] The number of students continuously rose, from a total of eight when the College was opened in 1885 to 545 in 1936.[11] This increase in the student body was accompanied by rising costs to operate the College, growing from US$35,800 in 1906 to US$180,000 in 1921.[12] In terms of finances, the basic problem was that the College was a private institution and thus did not receive public funding. Moreover, the students focused on community work instead of highly paid jobs, meaning that tuition fees and alumni donations would not suffice to finance the College in the long run or create an endowment. Receiving donations from wealthy individuals, but also from foundations, was thus of central importance in continuing to educate the rising number of US and foreign students.

In addition to wealthy donors from the Springfield-Hartford area, the Rockefeller family and their foundations provided large sums of money. Considering the strong competition between colleges in attracting donations, the Rockefeller contributions illustrate that the College's activities aligned well with their philanthropic and educational aims, while personal relations certainly were also of help. John D. Rockefeller, Jr., a friend of the well-known YMCA leader John R. Mott, heavily financed the YMCA.[13] In 1908, he donated US$2,250 under the condition that the College would attract additional money to pay back its mortgage, which it soon did. Five years later, he provided US$50,000 to support the College's expansion and US$100,000 more in 1921. Another YMCA donation appeal in the following year resulted in the Laura Spelman Rockefeller Memorial's promise to contribute US$500,000 if donors pledged two million dollars by 1925, the goal being reached shortly before the deadline.[14] As a consequence, during the 1920s, Rockefeller philanthropy contributed substantially to the International YMCA College's expansion and its aim to become more self-sustaining through creating its own endowment.

The donations from the Rockefeller family and others were crucial for maintaining a base of foreign students. Financial security allowed the College to grant foreign students waivers on tuition and rent, as well as a discount on boarding. The condition was that they agreed to return to their home countries after graduation to support the desired social transformation there instead of trying to find work in the United States or elsewhere. Moreover, the low salaries in non-Western countries would have put the graduates in financial trouble had they been expected to pay back their tuition fees after returning home. Between 1906 and 1916, the annual tuition fee for a three-year bachelor program in physical education (BPE) or humanics (BH) had been relatively low. However, to facilitate recognition of the degrees at other institutions such as the Teachers College of New York and Columbia University, in 1916 a four-year bachelor program was introduced, meaning that the overall tuition fee for bachelor students rose by one-third. Simultaneously, the College running costs and the annual room rent went up. Thus, the waiver on tuition and rent substantially reduced the living costs of foreign students.[15]

The admission of non-Western students was based on recommendations by their national YMCA committees, which normally were accompanied by a scholarship that seems to have sufficed to cover travel and living costs. In the fall of 1922, twenty foreign students from nine countries were enrolled.[16] However, the North American YMCA's foreign department decided in November 1924 to increase the number of scholarships for Chinese citizens from three to four, for Japanese from one to two, and to provide Indians (who already received at least two) with an additional one.[17]

The aim of the foreign department was to reduce the numbers of its officials working overseas by preparing "indigenous, self-governing" associations led by locals, as Doggett stated.[18] First, substituting American personnel with well-trained Asian personnel eased the burden on the foreign department's budget. In 1921, for instance, 179 Americans, paid by the foreign department, served in Africa, Asia and Latin America at a maintenance cost of US$775,400, which was about half of its total budget of US$1,467,396.[19] Substitution corresponded to the expectations of philanthropists, who wanted to create local YMCA structures that would not be permanently dependent on American money and personnel. Second, training Asian personnel discouraged accusations of American paternalism. Anti-colonialism intensified during and after World War I,[20] meaning that a permanent knowledge asymmetry would without question destabilize the working relationship between Americans and Asians. The belief was that the growing anti-colonialism could thus be controlled and channeled without severing the ties between the United States and Asian YMCAs.[21]

Attempts during the interwar period to create YMCA training schools abroad modeled on the International YMCA College underline the importance of the goals to train many more local YMCA officials and to intensify the knowledge transfer. In 1920, Harry C. Buck, a Springfield graduate, established the YMCA College of Physical Education in Madras (Chennai). All presidents and higher officials of the other physical education institutions that were founded in India during the next quarter-century graduated from his school.[22] Another Springfield graduate, together with a Chicago graduate, was strongly involved in founding the YMCA Training School (Instituto Técnico) in Montevideo. There, students graduated in physical education after a two-year course, preceded by a two-year course at the Montevideo YMCA, the Rio de Janeiro YMCA (whose course was headed by another Springfield graduate) or the Buenos Aires YMCA.[23] Moreover, the International YMCA College's president, Doggett, attempted to establish a YMCA physical education school in Geneva. The breakdown of the Russian, Ottoman and Austro-Hungarian Empires during World War I meant that the American YMCA became involved in the social transformation processes of the newly independent Central and Eastern European states as well as of Weimar Germany. In this context, amateur sports and the corresponding norms and values were meant to serve as a substitute for military gymnastics and encourage democratization. Reminiscent of events in the Asian part of the American "moral empire" and thus representing a global problem, the costs of encouraging democratization through American staff exploded and training locals seemed more economical. The 340 American YMCA officials serving in these European countries in 1920 were reduced to fifty-one in 1926, while the number of local YMCA officials went up to 150. Almost all of the local physical educators had been trained at the International YMCA College, hence the European plea to establish a physical education college in Europe modeled on Springfield to train more. As a consequence, in April 1926, Doggett again approached Rockefeller Jr., but his plans were rejected. Since the University of Geneva, the World YMCA (the YMCA's world headquarters in Geneva) and Rousseau Teachers' College (Collège Rousseau) offered assistance, the school nevertheless was opened and trained a number of students. During the Great Depression, it had to be closed due to a lack of funding, which is reminiscent of the YMCA's global financial problems.[24]

The Foreign Students at Springfield College

Foreign students enrolling at the International YMCA College between the 1910s and 1930s constituted an elite, since local YMCA training schools modeled on it were still in their infancy. Moreover, as mentioned above, non-Westerners were chosen by their national YMCA committees for leadership training in Springfield, further contributing to their special position. The College's curricula mirrored the aim of educating Christian (meaning Protestant) leaders. This did not exclude Catholic students, but their overall number at the College was low and later a maximum quota was implemented. For example, Catholic students from the Philippines, Europe and South America were allowed to enroll.[25]

Being a Christian affiliated with a church and a YMCA member were mandatory conditions for being admitted. Foreign students also needed to inform the school as to how many years they had been Christians and if they belonged to secret societies, clubs or orders.[26] While the first condition discouraged conversions for careerist purposes, the second addressed religious loyalty. Quite obviously, all these conditions served to increase the probability that the students after graduation would assist in spreading American Protestant norms, values and ideas in their home countries. The curricula were also not limited to practical skills. For example, the BPE curriculum of 1920 included several mandatory *theological* courses in the third and fourth years in addition to a variety of courses on physical education practices, medicine and general education (see tables 5.1–5.4).

According to Doggett, one of the most striking successes of Christian internationalism, egalitarianism and leadership training revealed itself at the 1936 Olympic Games in Nazi Germany. The gold medals won by Jesse Owens, an African American, certainly were of importance for challenging Nazi claims of Aryan supremacy. However, the marathon gold medal was won by another non-white athlete, Sohn Kee-chung (Japanese: Son Kitei). Sohn, a Korean who because of Japan's annexation of Korea needed to compete in the Japanese team, had been trained by the Seoul YMCA. Moreover, the Indian team that won the hockey gold medal had been trained by a graduate of Harry Buck's YMCA College of Physical Education in Madras. Finally, the Philippine team was not led by an American, but by three Filipino Springfield graduates, further underlining Asian capability of sportive self-government and refuting scientific racism.[27] Such examples indeed challenged Hitler's and many others' ideas of races as almost immutable biological units and of Aryan racial supremacy. Simultaneously, Doggett's examples demonstrate his very strong and paternalistic belief in the superiority of Protestant American civilization as *the* model that Asians needed to follow.

A noteworthy number of Springfield graduates returning home to Asia became prominent governmental officials with significant influence in physical education-related policy. Regino R. Ylanan (BPE 1920) served as the Philippines' second national physical director, a very high-ranking civil servant representing the leadership transfer from Americans to Asians. Among other duties, he accompanied teams to major sports events and was a central person in organizing the Tenth Far Eastern Championship Games (Manila 1934) and the Second Asian Games (Manila 1954). Candido Bartolome (BPE 1929, Master of Physical Education (MPE) 1929) for most of his life worked as physical director (a professorship) of the University of the Philippines. Hao Gengsheng (also Hoh Gunsun, BPE 1923) after the Chinese Civil War was the most important sports official of the Republic of China (Taiwan), who spent much of his time organizing events and battling the People's Republic of China (PRC) in IOC meetings (though himself never being co-opted into the IOC). Dong Shouyi (also Tung Shou-yi, BPE 1925), in contrast, worked as the PRC's IOC member, representing his country in the organization and combating Taiwan.

Sharajit Kumar Mukerjee (sometimes Mukerjie, BPE 1926) was not appointed an IOC member for India due to a power struggle among Indian sports organizations. In 1930, he led the very small Indian delegation (three athletes) to the Ninth Far Eastern Championship Games (Tokyo 1930), received a professorship at the University of Bombay (Mumbai) in 1931 and after India's independence went into business.[28] Ma Yuehan (John Ma, sometimes John Mo, BPE 1920, MPE 1926), the "father of Chinese physical education," became a professor at Tsinghua University (Beijing) and an extremely important sports official involved in organizing games and other events. He also served as the co-leader of the Chinese delegation to the 1936 Olympics.[29] Serafim Aquino (BPE 1922) and Geronimo Suva (BPE 1921) took over very important offices in the Philippines, Aquino working for the Department of Education and Suva eventually for the military.[30] However, significantly more in-depth research, starting with a statistical overview of Springfield College's exchange students, is necessary, since there were many other students whose long-term impact cannot be scrutinized here.

Conclusion

All in all, even this limited number of short biographical sketches of Asian Springfield graduates reveals that the Christian internationalist project of educating local leaders in physical education who were able to take over work from Americans had an important long-term impact. Organized and coordinated by various institutions of the YMCA's transnational network, a four-year BPE program, sometimes followed by a MPE program, taught a combination of scientific approaches to physical education, accompanied by a focus on hygiene, medicine, pedagogy and theology. Although statistical material is lacking, it also seems that a noteworthy share of graduates eventually left the YMCA. The YMCA did not necessarily discourage this, since it could facilitate networking with public institutions and "extension" (advisory work), but the phenomenon also reflected that governments increasingly took over the task of encouraging physical education among their populations. The growing governmental interest in topics such as public health and fitness thus often contributed to physical education's integration into nation-building projects. As a consequence, this integration quite often modified or, under drastic circumstances (like in the early PRC), even cut connections to the YMCA's Christian internationalist project.

Table 5.1 The BPE curriculum of 1920: Freshman

Subject	Hours per week	Terms
Biology	4	3
English	5	3
Personal Ethics	4	1
Teacher Training	4	1
Association History	5	1
Mathematics and Physics	5	3
Playground Administration	5	1
* Field Science (Laboratory Course)	2	3
* Camp Craft	5	1
Physical Education Practice	10	3

* Electives: students must select one of them
Source: International YMCA College, Springfield, MA, Thirty-Fourth Catalogue 1920–21, 33–34, Springfield College Archives and Special Collections, Springfield, MA

Table 5.2 The BPE curriculum of 1920: Sophomore

Subject	Hours per week	Terms
Anatomy	5	2
Chemistry	5	3
Psychology	5	3
Personal Hygiene	5	1
First Aid	2	1
* History of Physical Training	3	1
* Massage	5	1
* Rural Economics	5	1
* Rural Sociology	5	1
* Municipal Sociology	5	1
* Social Ethics	5	1
* Sociology	5	1
Physical Education Practice	10	3

* Electives: students must select three of them
Source: International YMCA College, Springfield, MA, Thirty-Fourth Catalogue 1920–21, 33–34, Springfield College Archives and Special Collections, Springfield, MA

Table 5.3 The BPE curriculum of 1920: Junior

Subject	Hours per week	Terms
Physiology	5	3
New Testament	5	3
Anthropometry and Physical Examination	5	1
Building and School Hygiene	5	1
Public Hygiene	2	1
History and Philosophy of Religion	3	1
History of Christianity	5	1
Old Testament	5	1
Physical Education Practice	7	3

Source: International YMCA College, Springfield, MA, Thirty-Fourth Catalogue 1920–21, 33–34, Springfield College Archives and Special Collections, Springfield, MA

Table 5.4 The BPE curriculum of 1920: Senior

Subject	Hours per week	Terms
Diagnosis and Prescription	5	1
Physiology of Exercise	5	1
Physical Education Administration (Indoor and Outdoor)	10	1
Psychology of Religion	3	1
Principles of Religious Education	3	1
Methods of Religious Education	5	1
* Modern English Literature	2	2
* County Work History and Methods	5	2
* Social Psychology	5	1
* Contemporary Civilization	5	2
* Economics	5	2
* History of Philosophy	5	1
* Medical Gymnastics	5	1
Thesis	5	3
Physical Education Practice	5	3

* Electives: Students must select three of them
Source: International YMCA College, Springfield, MA, Thirty-Fourth Catalogue 1920–21, 33–34, Springfield College Archives and Special Collections, Springfield, MA

Stefan Huebner is a research fellow at National University of Singapore's Asia Research Institute. He was awarded scholarships and fellowships at Harvard University, the Woodrow Wilson International Center for Scholars (Washington, DC), the German Historical Institute Washington, DC, the German Institute of Japanese Studies Tokyo and in a SIAS Summer Institute on "Cultural Encounters" (Wissenschaftskolleg

Berlin and National Humanities Center, NC). He received his Ph.D. from Jacobs University Bremen (Germany) in 2015. His book *Pan-Asian Sports and the Emergence of Modern Asia, 1913–1974* was published by the National University of Singapore Press.

Appendix: Dong Shouyi (1895–1978)

In the 1910s, Dong began practicing Western sports as a student at Tongzhou Xiehe Academy in Beijing, an educational institution operated by American missionaries. After his graduation, he worked in the physical education department of the Tianjin YMCA. In 1919, one of his students was Zhou Enlai, who later became one of the most important politicians of the early PRC. Dong also worked as a physical educator at Nankai University, until the YMCA sent him to Springfield, where he graduated (BPE) in 1925. After his return to China, he served as the director of the physical education departments of the Tianjin YMCA and of Nankai University. He also headed the basketball team to the 1936 Olympic Games and in 1941 was appointed as a member of the China National Amateur Athletic Federation, the national organization governing sport. In 1947, he was co-opted as an IOC member for the Republic of China. However, in contrast to the other Chinese IOC members, at the end of the Chinese Civil War (1945–1949), he decided to stay in the new PRC. For some years, the communist leadership seems not to have been aware of his presence. In 1952, when the PRC intended to participate in the Helsinki Olympics, Dong read about its conflict with the Republic of China (since 1949 limited to Taiwan) in the IOC. Both countries claimed that there was only one China, while the IOC decided to recognize two Chinas. Dong wrote a letter on the subject that eventually ended up in Zhou Enlai's hands and was "reactivated" as an IOC member. Until 1958, when China left the IOC and Dong resigned, he combated Taiwanese claims to represent "China."[31]

Notes

I would like to thank Giles Scott-Smith, Amanda Shuman and Ludovic Tournès for their feedback on my chapter. I am also grateful to Ryan Bean and the other staff of the Kautz Family YMCA Archives (Minneapolis, MN), as well as Jeffrey Monseau and Brian McGuinness of Springfield College's archives and international center (Springfield, MA), and Claude-Alain Danthe of the YMCA International (Geneva) for providing me with many of the sources used in this chapter. The German Research Foundation (DFG), the German Historical

Institute Washington, DC, the German Institute for Japanese Studies, Tokyo, the University Libraries of the University of Minnesota (Minneapolis) and Springfield College's international center generously supported this research.

1. Laurence L. Doggett, *Man and a School: Pioneering in Higher Education at Springfield College* (Digital Version, Springfield College Intranet, original version: New York: Association Press, 1943), 9.
2. Stefan Huebner, *Pan-Asian Sports and the Emergence of Modern Asia, 1913–1974* (Singapore: National University of Singapore Press, 2016), introduction and Chapter 1; Paul Christesen, *Sport and Democracy in the Ancient and Modern Worlds* (Cambridge: Cambridge University Press, 2012), Chapter 16; Steven J. Overmann, *The Protestant Ethic and the Spirit of Sport* (Macon: Mercer University Press, 2011); Fletcher S. Brockman, "Association Athletics as a Training in Democracy," *Physical Training* 17(2) (1919): 71–76.
3. Christopher Clark and Michael Ledger-Lomas, "The Protestant International," in Abigail Greene and Vincent Viaene (eds), *Religious Internationals in the Modern World. Globalization and Faith Communities since 1750* (Basingstoke: Palgrave Macmillan, 2012), 23–52; Nina Mjagkij and Margaret Spratt, "Introduction," in Nina Mjagkij and Margaret Spratt (eds), *Men and Women Adrift: The YMCA and the YWCA in the City* (New York: New York University Press, 1997), 1–21; Michael G. Thompson, *For God and Globe: Christian Internationalism in the United States between the Great War and the Cold War* (Ithaca: Cornell University Press, 2015), part 1.
4. Clifford Putney, *Muscular Christianity: Manhood and Sports in Protestant America, 1880–1920* (Cambridge, MA: Harvard University Press, 2001); David P. Setran, *The College "Y": Student Religion in the Era of Secularization* (New York: Palgrave Macmillan, 2007); William J. Baker, "Religion," in Steven W. Pope and John Nauright (eds), *Routledge Companion to Sports History* (London: Routledge, 2010), 216–28. More generally on the Progressive Era and transfers across the Atlantic, see Daniel T. Rodgers, *Atlantic Crossings: Social Politics in a Progressive Age* (Cambridge, MA: Harvard University Press, 1998).
5. Ian Tyrrell, *Reforming the World: The Creation of America's Moral Empire* (Princeton: Princeton University Press, 2010).
6. Ludovic Tournès, "La fondation Rockefeller et la naissance de l'universalisme philanthropique américain," *Critique Internationale* 35 (2007): 173–197.
7. Doggett, *Man*, 17.
8. Ibid., 23.
9. C. Howard Hopkins, *History of the Y.M.C.A. in North America* (New York: Association Press, 1951), Chapter 6; Clifford Putney, "Luther Gulick: His Contribution to Springfield College, the YMCA, and 'Muscular Christianity,'" *Historical Journal of Massachusetts* 39(1–2) (2011): 144–69.
10. Doggett, *Man*, 17; International YMCA College, Springfield, MA, Thirty-Fourth Catalogue 1920–21, 14–15, Springfield College Archives and Special Collections, Springfield, MA.
11. Doggett, *Man*, 27, 125, 153, 175.
12. Ibid., 125, 153.

13. C. Howard Hopkins, *John R. Mott, 1865–1955* (Grand Rapids: Eerdmans, 1979), 424–26, 538, 540, 546, 605–6, 670.
14. Doggett, *Man*, 119, 125, 151–52, 156–57, 171.
15. Ibid., 110; International YMCA College, Springfield, MA, Thirty-Fourth Catalogue 1920–21, 17–18, 108; Catalogue 1927–29, 99, both in Springfield College Archives and Special Collections, Springfield, MA.
16. Doggett, *Man*, 146.
17. Ibid., 110; Minutes of the Meeting of the Foreign Committee, Bankers Club, NY, 3 November 1924, 296–97, in International Work: Administrative Records, Box 6: Foreign Committee Meetings, Minutes, 1922–23 (1924), Kautz Family YMCA Archives, Minneapolis, MN (hereinafter KFYMCAA).
18. Doggett, *Man*, 109.
19. 1921 Foreign Work Budget of the YMCA of Canada and the United States, 3, 6, in International Work: Administrative Records, Box 6: Foreign Committee Meetings, Minutes, 1921, KFYMCAA.
20. Michael Adas, "Contested Hegemony: The Great War and the Afro-Asian Assault on the Civilizing Mission Ideology," *Journal of World History* 15(1) (2004): 31–63; Erez Manela, *The Wilsonian Moment: Self-Determination and the International Origins of Anticolonial Nationalism* (Oxford: Oxford University Press, 2007).
21. Huebner, *Pan-Asian Sports*, Chapter 2.
22. C.C. Abraham, "Physical Education in a Democracy," *Association Men* (India) 4(1–2) (1952): 6–7.
23. Claudia Guedes, "Changing the Cultural Landscape: English Engineers, American Missionaries, and the YMCA Bring Sports to Brazil, the 1870s to the 1930s," *International Journal of the History of Sport* 28(17) (2011): 2602–3; The Next Great Step Forward in Physical Education, 4, in Physical Education Program Records, Box 2: Physical Education Department Records, Reports and Correspondence, 1928–31, KFYMCAA.
24. Doggett to Rockefeller (28 April 1966) and Doggett to Colonel Franklin (5 July 1926), in USA, Training Institutes, Springfield College A-G, World YMCA Archives, Geneva.
25. Doggett, *Man*, 96–97.
26. International YMCA College, Springfield, MA, Thirty-Fourth Catalogue 1920–21, 106; Application for Admission (W.L. Wang), both in Springfield College Archives and Special Collections, Springfield, MA.
27. Doggett, *Man*, 179.
28. Huebner, *Pan-Asian Sports*, Chapter 2.
29. Shuman, *Politics*, 52–53, 87.
30. Regino R. Ylanan and Carmen W. Ylanan, *The History and Development of Physical Education and Sports in the Philippines*, 2nd edn. (Quezon City: University of the Philippines Press, 1974), 43–45, 47–48.
31. Amanda Shuman, "The Politics of Socialist Athletics in the People's Republic of China, 1949–1966," unpublished dissertation, (Santa Cruz: University of California, 2014), 86–88, 156–157, 213.

References

Abraham, C.C. "Physical Education in a Democracy," *Association Men* (India) 4(1–2) (1952): 6–7.
Adas, Michael. "Contested Hegemony: The Great War and the Afro-Asian Assault on the Civilizing Mission Ideology," *Journal of World History* 15(1) (2004): 31–63.
Baker, William J. "Religion," in Steven W. Pope and John Nauright (eds), *Routledge Companion to Sports History* (London: Routledge, 2010), 216–28.
Brockman, Fletcher S. "Association Athletics as a Training in Democracy," *Physical Training* 17(2) (1919): 71–76.
Christesen, Paul. *Sport and Democracy in the Ancient and Modern Worlds* (Cambridge: Cambridge University Press, 2012).
Clark, Christopher, and Michael Ledger-Lomas. "The Protestant International," in Abigail Greene and Vincent Viaene (eds), *Religious Internationals in the Modern World. Globalization and Faith Communities since 1750* (Basingstoke: Palgrave Macmillan, 2012), 23–52.
Doggett, Laurence L. *Man and a School: Pioneering in Higher Education at Springfield College* (Digital Version, Springfield College Intranet, original version New York: Association Press, 1943).
Guedes, Claudia. "Changing the Cultural Landscape: English Engineers, American Missionaries, and the YMCA Bring Sports to Brazil, the 1870s to the 1930s," *International Journal of the History of Sport* 28(17) (2011): 2602–3.
Hopkins, C. Howard. *John R. Mott, 1865–1955* (Grand Rapids: Eerdmans, 1979).
———. *History of the Y.M.C.A. in North America* (New York: Association Press, 1951).
Huebner, Stefan. *Pan-Asian Sports and the Emergence of Modern Asia, 1913–1974* (Singapore: National University of Singapore Press, 2016).
Manela, Erez. *The Wilsonian Moment: Self-Determination and the International Origins of Anticolonial Nationalism* (Oxford: Oxford University Press, 2007).
Mjagkij, Nina, and Margaret Spratt. "Introduction," in Nina Mjagkij and Margaret Spratt (eds), *Men and Women Adrift: The YMCA and the YWCA in the City* (New York: New York University Press, 1997), 1–21.
Overmann, Steven J. *The Protestant Ethic and the Spirit of Sport* (Macon, GA: Mercer University Press, 2011).
Putney, Clifford. "Luther Gulick: His Contribution to Springfield College, the YMCA, and 'Muscular Christianity,'" *Historical Journal of Massachusetts* 39(1–2) (2011): 144–69.
———. *Muscular Christianity. Manhood and Sports in Protestant America, 1880–1920* (Cambridge, MA: Harvard University Press, 2001).
Rodgers, Daniel T. *Atlantic Crossings: Social Politics in a Progressive Age* (Cambridge, MA: Harvard University Press, 1998).
Setran, David P. *The College "Y": Student Religion in the Era of Secularization* (New York: Palgrave Macmillan, 2007).

Shuman, Amanda. "The Politics of Socialist Athletics in the People's Republic of China, 1949–1966," unpublished dissertation (Santa Cruz, CA: University of California, 2014).

Thompson, Michael G. *For God and Globe: Christian Internationalism in the United States between the Great War and the Cold War* (Ithaca, NY: Cornell University Press, 2015).

Tournès, Ludovic. "La fondation Rockefeller et la naissance de l'universalisme philanthropique américain," *Critique Internationale* 35 (2007): 173–97.

Tyrrell, Ian. *Reforming the World: The Creation of America's Moral Empire* (Princeton, NJ: Princeton University Press, 2010).

Ylanan, Regino R., and Carmen W. Ylanan. *The History and Development of Physical Education and Sports in the Philippines*, 2nd edn (Quezon City: University of the Philippines Press, 1974).

6

MANAGING SCIENTIFIC EXCHANGE IN INTERWAR GERMANY
August Wilhelm Fehling and Rockefeller Foundation Fellowships

Judith Syga-Dubois

Introduction

The Laura Spelman Rockefeller Memorial and the Rockefeller Foundation supported the development of German social sciences during the interwar period by considerable means. In 1923, the Director of the Memorial, Beardsley Ruml,[1] began to consider the establishment of a Fellowship Program for European social scientists. His aim was to promote practically useful research and empirical methods to understand the problems of contemporary society.[2] In his opinion, European social sciences were, in general, too philosophical, and therefore more practical approaches had to be supported.[3] The objective of the Fellowship Program was to increase the number of social scientists able to conduct empirical research and to solve problems in a pragmatic way.

Between 1925 and 1940, about eighty young German social scientists received a Rockefeller fellowship to study abroad, and even more foreign fellows came to Germany. The German fellows were not chosen directly by the American Foundation, but by a German Advisory Committee that preselected the candidates. Acting as the Committee's secretary and the Rockefeller representative in Germany, the young historian August Wilhelm Fehling became the Foundation's most important contact person in Germany. He was also the designated official for German social scientists seeking a grant from the Foundation and he advised foreign fellows in Germany.

Based on archival research at the Rockefeller Archive Center (RAC) in Tarrytown and at archives in Germany, especially at the German

Federal Archive (Bundesarchiv Koblenz (BAK)) in Koblenz,[4] this chapter deals with the German-American processes of negotiation and adaptation involved in the transnational functioning of the European Fellowship Program. As Fehling was able to set priorities, define contents and impose his points of view on several crucial questions, he was much more than a simple administrator. Instead, he is best understood as a new type of scientific organizer and a competent negotiator on a transnational level.

August Wilhelm Fehling: Between New York and Berlin

Germany was integrated into the Memorial's fellowship plan following the first discussions in the early 1920s. The scientific boycott conducted against German scientists after World War I[5] contradicted the universal ideals of American philanthropy. In addition, the Memorial wanted to prevent a division of the international scientific community.[6] Two American professors, John J. Coss and Guy S. Ford, were sent to Europe to examine the possibilities of setting up a Fellowship Program. After having visited several German universities and talked to professors and students, they found that the main problem that German social scientists were facing was their intellectual isolation. "Intellectually as well as physically they have lived for ten years on their own flesh,"[7] they wrote to New York. They emphasized the "present emergency in the development of the next generation of scholars"[8] and recommended the support of the university libraries and the appointments of fellows.

In Germany, Coss' and Ford's principal interlocutor was Friedrich Schmidt-Ott, former Prussian Minister of Education and President of the Notgemeinschaft der Deutschen Wissenschaft (Emergency Association for German Science), an association organizing the financial support of scientific research in Germany.[9] Probably at their first meeting in March 1924 in Berlin, Schmidt-Ott drew their attention to his personal assistant, the twenty-eight-year-old historian August Wilhelm Fehling.[10] It is likely that Schmidt-Ott presented Fehling to the Americans because of his knowledge of English, his reliability and his high organizational skills. Fehling was born in 1896 to a merchant in Hamburg. After having participated in World War I, he studied history, philosophy and German in Rostock and Berlin and passed his doctorate examination in 1922. Due to economic difficulties, he had to interrupt his studies and worked for the Notgemeinschaft from 1923,[11] where he was responsible for the fields of fellowships, travel and the procuring of laboratory animals.[12] From 1927 to 1939, he was also the secretary of the Cecil Rhodes Trust in Germany.[13]

The Memorial asked Fehling to become its official representative in Germany. From July to December 1924, he sojourned in the United States and became acquainted with the Memorial's officers and eminent American social scientists.[14] This journey reinforced the personal relations between Fehling and the officers: Ruml invited him to a "picknick day" in his home[15] and Coss suggested they spend a weekend "out of town."[16] Half a year later, Fehling and Ruml met again, when the Director came to Germany to form a personal opinion about German social sciences.[17]

As representative of the Memorial in Germany, Fehling continued to work at the Notgemeinschaft.[18] He did the work for the Memorial at his home in Berlin Zehlendorf, assisted by his wife, who was paid for her secretarial help.[19] In 1925, he received the equivalent of US$80 per month as salary from the Notgemeinschaft, as well as US$62.50 from the Memorial.[20] In October, his American salary was raised to US$142.50 and one year later to US$250.[21] Gradually he reduced his working hours at the Notgemeinschaft, but he never gave up this second source of income and professional perspective.

Fehling started to search for potential fellowship candidates in December 1924. When the Trustees of the Memorial approved the fellowship plan for Germany, the Germany Advisory Committee, composed of five university professors[22] and administrated by Fehling, was officially appointed. In 1925, Germany was the only country where the selection of fellows was assigned to a committee and not only to the Laura Spelman Rockefeller Memorial national representative. Later, a second Committee would be appointed in Great Britain. The reasons for this special treatment of Germany seem to be diverse. Fehling did not have the reputation or the prestige to impose his decisions and Schmidt-Ott, chairman of the Committee, was a busy man with little time to manage the Fellowship Program. The scientific reputation of the Committee's members assured the acceptance of the decisions made in the academic community. Another reason may be that the scientific landscape in the social sciences seemed so fragmented that the Memorial deemed it unwise to concentrate on a sole decision maker.

The first Committee meeting took place in March 1925.[23] The most important task was now to find candidates representing the type of researcher requested by the Memorial. The officers chiefly wanted economists, sociologists and political scientists, and were secondarily prepared to accept some historians, psychologists and anthropologists. The fellows, after having already shown their ability to conduct original research, were to develop a specific research project. In the eyes of the officers, the selected fellows should offer promise of future leadership in their respective fields. Another condition was the definite intention to return to their countries of origin following the fellowship.[24] In most cases, the fellows were to receive a grant of US$1,800 per year and the reimbursement of travel expenses. The German Committee was asked to avoid any publicity or mention of the program in the press.[25]

The Committee decided not to send a general announcement of the Fellowship Program to the German universities immediately, but to collect propositions from the Committee members and some researchers of confidence.[26] For the first year, the selection process was highly opaque. In July 1925, three of ten applications were selected and sent to New York; later a fourth application was added. The Memorial accepted all propositions and at the end of 1925, the first four fellows arrived in the United States.[27] The group was composed of an economist from Kiel (Andreas Predöhl), a historian from Munich (Otto Vossler), a political economist (Eva Flügge) from Berlin and a jurist (and future resistance fighter) from Hamburg (Arvid R. Harnack).[28]

Fehling's Role in the Selection of Fellows: The Power of an Administrator

The German Committee was free to organize the selection process as it wished within the frame of the guidelines. Therefore, the members decided to apply supplementary criteria, such as the successful termination of a doctorate and the publication of a second substantial piece of research. For the second year, all social sciences faculties were informed about the program.[29] Candidates were asked to send Fehling their curriculum vitae, an outline of their research project, a photograph, a health certificate and all published scientific work.[30] All year round, Fehling corresponded with potential applicants. In the case of promising researchers, he asked their professors for confidential statements about their scientific and personal qualifications. Until the annual Committee meeting in spring, he controlled all the phases of the selection process. Some weeks before the meeting, Fehling sent all documents to the Committee members, often with a short presentation of each candidate, stressing their strong and weak points.[31] The Memorial, and later the Rockefeller Foundation, did not impose a fixed number of fellowships to every country, but often Fehling had information about a general order.[32] The Committee members could then accept an application and forward it for final decision to New York, reject it or propose a later reapplication. With one exception,[33] the German decisions were approved in the United States. Once the Committee assembled, Fehling's decisional power was limited to a role of expert on the fellowship guidelines. The outcome of the meeting was generally open, the discussions sometimes long and controversial. "It may also happen that a member of the Committee is too optimistic in regard to the ability of his own candidate. That means sometimes a delicate diplomatic task,"[34] wrote Fehling to Ruml.

Which criteria were the most important in the selection? The sociologist Christian Fleck, in his important study on the invention of empirical social research, has argued that the personal knowledge of the Committee members was decisive. He underlined that most of the fellows came from cities where the Committee members were active, like Berlin, Hamburg or Munich.[35] This was surely true for the first year, but thereafter other arguments are needed to explain the predominance of certain cities. Berlin and Hamburg were, like Kiel and Heidelberg, places where the Memorial and later the Rockefeller Foundation supported research institutions in which younger scholars were educated. These students already had the training requested by the Memorial and they were probably better informed about the program, for which no public announcement was made. Often, the members of the Committee did not personally know the successful candidates before they applied. Several times, candidates well-known by one of the Committee members, or even by a Foundation officer, were rejected.[36]

One of the difficulties encountered by Fehling was the relatively small number of applications: up to 1928, he never received more than twenty a year. He had to mobilize all his contacts at the Notgemeinschaft and the Akademischer Austauschdienst (Academic Exchange Service) to find candidates.[37] Often, he had the impression that the real "first class men" did not apply and that professors tended to recommend young social scientists who were only considered to be "pretty good."[38] High competition among researchers and lack of university appointments led to a situation that did not favor a stay abroad.[39] The number of applicants rose at the end of the 1920s, when the program became better known in university circles and was promoted by the first fellows returning to Germany.

Another problem was to find a balance between scientific and personal qualifications. The applicant's publications were scrutinized with great care. Whenever possible, the candidates were invited to discuss them with one of the Committee members. In addition, the candidates' personalities were analyzed with accuracy. The fellows were regarded as the elite of young social scientists and were to represent German science abroad. Fehling tried to see all the promising candidates in order to form an opinion about their personality and social manners. He found it very difficult to find individuals combining both scientific competence and personal reliability.[40]

Empirical research methods do not seem to have been one of the most important criteria: no candidate was rejected for using too "traditional" methods. Some of the fellows conducted rather conventional research projects, in political history for example, spending their time in foreign archives. Others used their stay abroad to discover new subjects and methods. Eva Flügge, for instance, used questionnaires to explore the American automobile industry and Rudolf Heberle started innovative research about social and geographic mobility. Political aspects were not part of the official fellowship guidelines, but they nevertheless embarrassed the Committee members in some cases. When the young economist Jürgen Kuczynski applied in 1926, Fehling asked his professors if there were a risk that his radical leftist political opinions would have negative consequences on the fellowship plan in Germany.[41] The Committee finally decided not to forward the application to New York.[42] When Fehling asked in the case of another communist applicant what the attitude of the Memorial would be in this case,[43] the Americans responded that "the Memorial is not interested in his convictions and will be glad to consider his application on the same basis as the others," as long as the fellow "desist[s] from political activities while on a fellowship."[44] Sometimes the proposed research plans were problematic, too: one applicant, of "national" political conviction, wanted to study German–American relations before World War I, especially before the immediate outbreak of the war. Fehling found this subject too delicate and advised the Committee members to avoid the selection of sensitive topics.[45] The candidate's application was not forwarded to the Memorial.

Difficult German–American Co-administration in the 1930s

In 1929, the Memorial was integrated into the larger Rockefeller Foundation.[46] The Fellowship Program continued as part of the Social Science Division under the direction of Edmund E. Day. More than fifty German fellows were chosen between 1929 and the beginning of World War II, most of them economists or political scientists. This selection reflected the Foundation's concentration on economic stabilization and international relations during the Great Depression. Most Germans still went to the United States, followed by England, France and Italy.

The Foundation decided to send an American representative of the social sciences to the Foundation's Paris Office, where the administration of the European Fellowship Program was now located. This permitted closer contact between Foundation officers and European social scientists, and thereby reduced the importance of the national advisors chosen by the Memorial.[47] The system of representatives, like Luigi Einaudi in Italy or Johan Huizinga in the Netherlands, was abolished in 1931. Thus, the European influence in the selection process was reduced. In Germany and Great Britain, the Committees were maintained[48] and both were requested to follow the Foundation's guidelines closely.

In Germany, Fehling had to deal with the changing objectives and new requests on the part of the Foundation. He was disappointed that the good, personal collaboration with Ruml had come to an end.[49] Fehling had a poor impression of the new organization: more bureaucratic, less individual handling of fellowships and the end of ambitious experiments.[50] In April 1929, Fehling was again invited to the United States, where Day explained the new business-like outlook of the Fellowship Program.[51]

In 1931, the Foundation asked the German Committee to select more mature candidates and to emphasize the learning of new methods. These two demands were judged to be contradictory by the Committee members who feared a transformation of the research into merely training fellowships.[52] Some German fellows were accused by the Foundation of having worked in too much isolation, without having established contacts with American researchers, and Fehling had to remind the newly selected fellows to develop close relations with at least some foreign social scientists. In 1932, the German Fellowship Program reached a peak with ten awards. This development came to an end with the National Socialists' rise to power.

In 1933, the Rockefeller officers had to decide whether the Fellowship Program and the other Foundation activities should be continued in National Socialist Germany. By then, the Memorial and the Foundation had already spent US$300,000 on the German Fellowship Program in the social sciences.[53] The officers followed the political situation in Germany very carefully.[54] The German Committee and the Rockefeller staff in Paris pleaded that the program be continued. The Paris officers decided to postpone a planned change in the Committee's members, some of them "relatively old men,"[55] to avoid political interference.[56] Only one Committee member, the jurist Albrecht Mendelssohn Bartholdy, proposed from his exile in Oxford to stop the selection of new fellows and to concentrate the Foundation's activities on assisting former fellows persecuted by the regime.[57]

The selection of the fellows posed new problems too. One of the principles of the Fellowship Program was that fellows should have good career prospects in their own countries. This was no longer the case for candidates considered as "non-Aryan," political opponents and women. Were "scholars who fail to sympathize with the Nazi movement or principles ... excluded from consideration?"[58] asked E.R.A. Seligman from Columbia University in May 1934. Day answered in the negative, but added that a person "definitely opposed to or excluded from the present regime in Germany would stand little chance of selection by the German committee for the simple reason that the Foundation has long taken the position that the fellow should have reasonable prospects of effective permanent careers in their respective countries of origin."[59] The Foundation continued to ask for "some assurance of a future position" for the candidates, but also found it necessary "to give a somewhat more liberal interpretation to this clause than in the past."[60] However, it refused to award fellowships to researchers who merely wanted to find an appointment abroad.[61]

In December 1933, the Trustees in New York decided to stop supporting research institutions in Germany.[62] One year later, the administrators ended the Fellowship Program in its existing form. In 1935, the German Committee was disbanded and Fehling was dismissed the following year. The political context, discussed at length in the Foundation, was definitely a reason for this, but reference to it was omitted in the letter sent to Fehling. More important was a general feeling of the Trustees that the Fellowship Program was too expensive, too broad and not sufficiently successful. From 1935 onward, fellowships had to be awarded only in connection with concrete research projects supported by the Foundation.[63] Fehling answered all inquiries with a "discouraging reply" and referred potential applicants to the Paris Office.[64]

Only five fellowships were awarded between 1936 and 1940, three of them to exiled German social scientists. The Foundation increasingly concentrated its activities on its refugee programs for deposed scholars, inaugurated in 1933, which assisted 190 Germans of all disciplines to leave Germany and find posts abroad.[65] In these programs too, Fehling was consulted by the Foundation: the officers frequently asked him to evaluate the personal and scientific qualifications of dismissed researchers. His responsibility was great in these cases as his decisions were likely to have far-reaching consequences for the applicants.

Conclusion

Fehling was the key figure in the Rockefeller Fellowship Program for the social sciences in interwar Germany. From 1925 to 1928, he instituted German–American cooperation together with the broadminded and generous Memorial Director, Beardsley Ruml. He executed Ruml's vision of the Fellowship Program with great care, but took also the liberty of introducing a relatively strict control of the German fellows. In 1929, the very liberal phase of the Fellowship Program ended and Fehling had to deal with new American priorities. With regret but also understanding, he adapted himself to the new situation.

For German social scientists, the Fellowship Program was a unique possibility to realize a stay abroad at the postdoctoral level. They often established durable contacts with the Foundation officers and with foreign social scientists. They were part of a large scientific network developed among research institutions supported by Rockefeller funds in a great number of countries. In Germany, the most important institutions were situated in Berlin, Kiel, Heidelberg and Hamburg, some of the favorite destinations of foreign Rockefeller fellows in Germany.

When this transnational cooperation came to an end in 1936, it was a harsh, but foreseen, break in Fehling's professional life. After 1937, he worked full-time for the Deutsche Forschungsgemeinschaft (German Research Foundation), as the Notgemeinschaft had been renamed.[66] He took part in World War II as a major and regimental commander and established himself in Kiel in 1945. He continued to work in the administration of science, this time in the Ministry of Education and the University of Kiel, and contributed to the re-establishment of the Deutsche Forschungsgemeinschaft and the Akademischer Austauschdienst.[67] In the 1950s, he kept in touch with some of the former Rockefeller officers.[68] He always took great care of his accurately organized Rockefeller archives and, following his death in 1964, his wife would pass them to the German Federal Archive in Koblenz for safekeeping.

Judith Syga-Dubois, former student of the International Selection of Ecole normale supérieure (ENS) in Paris, completed in 2016 a Ph.D. about the social sciences programs of the Laura Spelman Rockefeller Memorial and the Rockefeller Foundation in Germany in the interwar period at the EHESS (Paris) and Bielefeld University (Germany). She is currently Maître de conférences in German civilisation at the university of Mulhouse, France.

Appendix: Eva Flügge

For the German and American administrators of the LSRM's Fellowship Program, Eva Flügge incarnated the ideal type of fellow. Born in 1895, she studied economics, law, philosophy and art history in Berlin and Jena, before receiving her doctoral degree from Berlin University in 1922. She was one of the first German LSRM fellows and started her fellowship in November 1925 with a four-month stay at the London School of Economics, where she took part in language lessons and familiarized herself with the American bibliography in economics. Arriving in New York in March 1926, she chose Chicago as her first place of study and the American automobile industry as her research topic. Her empirical approach and the direct link to contemporary issues were in complete conformity with the aims of the program. Making full use of her fellowship, she studied at the University of Chicago, the Brookings Graduate School in Washington, DC (which became Brookings Institution in 1927), Harvard University and Columbia University; she also visited car manufacturers such as General Motors and Ford. Additionally, she got in contact with governmental services and associations, assembling an important collection of first-hand material. After three years as a Rockefeller fellow, she was allowed to extend her stay for some months to work with the economist Leon C. Marshall. In 1931, she used her monograph about the American automobile industry as a habilitation thesis at the University of Berlin. She worked as *Privatdozent* in political economics at the University until she followed her husband—the diplomat and former LSRM fellow Heinz von Trützschler—to Geneva. She probably died from pneumonia during World War II.

Notes

1. Martin and Joan Bulmer, "Philanthropy and Social Science in the 1920s: Beardsley Ruml and the Laura Spelman Rockefeller Memorial, 1922–1929," *Minerva* 19 (1981): 354; David L. Seim, *Rockefeller Philanthropy and Modern Social Science* (London: Pickering & Chatto, 2013), 104–5.
2. Donald Fisher, "American Philanthropy and the Social Sciences in Britain 1919–1939: The Reproduction of a Conservative Ideology," *Sociological Review* 28 (1980): 278.
3. Helke Rausch, "US-amerikanische 'Scientific Philanthropy' in Frankreich, Deutschland und Großbritannien zwischen den Weltkriegen," *Geschichte und Gesellschaft* 22 (2007): 85–87.
4. I wish to express my appreciation for the help and the great service of the staff of the RAC and the BAK.

5. Brigitte Schroeder-Gudehus, *Deutsche Wissenschaft und internationale Zusammenarbeit: 1914–1928. Ein Beitrag zum Studium kultureller Beziehungen in politischen Krisenzeiten* (Geneva: Dumaret and Golay, 1966), 91–124.
6. Katharina Rietzler, "Philanthropy, Peace Research, and Revisionist Politics: Rockefeller and Carnegie Support for the Study of International Relations in Weimar Germany," *GHI Bulletin Supplement* 5 (2008): 65–66.
7. G.S. Ford to B. Ruml, 12 March 1924, in Rockefeller Archive Center—Laura Spelman Rockefeller Memorial, Series 3.06, box 52, folder 558 (hereinafter RAC-LSRM, 3.06/52/558).
8. Their report is included in "Report of European Fellowship Program in the Social Sciences of the LSRM, 1923–1928," undated, in Rockefeller Archive Center—Rockefeller Foundation, RG 1.2, Series 100 ES, box 50, folder 380 (hereinafter RAC-RF, RG 1.2, 100ES/50/380), 3–5.
9. Sören Flachowsky, *Von der Notgemeinschaft zum Reichsforschungsrat. Wissenschaftspolitik im Kontext von Autarkie, Aufrüstung und Krieg* (Stuttgart: Franz Steiner Verlag, 2008), 68.
10. A.W. Fehling to F. Schmidt-Ott, 27 May 1935, in Bundesarchiv Koblenz (hereinafter BAK), NL 1106 A.W. Fehling, No. 43.
11. Curriculum vitae A.W. Fehling, undated, BAK, NL 1106 A.W. Fehling, No. 6.
12. Flachowsky, *Notgemeinschaft*, 204.
13. Franz Kock, "August Wilhelm Fehling," in Olaf Klose and Eva Rudolph (eds), *Schleswig-Holsteinisches Biographisches Lexikon* 4 (Neumünster: Wachholtz, 1974), 66.
14. Itinerary, in Geheimes Staatsarchiv-Preußischer Kulturbesitz (hereinafter GstA PK), HA Familienarchive und Nachlässe, NL F. Schmidt-Ott, No. 50.
15. Fehling to B. Ruml, 12 December 1924, BAK, NL 1106 A.W. Fehling, No. 6.
16. Telegram from F.M. Rhind to Fehling, 22 October 1924, BAK, NL 1106 A.W. Fehling, No. 6.
17. Ruml to Fehling, 8 August 1925, BAK, NL 1106 A.W. Fehling, No. 8.
18. Fehling to J.J. Coss, 31 January 1924 [1925], BAK, NL 1106 A.W. Fehling, No. 6.
19. Fehling to F.B. Stubbs, 19 July 1925, BAK, NL 1106 A.W. Fehling, No. 8.
20. Fehling to Ruml, 22 September 1925, BAK, NL 1106 A.W. Fehling, No. 8.
21. F. M. Rhind to Fehling, 5 October 1926, BAK, NL 1106 A.W. Fehling, No. 10.
22. The five Committee members were Friedrich Schmidt-Ott (chairman), Paul Kehr, Hermann Oncken, Albrecht Mendelssohn Bartholdy and Hermann Schumacher: see Christian Fleck, *Transatlantische Bereicherungen. Zur Erfindung der empirischen Sozialforschung* (Frankfurt am Main: Suhrkamp Verlag, 2007), 74–76.
23. Minutes of the Committee meeting to select the LSRM fellows on 7 March 1925, in Landesbibliothek Oldenburg (hereinafter LB Oldenburg), NL H. Schumacher, HS 362.2200.1.
24. T.B. Kittredge, "Report on Social Science Fellowship Program (1924–1941)," 19 January 1942, RAC-RF, RG 1.2,100 ES/49/378, 4.
25. Minutes of the Committee meeting to select the LSRM fellows on 7 March 1925, LB Oldenburg, NL H. Schumacher, HS 362.2200.1.

26. Ibid.
27. Ruml to Fehling, 8 August 1925, BAK, NL 1106 A.W. Fehling, No. 8.
28. Minutes of the Committee meeting to select the LSRM fellows on 9 July 1925, LB Oldenburg, NL H. Schumacher, HS 362.2200.5.
29. Fehling to the faculties concerned, undated, BAK, NL 1106 A.W. Fehling, No. 8.
30. Fehling to the Faculty of Philosophy, Bonn University, 19 April 1926, BAK, NL 1106 A.W. Fehling, No. 9.
31. Fehling to P. Kehr, 28 February 1927, BAK, NL 1106 A.W. Fehling, No. 11.
32. So, in 1927, the Committee was to send not more than ten applications to New York (Minutes of the third Committee meeting to select the Laura Spelman Rockefeller fellows on 22 April 1927, GeStA-PK, VI. HA. Familienarchive und Nachlässe, NL F. Schmidt-Ott, No. 50).
33. Fehling had presented the candidate as "not as brilliant as some of her competitors" and "rather shy." This might have led to the rejection (Fehling to the LSRM, undated, BAK, NL 1106 A.W. Fehling, No. 15).
34. Fehling to Ruml, 24 March 1927, BAK, NL 1106 A.W. Fehling, No. 11.
35. Fleck, *Transatlantische Bereicherungen*, 94.
36. Fehling to F. Schmidt-Ott, GstA PK, VI. HA Familienarchive und Nachlässe, NL F. Schmidt-Ott, No. 50.
37. Fehling to A. Bergstraesser, 12 January 1929, BAK, NL 1106 A.W. Fehling, No. 18.
38. Fehling to Ruml, 24 March 1927, BAK, NL 1106 A.W. Fehling, No. 11.
39. Ibid.
40. Fehling to S. Kähler, 28 November 1928, BAK, NL 1106 A.W. Fehling, No. 17.
41. Fehling to P. Hensel, 29 April 1926, BAK, NL 1106 A.W. Fehling, No. 9.
42. Fehling to J. Kuczynski, 20 July 1926, BAK, NL 1106 A.W. Fehling, No. 10.
43. Fehling to E.E. Day, 26 March 1928, BAK, NL 1106 A.W. Fehling, No. 15.
44. M.C. Cole to Fehling, 4 April 1928, BAK, NL 1106 A.W. Fehling, No. 15.
45. Fehling to H. Oncken, 18 September 1926, BAK, NL 1106 A.W. Fehling, No. 10.
46. Earlene Craver, "Patronage and the Directions of Research in Economics: The Rockefeller Foundation in Europe, 1924–1938," *Minerva* 24 (1986): 210.
47. T.B. Kittredge (?), "Social Science Fellowship Program in Europe—Rockefeller Foundation," undated, in RAC-RF, RG 1.2, 100ES/50/384, 6.
48. T.B. Appleget, "Report on Fellowship Programs of the Rockefeller Foundation," 1932, in RAC-RF, RG 1.2, 100E/43/318, 53.
49. Fehling to Ruml, 15 January 1929, BAK, NL 1106 A.W. Fehling, No. 18.
50. Fehling to A. Mendelssohn Bartholdy, 19 January 1929, BAK, NL 1106 A.W. Fehling, No. 18.
51. Day to Fehling, 11 February 1929, BAK, NL 1106 A.W. Fehling, No. 18.
52. Minutes of the seventh Committee meeting to select the German social sciences fellows on 2 March 1931, GeStA-PK, VI. HA. Familienarchive und Nachlässe, NL F. Schmidt-Ott, No. 50.
53. J. Van Sickle, "Report on Rockefeller Foundation activities in Germany, Social Sciences," undated, RAC-RF, RG 2 (1933–34), 717/93/736.

54. Malcolm Richardson, "Philanthropy and the Internationality of Learning: The Rockefeller Foundation and National Socialist Germany," *Minerva* 28 (1990): 27.
55. T.B. Kittredge, "Memorandum: Present Situation of German Advisory Committee—conversations TBK with AWF and various professors in Berlin and Kiel—Nov. 1-4, 1934," RAC-RF, RG 1.1, 717/16/151, 2.
56. Van Sickle to Day, 1 December 1933, RAC-RF, RG 1.1, 717/16/151.
57. T.B. Kittredge, "Memorandum. Fellowship Program in Germany. Conversation of TBK with Prof. Mendelssohn-Bartholdy, Paris, January 17, 1935," RAC-RF, RG 1.1, 717/16/151.
58. E.R.A. Seligman to Day, 23 May 1934, RAC-RF, RG 1.1, 717/16/151.
59. Day to Seligman, 8 June 1934, RAC-RF, RG 1.1, 717/16/151.
60. Kittredge to Fehling, 30 October 1933, RAC-RF, RG 1.1, 717/16/151.
61. Ibid.
62. M. Mason to G.K. Strode, 18 December 1933, RAC-RF, RG 2 (1933), 700/91/720.
63. Kittredge to Fehling, 10 January 1935, in RAC-RF, RG 1.1, 717/16/151.
64. Kittredge to S. May, S.H. Walker and J. Van Sickle, 8 December 1936, RAC-RF, RG 1.1, 717/16/151.
65. T.B. Appleget, "The Foundation's Experience with Refugee Scholars," 5 March 1946, RAC-RF, RG 1.1, 200/47/545 A, retrieved 22 March 2017 from http://www.rockarch.org/collections/rf/refugee.php.
66. Fehling to B. Pfister, 10 December 1936, BAK, NL 1106 A.W. Fehling, No. 45.
67. Kock, "August Wilhelm Fehling," 65–67.
68. Fehling to Van Sickle, 25 January 1950, BAK, NL 1106 A.W. Fehling, No. 5.

References

Bulmer, Martin, and Bulmer, Joan. "Philanthropy and Social Science in the 1920s: Beardsley Ruml and the Laura Spelman Rockefeller Memorial, 1922–1929," *Minerva* 19 (1981): 347–407.
Craver, Earlene. "Patronage and the Directions of Research in Economics: The Rockefeller Foundation in Europe, 1924–1938," *Minerva* 24 (1986): 205–22.
Fisher, Donald. "American Philanthropy and the Social Sciences in Britain 1919–1939: The Reproduction of a Conservative Ideology," *Sociological Review* 28 (1980): 277–315.
Flachowsky, Sören. *Von der Notgemeinschaft zum Reichsforschungsrat. Wissenschaftspolitik im Kontext von Autarkie, Aufrüstung und Krieg* (Stuttgart: Franz Steiner Verlag, 2008).
Fleck, Christian. *Transatlantische Bereicherungen. Zur Erfindung der empirischen Sozialforschung* (Frankfurt am Main: Suhrkamp Verlag, 2007).
Kock, Franz. "August Wilhelm Fehling," in Olaf Klose and Eva Rudolph (eds), *Schleswig-Holsteinisches Biographisches Lexikon 4* (Neumünster: Wachholtz, 1974): 65–68.

Rausch, Helke. "US-amerikanische 'Scientific Philanthropy' in Frankreich, Deutschland und Großbritannien zwischen den Weltkriegen," *Geschichte und Gesellschaft* 22 (2007): 73–98.

Richardson, Malcolm. "Philanthropy and the Internationality of Learning: The Rockefeller Foundation and National Socialist Germany," *Minerva* 28 (1990): 21–58.

Rietzler, Katharina. "Philanthropy, Peace Research, and Revisionist Politics: Rockefeller and Carnegie Support for the Study of International Relations in Weimar Germany," *GHI Bulletin Supplement* 5 (2008): 61–79.

Schroeder-Gudehus, Brigitte. *Deutsche Wissenschaft und internationale Zusammenarbeit: 1914–1928. Ein Beitrag zum Studium kultureller Beziehungen in politischen Krisenzeiten* (Geneva: Dumaret and Golay, 1966).

Seim, David L. *Rockefeller Philanthropy and Modern Social Science* (London: Pickering & Chatto, 2013).

 7

WEDGES AND WEBS
Rockefeller Nursing Fellowships (1920–40)

Pierre-Yves Saunier

Introduction

Browsing the two directories that have been published by the Rockefeller Foundation to compile the results of its Fellowship Program, one gets the impression that the latter was a single, continuous enterprise culminating in the emergence of leaders and paradigm setters.[1] Introducing the *Rockefeller Foundation Directory of Fellowships and Scholarships 1917–1970*, J. George Harrard emphasized that it was the "oldest continuing activity of the Rockefeller Foundation."[2] This view of the Fellowship Program as a constant and stable policy for "three generations of scholars" also received the support of historians. Stanley Coben described it as a major innovation, emphasizing the role of the General Education Board and the Laura Spelman Rockefeller Memorial,[3] which started in 1923 and 1924 respectively, and Darwin Stapleton has emphasized the fine mechanics of the International Health Board and Division fellowships.[4] Nurses seem to be miles away from the persons we usually associate with the fellowships, such as winners of the Nobel Prize in Physics, biology luminaries or top social scientists. Indeed, nursing fellowships, despite their having been numerous in both absolute and relative terms,[5] stand in contrast with the bulk of Rockefeller fellowships: they were not research-oriented, they were given to members of a specific profession that was not an established discipline, they could be awarded for undergraduate training and they went overwhelmingly to women. These very differences are why nurses matter.

When general fellowship rules and goals were devised, probably sometime in 1922,[6] their stated goal was to provide training abroad for selected nationals of countries in domains where such training was not available, before returning them to the homeland so that they would "raise standards" in their field. By then, a number of nursing fellowships had already been awarded. Within the context of Rockefeller Foundation fellowships, nursing fellowships thus stand out for their precocity as they developed in the absence of any well-established fellowship policies. They were, indeed, one important place where these policies were devised, defined and accepted. In the nursing domain, fellowships were quickly identified by Foundation officers and trustees as the ideal device to explore a country without committing large sums of money, all the more so since nursing was not seen as a priority. The autonomous or ancillary status of this fragile domain was a subject of almost constant debate between women nursing officers of the Foundation and the men who presided over the more prestigious programs in medicine or public health. But the importance of nursing fellowships and their impact on nursing were not merely a byproduct of the institutional inferiority and insecurity of nursing within the Foundation. Fellowships were cunningly used as a double-edged device by the inventive female nursing officers who worked for the Foundation. On the one hand, they were a wedge to penetrate existing national and local nursing institutions and organizations, especially into difficult local or national contexts. On the other hand, fellowships created webs of connections between the different regional, national or cultural nursing contexts where the Rockefeller Foundation and its subsidiaries were active. This chapter will approach these innovative conceptions of fellowships in the different countries where they were invented and developed between 1920 and 1940, chiefly but not only in Europe.

Of Serpents and Doves: Fellowships as a Wedge

The idea of the nursing fellowship as a leeway to change a local environment seems to have emerged from Elisabeth Crowell's work in France. Following her work with the Commission for the Prevention of Tuberculosis in France during World War I, she subsequently embarked on a larger attempt to strengthen nursing in that country. In the early 1920s, this experienced US nurse was trying to work with the nursing service of the public hospitals in the French capital city. Her idea was to place French but foreign-trained instructing nurses in the wards where student visiting nurses from schools supported by the Commission for the Prevention of Tuberculosis in France took their hospital training. This was a demonstration of good nursing education and practice aimed at doctors and administrators, which should open the way and gradually raise nursing standards in all the hospitals of the Parisian public system. In his diary, Rockefeller Foundation President George E. Vincent put down Crowell's "plans for introducing an entering wedge into the Service de Santé."[7] This was the lesson of five years of work in France, and some exploratory work in Belgium, Czechoslovakia and Poland, where she had learned that it took more than American energy, time and money to change the status quo. The fact that Crowell's Paris plan eventually failed did not alter her opinion; the reorganization of nursing in Europe would take place through European nurses. Fellowships would allow Europeans nurses to receive advance training in the principles of "modern nursing" abroad, make them their own and spread the gospel in the home country. Foundation secretary Edwin Embree came to endorse the strategy during his European tour with Crowell in the summer of 1923, and noted to his superiors that the Foundation people had to be "wise as serpents and harmless as doves" to impact nursing in Europe.[8] The fact that the Division of Studies multiplied fellowships in the following years is a clue that this cautious and incremental roadmap was followed. In Europe, wedges were provided by European fellows whose careful selection and monitoring was to open the different countries to the benefits of "modern nursing": these fellows would staff the schools supported by the Foundation in different countries, and their contribution in the classroom, the dispensaries and the school-wards would win the day. This was the kind of typical Rockefeller demonstration project that had gained a grip during the hookworm campaign earlier in the century.[9]

The wedge strategy apparently ruled out the project to bring in trained leaders from the outside, which was part of Crowell and Embree's initial 1923 Program for aid in nurse training in Europe. But some were already on location (for instance, in Poland), while Crowell and her assistants (who turned out to be American, Canadian, English or French) were always available for counsel and advice, and spent a lot of time in organizing schools, wards and dispensaries all across Europe. In Asia, it was also chiefly missionary nurses, North American nurses or nationals with previous training or work experience in the United States who were offered fellowships to return to Japan, Siam or the Philippines in order to teach and supervise work in schools, hospitals and dispensaries. In the four Asian countries where fellowships were offered between 1920 and 1940, a clear distinction was made: fellows from the countries in question were trained as instructors or for second-tier supervision, but very seldom for general supervision. For instance, while six third-year Siamese nursing students were offered fellowships to the Philippines to be trained as ward supervisors and instructors, it was the American nurse Vera Hickox who received a fellowship to England and Denmark, to be trained as a director of the midwifery school in Bangkok. The wedge was not always of the same wood as the tree it was meant to splint, and a combination of foreign and native fellows was used to develop the nursing activities of the Foundation.

The effectiveness of fellowships was not just about pushing people into strategic positions of teaching or leadership. Current and former fellows also weaved a network of complicity that helped the nursing officers to foster their "wedge work." As Crowell contemplated fellowships for Yugoslavian Catholic nuns to train in England, she invited high-ranking sisters of their order to tour Europe, with a precise plan in mind. In Brussels, in England and in Lyon (France), the Yugoslavian sisters were shown around by former fellows, so that they would see the light. Crowell's assistant then wrote to Miss Bauer, assistant director of the Lyon nursing school and herself a former fellow: "we have practically achieved the point with Soeur Thecla where she is interested in having some of her sisters going to England. You will see how important it is that she be given a good impression of results obtainable from such studies, although it will be preferable that she does not realize you have any knowledge of the project."[10] At the very moment where six Catholic sisters from the Lyon hospitals were receiving training in English hospitals, Bauer was expected to provide the Yugoslavian nuns with all the necessary clues and proof that such a scheme could be worked out profitably and safely for religious nurses. Following that tour, six nurses from Zagreb received a fellowship between 1925 and 1927.

This situates fellowships as a crucial element within Crowell's overall strategy: let Europeans teach themselves about nursing and learn best practices through observation of different experiences that had already been influenced by the appropriation of and translations from "modern nursing." The webs of connections fellows eventually created en route were an essential asset in their training, as fellows and travelers went from one place to another within Europe and beyond. One of the major impacts of the Fellowship Program and its consequences was therefore to place specific nursing communities within a wider world of nursing references and experiences.

Fellowships as a Web: Follow the Fellows

The circulation of fellows themselves had the effect of placing nurses in foreign training contexts. The Manila General Hospital and Peking Union Medical College were used to train Siamese (six fellowships in 1929) and Japanese nurses (two fellowships in 1923) respectively. And one of the justifications for supporting Saint Luke's hospital nursing school in Tokyo was Embree's conviction that improvements in Japan would affect a wide group of neighboring countries.[11] Clues as to the conception of regional training areas were even more obvious in Europe. As she tried to defend the scope of nursing activities to the head of the Medical Education Division Richard Pearce in 1927, Crowell sold the Lyon school of nursing as a "possible model not only for France but also for French speaking countries in general," a "training and demonstration centre for all French speaking people in Europe" and "one of three supercentres to serve all Europe and its colonies, their location to be decided by the progressiveness and efficiency of a given country, by its past and present influence on surrounding and foreign countries and above all by the particular language facilities it offers."[12]

But to Crowell, this allegiance to domino theory might have been more of a convenient selling point than the core of her thinking. If she might have had a clear vision of the geopolitics of nursing in Europe, she was above all sold on the idea that nursing circles in the different regions covered by Rockefeller activities should be plugged into one another. The work of her nursing officer colleagues shared a similar trend, and this was embodied in the itineraries of the nursing fellows. Their geographic diversity seems to have been wider than those in public health, for example. The 1945 report on public health fellowships mentioned that 81 percent of fellowships were given for study in the United States, and an additional 11 percent for work in Canada.[13] The map of nursing fellowships is quite different. From the twenty-nine fellowships active in March 1926, ten took their beneficiaries to the United States and Canada, nine to England, and ten to a mix of European countries that included France, Belgium and Austria. Between 1920 and 1940, Chinese nurses took their training in midwifery in England, and Siamese students went to Manila General Hospital as often as they did to the United States. Itineraries that brought nurses successively to Austria, Belgium, Hungary and Yugoslavia were no less common than North American combinations, and Canadian schools and sites were as important as US ones.

Yet, the nursing officers' world was not flat. They had a sense that the kind of nursing they wanted to promote could be showcased mostly (not exclusively) in the schools and hospitals the Foundation was supporting. As soon as the fellowship applications were started, the Foundation nursing officers began to devise the fellows' itineraries and activities, through conferences and correspondence with the fellows' superiors and with correspondent nurses in countries and cities to be visited, themselves very often past or future fellows. These itineraries were tailored to match the future position of the fellows, and fellows were eventually assigned to a limited number of specific locations. Bedside nurses who received a fellowship "to be equipped" as head nurses and supervisors went to Philadelphia General Hospital (United States), to the London General Hospital or to University College London (England). Those targeted for responsibilities in nursing education would meet one another at the Yale University School of Nursing or on the bench of the Teachers College at Columbia University, while would-be public health education supervisors gathered at the University of Toronto Department of Public Health Nursing and its field assignments. Public health nurses received practical field training in several locations with a preference for the East Harlem Nursing and Health Service in New York City and the Vanderbilt dispensary in Tennessee, according to the "rural" or "urban" nature of their future assignment in the home country. Likewise, a fellowship or a travel grant for European nurses who were expected to operate in pediatric nursing was inherently linked with a stay under Professor Von Pirquet at the Kinderklinik in Vienna (Austria). Midwifery training took place at the British Hospital for Mothers and Babies in Woolwich (London) for Chinese fellows in the 1920s or at the Lobenstine Clinic in New York City for US fellows of the 1930s. Matters of nationality, language or color also influenced the assignment of fellows to specific institutions, in order for them to band against homesickness, benefit from the language skills of a specific instructor, or circumvent the color line that made it difficult for nurses from Asia to be welcomed in US nursing institutions. Thus, the principal of the School for Nurses at Johns Hopkins University, when approached to host Chinese nurses in 1918, responded: "unless they should be in appearance very definitely Chinese, I do not believe this far South we could admit a student who might bear resemblance to a colored person."[14]

The locations that structured the itineraries of nurse fellows were closely interlinked, carefully chosen and renewed. Concentration is clear when one looks at the itineraries of fellows studying in North America. The Philadelphia General Hospital, Yale University School of Nursing, the University of Toronto School of Nursing, Columbia University Teachers College Department of Nursing Education,

Vanderbilt University School of Nursing, Johns Hopkins University School of Hygiene in Baltimore, Simmons College and Boston University in Boston were successively or simultaneously focal points for fellows between the 1920s and the 1940s. Some public health agencies were systematically visited by almost every nurse fellow or travel grantee when they were in North America, like the City of Toronto Health Department and the East Harlem Nursing and Health Center in New York City; the latter ceased to be a compulsory stage during the 1940s and the former a bit later. Likewise, fellows specialized in public health nursing were typically sent to the dispensaries of the Department of Health of Alabama State Board of Health and the Tennessee State Health Department for observation work during the late 1920s. Ten years later, visitors flocked to the Eastern Health District in Baltimore and the Newton Health Department in Massachusetts to learn from its school hygiene program. These were not random centrifugal tendencies. From the mid 1920s, when nurse Mary Beard was hired at the New York headquarters to supervise the sojourn of foreign fellows in North America, she arranged and rearranged systematic circuits that fellows would ride for a few days to several months. In 1927, for instance, she had her "usual visits" for all the fellows who had completed their course of study at Toronto: the Yale University School of Nursing, the Providence Visiting Nurses Association, the General Hospital and the Phipps Institute in Philadelphia and the East Harlem Nursing and Health Center had to be experienced. The expected learning outcomes of such circuits of study, visit and observation included nursing gestures and knowledge, ability to teach and organize teaching, but also ideas about nursing leadership and professional organization. Whence the frequency of visits to the headquarters of US professional organizations of nurses, to their conferences or to the headquarters of the American Red Cross in Washington, DC. Similar "Grand Tour" itineraries existed in Europe, with the stages changing as the Foundation built or supported new nursing schools or new public health centers. It is this detailed topography of immersion, impression and appropriation that helps us to understand what fellows saw, heard, read or missed in their individual experience.

The material on the fellowships processed so far underlines the collective dimension of that experience, beyond the mere fact that fellows attended class, did fieldwork or observed nursing work in the same places. The web of nursing was weaved by the officers in order to build ties between the fellows and themselves, and among the fellows.

Once the fellows arrived on location, nursing officers carefully nurtured the fellows at each moment of their fellowship, relentlessly offering company for travel, food or entertainment and visiting regularly to places where fellows studied. This social aspect was quite specific to nursing fellowships. When comparing nursing officers' diaries with those of Alan Gregg, who represented the Division of Medical Education in Europe, differences in the handling of future, current and former fellows are obvious. Systematic interviews of possible nursing fellows were conducted by nursing officers themselves, and great care was given to the evaluation of their social background, moral and educational characteristics, as well as their engaging personality, leadership aptitudes, education level and professional ability. Nor are there any mention of Gregg visiting sick former fellows when in town, nor of the tea, lunch or dinner parties that nursing officers never failed to offer to current or past fellows while they visited Debreczen, Lyon or Cracow, or in Crowell's home in Paris. Nursing officers of the Foundation interwove evaluation, empathy and advice on all these occasions. Besides being part of the monitoring process, such bonds echo the emphasis on sisterhood that was a hallmark of women's movements in the nineteenth century, and also characterized the community of North American nurses, at the training level as well as in professional activities.[15] Creating a community was also part and parcel of the professional ethos that the Rockefeller nursing officers were striving to establish. Their commitment to social bonds was a first-hand example of how nurses should stick together and strive for their profession to be recognized. In any case, this concern to be close to one another bonded nursing officers and fellows together, and this was without equivalent in other sectors, where the relationship between fellows and Foundation officers was patterned on academic lore, rank and status.

This socialization aspect is another clue to how fellowships were used by officers to build up nursing internationally. Nursing officers treated fellowships as a cumulative process that continuously fed resources into their collective brain. Current and recent fellows brought information: news about people and facilities, comments on differences between schools, hospital wards or dispensaries in Europe, compared evaluations of performance of the institutions they had visited, and hints of discrepancies and relevance of training in the United States. Both serious talk and gossip provided vital elements for the officers to monitor the evolution of each institution to which they sent fellows, and to adjust the Fellowship Program and the Nursing Program as a whole. Their diaries and memos were a sort of perpetual online bulletin board where news of nursing institutions and individuals all around the world were, selected, classified and analyzed. Past fellows were also regularly received in the Paris office or in Crowell's home, just like most nurses from around the world who passed through Paris. In New York City, Mary Beard frequently brought foreign and US fellows together for dinners or Christmas parties at her home or organized parties and picnics. Socialization among fellows studying in North America was also favored beyond her presence, beginning with the fact that nursing fellows most frequently boarded in the nursing schools and hospitals where they studied. This daily cohabitation was completed by special events: fellows shared a week of recess at the Convalescent and Vacation House for Nurses of Babylon, Long Island, or traveled together for observation and visits. Nurses from the same country or school especially enjoyed these moments where they would enjoy complicity, but such groups could also be (smartly) composed of fellows from different countries: French nurse Anna Fressenon, from the school of nursing in Lyon, accomplished her 1928 summer program with three Yugoslavian fellows, just like Miss Tjellstrom from Sweden shared her observation visits with three Danish nurses in 1940.

These opportunities for ties among fellows were paralleled by an effort to have foreign visitors socialize with domestic nurses, especially on American soil. In addition to the propinquity in the hospital wards, on the school bench or in the Nurses Home, foreign fellows were sent to conferences of US and Canadian nursing societies. Travel grantees, when in New York, were often invited to lunches or dinners where Mary Beard convened elite nurses from the East Coast, featuring major leaders like Adelaide Nutting, Annie Goodrich and others. This inter-foreign and foreign–domestic liaison work would often rely on previous ties that the nursing profession had built between and through countries and institutions. Some fellows were already acquainted to one another because they had followed the course of the International League of Red Cross Societies in London,[16] and several entertained earlier acquaintances with US or Canadian nurses from war work, International Council of Nurses meetings or international visits in other settings. It was not just the Foundation that internationalized nurses, but nurses with some international characteristics who were selected as fellows by the Foundation. In any case, their experience on location did not boil down to individual trajectories of study and observation in different nursing centers, but took the form of a series of collective interactions with domestic nurses and other foreign fellows.

Similar gatherings or conversations were invariably sought every time a nursing officer visited a place where a former fellow worked. All across Europe, but also in China, Japan and Siam, former fellows became directors of schools and dispensaries, government advisors or administrators, instructors and head nurses in hospitals, and they were first-class informants on the whereabouts of nursing in their countries and their institutions. They constituted a web of nursing crisscrossed by blueprints of nursing school buildings, curricula and course outlines, professional and governmental nursing regulations, textbooks and practical "how to?" information (management of statistical records for health centers, compilation of monthly reports, arrangement of course blocks or installation of a diet kitchen). Foundation nursing officers were the pivots of that circulation, seconded by fellows and by the travels of "VIP nurses" that were started following Crowell and Embree's 1923 program. Just like these travel grants, fellowships were given to individuals, but eventually created a group of nurses who shared affections as much as professional commitments and information.

Conclusion

Within the world of nursing, fellowships complemented the support given by Rockefeller organizations to nursing schools, dispensaries, professional organizations and the establishment of national nursing policies and agencies. In that Rockefeller galaxy, nursing was tackled as a discipline, a profession and a form of knowledge. Such a degree of integration was not attained in other fields. The role of fellowships, as a result, can be roughly assessed as having been the spider silk wherefrom a web of nurses and nursing institutions was supported, expanded and maintained during the 1920s and 1930s, across nations, across cultural areas and across land masses. The outcome was to expand a common platform for nurses "throughout the world." Though not without differences and gaps, hundreds of nurses from very different contexts came to rely on a common language of gestures, values, organizational features and training devices. The circulation of Rockefeller fellows and the nursing activities of the Foundation and its subsidiaries were not the only factors in that development. Private and personal links, bilateral relations among nursing associations, and the activities of other international associations and agencies such as the International Council of Nurses or the League of Red Cross Societies contributed in an important manner. The Rockefeller fellowships, though, were unique in creating an elite internationalized cadre of nursing in different countries. When the first nursing expert committee was created at the World Health Organization in the fall of 1949, most of its members had previously benefited from a Rockefeller fellowship.[17]

However, the study of nursing fellowships has relevance beyond the domain of nursing. It also brings food for thought in relation to the understanding of the larger impact of scholarship programs. Thus, the idea that networks of fellows could be an end in themselves, because they would create communities of thought, belief, behavior and information, is usually associated with the Cold War era.[18] The history of nursing fellowships suggests that such an aim has been contemplated and pursued before the Cold War, in a very different context, and for reasons that had more to do with professional politics. As such, the case of nursing fellowships should help to sharpen arguments for or against interpretations in terms of americanization and hegemony, which usually rely on activities in fields endowed with higher political or scientific importance.

Pierre-Yves Saunier is a professor of European history at Université Laval (Quebec City, Canada). He is the coeditor, with Akira Iriye, of the *Palgrave Dictionary of Transnational History* (Palgrave Macmillan, 2009). His latest significant publication is a methodological and historiographical primer, *Transnational History* (Palgrave Macmillan, 2013). His imagination, curiosity and energy are currently absorbed by his attempts to be a decent professor, but he has not renounced his research interest for international governmental and nongovernmental organizations in the nineteenth and twentieth centuries.

Appendix: Katarina Stipetic

Sister Blanda (her religious name) was thirty-seven years old when she received a Rockefeller Foundation fellowship in 1926. She had joined the Sisters of Mercy of Saint Vincent de Paul, who staffed an hospital in Zagreb, Croatia, in 1912. She received special training in Vienna in the early 1920s, to equip her as teaching staff for the nursing school that was being set up in Zagreb by governmental authorities. As a Rockefeller fellow, she was "to study bedside nursing and hospital organization." She began training at the London Hospital in January 1927, with two other sisters of her order, followed by a study tour in North America that began on 6 August 1927. The tour began in Rochester, Minnesota, at the Saint Mary's Hospital—managed by the Sisters of Saint Francis. However, Sister Blanda did not relish the experience. Her stint at the School of Nursing of the University of Toronto, where they spent a couple of months at the end of 1927, she enjoyed much more, but we do not know what she thought of her final New York City sojourn with attendance to Teachers College conferences (Columbia University), conversations with nursing leaders and a visit to the Henry Street Settlement. By and large, it was the Philadelphia General Hospital that she assessed as the best organization and teaching nursing operation they had seen. Miss Clayton, the nursing superintendent of that hospital, later declared that the nuns were very radical in their views about the needs for nursing reform in Yugoslavia, and that their fire would certainly win the day.

In her debriefing interview at the beginning of 1928, Sister Blanda was very responsive to Crowell's prod about the educational work to be done in Zagreb: just like the fellows in Lyon, Blanda was to promote a different understanding and organization of nursing among students, religious superiors and hospital doctors. In fact, Sister Blanda went beyond calling; she stated her plans to return to Zagreb via Vienna, so that her two companions would see the upscale gynecological and maternity care given by religious nuns there. Blanda also voiced her resolution to push the Croat Catholic hierarchy to modify the restrictions on the kind of nursing care provided by the nuns. Crowell visited her regularly in subsequent years, and her last diary entry about Stipetic, in 1938, stated that: "Money spent on her fellowship has certainly been productive."

Notes

Thanks to Clifford Rosenberg for revising the initial version of this text.

1. Rockefeller Foundation, *The Rockefeller Foundation Directory of Fellowship Awards 1917–1950* (New York: Rockefeller Foundation, c. 1951); *Directory of Fellowships and Scholarships 1917–1970* (New York: Rockefeller Foundation, 1972).
2. *Directory of Fellowships* (1972), vii.
3. Stanley Coben, "Foundation Officials and Fellowships: Innovation in the Patronage of Science," *Minerva* 14 (1976): 225–40.
4. Darwin H. Stapleton, "Fellowships and Field Stations: The Globalization of Public Health Knowledge, 1920–1950," Explorations in Public Health History Conference, Bellagio, Italy, 2003.
5. According to the 1951 *Directory* (*The Rockefeller Foundation Directory*, x), 689 nurses had by then received Rockefeller Foundation fellowships, out of a total of 6,000 fellows. This number proves to be underestimated when one returns to the original material, and some 718 had been awarded to nurses by the end of 1950.
6. Stapleton, "Fellowships and Field Stations," 7.
7. Rockefeller Archive Centre (hereinafter RAC), Rockefeller Foundation papers (hereinafter RF), Record Group (hereinafter RG) 12, Vincent diary, 27 February 1922.

8. RAC, RF, RG 1.1, series 700 C, box 20, folder 137 (hereafter 700C/20/137), Embree to Vincent, 12 August 1923.
9. John Ettling, *The Germ of Laziness: Rockefeller Philanthropy and Public Health in the New South* (Cambridge, MA: Harvard University Press, 1981).
10. École Rockefeller Archives, Lyon, pink folder "Correspondence with the Rockefeller Foundation," Adams to Bauer, 14 August 1926.
11. RAC, RF, RG 3.1, 908/7D/86.052, History—Greer Williams' notes—nursing.
12. RAC, RF, RG.1.1, 700/20/141, Crowell to Pearce, April 29, 1927.
13. Stapleton, "Fellowships and Field Stations."
14. RAC, China Medical Board, RG. 4, 1/7/80, letter from June 27, 1918.
15. Edith F. Hurwitz, "The International Sisterhood," in Renate Bridenthal and Claudia Koonz (eds), *Becoming Visible: Women in European History* (Boston: Houghton Mifflin, 1977), 325–45; Susan Armstrong-Reid, *Lyle Creelman: The Frontiers of Global Nursing* (Toronto: University of Toronto Press, 2014).
16. Susan McGann, "Collaboration and Conflict in International Nursing, 1920–39," *Nursing History Review* 16 (2008): 29–57.
17. WHO 602-4-2 "Nursing Expert Committee," Eliot to Chisholm, 19 August 1949, World Health Organization archives, Geneva; Armstrong-Reid, *Lyle Creelman*.
18. Edward H. Berman, *The Influence of the Carnegie, Ford and Rockefeller Foundations on American Foreign Policy* (Albany, NY: SUNY Press, 1983), 60.

References

Armstrong-Reid, Susan. *Lyle Creelman: The Frontiers of Global Nursing* (Toronto: University of Toronto Press, 2014).
Berman, Edward H. *The Influence of the Carnegie, Ford and Rockefeller Foundations on American Foreign Policy* (Albany, NY: SUNY Press, 1983).
Coben, Stanley. "Foundation Officials and Fellowships: Innovation in the Patronage of Science," *Minerva* 14 (1976): 225–40.
Ettling, John. *The Germ of Laziness: Rockefeller Philanthropy and Public Health in the New South* (Cambridge, MA: Harvard University Press, 1981).
Hurwitz, Edith F. "The International Sisterhood," in Renate Bridenthal and Claudia Koonz (eds), *Becoming Visible: Women in European History* (Boston, MA: Houghton Mifflin, 1977), 325–45.
McGann, Susan. "Collaboration and Conflict in International Nursing, 1920–39," *Nursing History Review* 16 (2008): 29–57.
Stapleton, Darwin H. "Fellowships and Field Stations: The Globalization of Public Health Knowledge, 1920–1950," Explorations in Public Health History Conference, Bellagio, Italy, 2003.

 8

FELLOWSHIP PROGRAMS FOR PUBLIC HEALTH DEVELOPMENT

The Rockefeller Foundation, UNRRA and the WHO (1920s–1970s)

Yi-Tang Lin, Thomas David and Davide Rodogno

Introduction

This chapter offers an overview of fellowship programs in public health and medical sciences and uses them as useful prisms to demonstrate the transfer of knowhow between different organizations. We claim that, as far as fellowships programs in medical sciences and public health are concerned, World War II does not represent a rupture. We argue that the original template conceived and developed by the Rockefeller Foundation (RF), which has its origins in a specific US domestic context, was appropriated by other US institutions (for instance, the Carnegie Foundation and the Millbank Memorial Fund) and eventually by international organizations such as the League of Nations, the United Nations Relief and Rehabilitation Administrations (UNRRA) and by other United Nations (UN) agencies such as the World Health Organization (WHO), the United Nations International Children's Emergency Fund (UNICEF), the United Nations Educational, Scientific and Cultural Organization (UNESCO) and the Food and Agriculture Organization (FAO).

We wish to demonstrate that meaningful connections exist between the programs conceived and implemented by the RF, the League of Nations, UNRRA and the WHO. These connections concern: (1) the purposes and objectives of these programs; (2) the people involved; (3) the networks they created, by design or otherwise; and (4) their administration, such as the selection criteria.[1] From the interwar period onward, there was an increase in the use of exchange programs to offer training in technical and professional fields. Some countries created agencies that developed bilateral or binational exchanges, which coexisted with international fellowship programs. In an UNRRA draft document entitled "Proposal for an International Fellowship Program" from October 1946, the author defended the merits of these international exchanges in comparison with binational ones: "extensive as is this growing interexchange of educational personnel between countries, it is not yet truly international ... What is indicated therefore is the need for some operating agency to facilitate a truly international exchange of educational personnel, one that will assign specialists from one country to best facilities available anywhere, without special reference to the country in which these facilities are located."[2]

This chapter represents a preliminary overview and we are aware that there are several ways of writing the history of these programs.

The Common Rationale of the Fellowship Programs

One common feature of fellowship programs in public health in the first half of the twentieth century is that they were never started in a vacuum. They had a political objective. They were also based on the donor institutions' visions concerning what is public health and how it should be achieved. For instance, the RF's definition of public health was intimately connected with its endeavors in the United States. The RF officers assumed that the way in which public health was taught at Harvard and Johns Hopkins—both institutions had been funded or created thanks to the Foundation's financial aid—was the best possible way. The RF officers had information about the countries where fellowship programs were set up, and their reports reflected how they presumed fellowships would function to promote a particular type of public health service.

What the RF and international organizations such as the League of Nations, UNRRA and the WHO had in common was the intrinsic value that they attributed to, and the expectations they placed on, fellows. They believed fellows were the "human capital," an investment worth making to reach specific objectives such as the improvement of living conditions worldwide. As early as 1924, the RF claimed:

> Fellowships were an organic part of the institution's policy; they were a means of carrying out plans in health and education, not an end in themselves ... The aim is to prepare them (i.e. fellows) for better service in their home lands.[3]

Thirty-four years later, in 1958, the Director-General of the WHO wrote about fellows in very similar terms:

> Fellows are making contributions in informing and training others, in improving or expanding existing services or establishing new ones, in carrying out research and in providing leadership.[4]

These two quotes encapsulate the objectives of fellowship programs: improving public health services in their countries of origin, informing and training others, and leadership. On "leadership" there is a lot to say, because it was conspicuously present in missionary educational programs and discourses in colonial contexts around the world. The RF—as well as international organizations—inherited and/or shared the same ambitions as missionaries concerning the education of elites and leaders. No matter what kind of program a fellow attended, he or she was expected to become a leader in her or his field. As late as 1975, Bruce-Chwatt of the WHO wrote:

> The principal aim of WHO is to raise the level of health in all countries through technical and other types of assistance given to national administrations. This can be achieved through the strengthening of health services and through improvement of the standards of teaching and training of the medical and health personnel. Better cooperation between the scientific, educational and operational staff within the country and between various countries contribute to the advancement of health. One of the important ways in which WHO attempts to achieve these goals is through its fellowship programme.[5]

The implicit corollary of this aim was that fellows would return to their own countries. The RF, UNRRA and the WHO ensured that their fellowship programs collaborated closely with governmental institutions. Neither the RF nor the UN agencies granted aid to individuals who were planning to become private practitioners or commercial laboratory workers. There were strings attached to the fellowship programs insofar as the RF and the WHO would request official assurances that positions would be available when the training had been completed.

The RF Fellowship Program: A Global Ambition

The RF mission was to "promote the well-being of mankind throughout the world."[6] It concentrated its funds on governmental programs and put forward a plan for "human betterment" revolving around research, education and public health. From as early as 1913, these three goals were intertwined in RF planning, and fellowships were key for achieving them. During the winter of 1913, the RF began a fellowship program with two medical institutions in Brazil and started its medical work in China. By 1916, the China Medical Board granted fellowships to twenty-seven missionary physicians and to seven Chinese physicians. The cost of these allocations in 1916 was US$86,750.[7] While during the war the amount of money allocated for fellows dwindled, as early as 1918, the RF reverted to its previous policies and increased the amount of money available. It deemed the wise provision of stipends for the training of such persons to be a fundamental contribution to progress in each nation, and a means of promoting international understanding and goodwill.

The RF devised the Fellowship Program as the human resource allocation program for the RF public health work in various countries. Victor Heiser's letter to John B. Grant, the Director of the Department of Public Health and Preventive Medicine of the Peking Union Medical College (PUMC), faithfully confirmed that the above rationales lay behind the RF Fellowship Program. In his letter, Heiser insisted that the fellowships should enable "younger men to prepare them for certain definite technical or administrative positions in public health work."[8] Through its Division of Medical Education, in 1920 the RF began allocating scientific journals and books, funds for laboratory supplies, and fellowships, including "physicians and medical students from Brazil, from China, and Europe to pursue courses in leading medical schools of the United States."[9] The purpose of this decision was to begin a transition from a policy of "emergency relief to a plan of developmental aid."

The very first International Health Board (IHB) fellowships were granted to Brazilian fellows, who became leaders of public health work in Brazil as soon as they returned. Satisfied by the usefulness of the fellowships, the IHB increased their number.[10] The RF would gradually lower the number of American missionary (on furlough back home) recipients of fellowships and increase the number of European, Brazilian and Chinese fellows in medicine and public health. In China, the number of Chinese fellows outgrew that of foreign fellows in 1924.[11] Fellows were both graduate physicians and undergraduate medical students (for instance, they were students of the Harvard Medical School of China).

As noted in the 1919 RF Annual Report, the purpose of fellowships for graduate study was the "excellent prospect that men well trained in the more essential requirements of public health administration may return to their countries and achieve leadership in public health affairs."[12] The RF sought to train teaching of hygiene and public health, because it firmly believed that this would be of crucial importance for achieving better living conditions worldwide. Through the Fellowship Program, it hoped to train teachers for schools of hygiene and public health campaigns in countries in need, as well as chairs of public health to provide undergraduate teachings in medical schools. In many countries this meant setting up such schools and/or chairs. The RF's fellowship policy was therefore closely connected to political strategies coordinated by the Foundation, aiming to persuade national governments to establish schools of public health and setting up related positions.[13]

From the 1920s, the RF considerably expanded its Fellowship Program in Europe, Latin America and Asia. The Foundation also began its cooperation with the League of Nations, which included the international exchange of health personnel program. The League of Nations Health Organization (LNHO) officers organized group visits for national health officials to other countries' public health institutions. Quite different from the RF fellowships, the LNHO program was only three months long. The main goal was to inform public health officials about what had been done in other member countries.[14] As Ludwik Rajchman indicated in a letter to Wickliffe Rose, the Director of the RF-IHB, the program aimed to create "a new spirit of collaboration."[15]

In the mid 1930s, the RF seemed satisfied with the outcome of its Fellowship Program, given that most fellows were now occupying positions of importance and distinction worldwide. The Foundation did not assume that the fellows' leadership and their contribution to scientific thought were the results solely of their fellowship experience. UNRRA and the WHO would adopt the RF model, because they seemed persuaded of its soundness. It is noticeable that UNRRA and WHO experts in charge of setting up and running these programs had previously been RF fellows or had worked for the RF themselves.

There were no fundamental changes in the assumptions, guiding principles or purposes of the RF's Fellowship Program during the interwar period. Of course, the number of fellows varied. During the 1930s, the program was affected by economic conditions and the countries from where fellows came from varied. As early as 1940, the Foundation started to reflect on its postwar role, but it was only in 1948–49 that it eventually put forward its new policy. The Foundation's new vision was shaped by the profound political changes brought about by the Cold War, which prevented it from operating in several countries, including in Central and Eastern Europe and China. The RF was also aware of the discrepancy between the resources of any privately endowed philanthropic organization and the magnitude of funds by that time provided by governmental agencies for large-scale research or educational enterprises. For these reasons, the RF started financing smaller projects and would restrict the fields of its Fellowship Program in public health. The creation of the WHO also explains the change of the RF fellowship policy. In an internal report from 1954, the Foundation explained that for many years it was practically alone in this field. However, since the beginning of World War II, a multiplicity of agencies, both governmental and private, had been created or expanded, most of which included a fellowship program patterned after that of the Rockefeller Foundation. Therefore, the Foundation gradually withdrew from these areas to devote its attention to newer fields in which there seemed to be "opportunity for advancement or application of knowledge."[16]

The UNRRA Fellowship Program: A Rehabilitation Program

In 1943, UNRRA, the first UN agency, was created to oversee and direct relief programs across the world.[17] It also played an important but underestimated role in health relief and national public health rehabilitation in Europe and Asia. Scholarly studies mentioned UNRRA as a precursor of the WHO,[18] whereas contemporaries grasped its wider significance. Wilbur A. Sawyer, UNRRA Director of Health, argued that "when the future historian evaluates the work of UNRRA's Health Division, he will probably attribute greater significance to its service in bridging the war-caused gap in the evolution of international health organization than to its relief operations of a purely emergency nature."[19] Comparing the importance of UNRRA's efforts with other international organizations (the League of Nations or the RF), Sawyer proclaimed that the Health Division of UNRRA "became by far the largest international health organization which the world has yet seen."[20] Sawyer was well-placed to make such a comparison as he had been one of the most influential figures of international public health during the interwar period. He had worked for many years for the RF International Health Board (renamed the International Health Division in 1929), which he had joined in 1919, before becoming its director (1935–44) when he eventually joined UNRRA. His professional trajectory shows that UNRRA was in many ways influenced by the RF and its staff.[21] This influence was particularly blatant when one examines the UNRRA Fellowship Program. Oscar J. Falnes, the director of the program, wrote that from the beginning, "the administration of these fellowships might be similar to those offered by the Rockefeller Foundation."[22]

During the War, the UNRRA administration decided to create a training program in response to a Chinese government request to send Chinese relief workers to the United States for training. This anticipated the 1946 UNRRA Fellowship Program, which was "not really an educational programme but primarily a rehabilitation programme being designed to bring a number of specialists and key personnel out of UNRRA receiving countries to study in countries not ravaged or devastated by war. These specialists ... were not concerned with education as an individual process; rather they were the instruments in a larger programme designed to help rehabilitate their respective countries."[23] Here rehabilitation meant that fellows would come back to their home countries after the completion of their education abroad.[24]

During its short life, UNRRA managed to send 155 fellows abroad. Most of them went to the United States (around 80 percent), while others went to the United Kingdom, France or neutral countries such as Sweden and Switzerland.[25] Most of these fellows came from Eastern and Southern Europe (Czechoslovakia, Poland, Ukraine, Yugoslavia and Greece) and China.

The choice of the candidates was made collectively by UNRRA missions and the respective governments.[26] The operating divisions of UNRRA, in collaboration with the Training Branch, screened the applications. UNRRA headquarters seldom rejected recommendations made by mission personnel, as the latter were in a position to know the immediate needs and priorities of the countries where they operated.[27] Sometimes candidates were selected because "political colour weighs more than technical suitability."[28] UNRRA fellows had a quite typical and specific profile: "the holder of an UNRRA fellowship uniformly was a more mature person, occupying a key position in his home country. He was not a trainee but rather a person who on returning home would supervise trainee[s]."[29] Again, as with the RF, UNRRA recognized the need to educate national elites and future leaders.

Fellows were sent to the United States or Europe, where a program of orientation was organized on their behalf. In the United States, the program included information about "American life," American customs, a consideration of the fellows' relationship to UNRRA, and a meeting with technical advisers to organize the fellows' activities and, in particular, their internship.[30] Contrary to the practice in the more academic type of fellowships, such as the RF programme, "in the UNRRA fellowships formal enrolment in colleges and universities was at a minimum and assignment in governmental agencies, industrial and commercial firms at a maximum."[31]

UNRRA fellowships covered public health, welfare, public services, agricultural rehabilitation and industrial rehabilitation. Connections with the RF were the most evident in public health: "placement for the fellows in the field of health was in some respects less of a pioneering effort than in other fields because of work in the past by large foundations, notably the Rockefeller Foundation, in subsidizing health fellowships ... The technical advisers for the health fellows found it advisable to work largely through two main organizations, namely the Rockefeller Foundation's International Health Division and the Office of International Health Relations of the United States Public Health Service."[32]

In 1947, UNRRA's resources and activities were transferred to newly created UN agencies such as the WHO, UNICEF and UNESCO. The Fellowship Program was transferred to UNESCO and the WHO under the supervision of Joseph Vasely. Vasely embodies the continuity between the Rockefeller, UNRRA and WHO programs. Born in 1894 in the Austro-Hungarian Empire, as soon as he received his PhD in medicine in 1920 at Charles University, he took on a Rockefeller fellowship. For a number of years, he was Director of Public Health in Czechoslovakia. During World War II, he was Deputy Director of Health at UNRRA and then Chief of the Section of Fellowships and Training at the WHO.[33]

WHO Fellowship Program: Decentralizing the Administration

As mentioned above, WHO Fellowship Program followed on from that of UNRRA.[34] The UN system as a whole also placed great importance on the international fellowship program. As early as 1947–48, more than 1,135 international fellowships were awarded among member states by the WHO, UNICEF, the FAO and UNESCO.[35] WHO fellowships grew rapidly from 1947 to 1974 (see Figure 8.1). These programs varied in terms of duration and the nature of education provided. Some lasted only three weeks, while others involving study for a diploma at a foreign university would last up to two years. From 1947 to 1968, about 3,0000 fellowships were awarded by WHO, plus over 11,000 special fellowships granted for participation in group educational activities, way beyond the amount of Rockefeller fellowships.[36] Notwithstanding the rapid budget growth of the WHO, from 1960 to 1974, the Fellowship Program represented consistently around 9–12 percent of the regular budget.[37]

Following both the RF and UNRRA models, WHO devised a fellowship program as a means to provide public health manpower for

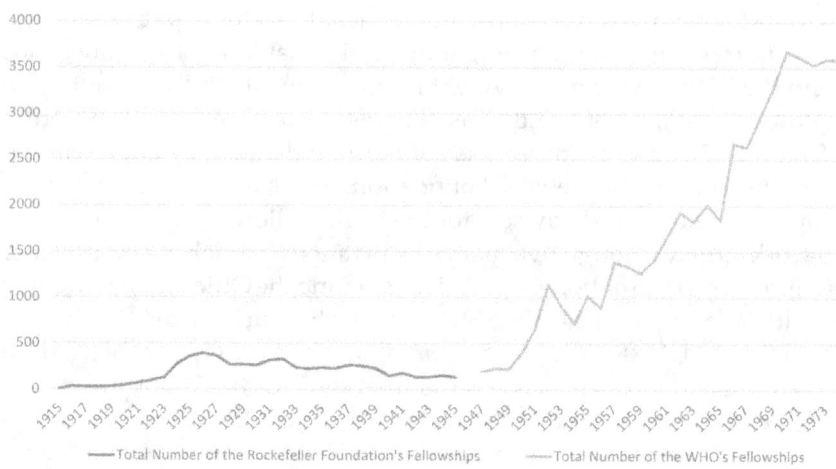

Figure 8.1 Number of fellowships in public health granted by the RF, 1915–1945, and the WHO, 1947–73

Source: RAC, RF/ 1.2/ 100 International/ 43/320 and WHO Library, L.J. Bruce-Chwatt, Report on the WHO Fellowships Programme, October 1975 (unpublished)

its member countries. During the eleventh World Health Assembly, Marcolino Candau, the Director-General of the WHO and a former Rockefeller fellow, explained their purpose:

> The organization regards the Fellowship Programme as a mean for improvement of health of all countries, but particularly those of the developing world. It is an indirect approach to bringing to the country, in a permanent way, through its own nationals, the benefits of rapid advance.[38]

Candau emphasized once again the role of local authorities in determining specific needs for the Fellowship Program. This was perhaps the main difference between the WHO and the RF. The WHO fully endorsed the national governments to propose fellowship subjects and candidates, while the local RF officials would often assume full responsibility to decide on the subjects, candidates and training institutions. UNRRA was in between, choosing candidates based on the needs of their missions and local authorities.

The case of the Republic of China (ROC), the official China government recognized by the UN from 1946 to 1971, offers insights into the government's use of WHO fellowships. In order to secure the nation's international image, ROC public health fellows were chosen based on experience and political ideology. Alongside the testing of language skills, security checks were included in the admission process.[39] The candidates and their guarantors were also required to sign a form indicating that they would take full responsibility for any misbehavior by the candidates that might jeopardize the nation's reputation.[40] Sending a public health expert abroad represented not merely the quest for expertise, but also sought to improve the nation's reputation in the Cold War context.

The WHO Fellowship Program also operated in a regional context. From the 1950s, Regional Offices were responsible for administering fellowships and for evaluating the results. Every Regional Office employed an educational advisor to take on fellowship-related matters. In this way, the WHO granted more intraregional than interregional fellowships.[41] It established a list of criteria to evaluate success, such as the relationship between the fellowship training and the eventual employment of the returned fellow. According to the WHO's Western Pacific Regional Statistician: "The success or the failure of a WHO fellowship depends on whether the returned fellow has been appropriately utilized by his government, and the extent to which he has been able to contribute to the improvement of his country's medical and health services."[42] Using the same criterion, in 1957 the WHO conducted a study based on 1,053 returned fellows' contributions to their countries, which showed that only 8 percent had not fully used their skills following the training.[43]

Inspired by the RF's achievements, the WHO regarded the Fellowship Program as an instrument to secure its member states' health development. In contrast to the RF, whose officials were in charge of defining the specific needs of other countries, the WHO's fellowship administration was decentralized: national governments decided which fellowship training was the most needed, and the regional officers had considerable autonomy in distributing their budget. The Fellowship Program remains an important instrument for the WHO. The shift from mass eradication programs to community health in the late 1970s did not alter the position of the Fellowship Program in WHO policy.

Conclusion

The reciprocal influences and quasi-symbiotic relationship we referred to in this chapter largely explain the continuities in the fellowship programs during the twentieth century. Therefore, contrary to the commonly held view of the post-1945 period as a completely new era in the history of international organizations, we argue that significant continuities with the first half of the twentieth century prevail. We argued that, first for the three institutions we examined, fellowship programs were complementary to related activities in the realm of public health, such as campaigns against communicable diseases or the setting up and enforcement of public health administrations in "developing" countries. Second, for the RF as well as for UNRRA, and to some extent the WHO, fellowship programs were intrinsic to emergency relief programs. Nevertheless, they did not end with the end of emergencies, but persisted and were eventually expanded when broader and more ambitious development programs replaced initial relief programs. Third, these programs were set up to enhance investment in human capital in "developing" countries. For this reason, it was of crucial importance to ensure that fellows should return to their home countries to avoid any "brain drain." As Bruce-Chwatt wrote in a 1975 WHO report, any fellow who did not return home was a failure.[44] Last not but least, fellows generally were mature persons who occupied senior and/or key positions in their home countries as public health administrators. Institutions aimed to train key persons with recognized knowledge and skills, enabling them to train other workers in their native countries. As a matter of fact, a large percentage of these fellows would continue their careers in regional or national public health administrations.

Lastly, despite having highlighted the continuities, it would be incorrect to overlook conspicuous ruptures that took place after World War II. First, the RF and UNRRA privileged what they referred to as "West Points of Public Health," namely the schools of public health of Johns Hopkins and Harvard:[45] between 1917 and 1949, more than two-thirds of public health fellows attended courses in one of these academic institutions. The very strong ties with Johns Hopkins or Harvard led to some criticism and self-critiques. For example, the Commission on Review on the International Health Division of the RF, which was supposed to devise the new policy in public health for the Foundation, argued that: "first, there is the question as to whether or not we accomplished the most good by insisting on American standards throughout the world rather than adapting our techniques to local conditions. Even in the United States, I have twice heard the statement 'the RF has done damage to schools of public health by imposing on them the IHD pattern of separateness from other allied, often parallel and contributing disciplines.'"[46] Hence, it is not at all surprising that the WHO adopted a different policy and, since the early 1950s, it increased intraregional exchanges. Second, and partially related to the abovementioned point, on the one hand, the RF and UNRRA had a centralized administration of fellowships, while on the other hand, the WHO implemented a decentralized policy entrusting the attribution and management of fellowships to its regional offices and member countries.

Yi-Tang Lin is a Ph.D. student in international history at the University of Lausanne. After completing a B.A. in Sociology from National Taiwan University (2008), she took a M.A. in Interdisciplinary Practice of Humanities and Social Sciences from ENS/EHESS (Paris) with a thesis on the globalization of Taiwanese healthcare system (2012). As a member of the Swiss National Fund (SNSF) "Sinergia" program on a project entitled "Patterns of Transnational Regulations," she is currently finalizing her dissertation entitled "Statistics as a World Language for Public Health? International organizations, transnational actors and local agencies in China(s), 1917–1950s."

Thomas David is Professor of International History at the University of Lausanne and at the Ecole Polytechnique Federale of Lausanne, where he is the Director of the College of Humanities. His recent researches have focused on the history of philanthropy, of elites and of the WHO. Between 2013 and 2016, he was one of the coordinator of the Swiss National Fund "Sinergia" program on a project entitled "Patterns of Transnational Regulations." His publications include *The Power of Corporate Networks: A Comparative and Historical Perspective* (Routledge, 2014, with G. Westerhuis) and *Les élites économiques suisses au XXe siècle* (Alphil, 2016, with F. Bühlmann, S. Ginalski and A. Mach).

Davide Rodogno is Professor in International History at the Graduate Institute of International and Development Studies, Geneva. He is the author of *Fascism's European Empire* (Cambridge University Press, 2006) and *Against Massacre: Humanitarian Interventions in the Ottoman Empire (1815–1914), the Birth of a Concept and International Practice* (Princeton University Press, 2011). He has coedited and authored a volume on *Transnational Networks of Experts* (Berghahn Books, 2014), another on *Humanitarian Photography* (Cambridge University Press, 2015) and a third on the *League of Nations' Work on Social Issues* (UN Press, 2016). He is currently works on a monograph tentatively entitled: *Night on Earth: Humanitarian Organizations' Actions on Behalf of Civilian Populations in the Aftermath of the First World War*.

Notes

1. Some historiographies have shown the connection between the RF and the LNHO fellowship programs, See Josep L. Barona, *The Rockefeller Foundation, Public Health and International Diplomacy, 1920–1945* (London: Routledge, 2015); Ludovic Tournès, *Les États-Unis et La Société Des Nations (1914–1946): Le système international face à l'émergence d'une superpuissance* (Bern: Peter Lang, 2015).
2. "Proposal for an International Fellowship Program," 17 October 1946, S-1310-0000-1352, United Nations Archives (UNA).
3. Rockefeller Foundation, "The Rockefeller Foundation Annual Report 1924," 1924, 46, retrieved 24 March 2017 from https://www.rockefeller foundation.org/app/uploads/Annual-Report-1924.pdf.
4. World Health Assembly, *Eleventh World Health Assembly, Minneapolis, May 28–June 13, 1958: Verbatim Records* (Geneva: WHO, 1958), 444, retrieved 24 March 2017 from http://www.who.int/iris/handle/10665/85706.
5. L.J. Bruce-Chwatt, "Report on the WHO Fellowship Programme," October 1975, WHO Library.
6. Rockefeller Foundation, "The Rockefeller Foundation Annual Report 1913–1914," 1914, 7, retrieved 24 March 2017 from https://www.rocke fellerfoundation.org/app/uploads/Annual-Report-1913-1914.pdf.
7. Aid grants were made to several, mainly Protestant, missionary organizations (Rockefeller Foundation, "The Rockefeller Foundation Annual Report 1916," 1916, 18, retrieved 24 March 2017 from https://www.rocke fellerfoundation.org/app/uploads/Annual-Report-1916.pdf).
8. Victor Heiser, "To Grant," 12 April 1923, RF/5/1.2/173/2236, Rockefeller Archive Center (hereinafter RAC).
9. Rockefeller Foundation, "The Rockefeller Foundation Annual Report 1918," 1918, 44–45, retrieved 24 March 2017 from https://www.rocke fellerfoundation.org/app/uploads/Annual-Report-1918.pdf.
10. International Health Board, "Working Program for 1921," 26 October 1920, 20193, IHB Minutes/1920, RAC.
11. China Medical Board, "Fellowship for Study in America or Europe 1915–1928," RF/1/601/42/346a, RAC.
12. Rockefeller Foundation, "The Rockefeller Foundation Annual Report 1919," 1919, 111, retrieved 24 March 2017 from https://www.rockefeller foundation.org/app/uploads/Annual-Report-1919.pdf.
13. Elizabeth Fee, *Disease and Discovery: A History of the Johns Hopkins School of Hygiene and Public Health, 1916–1939* (Baltimore, MD: Johns Hopkins University Press, 1987), 219–20.
14. For the LNHO exchange programs, see Iris Borowy, *Coming to Terms with World Health: The League of Nations Health Organization* (Berlin: Peter Lang, 2009); Barona, *The Rockefeller Foundation*; Tournès, *Les États-Unis*.
15. Ludwik Rajchman, "To Wickliffe Rose," 23 May 1923, 12B/R839/21836, League of Nations Archives, Geneva.

16. Rockefeller Foundation, "DMPH: Fellowship Program," 18 October 1954, RF/1.2/100 International/50/386, RAC.
17. Jessica Reinisch, "Internationalism in Relief: The Birth (and Death) of UNRRA," *Past & Present* 210(6) (2011): 258–89.
18. Mark Zacher and Tania Keefe, *The Politics of Global Health Governance: United by Contagion* (New York: Palgrave Macmillan, 2008), 38. On the importance of UNRRA for development policy, see also Eric Helleiner, *Forgotten Foundations of Bretton Woods: International Development and the Making of the Postwar Order* (Ithaca, NY: Cornell University Press, 2016).
19. Wilbur A. Sawyer, "Achievements of UNRRA as an International Health Organization," *American Journal of Public Health and the Nation's Health* 37(1) (1947): 41–58.
20. Ibid., 41. For recent research on the role of UNRRA in the field of health, see Sunil S. Amrith, *Decolonizing International Health: India and Southeast Asia, 1930–65* (Basingstoke: Palgrave Macmillan, 2006), 55–69; Rana Mitter, "Imperialism, Transnationalism and the Reconstruction of Postwar China: UNRRA in China, 1944–7," *Past & Present* 218(8) (2013): 51–69.
21. On the structural continuity of both organizations, see Ludovic Tournès, "The Rockefeller Foundation and the Transition from the League of Nations to the UN (1939–1946)," *Journal of Modern European History* 12(3) (2014): 331; Anne-Emanuelle Birn, "Backstage: The Relationship between the Rockefeller Foundation and the World Health Organization, Part I: 1940s–1960s," *Public Health* 128(2) (2014): 129–40.
22. Oscar J. Falnes, "A History of the UNRRA Fellowship Program," 1947, 6, S-1021-0005-06, UNA.
23. Ibid, 1. Fellowships were not the only training programs developed by UNRRA; it also sent technical experts in its foreign missions (UNRRA, "Extension of Training Assistance to Member Nations," 10 January 1946, S-1271-000-0081, UNA).
24. F.H. La Guardia, "To Rajchman," 30 December 1946, S-1271-000-0081, UNA.
25. Advisory Committee of Fellowships, "Minutes of the Third Meeting," 28 February 1946, 1, S-1271-000-0081, UNA.
26. Falnes, "A History," 35.
27. Advisory Committee of Fellowships, "Minutes of the Fourth Meeting," 11 April 1946, S-1271-000-0081, UNA.
28. "Notes of Discussion between Snyder and Topping," 8 May 1946, S-1271-000-0081, UNA.
29. Falnes, "A History," 97.
30. Advisory Committee of Fellowships, "Minutes of the Fourth Meeting."
31. Falnes, "A History," 75.
32. Ibid., 83.
33. Brief biography of Dr Joseph Vesely, RF/2-1952/100/ 8/44, RAC.
34. The Secretariat of the United Nations, "A Report on the International Fellowship Programmes Administered by the United Nations, the World Health Organization, the United Nations Educational, Scientific and Cultural Organization, and the United Nations International Children's Emergency Fund," January 1949, 29, 615-2-10, WHO Archives.

35. Ibid.
36. Marcolino Candau, "Executive Board 45th Session, Agenda Item 3.2, Evaluation of WHO Fellowship Programme, Report of the Director-General," 22 January 1970, EB45/WP/4, WHO Library.
37. Bruce-Chwatt, "Report on the WHO Fellowship Programme," 112.
38. World Health Assembly, *Eleventh World Health Assembly, Minneapolis, May 28–June 13, 1958: Verbatim Records*, 436.
39. Taiwan Provincial Government, "Security Check for Go Abroad Staffs [in Chinese]," May 1956, Provincial Public Health Bureau Archives/061000000055A, Taiwan Historica.
40. "Warranty for Wong Bin-Nan [in Chinese]," 1958, 028000002332A, Academia Historica.
41. Bruce-Chwatt, "Report on the WHO Fellowship Programme," 106.
42. S.K. Quo, "Analysis of WHO Fellowships Awarded during the Period 1957–1963 and Evaluation of Those Awarded during the Period 1955–1961 in the Western Pacific Region," 25 May 1964, S5/418/3 (WPR/STAT/15), WHO Archives.
43. WHO, "Eleventh World Health Assembly, Provisional Agenda Items 6.3 and 6.4: Report on a Review and Appraisal of the WHO Fellowships," 2 April 1958, 5, All/P&B/5, WHO Library.
44. Bruce-Chwatt, "Report on the WHO Fellowship Programme."
45. Elizabeth Fee, *Disease and Discovery: A History of the Johns Hopkins School of Hygiene and Public Health, 1916–1939* (Baltimore, MD: Johns Hopkins University Press, 1987).
46. Rockefeller Foundation, "Commission on Review on the IHD," March–May 1950, RF/3/908/13/140, RAC.

References

Amrith, Sunil S. *Decolonizing International Health: India and Southeast Asia, 1930–65* (Basingstoke: Palgrave Macmillan, 2006).
Barona, Joseph L. *The Rockefeller Foundation, Public Health and International Diplomacy, 1920–1945* (London: Routledge, 2015).
Birn, Anne-Emanuelle. "Backstage: The Relationship between the Rockefeller Foundation and the World Health Organization, Part I: 1940s–1960s," *Public Health* 128(2) (2014): 129–40.
Borowy, Iris. *Coming to Terms with World Health: The League of Nations Health Organization* (Berlin: Peter Lang, 2009).
Fee, Elizabeth. *Disease and Discovery: A History of the Johns Hopkins School of Hygiene and Public Health, 1916–1939* (Baltimore, MD: Johns Hopkins University Press, 1987).
Helleiner, Eric. *Forgotten Foundations of Bretton Woods: International Development and the Making of the Postwar Order* (Ithaca, NY: Cornell University Press, 2016).
Mitter, Rana. "Imperialism, Transnationalism and the Reconstruction of Postwar China: UNRRA in China, 1944–7," *Past & Present* 218(8) (2013): 51–69.

Reinisch, Jessica. "Internationalism in Relief: The Birth (and Death) of UNRRA," *Past & Present* 210(6) (2011): 258–89.

Rockefeller Foundation. "The Rockefeller Foundation Annual Report 1913–1914," 1914. Retrieved 24 March 2017 from https://www.rockefellerfoundation.org/app/uploads/Annual-Report-1913-1914.pdf.

Rockefeller Foundation. "The Rockefeller Foundation Annual Report 1916," 1916. Retrieved 24 March 2017 from https://www.rockefellerfoundation.org/app/uploads/Annual-Report-1916.pdf.

Rockefeller Foundation. "The Rockefeller Foundation Annual Report 1918," 1918. Retrieved 24 March 2017 from https://www.rockefellerfoundation.org/app/uploads/Annual-Report-1918.pdf.

Rockefeller Foundation. "The Rockefeller Foundation Annual Report 1919," 1919. Retrieved 24 March 2017 from https://www.rockefellerfoundation.org/app/uploads/Annual-Report-1919.pdf.

Rockefeller Foundation. "The Rockefeller Foundation Annual Report 1924," 1924. Retrieved 24 March 2017 from https://www.rockefellerfoundation.org/app/uploads/Annual-Report-1924.pdf.

Tournès, Ludovic. "The Rockefeller Foundation and the Transition from the League of Nations to the UN (1939–1946)," *Journal of Modern European History* 12(3) (2014): 323–41.

Tournès, Ludovic. *Les États-Unis et La Société Des Nations (1914–1946): Le système international face à l'émergence d'une superpuissance* (Bern: Peter Lang, 2015).

World Health Assembly. *Eleventh World Health Assembly, Minneapolis, May 28–June 13, 1958: Verbatim Records* (Geneva: WHO, 1958). Retrieved 24 March 2017 from http://www.who.int/iris/handle/10665/85706.

Sawyer, Wilbur A. "Achievements of UNRRA as an International Health Organization," *American Journal of Public Health and the Nation's Health* 37(1) (1947): 41–58.

Zacher, Mark, and Tania Keefe. *The Politics of Global Health Governance: United by Contagion* (New York: Palgrave Macmillan, 2008).

 9

NEW MISSIONARIES FOR SOCIAL DEVELOPMENT
The ILO Internship Program (1950–63)
Véronique Plata-Stenger

Introduction

In 1961, Robert Lafrance, several times director of study of the International Labour Organization (ILO) Internship Program, insisted on its role in widening the ILO's influence in developing countries: "each alumnus coming home become a kind of missionary of ILO's aims, methods, and activities."[1] The study of the ILO Internship Program is part of a broader analysis of international technical cooperation programs that developed rapidly after World War II. The ILO's involvement in technical cooperation was in line with the resolutions adopted at the international conferences of 1941, 1944 and 1945.[2] The 1944 Declaration of Philadelphia, adopted under the leadership of the United States and Great Britain, proclaimed the commitment of the ILO "to promote the economic and social advancement of the less developed regions of the world."[3] This declaration in particular reflected the important transformation the ILO had undergone since the 1930s. After 1945, the ILO became one of the main forums where development discourse and practices were elaborated.[4] Besides, in 1949, following the Point Four Program for developing countries announced by US President Harry S. Truman on 20 January, the United Nations (UN) launched the Expanded Program of Technical Assistance (EPTA), which put into practice, on a global scale, the concept of exchanging economic and social expertise. The raising of the standard of living and the steering of economic progress, following the model of Western industrial societies, were the main objectives of international technical assistance programs designed to help "Third World" countries through their decolonization processes.[5] In the framework of these activities, international organizations developed instruments to facilitate the transfer of technical knowledge and knowhow to developing countries. Internship programs, missions of technical assistance, training courses and seminars were the principal instruments of international development, and are still in use today.

Research on scholarship programs is growing, but the contribution of international organizations in their development still needs to be studied.[6] Besides, while the issue of international development is gaining interest among researchers, the ILO is still marginalized.[7] The main reason is that the ILO, which was created by the Treaty of Versailles in 1919, was originally set up as a body for elaborating international labor standards through international conventions.[8] However, in the context of the Great Depression of the 1930s, it expanded its activities to new fields like economic planning, regulation of trade and the study of problems raised by industrialization in colonies and developing countries.[9] The civil servants of the ILO also developed operational activities, providing technical assistance in Eastern and Southeastern Europe, Asia, Middle East and Latin America.[10] These activities continued during and after World War II.

This chapter emphasizes the ILO's development work through the analysis of its Internship Program, established in 1950. The commitment of the ILO to exchange activities after 1945 was based on a particular conception of technical assistance, where research, expertise, social policy and labor legislation were interconnected. The Internship Program was conceived as a tool for the planning and development of social policy by linking together international experts, national administrators, trade union officials and members of employers' organizations. The way in which these internships were organized also highlights another central objective—to educate social professionals in international cooperation. First, the evolution of ILO's activities in scholarship programs from the interwar period up to the establishment of the Internship Program will be traced. The ways in which the ILO tried to secure its participation in UN scholarship programs against the political background of the Cold War will then be discussed. Finally, I will analyze the training courses, the profile of trainees and the trainees' reports to highlight the role of the ILO Internship Program in fostering social development according to the organization's principles.

The ILO's International Scholarship Activities: A Historical Perspective

The ILO's scholarship activities date back to the interwar period, but these were mostly performed on an ad hoc basis. At the International Labour Office, the permanent secretariat of the ILO, it was not uncommon to see brand-new trainees being assigned to the cabinet of the first Director, the French socialist Albert Thomas. The League of Nations' technical services also set up individual scholarships, in collaboration with the Rockefeller Foundation.[11] The United States joined the ILO in 1934 and Harold Butler, the second Director of the International Labour Office, initiated attempts at rapprochement between the Foundation and the ILO. However, opposition from US trade unions prevented the development of cooperative projects. One of the reasons for this opposition was that American workers did not make the distinction between the Rockefeller Foundation and the Industrial Relations counselors—an institute dedicated to the study of industrial relations—created in 1921 by John D. Rockefeller, which was from the start seen as a rival body by trade unions.[12] Collaborations with the Rockefeller Foundation were thus very rare. For example, the Frenchman Adrien Tixier, head of the Social Insurance Section of the ILO, sought in 1935 to organize fellowships for Latin American experts to be trained in social insurance. A lack of ILO's funds brought him to ask in 1937 for Rockefeller support.[13] However, Tixier feared that both organizations did not share the same philosophy on social insurance. Support from the Rockefeller Foundation for the Health Organization of the League, whose activities relied on a conception of social insurance based on voluntary and charitable organizations, clashed with ILO's support for the principle of compulsory social insurance systems promoted by governments and sanctioned by law. Because of these concerns, the ILO and the Foundation reached agreement in 1938 for only one fellowship, granted to Edgardo Rebagliati, manager of the National Social Security Fund in Lima.[14]

The 1941 International Labour Conference (ILC), which was held following the publication of the Atlantic Charter, directly inscribed the development of social policies during World War II as part of the fight against totalitarian regimes.[15] The context of war and the financial difficulties of the ILO prevented the development of large-scale scholarship programs before 1945. Nevertheless, the war increased the need for Latin American countries to organize their systems of social insurance.[16] In this context, the International Labour Office organized actuarial training seminars in 1943 and 1944.[17]

The Development of the ILO's Scholarship Programs after World War II

Between the late 1940s and the early 1950s, the participation of the ILO in various UN scholarship programs faced difficulties due to the growing competition among international organizations and the context of the Cold War. The need to avoid duplication in international scholarship programs quickly called for coordination measures between the specialized agencies. This issue was raised at the December 1948 ILO Governing Body's session, where the decision was taken to allow the American David Morse, General Director of the International Labour Office from 1948 to 1970 and former New Dealer, to enter into negotiation with the UN in order to coordinate and rationalize the diverse international fellowship programs.[18] The multiplication of international organizations called for a division of labor that was, however, not always to the advantage of the ILO.[19] The tensions were particularly acute with the UN Division of Social Affairs. In 1949, at a meeting of the UN working group on the coordination of fellowship programs, Raphael Cilento, Director of the Division of Social Affairs and former Director of the United Nations Relief and Rehabilitation Administration (UNRRA) in the British zone of occupied Germany, violently attacked the ILO's exclusive position in the field of social policy.[20] The ILO saw, in particular, the development of the UN European Social Welfare Program as a threat to its own activities.[21] The 1949 report of the UN Administrative Coordinating Committee, which saw the impossibility of rationalizing and coordinating all fellowship programs, highlighted the lack of agreement on common rules and the institutional competition that existed, and also a lack of coordination within governments between the various departments concerned with these programs.

The position of the ILO was also weakened by the absence of the USSR, which only became a member of the organization in 1954. The organization was the scene of ideological struggles that made the development of technical cooperation activities with socialist countries difficult. At the 1949 ILC, the Polish government delegate strongly opposed the resolution on technical assistance for economic development, which he considered a new form of imperialism promoted by the capitalist countries.[22] The appointment of Morse reinforced this atmosphere of suspicion. Morse's New Deal experience and the role he played in promoting democratic labor organization during World War II obviously marked his intellectual vision on modernization.[23] At the meeting of the UN working group in 1949, Raphael Cilento pointed to the ILO's "geographical gaps," which, according to him, justified UN incursions in its competences. The same year, after the takeover by the Communists in February 1948, the Ministry of Social Affairs of Czechoslovakia had informed Cilento that requests for technical assistance covering the fields of wage policy, vocational training, training within industry and technical labor inspection should not be passed to the ILO.[24] Yet the break with the ILO was not complete. Beyond the ideological oppositions, forms of circulation and exchanges developed during this period, sometimes thanks to individuals involved with the ILO since the interwar period.[25]

Because of the problems raised in particular by the coordination of scholarship programs with other international organizations, the ILO decided to develop programs under its regular budget. The first fellowship program followed the first ILO's international technical cooperation program, the Manpower program, which was launched in 1948 as a response to the changing post-World War II environment and growing concerns about the need to raise economic productivity in all countries in order to limit the influence of communism.[26] The Manpower program allowed the ILO to fund a fellowship program for the organization of employment, vocational training and vocational guidance.[27] This program was originally intended for Europe, as an auxiliary to the reconstruction projects devised under the Marshall Plan, before being deployed elsewhere.[28] From 1965, the Turin Centre, still the ILO's main training location, supported vocational training activities.[29] In March 1949, the Governing Body also accepted in principle the implementation of an internship program, with the full support of workers' representatives.[30] In June 1949, it accepted the proposition of the Budget Committee to provide US$75,000 to the ILO's fellowship programs, of which US$10,000 was earmarked for grants to the study of the functioning and the activities of the ILO.[31] At the 110th session of the Governing Body in 1950, it was decided to allow each year twelve grants to trainees to study the structure and activities of the ILO for a period of two months. Several volunteers were also added. Between 1950 and 1958, 136 people participated to the Internship Program.[32]

Between Training in International Cooperation and International Acculturation

The ILO Division of Technical Assistance was responsible for the Internship Program. In accordance with the principles established under the EPTA, international scholarship programs should allow developing countries full and complete access to "scientific and technical progress that has already significantly altered the economy of many developed regions."[33] As shown by the report of the technical working group on fellowship programs in 1950, the representatives of all specialized agencies agreed with the UNESCO policy that fellowships should be related to a particular project of economic development.[34]

The ILO Governing Body decided each year the countries that were awarded an internship and then proposed candidates to the General Director of the International Labour Office, who made the appointments. Initially, grants were to be distributed on as wide a geographic basis as possible and did not exclude the more developed countries. However, discussions in the Governing Body between 1949 and 1950 indicate that ILO members wanted these grants to be primarily given to countries where labor organizations were weak. As underlined by Daniel Maul, the realization of the principles of freedom of association and collective bargaining in less developed countries were in particular seen as a means to economic progress and a guarantee of enduring development.[35] Between 1950 and 1963, trainees mainly came from Latin America, Asia, the Middle East, Africa and the Pacific. In several cases, the rotation established for internships closely followed the rhythm of new members in the ILO. For example, Jordan and Sudan obtained a grant in 1957 and Tunisia in 1958. Sometimes the internship even preceded independence, as evidenced by the participation of Madagascar in 1955. Malaya was also granted an internship in 1955, but did not send anybody. In 1959, Nigeria, where decolonization officially began in 1958, also participated in the ILO Internship Program.

The Internship Program was designed to ensure better understanding and wider publicity of ILO's activities. As noted by the French employer delegate Pierre Waline in 1949, "it must be recognized that the International Labour Organization does not find in the press as much interest as other international organizations. Fellows who have been able to acquire direct knowledge of the work of the Organization will become the best propagandists."[36] The ILO thus turned itself into a form of university, as David Morse described it during a speech to the Commonwealth Club in San Francisco in 1948.[37] Because of the ILO's tripartite structure, several delegates of the Governing Body insisted in 1949 that trainees should come to Geneva when tripartite meetings were held. The Australian governmental delegate declared: "Indeed, it is useful to have a theoretical knowledge of the tripartite character of the Organization and to see its impact on the daily work of the Office; it is even more interesting to provide an opportunity for fellows to be in personal contact with the functioning of tripartite conferences."[38] The

Internship Program was also organized in a tripartite fashion, with four candidates proposed by governments, four by employers and four by workers' organizations. This tripartite mode of organization gave the opportunity to kill two birds with one stone: in addition to the acculturation with international activities, trainees were able to experience the process of social dialogue, one of the founding principles of the ILO.

The courses were also intended to foster a process of acculturation to international life for people who were, for the first time, in contact with international institutions. As with other fellowship programs, in particular those of the philanthropic foundations, they were thought to be "effective in breaking down national isolation."[39] In 1952, the presence in the group of trainees of an Israeli employer and a civil servant of the Lebanese government underlines the usefulness of these trips abroad for connecting individuals who would otherwise rarely meet. The ILO's internships were especially meant to overcome cultural barriers in social policy, to help to build a common bond for the solution of social problems and to promote the development of an international elite.

The Diffusion of Modern Principles on Social Development

The ILO's method of supervision managed to create a new space for the diffusion of modern principles and ideas on social development. The training courses started with a general conference on ILO's principles, underlining the need for international regulation of working conditions. The miserable living conditions of workers and the need for more equality were used as arguments to reduce global competition due to market expansion, the "elimination of despair that leads to extreme solutions," and greater global solidarity.[40] From 1954 onward, the procedure was formalized and the ILO also sent a memorandum to the candidates containing information on the structure of the organization and its main activities. During their stay, trainees also attended conferences of ILO personnel. Afterwards, the trainees were given time to read publications selected by the head of the ILO Division of Technical Assistance.[41] Internships were thus an ideal space for the diffusion of an ILO self-reflexive discourse: progress could be achieved through the adoption of international norms and technical assistance.

The training courses also provided practical knowledge. Visits to the various ILO's technical sections punctuated the internship and were an opportunity for trainees to see how international civil servants worked, and to obtain technical information on specific issues concerning their own countries. Trainees were also invited to participate as observers in the work of certain technical committees. Lastly, trainees visited various international institutions located in Geneva. Instruction films on international technical cooperation projects followed visits to these locations.

Ten years after the launching of the program, Robert Lafrance emphasized the results obtained: "as a public relations effort alone the program can be considered worthwhile, reaching actual or potential leaders of government ministries and of employers' and workers' organizations."[42] Trainees with whom contact was maintained were valuable resources for the ILO in the newly independent countries, where its activities were little known. In 1958, an Association of Interns was even created with a secretariat in Bonn to further diffuse knowledge and understanding of the ILO.[43] However, because of the ILO's general policy not to get involved in the editorial work of non-governmental organizations (NGOs), this association seems to have disappeared by 1960, due to a lack of resources and the geographic dispersion of its members.[44]

The Internship Program was more successful in fostering international policy education and in promoting the participation of trainees at international conferences. For example, in 1957, seventeen former trainees were members of the delegation of their country to the ILC and four former trainees were members of the Maritime Technical Conference. Other former trainees would become associate members of the Governing Body.[45] Research and observation at the international level could also be an incentive for political action. In 1952, Kazuo Motoyama, a Japanese worker trainee who became interested in the ILO's industrial committees, wrote in his report that the Japanese miners' union would press the government to improve working conditions on the basis of the findings of the ILO's committee on the coal industry.[46] In 1959, L.L. Borha wrote in his report: "the internship made a very useful contribution towards stimulating a better informed Nigerian Trade Union Movement, which will consequently be able to exert more constructive influence."[47] Behind these declarations lies the main effect that ILO's internships could have on trade union and labor organization leaders—the promotion of collective bargaining in developing countries. Internships were thought to be a very effective way to spread this principle.

The Profile of the Trainees and Their Perception of Technical Assistance

The importance of the Internship Program as a tool for the diffusion of ILO's activities and principles around the world required finding the right people with the right competencies. The trainees had all experienced a degree of professionalization in the social field at the national level and were mostly in the age range of thirty to forty years (although few of them were women). If the internship was not specifically designed to prepare these people for an international career, it nevertheless sought to provide them with the tools necessary for their likely participation at the ILC as advisors or delegates. The necessity of educating them was highlighted by the Frenchman Henri Gallois, director of study in 1952: "the need for general knowledge was illustrated by another revealing fact. I have found that trainees delegated to the conference and having a broad general culture were totally ignorant of the scope of the decisions they were voting."[48] The governmental group was composed of civil servants, usually employed by the ministries of labor or foreign relations. The employers' group brought together professionals of employers' associations, industrial organizations, lawyers and teachers. In the workers' group were many secretaries of trade unions and labor inspectors, with the union nominees usually members of unions supported by their governments.

In general, trainees had a high cultural level, which facilitated a better understanding of the work of the ILO. They all adhered to the philosophy of internationalism. Robert Lafrance noted in 1960 that in their reports "the usefulness of the program is hardly criticized."[49] In 1963, K.K. Soni, the administrative and organizing secretary of the Kenya Distributive and Commercial Workers' Union, wrote in his report: "I do not hesitate to declare that we shall be grateful to all and any source for providing us technical and financial help for any potential projects in our country for all time to come."[50]

Most of the trainees insisted on the needs of their country for technical assistance. The reports highlight the full commitment of these national elites to the principle of a planned economy. Reports from the few socialist countries that participated in ILO's internships after 1954 were no exception, often highlighting the merits of economic socialist planning. However, the 1963 report of V.I. Peshkov, governmental intern from Belarus, who criticized the fact that the economic and social research of the ILO was based solely on the work of Western economists, highlights the dividing line that existed between socialist countries and Western democracies.⁵¹ The interns' presentations, which provided a general summary of their government's labor management policy, reproduced to a large extent the discourse of international organizations on the need to establish a rational organization of societies. The processes of decolonization also gave a nationalist character to the discourse of some trainees on the need for development. In 1961, the Tunisian worker Hadi Bel Hadj entitled his presentation: "From Political Independence to the Liberation and Economic and Social Development and Progress, or How Tunisia Deals with its new Problems."⁵² In 1963, K.K. Soni devoted a portion of his report to describe the horrors of British colonialism and the nationalist movement for independence.⁵³

Conclusion

World War II provided the context for the institutional foundations of technical assistance programs after 1945. Yet the ILO Internship Program has always remained very small in scope. In the 1950s, the development of ILO's scholarship programs remained precarious due to a lack of coordination with the UN specialized agencies and the context of the Cold War. Nevertheless, the analysis of this program underlines the importance of education as a means for the ILO to fulfill its mission of promoting social development, in particular in developing countries. The Internship Program, by bringing together civil servants, trade unionists and members of employers' organizations, with international experts, allowed the ILO to diffuse a democratic model of social development, while helping these individuals to formulate their political and social demands. From 1963, the Internship Program was taken over by the International Institute for Labor Studies (IILS), which was established in 1960, as part of its Management program.⁵⁴ The creation of the IILS can be seen as a continuity of the role that the ILO wanted to play in the international education of labor specialists.

Véronique Plata-Stenger is a lecturer of modern history at the Department of History, University of Geneva. She completed in 2016 her Ph.D. dissertation entitled "Une voie sociale pour le développement. Le Bureau international du travail et les débuts de la coopération technique (1919–1949)." She has published several articles and book chapters in French, English and Spanish, mainly related to social policies, international development and the ILO.

Appendix: Fresia Carballo de Mendoza

Fresia Carballo de Mendoza was one of the rare women who in 1960 received in 1960 a grant to participate to the ILO Internship Program, as a governmental nominee.[55] Born in 1937 in Bolivia, she studied humanities at the Colegio Frances de los Sagrados Corazones. She then studied labor law at the Colegio Italiano Santa Ana and graduated from the Instituto Internacional Antonio Quijarro, where she specialized in the history of international organizations. She did several temporary missions for the Ministry of Foreign Relations in La Paz before becoming an official. At the time she participated in the ILO Internship Program, she handled relations with international organizations. Fresia Carballo de Mendoza was also deeply involved in feminist networks and associations. She was a member of the Ateneo Feminino, created in 1923, where many socialist activists were promoting women rights and the right to work for mothers in Bolivia. From 1945, the Ateneo Feminino was involved in the fight for civil and political rights, equal pay and free access to free education for women. Fresia Carballo de Mendoza was also member of the Inter-American Commission of Women, created in 1928, which was the first intergovernmental organization established to promote the recognition of children and women's rights. She also became a member of the Alianza de Liberación de la Mujer Americana, created in 1959 to promote women's emancipation and gender equality in Latin America. During her internship, Fresia Carballo de Mendoza was mainly interested in ILO's activities regarding social protection for women and mothers.

Notes

1. FS 5-03 (1961), ILO archives (hereinafter ILOA).
2. Akira Iriye, *Global Community: The Role of International Organizations in the Making of the Contemporary World* (Berkeley, CA: University of California Press, 2002)
3. The text of the Declaration is available at: http://www.ilo.org/dyn/normlex/en/f?p=NORMLEXPUB:62:0::NO::P62_LIST_ENTRIE_ID:2453907.
4. Daniel Maul, *Human Rights, Development and Decolonization: The International Labour Organization, 1940–70* (Basingstoke: Palgrave Macmillan, 2012); Daniel Maul, "'Help Them Move the ILO Way': The International Labor Organization and the Modernization Discourse in the Era of Decolonization and the Cold War," *Diplomatic History* 33(3) (2009): 387–404.
5. Andreas Eckert, Stephan Malinowski and Corinna R. Unger, "Modernizing Missions: Approaches to 'Developing' the Non-Western World after 1945," *Journal of Modern European History* 8(1) (2010): 135.

6. Corinna R. Unger, "Histories of Development and Modernization: Findings, Reflections, Future Research," (2010), retrieved 29 March 2017 from http://www.hsozkult.de/literaturereview/id/forschungsberichte-1130.
7. As an exception, see Sandrine Kott and Joëlle Droux (eds), *Globalizing Social Rights: The International Labour Organization and Beyond* (Basingstoke: Palgrave Macmillan/ILO, 2013); Maul, *Human Rights*.
8. International Labour Office, *ILO Conventions and Recommendations, 1919–1999* (Geneva: International Labour Office, 2000).
9. Véronique Plata-Stenger, "Une voie sociale pour le développement: Le Bureau international du travail et les débuts de la coopération technique (1919–1949)," Ph.D. dissertation (Geneva: University of Geneva, 2016).
10. Ibid. See also Antony E. Alcock, *History of the International Labour Organization* (London: Macmillan, 1971); George A. Johnston, *The International Labour Organization: Its Work for Social and Economic Progress* (London: Europa Publications, 1970).
11. Ludovic Tournès, *Les Etats-Unis et la Société des Nations: le système international face à l'émergence d'une superpuissance (1919–1946)* (Bern: Peter Lang, 2015), 178–79.
12. Ibid., 257–58.
13. Rockefeller Foundation archives, RG 1/100S/108/973. Rockefeller Archive Center, Tarrytown, NY.
14. Albert Thomas Cabinet Files, CAT 61-1-1, ILOA.
15. Sandrine Kott, "Fighting the War or Preparing for Peace: The ILO during the Second World War," *Journal of Modern European History* 12 (2014): 359–76.
16. Jill Jensen, "From Geneva to the Americas: The International Labor Organization and Inter-American Social Security Standards, 1936–1948," *International Labor and Working-Class History* 80(1) (2011): 215–40.
17. SI 21, Jacket 1 "Social security: seminars—travel arrangements for meetings of social security administration Board, Washington, 02-03 Jan 1945; 1944 trends in Latin America as summarized by the Inter-American Committee on Social security; Nov meeting in Montreal of actuaries from Brazil, Chile, Costa Rica, Ecuador, Mexico," ILOA.
18. GB, 107th session, December 1948: 94, ILOA.
19. Manuela Tortora, *L'OIT, Institution spécialisée et organisation mondiale: étude des relations de l'OIT avec la SdN et l'ONU* (Brussels: E. Bruylant, 1980).
20. Cinquième rapport du Comité administratif de coordination au Conseil économique et social, E/1340, 25 May 1949, United Nations Archives (hereinafter UNA).
21. Resolution 155 (VII) of the Economic and Social Council, 13 August 1948 on advisory social welfare activities, UNA; Karen H. Lyons, Terry Hokenstad, Manohar Pawar, Nathalie Huegler and Nigel Hall (eds), *The SAGE Handbook of International Social Work* (London: Sage, 2012), 165–68.
22. ILC, 32nd session, 1949: 336–38, ILOA.
23. Jason Guthrie, "The ILO and the International Technocratic Class, 1944–1966," in Kott and Droux (eds), *Globalizing Social Rights*, 120–121.

24. Correspondence between A. Evans, UN economic section, and Wilfred Jenks, 15 April 1949; FS 1000.3 "Working Group on Fellowship Programmes. Meeting. Lake Success, 14th–15th March, 1949," ILOA.
25. Sandrine Kott, "Par-delà la guerre froide. Les organisations internationales et les circulations Est-Ouest (1947–1973)," *Vingtième Siècle. Revue d'histoire* 109 (2011): 142–54.
26. Dominique Barjot, *Catching up with America: Productivity Missions and the Diffusion of American Economic and Technological Influence after the Second World War* (Paris: Presses de l'Université de Paris-Sorbonne, 2002).
27. *International Labour Review* LIX/4 (1949): 399–429, ILOA.
28. For a European perspective, see Lorenzo Mechi, *L'Organizzazione Internazionale del Lavoro e la ricostruzione europea* (Rome: Ediesse, 2013).
29. See the official website: http://www.itcilo.org/fr.
30. GB, 108th session, March 1949: 25, ILOA.
31. GB, 109th session, June 1949: 36, ILOA.
32. FS 5-05: Association of ILO interns, ILOA.
33. Assistance technique en vue du développement économique. Plan d'un programme pour l'extension de la collaboration par l'entremise de l'Organisation des Nations Unies et des institutions spécialisées. Report by the General Secretary in consultation with general administrators of specialized agencies, through the Administrative Committee on Coordination in accordance with Resolution 180 (VIII), 1949, UNA.
34. FS 7-13. June 1950, ILOA.
35. Maul, *Human Rights*, 392.
36. GB, 108th session, March 1949: 25, ILOA.
37. "The United States and World Labor," address by David Morse before the Commonwealth Club, San Francisco, 25 June 1948, as Acting Secretary of Labor and US Government Delegate to the 31st session, International Labor Conference, David Morse Papers, Princeton, Princeton University.
38. GB, 108th session, March 1949: 28, ILOA.
39. Frank A. Ninkovich, *The Diplomacy of Ideas: US Foreign Policy and Cultural Relations, 1938–1950* (Cambridge: Cambridge University Press, 1981), 15.
40. FS 5: ILO internships 1953 Programme (General), ILOA.
41. Report by Henry Gallois, 1 September 1952—31 October 1952. FS 5, ILOA.
42. FS 5-03 (1961), ILOA.
43. The first national association of former UN fellows was founded in France in 1951. FS 5-05, ILOA.
44. Internal note of 27 February 1959 by R.P. Lopes, Chief of the Educational Programmes Unit. FS 5-05, ILOA.
45. This was the case for two former trainees: Juan Diaz-Salas from Chile and Shlomo Moriel from Israel. Internships 1958. Report of the Director of Studies. FS 5-04, ILOA.
46. FS 5-03 (1952), ILOA.
47. FS 5-03 (1959), ILOA.
48. Ibid., 4.
49. FS 5-03 (1960), ILOA.
50. FS 5-08 (1963), ILOA.

51. Ibid.
52. FS 5-03 (1961), ILOA.
53. Internship program. Textes des Exposés faits par les stagiaires. FS 5-08 (1963), ILOA.
54. International Institute for Labour Studies: Course Internship (from 1962 to 1964). INST 14-1, ILOA. This transfer was decided on 5 November 1963, following a proposal from David Morse.

References

Alcock, Antony E. *History of the International Labour Organization* (London: Macmillan, 1971).
Barjot, Dominique. *Catching up with America: Productivity Missions and the Diffusion of American Economic and Technological Influence after the Second World War* (Paris: Presses de l'Université de Paris-Sorbonne, 2002).
Eckert, Andreas, Stephan Malinowski and Corinna R. Unger (eds). "Modernizing Missions: Approaches to 'Developing' the Non-Western World after 1945," *Journal of Modern European History* 8(1) (2010): 1–138.
Guthrie, Jason. "The ILO and the International Technocratic Class, 1944–1966," in Kott Sandrine and Joëlle Droux (eds), *Globalizing Social Rights: The International Labour Organization and Beyond* (Basingstoke: Palgrave Macmillan/ILO, 2013), 115–34.
Iriye, Akira. *Global Community: The Role of International Organizations in the Making of the Contemporary World* (Berkeley, CA: University of California Press, 2002).
Jensen, Jill. "From Geneva to the Americas: The International Labor Organization and Inter-American Social Security Standards, 1936–1948," *International Labor and Working-Class History* 80(1) (2011): 215–40.
Johnston, George A. *The International Labour Organisation: Its Work for Social and Economic Progress* (London: Europa Publications, 1970).
Kott, Sandrine and Joëlle Droux (eds). *Globalizing Social Rights: The International Labour Organization and Beyond* (Basingstoke: Palgrave Macmillan/ILO, 2013).
Kott, Sandrine. "Fighting the War or Preparing for Peace: The ILO during the Second World War," *Journal of Modern European History* 12 (2014): 359–76.
———. "Par-delà la guerre froide: Les organisations internationales et les circulations Est-Ouest (1947–1973)," *Vingtième Siècle. Revue d'histoire* 109 (2011): 142–54.
Lyons, Karen H., Terry Hokenstad, Manohar Pawar, Nathalie Huegler and Nigel Hall (eds). *The SAGE Handbook of International Social Work* (London: Sage, 2012).
Maul, Daniel. "'Help Them Move the ILO Way': The International Labor Organization and the Modernization Discourse in the Era of Decolonization and the Cold War," *Diplomatic History* 33(3) (2009): 387–404.
———. *Human Rights, Development and Decolonization: The International Labour Organization, 1940–70* (Basingstoke: Palgrave Macmillan, 2012).

Mechi, Lorenzo. *L'Organizzazione Internazionale del Lavoro e la ricostruzione europea* (Rome: Ediesse, 2013).

Ninkovich, Frank A. *The Diplomacy of Ideas: US Foreign Policy and Cultural Relations, 1938–1950* (Cambridge: Cambridge University Press, 1981).

Plata-Stenger, Véronique. "Une voie sociale pour le développement: Le Bureau international du travail et les débuts de la coopération technique (1919–1949)," Ph.D. dissertation (Geneva: University of Geneva, 2016).

Tortora, Manuela. *L'OIT, Institution spécialisée et organisation mondiale: étude des relations de l'OIT avec la SdN et l'ONU* (Brussels: E. Bruylant, 1980).

Tournès, Ludovic. *Les Etats-Unis et la Société des Nations: le système international face à l'émergence d'une superpuissance (1919–1946)* (Bern: Peter Lang, 2015).

Unger, Corinna R. "Histories of Development and Modernization: Findings, Reflections, Future Research" (2010), retrieved March 29, 2017 from http://www.hsozkult.de/literaturereview/id/forschungsberichte-1130.

PART III

THE COLD WAR

A GOLDEN AGE OF SCHOLARSHIP PROGRAMS

 10

THE FULBRIGHT PROGRAM AND THE PHILOSOPHY AND GEOGRAPHY OF US EXCHANGE PROGRAMS SINCE WORLD WAR II

Lonnie R. Johnson

Introduction

The end of World War II, the beginning of the Cold War and its conclusion, and the beginning of the global War on Terror have been defining moments for US foreign policy. They provide a framework for dividing the history of US governmental education exchange into four distinct periods, each of which reflects different exchange philosophies, policies and geopolitical interests. A brief liberal internationalist phase after the end of World War II in 1945 lasted until the beginning of the Cold War in 1947–48, and it was followed by a protracted Cold War period of East–West conflict that dominated and defined the institutions of US public diplomacy for over four decades until 1989–91. A transitional post-Cold War period of disorientation and reorientation lasted just over a decade and ended abruptly on September 11, 2001, which marks the beginning of the current post-9/11 era that has been driven by an array of North–South defense, security, intelligence and development concerns related to the so-called global War on Terror.

The optimistic philosophy of liberal internationalism and the ideological demands of Cold War propaganda both informed the inception of US postwar government exchange programs. Between 1946 and 1948, the US Congress passed two pieces of landmark legislation that laid the foundations for U.S government exchanges. J. William Fulbright, a junior Senator and Democrat from Arkansas who had studied in Oxford as a Rhodes Scholar between 1925 and 1928, said that "the atomic bombing of Hiroshima and Nagasaki focused his thoughts" on international educational exchange,[1] and less than one year later on August 1, 1946, President Harry S. Truman signed an act into law that brought the visionary academic exchange program that came to bear Fulbright's name into being. The Fulbright Program was a quintessential expression of the liberal internationalist optimism that *preceded* the Cold War and informed international institution building in the immediate postwar period.[2]

By 1948, however, the Cold War was in full swing, and the United States saw the urgent need to vigorously counteract Soviet propaganda in a global struggle for allies and for hearts and minds. The US Information and Educational Exchange Act of 1948—better known by the names of its Congressional sponsors Smith-Mundt—laid the foundations for the US government's institutionalization of public diplomacy, and it provided the basis for the establishment of the United States Information Agency (USIA) in 1953 that encompassed "fast media," such as radio and film, and "slow media," like publishing, libraries and exchanges.

The Smith-Mundt Act also provided the basis for the United States' second big postwar exchange program: the Foreign Leader Program (FLP), which was inaugurated in 1949–50. This visitation program was conceived to identify up-and-coming foreign elites and to bring them to the United States on shorter-term programs tailor-made to meet their professional needs (and renamed the International Visitor Program (IVP) in 1965 and the International Visitor Leadership Program (IVLP) in 2004).[3] In this respect, the history of US government postwar exchange programs is a history of the Fulbright and the FLP-IVP-IVLP programs to a great extent: by 2015, Fulbright as the "flagship international educational exchange program sponsored by the US government"[4] had over 360,000 alumni and IVLP as "the US Department of State's premier professional exchange program"[5] had over 200,000.

However, there are important philosophical and structural differences between Fulbright as a government-sponsored *academic exchange* program and FLP-IVP-IVLP as a government sponsored *professional visitation* program. Academic exchange has ultimately been based on the idea of bilateral reciprocity, has entailed the joint articulation of interests and objectives and has been driven by non-governmental actors: students, scholars and institutions of higher education. Governmental visitation programs are substantially unilateral, informed by specific policy objectives, and frequently entail the identification of existing or potential "elites" with the intention of exposing them to specific US values and institutions or—as is the case for the extensive visitation programs of the Department of Defense[6]—for advanced training.

The history of US government exchange programs is also a history of the presidential administrations that have funded them, US government agencies entrusted with their oversight and management, and the ongoing struggle between the non-partisan advocates of the diffuse, long-term benefits of educational and cultural exchange and the usually partisan proponents of short-term, results-oriented information programs driven by policy objectives and messages, and informed by the prevailing definition of a presidential administration's definition of the US national interest. Any history of exchanges must take the recurrent tensions between these philosophies of cultural exchange and "information" into account. Furthermore, the exchange philosophy of the Fulbright Act preceded the Cold War, whereas the information philosophy of the Smith-Mundt Act was an immediate reflection and product thereof.

The tensions between these two philosophies are reflected in the administrative history of US government exchange programs too, which can be divided into three periods: from 1945 to 1977, from 1977 to 1999 and from 1999 to the present. It is an underexposed fact that Senator Fulbright went to great lengths to keep US government exchange programs out of the portfolio of programs managed by the United States Information Agency (USIA) when it was established in 1953, and he objected to their incorporation into the USIA in 1977 because he felt that their independence and integrity would be compromised if they were subordinated to an agency responsible for message-driven "information."[7]

Fulbright noted in the mid 1960s that: "The objectives of the educational exchange program cannot be quickly realized and are not measurable in immediate tangible returns." And he added: "unfortunately, the distinction between education and propaganda is sometimes forgotten and pressures are brought to bear to use educational exchange for short-range and shortsighted political purposes."[8]

However, in the course of a major reorganization of governmental agencies in 1977, the Bureau for Educational and Cultural Affairs was transferred from the State Department to the USIA, and this migration brought a different set of institutional pressures to bear on exchanges. They became more closely associated with the centralized planning and the messaging that was part of the USIA's central task as an information agency conceived to inform and influence international public opinion: "telling America's story to the world."[9]

The Foundational Years

The establishment of the Fulbright Program in 1946 was based on Fulbright's ingenious amendment to a piece of legislation that had nothing to do with educational exchange: the Surplus Property Act of 1944. With amazing brevity, a two-page amendment provided funding for an educational exchange program from revenues generated by the sale of US stockpiles of war-related materials overseas. It funded the first US government postwar educational exchanges without recourse to the federal budget because it fundamentally involved spending offshore windfall foreign currency income. In addition, the Fulbright Program could only initially be funded in a handful of countries—predominantly in Europe and Asia—where such surpluses and revenues were available.[10] However, the location of these surpluses corresponded well to the geopolitical interests of the United States in postwar Europe and Asia. A list of the twenty-seven countries that concluded Fulbright agreements with the United States between 1947 and 1953 reads like a catalog of the United States' postwar European and Asian friends and allies, both large and small: Australia, Austria, Belgium, Burma, Ceylon, China, Denmark, Egypt, Finland, France, Germany, Greece, India, Iran, Italy, Japan, Korea, the Netherlands, New Zealand, Norway, Pakistan, the Philippines, South Africa, Sweden, Thailand, Turkey and the United Kingdom.[11]

One of the structural challenges for the Fulbright Program was to identify funding for exchanges where revenues from the sale of wartime surpluses were not available (as was the case, for example, in most of Africa, the Near and Far East, and Latin America). Indeed, the importance of the Smith-Mundt Act of 1948 for the Fulbright Program was that it provided for regular US government funding for exchanges in US dollars from the federal budget, thus providing funding in *US dollars* for the *stateside* operating costs of the program as a two-way exchange (with US universities bearing the lion's share of costs for incoming grantees in the United States in the form of tuition remissions, scholarships and grants). This also included funding for Fulbright awards managed by US embassies in countries without executive agreements or binational Fulbright commissions and provided the basis for smaller contingents of "post-based" or "embassy-based" Fulbright grantees.

The Fulbright Act consisted of four major points. First, it provided for the foundation of a presidentially appointed "Board of Foreign Scholarships" (BFS)[12] responsible for the articulation of program policy.

There was no grand statement of purpose in the Fulbright Act about the objectives of the program, and it was initially unclear how the program would be structured in detail. The philosophy of the program was inherent in some of its organizational principles, but ultimately articulated in detail by policies and practice.[13] The truly promethean achievement of the founding members of the BFS in the initial years of the program was to establish the principles and guidelines for its execution and to orchestrate the various governmental and nongovernmental institutions responsible for the recruitment of outgoing US students and scholars and in-country management and funding of incoming foreign grantees.[14]

Second, one of the unique and far-reaching provisions of the Fulbright Act was that it called for the conclusion of "executive agreements" between the United States and the governments of participating countries.

Third, these agreements established "commissions": binational entities capable of receiving and disbursing funds that also assumed a wide range of responsibilities for the execution of the program. These commissions were based on the establishment of binational boards of experts and academics with US members appointed by US ambassadors on behalf of the Secretary of State (and usually including the local embassy US cultural affairs officer) and partner government board members appointed by foreign governments.

Fourth, these commission boards, in turn, were responsible for hiring "executive directors" and staffing secretariats responsible for the onsite administration of the outgoing and incoming grantees. The "local" tasks of the first generation of the twenty-seven Fulbright commissions established by the conclusion of binational executive agreements between 1947 and 1952 were analogous to the tasks of the BFS in the United States. They had to reach out to the audiences the Fulbright Program was conceived to serve and to establish "local" procedures and institutions to manage it. Furthermore, in 1953–54, the US Congress authorized the use of other US government revenues accrued overseas for educational exchange—for example, from the sale of US agricultural surpluses. This led to the establishment of a "second wave" of fifteen new commissions between 1955 and 1960, eight of which were in Latin America: Argentina, Brazil, Chile, Colombia, Ecuador, Iceland, Iraq, Ireland, Israel, Paraguay, Peru, Portugal, Spain, the United Arab Republic and Uruguay.[15]

The fact that the Fulbright Act called for the establishment of binational commissions based on intergovernmental agreements had a number of enduring consequences. Although the initial funding for the

Fulbright Program came exclusively from US government revenues, it embodied an exchange philosophy that was based on the ideas of collaborative decision making, joint proprietorship and bilateral reciprocity. Furthermore, the Fulbright Program was highly decentralized because it entrusted the individual binational commissions with the responsibility for "local" decision making, and its governance structures relied predominantly on nongovernmental actors. Above all, binational commissions provided partner governments with a tremendous incentive to buy into and identify with the program. The establishment of fifty binational Fulbright commissions in the first two decades of the program's history and the larger volume of grantees participating in these programs is the structural explanation for the fact that grantees from programs managed by binational commissions account for almost 80 percent of the Fulbright Program's alumni to date.[16]

Finally, the Fulbright Program was conceived as an *academic* exchange program. The overwhelming majority of the appointees to the BFS from the late 1940s to the late 1960s were representatives from leading universities in the United States. The role of *academics* in articulating the principles of the exchange program made *academic freedoms*—such as the freedom of expression and the freedom on inquiry—guiding principles of the program from the start and, in turn, they made the Fulbright Program incompatible with most short-term partisan policy concerns. According to the BFS, the purpose of Fulbright commissions was to "administer the educational exchange program on an impartial and binational basis, to ensure that the grantees and educational institutions participating in the program are qualified to do so, and to plan and propose educational exchanges that are in keeping with the needs and educational resources of each country."[17]

The Consolidation of the Fulbright Program

The exhaustion of the initial wartime surplus funding for the Fulbright Program in the 1950s made it necessary to place the program on a new statutory basis to fund the program in the future. The Fulbright-Hays Act of 1961 (the Mutual Educational and Cultural Exchange Act), which provided funding as a line item appropriation in the federal budget, reflected the experience of fifteen years of program administration. Its preamble also eloquently rearticulated the principles of liberal internationalism, a statement of which was missing in the initial Fulbright Act.[18] It also reaffirmed binational commissions as the core organizational principle of the program.

Fulbright-Hays facilitated the establishment of nine new binational commissions that brought the global total of Fulbright commissions to fifty-one by 1966. Most importantly, it put the funding of the Fulbright Program on a new binational basis by providing foreign governments as well as other private and public entities inside and outside of the United States with opportunities to contribute to the program, and many foreign governments enthusiastically began to support the program with their own resources.

The initial consolidation of the Fulbright Program is perhaps best expressed by the fact that federal funding for the program peaked at US$38.8 million in 1966. However, it began to slip immediately thereafter and was subject to a dramatic cut from US$32 million to US$20 million in 1969 (with the number of Fulbright grantees dropping over 30 percent from 4,556 in 1968–69 to 3,146 in 1969–70).[19] This cut was precipitated in part by a falling-out between President Lyndon B. Johnson and Senator Fulbright, who had become a leading critic of President Johnson's foreign policy and the Vietnam War.[20] According to an analysis drafted by the Bureau for Educational and Cultural Affairs, the cuts resulted in "total uncertainty surrounding the future" and jeopardized "in many cases the existence of the binational commissions."[21] The provisions of the Fulbright-Hays Act enabling foreign governments to cofund the program were critical at this juncture. As a response to the 1969–70 US cuts, governments of countries with binational Fulbright commissions in Europe maintained or increased their contributions to the Fulbright Program and thus collectively funded it better than the US government.[22]

This illustrates the prescient nature of the Fulbright-Hays Act's provisions for partner country cofunding and the establishment of patterns of partner government funding that have proved to be enduring—a critical but underexposed fact in the Fulbright Program's historical narrative. Support for the Fulbright Program from abroad has increased from zero in 1961 to almost US$110 million in the fiscal year 2013: a sum approaching half of the US government allocation of US$242.8 million. Furthermore, the overwhelming majority of foreign governmental as well as foreign private and in-kind support—94 percent of US$109.6 million—came from the forty-nine countries with binational Fulbright commissions,[23] many of which contributed more to the program than the US.[24]

Starting in the late 1970s, USIA moved away from concluding new bilateral Fulbright agreements and focused the further expansion of the Fulbright Program on embassy-based programs that were devoid of "local" binational commissions and boards, funded unilaterally by the US government for the most part, and managed by USIA cultural affairs officers and US embassy personnel inhouse.

It took twenty-five years for educational exchange funding to reapproach the level it had been at before the 1969 cuts in inflation-adjusted terms. The recovery of funding was fueled by the public diplomacy ambitions of the two presidential administrations of Ronald Reagan, who after years of detente took a more confrontational stance with the communist world between 1980 and 1988, and by the George H.W. Bush administration before and after the collapse of communism in Europe in 1988–92. Between 1981 and its peak year of 1994, USIA funding increased almost threefold (from US$458 million to US$1.268 billion), with the budget of the Bureau for Educational and Cultural Affairs (ECA) increasing over fivefold (from US$67 million to US$351 million).[25] In the wake of the regime transitions after 1989, six new binational Fulbright commissions were established in the "new democracies" of Poland, the Czech Republic, the Slovak Republic, Hungary, Romania and Bulgaria; Fulbright "offices" opened in Moscow, Kiev and Beijing; and existing and new programs for young and midcareer professionals and scholars—the Hubert H. Humphrey Program and the Edmund S. Muskie Program—were extended to postcommunist Eastern Europe. Exchanges were a key public US diplomacy tool in the "transitions to democracy."

From the Fall of the Berlin Wall to the Global War on Terror

Ironically, the end of the Cold War deprived the USIA of one of the most important arguments it had articulated to justify itself and its funding during the Cold War. If the purpose of the USIA had primarily been to wage the Cold War on the all-important front of information, the end of the Cold War explicitly called the existence of the USIA into question. The logic of this argument was devastatingly simple. The Cold War was over. The United States had won. Therefore, it was not necessary to spend as much time, energy and money on public diplomacy; this kind of "big government" was no longer necessary.

The fate and the funding of exchanges were institutionally bound to the USIA, which slid into a fiscal and institutional crisis in the mid 1990s. A variety of politically divergent interests coincided to create a perfect storm. President Clinton battled with Newt Gingrich and a Republican-controlled Congress over "right-sizing" government. Furthermore, Secretary of State Madeleine Albright and the Republican Senator Jesse Helms agreed—albeit for different reasons—that it would be a good idea to "consolidate" the USIA with the State Department, and in 1999 the USIA ceased to exist as an autonomous government agency when most of its component parts were incorporated into the State Department.[26]

Between 1994 and 1996, total funding for public diplomacy fell over 25 percent from US$1,478 million to US$1,077 million, with broadcasting—Radio Free Europe and Radio Liberty—taking the biggest hit (from US$210 million to US$70 million), followed by the Bureau for Educational and Cultural Affairs (with cuts from US$351 million to US$200 million).[27] It had taken the Fulbright Program twenty-five years to recover most of the funding lost in the Johnson administration's 1969 cuts. The 1994–96 Clinton administration "right-sizing" cuts brought it down again by over 20 percent from US$120 million to US$98.9 million. These cuts also corresponding increased the relative levels of partner government funding for the program.[28]

The "consolidation" of the USIA with the State Department in 1999 and the 9/11 terrorist attacks in 2001 thrust exchange programs into a dramatically different hierarchical, partisan and short-term results-oriented institutional culture at a time of national crisis. The global image of the United States deteriorated dramatically in the wake of the US invasions of Afghanistan in 2001 and of Iraq in 2003. The United States urgently needed to explain its policies to foreign audiences and to marshal support in those regions of the world that had historically been of subordinate interest to the United States. As part of its post-9/11 public diplomacy, the George W. Bush administrations steadily increased funding for educational and cultural exchanges, especially for the Muslim world.

The budget for the Bureau for Educational and Cultural Affairs increased dramatically from US$205 million in the fiscal year 2000 to UD$635 million in the fiscal year 2010 and globally recovered ground lost as a result of the Clinton administration cuts in the mid-1990s. However, the regional distribution of the funding inside the Fulbright Program meant that "traditional" policy regions in most of Europe, the Americans and parts of the Pacific barely participated in increases because increased funding flowed into the "new" priority regions of the Muslim world in the Near East and Asia or the former Soviet Union.

The reasons for the major policy shifts of US foreign policy after 9/11 from Europe and the Western Hemisphere to the Near East, Sub-Saharan Africa, Asia and the Pacific are obvious. Combatting global terrorism and outreach to Muslim communities go hand-in-hand with traditional US foreign policy objectives such as the promotion of democracy, human rights and economic opportunity. The "3Ds" of diplomacy, development and defense "provide the foundation for promoting and protecting US national security interests abroad,"[29] and the demographics of these regions with their young and rapidly growing populations make reaching out to youth and empowering women high-priority concerns.

US federal budget proposals for exchanges since 2010 illustrate two trends. First, federal funding for exchanges has slipped from its post-9/11 peak of US$635 million in 2010 to US$590 million for the fiscal year 2016. Funding for Fulbright has fallen 7 percent from US$253.8 million to US$236 million—15.6 percent in inflation-adjusted terms—in this time period due to sequestering, budget consolidation measures, the desire to divert funding to other or newer programs and benign neglect.[30] Second, the National Security Council has shown an unprecedented interest in the detailed planning of exchanges in recent years, and it has attempted in this restrictive budget environment to fund new initiatives at the expense of established programs.

In the fiscal year 2015, the federal budget proposed moving US$43.5 million out of traditional long-term educational and cultural exchange programing (US$30 million or 13 percent from the Fulbright budget and US$13.5 million or 14 percent from Citizen Exchange Programs) to fund new short-term "signature presidential Youth Leadership Initiatives targeting young private, public, and civil society sector leaders"[31] from Africa, Southeast Asia and the Americas, as well as an "exchanges rapid response fund."[32] However, the respective Congressional appropriations committees restored the funding for Fulbright and Citizen Exchange Programs in the federal budget proposal for 2015—partially informed by the advocacy of an online, global, grassroots Fulbright alumni platform and initiative (www.SaveFulbright.org)—while modestly funding the new youth leadership initiatives. In doing so, they explicitly criticized the "lack of long-term planning"[33] that the proposed cuts reflected.

Conclusion

This episode illustrates three interlocking issues: the dramatic regional shift of emphasis in US public diplomacy since the end of the Cold War; the budgetary, institutional and political pressures that have been brought to bear on traditional exchanges since 9/11; and either an institutional lapse of historical memory or an intergenerational change of opinion among policymakers regarding the value of the Fulbright Program. Fulbright has traditionally been acknowledged as the "flagship" of the US exchanges: a global and globally recognized, bilateral, nonpartisan, academic exchange program with an established reputation for long-term impacts. How it will continue to fare in a political and policy environment driven by an apparent partisan preference for specific regional, unilateral, shorter-term and policy-driven visitation programs is an open question that the powers that be in Washington, DC will decide in the process of their budgeting exercises in the future.

Lonnie R. Johnson (Dr phil., University of Vienna), a native of Minnesota, moved to Vienna to study abroad for one year in the mid 1970s and subsequently enrolled at the University of Vienna to study history and philosophy. He worked with various educational exchange organizations—including IES Abroad, Vienna and the Austrian Academic Exchange Service—before becoming the executive director of the Austrian-American Fulbright Commission in 1997. His most recent book is *Central Europe: Enemies, Neighbors, Friends* (3rd revised ed., Oxford University Press, 2011). His current research focuses on the history and structure of the Fulbright Program.

Appendix: The Long-Term Impact of the Fulbright Program An Assessment by Bronislaw Marciniak

"I had an opportunity to work as a Fulbright Scholar (1991–92) in one of the best laboratories in the area of photochemistry—the Radiation Laboratory at the University of Notre Dame (UND)—and collaborate with the best experts in the field. The laboratory had unique equipment, at that time not unavailable in Poland. It allowed me to conduct the experiments necessary for my project. The results of my research work were published jointly with Dr Gordon Hug, who was my host, in the leading chemistry journals and presented during several international conferences. This collaboration has continued after my return to Poland and led to over fifty joint publications. Our cooperation paved the way to the formation of a research team within which my students repeatedly visited the Radiation Lab, while our Department has hosted Dr Hug twice on nine-month-long Fulbright scholarships in addition to his and other Notre Dame faculty members' short-term visits. Finally this led to a bilateral agreement between the two universities. During my scholarship, I also had the opportunity to learn about the organization of research and teaching at UND and about the modern methods of planning and performing research as well as governing university communities. The Fulbright experience was one of the major reasons for my election to various academic positions, then as the rector of Adam Mickiewicz University (Poznan) and finally as the president of the Conference of Rectors of Polish Universities. In addition, my own personal benefit from the Fulbright grant was that I (and my family) found genuine friends in the US" (Interview with the author, April 2016)

Notes

1. Randall Bennett Woods, *Fulbright: A Biography* (New York: Cambridge University Press, 1995), 129.
2. Randall Bennett Woods, "Fulbright Internationalism" and Harry P. Jeffrey, "Legislative Origins of the Fulbright Program," *The Annals of the American Academy of Political and Social Science* 491 (1987) [The Fulbright Experience and Academic Exchanges]: 22–35 and 36–47; Kurt Tweraser, "The 'Operational Code' of Senator Fulbright and International Education: Belief Systems, National Missions, Political Contexts," *Österreichische Zeitschrift für Politikwissenschaft* (ÖZP), 41(1) (2012): 23–35.
3. Giles Scott-Smith, *Networks of Empire: The US State Department's Foreign Leader Program in the Netherlands, France, and Britain, 1950–70* (Brussels: PIE Peter Lang, 2008).
4. This is the classic formulation on the US Department of State's website at http://eca.state.gov/fulbright.
5. Retrieved 29 March 2017 from the US Department of State's IVLP website: http://eca.state.gov/ivlp.
6. The "civilian" exchanges funded by the US Department of State are dwarfed by the military "exchanges" funded by the Department of Defense. See Carol Atkinson, *Military Soft Power: Public Diplomacy through Military Educational Exchanges* (Lanham: Rowman & Littlefield, 2014).
7. Richard T. Arndt, *The First Resort of Kings: American Cultural Diplomacy in the Twentieth Century* (Dulles, VA: Potomac Books, 2005), 258–87.
8. Walter Johnson and Francis J. Colligan, *The Fulbright Program: A History* (Chicago, IL: University of Chicago Press, 1965), viii and 68–87.
9. Harilaos Stecopoulus, "Telling America's Story to the World," *American Quarterly* 63(4) (2011): 1025–37.
10. Sam Lebovic, "From War Junk to Educational Exchange: The World War II Origins of the Fulbright Program and the Foundations of American Cultural Globalism, 1945–1950," *Diplomatic History* 37(2) (2013): 280–312.
11. For a list of dates for the conclusion of agreements with current commissions, see the J. William Fulbright Scholarship Board *2014 Annual Report*, 21–5.
12. Later renamed as the Fulbright Foreign Scholarship Board or FFSB.
13. Donald B. Cook and J. Paul Smith, "The Philosophy of the Fulbright Program," *UNESCO: International Social Science Bulletin* VIII(4) (1956): 615–27.

14. For the standard history of the program's early years, see Johnson and Colligan, *Fulbright Program*.
15. Board of Foreign Scholarships, *International Educational Exchange: The Opening Decades: 1946–1966*, 4–5.
16. Based on the 1949–2014 "Fulbright by Numbers and Regions" online Excel sheet addendum to the FFSB's *2014 Annual Report*, retrieved 27 March 2017 from https://eca.state.gov/fulbright/about-fulbright/j-william-fulbright-foreign-scholarship-board-ffsb/ffsb-reports.
17. For this formulaic language, see Board of Foreign Scholarships, *Toward Mutual Understanding*, Sixth Annual Report, October 1968 (US Department of State, 1968), 22.
18. See the Mutual Educational and Cultural Exchange Act of 1961, Congressional Statement of Purpose, Sec. 2451, Public Law 87-256, 21 September 1961, retrieved 27 March 2017 from https://www2.ed.gov/about/offices/list/ope/iegps/fulbrighthaysact.pdf.
19. Board of Foreign Scholarships, *Continuing the Commitment*, Eighth Annual Report, October 1970 (US Department of State, 1970), 5.
20. Randall Woods, *Fulbright*, 385, 490.
21. "Effects of the Fiscal Year 1969 Budget Cut: Backup Budget Statement," University of Arkansas Special Collections Division, MC 468, Bureau for Educational and Cultural Affairs Historical Collection (CU), Box 41-4.
22. Unclassified Cable, No. CA 10930, 17 September 17, 1968, Austrian-American Educational Commission Archives, General Files, 9/67-74. The US government allocation for the Fulbright Programs in Europe was US$1,318,981 and European partner countries with Fulbright Commissions contributed US$1,565,886. The countries that outfunded the United States were, in alphabetical order, Austria, France, Germany (US$500,000 compared to the US figure of US$136,000), Italy, the Netherlands, Spain and the United Kingdom.
23. FFSB, *2014 Annual Report* (US Department of State), 56. Percentages based on tallying the Fulbright commission numbers reported for the fiscal year 2013, 57–58.
24. Based on self-reported numbers provided by European Fulbright Program executive directors at a regional meeting in Lisbon, 15–17 April 2015, the ratio of the overall cash and in-kind contributions of countries with Fulbright commissions to the US government allocations for commissions was 2:1. Individual countries exceeded the US contributions in bilateral terms by higher multiples in many cases.
25. For comparative budget figures from 1981 to 1996, see United States General Accounting Office (GAO), *Report to the Chairman, Committee on the Budget, House of Representatives: US Information Agency: Options for Addressing Possible Budget Reductions*, GAO/NSIAD-96-179 (Washington, DC: GAO 1996), "Funding for Public Diplomacy by Account," 18–19, retrieved 27 March 2017 from http://www.gao.gov/assets/160/155584.pdf.
26. Nicholas J. Cull, *The Decline and Fall of the United States Information Agency: American Public Diplomacy, 1989–2001* (New York: Palgrave Macmillan, 2012).

27. For figures, see GAO, *US Information Agency: Options for Addressing Possible Budget Reductions*, 18–19.
28. For a tabular representation of US government support for the Fulbright Program in annual and constant dollars, see *Fulbright Fiftieth: 1946–1996: The 33rd Annual Report of the J. William Fulbright Scholarship Board* (Washington, DC: USIA, 1996), 29. This table has been updated as "US Government Support of Fulbright, 1947–2013" in constant (1971) and current dollars in the FFSB, *2014 Annual Report*, 10.
29. See the USAID 3 D Planning Guide (31 July 2012), 4, retrieved 27 March 2017 from https://www.usaid.gov/documents/1866/diplomacy-development-defense-planning-guide.
30. The ups and downs of the funding history of the Fulbright Program are analogous to a rollercoaster ride. It is worth noting that it is still 15 percent below its peak funding level of 1966 in constant dollars: US$38 million 1996 dollars would be US$279 million in 2016 according to the CPI Inflation Calculator of the US Department of Labor (retrieved 27 March 2017 from http://www.bls.gov/data/inflation_calculator.htm).
31. This is how these programs are described in the *Congressional Budget Justification—Department of State, Foreign Operations, and Related Programs*, Fiscal Year 2016, 31.
32. The Young Africans Leaders Initiative (YALI, then renamed the Mandela Washington Fellowships for Young African Leaders) and the Young Southeast Asian Leaders Initiative (YSEALI) were established in 2015 and the Young Leaders in the Americas Initiative in 2016.
33. Department of State, Foreign Operations, and Related Programs Appropriations Bill, Report, 19 June 2014, 23, cited in the Alliance for International Educational and Cultural Exchange Policy Monitor, 19 June 2014.

References

Arndt, Richard T. *The First Resort of Kings: American Cultural Diplomacy in the Twentieth Century* (Dulles, VA: Potomac Books, 2005).

Atkinson, Carol. *Military Soft Power: Public Diplomacy through Military Educational Exchanges* (Lanham: Rowman & Littlefield, 2014).

Cook, Donald B., and J. Paul Smith. "The Philosophy of the Fulbright Program," *UNESCO: International Social Science Bulletin* VIII(4) (1956): 615–27.

Cull, Nicholas J. *The Decline and Fall of the United States Information Agency: American Public Diplomacy, 1989–2001* (New York: Palgrave Macmillan, 2012).

Jeffrey, Harry P. "Legislative Origins of the Fulbright Program," *Annals of the American Academy of Political and Social Science* 491 (1987) [The Fulbright Experience and Academic Exchanges]: 36–47.

Johnson, Walter, and Francis J. Colligan. *The Fulbright Program: A History* (Chicago, IL: University of Chicago Press, 1965).

Lebovic, Sam. "From War Junk to Educational Exchange: The World War II Origins of the Fulbright Program and the Foundations of American Cultural Globalism, 1945–1950," *Diplomatic History* 37 (2) (2013): 280–312.

Scott-Smith, Giles. *Networks of Empire: The US State Department's Foreign Leader Program in the Netherlands, France, and Britain, 1950–70* (Brussels: PIE Peter Lang, 2008).

Stecopoulus, Harilaos. "Telling America's Story to the World," *American Quarterly* 63(4) (2011): 1025–37.

Tweraser, Kurt. "The 'Operational Code' of Senator Fulbright and International Education: Belief Systems, National Missions, Political Contexts," *Österreichische Zeitschrift für Politikwissenschaft* (ÖZP), 41(1) (2012): 23–35.

Woods, Randall Bennett. "Fulbright Internationalism," *Annals of the American Academy of Political and Social Science* 491 (1987) [The Fulbright Experience and Academic Exchanges]: 22–35.

———. *Fulbright: A Biography* (New York: Cambridge University Press, 1995).

 11

Grassroots Diplomacy
Fighting the Cold War on the Family Farm with the International Farm Youth Exchange

Peter Simons

Introduction

In the early summer of 1952, a college student from Ohio named Joann Campbell was sailing toward a five-month stay in Finland. She was one of eight hundred students aboard the MS *Nelly*, a converted cargo ship and aircraft carrier that had left New York City bound for Le Havre. The *Nelly* had served as an emigration ship immediately after the war, taking Europeans to new homes throughout the British Empire, but on this June voyage it had become a "floating campus" carrying US students to participate in exchange programs throughout Europe.[1] Joined by two other vessels chartered to satisfy the enormous demand for passage to Europe, the trio carried a total of 3,500 students representing 170 educational institutions that ranged from glee clubs to religious organizations volunteering for hard labor.

But despite her college background, Campbell was not headed to the University of Helsinki as a Fulbright scholar or as part of another educational exchange. She was instead one of thirty-nine students traveling to live on European farms as participants in the International Farm Youth Exchange (IFYE). The program was inspired by former GIs studying agriculture at Cornell University and, since 1948, had been sponsored by the 4-H—a farm youth organization—and the US Department of Agriculture. The IFYE placed college-aged students from farms in the United States, like Campbell, on European farms and conversely brought European farm youth to the United States. However, unlike the postwar agricultural programs that sent foods, supplies and experts to rebuild European farming and secure allies for the United States, these students were working with little training and no materials to promote the abstract goal of mutual understanding.

Although the IFYE operated with far fewer people and resources than government-run exchange programs like the Fulbright Program and technical assistance projects under the Marshall Plan, it is an important piece in explaining the transition between international cooperation at the end of World War II and Cold War belligerence just a few years later.[2] The program further underscores the depth and breadth of Americans' involvement in the Cold War as it attracted farm youth who, often unwittingly, helped wage the early cultural and agricultural battles against communism that would lead to the better-known development programs of the 1950s and 1960s.

Agricultural exchange in the Americas dates back to European colonization, and beginning the late nineteenth century it became the focus of US missionaries and technical experts hoping to improve the welfare of others abroad.[3] World War II rapidly accelerated these exchanges as US-grown food went to allies around the world and an international collection of workers came to the United States to raise wartime crops. Moreover, US farmers turned soldiers, like those who created the IFYE, returned from the war with perspectives on overseas agriculture that helped cultivate a more cosmopolitan worldview among their fellow farmers.[4] These experiences abroad coupled with wartime prosperity at home fostered an urge to support agricultural rehabilitation and food aid after the war. In the face of the US government's bare-shelf policy, which inadequately addressed Europe's food needs in the interest of avoiding a domestic recession, farmers recognized their moral obligations and interests in maintaining newfound profits through food aid.[5] They sent private shipments of food overseas, participated in programs to redirect military rations to civilians, and volunteered to travel abroad to rebuild European agriculture. But it was not until the Marshall Plan began in 1948 that the US government gave full support to agricultural aid, after officials had recognized agriculture's ostensibly apolitical nature as a means of reaching international political goals. Just as US agriculture had served as a testing ground for state capacity during the New Deal, overseas farming provided an avenue for international engagement under the cover of humanitarianism. John Maynard Keynes, for example, chided Franklin D. Roosevelt for starting with the "vitamins" when he used the Food and Agricultural Organization to demonstrate the United States' commitment to international cooperation, and the United Nations in particular, but it proved to be a politically savvy move for gaining public support in the United States.[6] In response, internationally minded farmers expressed their concern at the program's inability to satisfy the nutritional needs of its recipients and at its political motives, which led to unfairly distributed food.[7] Programs such as the IFYE thus operated at cross-purposes—they embodied the altruistic goals of international cooperation and mutual understanding held by participants such as Joann Campbell, while also serving sponsors' goals of fighting communism.

Grassroots Diplomats

The twenty-year-old Campbell had grown up on a cattle farm in Ohio and had studied rural sociology at Earlham College, a Quaker college in Indiana that would have immersed her in the ferment to avoid war through international cooperation.[8] The prosperity of her family's farm had paid for her college education, allowed her to travel overseas and even covered the sponsorship of a British family's immigration to the United States. Although the five months Campbell spent on farms in Finland were not necessarily representative of other delegates' experiences, IFYE leaders considered her an archetypical delegate, based on her background, and so her experiences illuminate the early goals of the program as well as the ways in which private organizations and the federal government helped cement Cold War animosities after a period of postwar international cooperation.[9]

Campbell and six other college-aged farmers were selected to represent the state of Ohio through a competitive application and interview process. Her application essay focused on international friendship, but also pointed out several characteristics considered ideal for prospective IFYE delegates, or Iffys as they were commonly called: she had traveled overseas before, for ten years she had been a member of her local 4-H club (which was part of the US agricultural bureaucracy) and she had demonstrated a proficiency at public presentations, which would later win her recognition from officials in Washington, DC.

Delegates from Ohio began participating in the IFYE in 1950, after students secured funding from the Ohio branches of 4-H, the Grange and Farm Bureau. The following year, the national IFYE transitioned from an independently financed, experimental project of the US Extension Service to become a permanent program. With funding from the Ford Foundation as well as "internationally minded" corporations (usually those that would profit from selling agricultural equipment abroad), the IFYE also expanded its geographic scope and began sending delegates to Latin America and Asia.[10] In 1952, Campbell therefore found herself joining the program in a watershed period, as it moved beyond Europe and saw its US delegates increase in number to 123 from just seventeen in 1948.

Before traveling overseas, IFYE delegates gathered in Washington, DC to meet fellow participants and prepare for life in unfamiliar circumstances. There they met officials from the Department of State and the US Information Agency, who were careful to point out that they were not engaging in propaganda. The government officials instructed delegates, often dubbed "grassroots diplomats," to not promote US methods as superior while working on overseas farms, but instead to participate in farm work and take in cultural differences as a point of mutual understanding. In fact, despite the requirement that all participants had to have a farm background, delegates received no explicit charge to transmit agricultural knowledge apart from distributing literature and promoting the 4-H. They instead heard lectures on "moral standards," customs and how to deal with "knotty problems" such as race relations if they were to arise in conversation with host families.[11] Reflecting the assumed superiority of the United States, and especially its farm youth, organizers argued that they were simply helping the grassroots diplomats to present the information that they knew "almost instinctively."[12]

Campbell diligently packed the 4-H pamphlets she was instructed to distribute abroad, but otherwise arrived in New York with a limited ability to influence, let alone speak with her overseas hosts. Although she had received Finnish language records, she boarded the *Nelly* only able to recognize a few Finnish words. Her traveling companions to Finland were in similar positions. One had grown up on a Finnish settlement in the United States, but did not have the language skills he claimed he did, and the other had been mistakenly sent a Swedish language record. As a result of this practical dilemma, the group embarked for Le Havre hoping to encounter Finns with some knowledge of English and relying on the US diplomats who would periodically accompany them during their time abroad. Later realizing the gravity of not speaking Finnish, Campbell complained that Dave Patterson, the alleged Finnish-speaker, had "fouled up" their exchange because organizers assumed that he could serve as an interpreter.[13] But the Finland-bound delegates were not unusual. Linguistic indifference had existed since the first seventeen Iffys (as they became known) traveled to Europe with no foreign language ability. Even several years into the program, delegates reported that the vinyl language records they received in preparation for the exchange were more novelties than learning tools. They consequently arrived knowing that they would need to rely on smiling, pointing or encountering someone who could speak English.[14]

Although a Missouri delegate recounted that his inability to communicate encouraged him to trust his Swiss host family more, European host families often interpreted the lack of language skills as American indifference or an assumption of superiority.[15]

After arriving at her first farm stay, a fourteen-acre farm three miles from the Soviet border, Campbell lamented to her parents that she barely said over twenty words a day and could not talk to anyone.[16] Meetings with agricultural officials involved her laughing at incomprehensible jokes and otherwise enduring undecipherable conversations. This continued throughout her stay as she learned a basic vocabulary to complete farm chores, but never enough to actually speak with anyone around her. With little ability to communicate and no agricultural expertise to provide, she and other Iffys were left to help with farm chores, promote the International 4-H program and demonstrate to their hosts that not all Americans smoked and drank.

But despite these limitations, delegates could still do what organizers considered a significant responsibility of IFYE delegates: report on their travels to audiences in the United States. Campbell regularly wrote to her family on the trials of living abroad, mentioning, for example, that if her family could see the way dishes were washed and bread was baked, they would understand why she needed to get a typhus shot. She complained to them about the flies in her coffee and the black flakes that permeated all food cooked in her host's cast-iron skillet. With a diet largely consisting of starches and sugars complementing the seemingly endless manual farm labor, Campbell seemed to be in misery during her first month abroad. Even presenting the slideshow of her family's Ohio farm became exhausting because she could not tell her audiences what they were seeing. Campbell noted the villagers' bad teeth, the poor condition of her host family's farm and her unsmiling neighbors. With no one to speak to, she declared that she had long since lost her identity and that she shared more in common with the family dog, who knew about as much of what was going on as she did.

Likely unwilling to air her grievances publicly or upset the benefactors who had paid for her exchange, Campbell's weekly articles written for the *Daily News* in Dayton, Ohio focused instead on the oddities of life in Finland and the shortcomings of that country's agriculture. She wrote about the "hidden values" of the sauna, noted that women and children did the majority of heavy labor on Finnish farms, and that men back in the United States who felt "henpecked from the work they did at home should move to Finland."[17] This was a common thread among other Iffys as well, who focused not only on the lack of farm equipment abroad but also scrutinized unfamiliar work practices while ignoring labor inequalities in the United States. Through all the oddities of life overseas, Campbell was able to hold out the possibility of international friendship. But even that found its limit in the "shadow of the Iron Curtain." She described the Finnish-Soviet border as "the edge of the earth" and a "place where men could no longer stand together." Although she held out hope that "someday the trees will grow again and the boundary ... will disappear," it was not until 1961 that the IFYE entered the Eastern Bloc, and then only in Poland.[18]

In her five months away from home, Joann Campbell lived on three Finnish farms, attended the Olympic Games in Helsinki and saw a performance of the Fisk Jubilee Singers. She distributed the 4-H pamphlets and personalized pencils she brought as gifts and accumulated a suitcase of souvenirs to bring home. She was well-liked by her Finnish hosts, to whom she continued to write for years after her exchange. She even expressed sadness upon leaving, contending that the language barrier was not as important as it seemed and concluding that staying on an "average" farm without plumbing or other conveniences allowed her to "accomplish the mission behind" her trip.[19] Once back in the United States, Campbell, like all returning IFYE delegates, was obligated to stay in her home state for at least three months, taking leave from school if necessary, in order to "present slides, develop newspaper articles, teach new recipes learned overseas, or just chat with friends about the impact of the cross-cultural experience on the individual's outlook on life."[20] Aided by her large collection of slides, she presented to 150 groups over the next three years, spoke on radio shows in Chicago and Cincinnati, and even appeared on television.

Reports from Campbell's fellow delegates suggested that the program was improving Americans' agricultural knowledge about the rest of the world, explaining that the rocky soil and humidity of Norway prevented the wider adoption of machinery and that the need for employment in Italy explained why farm laborers could just as well do the work of farm machinery.[21] Bill Upton, a delegate from North Carolina, even noted the advantage his Japanese hosts had in owning their land compared to the growing numbers of farmers in the United States who were forced to rent their land and take out loans for seed and machinery.[22] But for each of these more thoughtful observations, there were dismissals of outdated farm machinery, backward techniques, and women forced to perform too much heavy labor. The framework of US politics especially shaped delegates' perspectives on events abroad, such as creeping communism, high taxes and the English health plan that was as bad as English coffee.[23] These reports suggested that in place of mutual understanding, delegates accumulated anecdotal evidence in order to support their preconceived notions about the rest of the world.

"America as it Really is"

Exchanges like Campbell's reaffirmed the superiority of life in the United States for delegates and those they came in contact with, but the best way to do this for foreign farmers was to welcome them to live on US farms. Like their delegate counterparts, exchangees (the term used by 4-H to distinguish foreign participants from American "delegates") coming to the United States stayed with a variety of host families over the course of three to six months, often spread across different crop regions such as the Midwest, South and Pacific Coast. They were similarly selected through a competitive process that privileged members of agricultural organizations, but unlike US delegates, they were required to have some proficiency in English. Also, whereas the US delegates were instructed not to argue for US agricultural superiority while abroad, host families in the United States regularly demonstrated it to their foreign visitors.[24] This was in part due to the affluence of host families compared to average farmers in the United States. A survey of IFYE hosts in Ohio, for example, found that their farms were on average 228 acres, more than double the 105-acre average in that state.[25] Exchange reports continually noted the quantity of farm machinery, how much land one US farmer could cultivate, the modern homes farmers lived in, and the conveniences that seemed to make urban and rural life indistinguishable.[26] A participant from Argentina "marveled" at the many quotidian conveniences around his Iowa host's farm, such as gravel roads, rural mail delivery and electricity, as well as the grain-fed beef that surpassed his family's grass-fed cattle.[27] The unstated campaign to overwhelm the foreign visitors with the abundance of farm life in the United States even raised fears that the participants would not return home. A State Department evaluator suggested that agricultural exchanges were better suited for immigrants because they encouraged the participants to "put down roots in a favorable environment" rather than inspire them to return home with new ideas.[28]

In addition to highlighting the desirability of farm life in the United States, the experiences of the foreign participants burnished the country's agrarian mythology. They reported arriving with images of profligate living in New York and Hollywood, but encountered a wholly different culture on the farm. This discovery did not change their general impression of the United States, but it did excise rural Americans as a more wholesome group within the broader population and provided a "right picture" of life on US farms not provided in popular culture.[29] Even President Dwight Eisenhower affirmed this perspective in 1954 when he stated to a group of farmers from India and Pakistan that he was happy that they could "see America as it really is," while dismissing cities as "really only a small phase of American life."[30]

In evaluating the early effectiveness of the program, two Iffys from the program's first year declared that its results "are to be measured in terms of international Christianity, good will and understanding. They are, therefore, intangible but everlasting."[31] But these amorphous goals failed to produce the concrete results that funders and sponsors hoped for. Delegates failed to maintain contact with their host families as intended, moving on with their lives and remembering the exchange as a youthful adventure.[32] Host families in the United States similarly seemed to demonstrate little change in thinking about the world, instead rationalizing their long-held views to fit the experiences of hosting foreign farm youth.[33] Even the US Extension Service staff overseeing the program wondered, for example, how much better the farm hosts' knowledge of India was after the visits, suggesting that basing conclusions "about India from the acquaintance with from one to five well-educated, carefully chosen young men must certainly lead to the development of new stereotypes as misleading as the old ones."[34] The motivations of hosts were also suspect, as they occasionally cited an interest in doing something for peace and world understanding, but more commonly admitted that they hosted students because their children wanted the experience, while others more brazenly hoped to show how much better Christianity was or to get "paid back" for the work their child had performed in other countries.[35] More innocuously, hosts claimed that the experience served as a vacation at home, with the foreign visitor providing "zest" and "lift" to ordinary farm life.[36]

Conclusion

With the fleeting influence on delegates and mixed motivations of hosts in the United States, the early years of the IFYE therefore appear to be of limited consequence. While Joann Campbell maintained contact with her host families longer than others and spoke to thousands about her experiences, she chose not to finish college, was married and settled on a farm across the road from her parents. For many delegates, the exchange was a subsidized vacation that had little bearing on their adult lives. And based on their harsh assessments of host countries, the delegates appeared to confirm recent research indicating that exchange programs actually build nationalism rather than international cooperation.[37]

But among the thousands of delegates in the ensuing years, a strong tie developed between the program and later work for the US Agency for International Development, the State Department and transnational food and agricultural companies. Not only did IFYE alumni go on to work with internationally focused government agencies and corporations, but a symbiotic relationship also formed, which continues today, in which US development projects followed earlier work by the IFYE, and the IFYE enjoyed greater support from the US agrodiplomatic apparatus.[38] Likewise, exchangees commonly went on to work in ministries of agriculture, universities and the food industry. In providing early support, the Ford Foundation was explicit about its hopes to foster farm organizations and in turn rationalize agriculture abroad. And as the program spread beyond Europe, its mission widened as well. Early delegates like Joann Campbell were briefed in Washington to "[bend] over backwards to avoid criticism of one nation's standard of living" in order to overcome the "suspicion that so often jeopardizes international experiments."[39] This accommodation in turn permitted the IFYE program to build a reputation that fostered its rapid expansion. But as historian Amrys Williams notes, soon after Campbell's experience in Finland, the IFYE shifted its mission from the postwar reconstruction of Europe to the development of commercial agriculture in the postcolonial world.[40] Campbell and her fellow Iffys were, in effect, the thin end of the wedge that opened the way for subsequent technical assistance, first with publicly financed development projects and then private investment, including many of the farm machinery manufacturers that helped fund the IFYE.[41]

Despite the basic language barriers and the prohibition against promoting US methods, the program maintained an implicit propagandistic impulse. The requirement that all participants had to be college students excluded the vast majority of US farm youth in favor of those who had access to higher education and were predisposed to the industrial modes of agriculture taught at land grant universities. Moreover, the competitive process used to select participants ensured that those most involved with farm organizations and the federal agricultural bureaucracy would be chosen. And while the IFYE touted its private funding and sponsorship, it operated in cooperation with the state and its corporate partners, including the New York "bon voyage luncheon" hosted by the Grocery Manufacturers of America.[42] The IFYE and similar programs therefore had real environmental and human consequences, especially as they moved beyond Europe to countries that received greater attention for development and modernization projects.

Farm exchanges such as the IFYE also demonstrated that while agriculture seemed to occupy a marginal place in a largely industrial United States, it remained essential to the country's Cold War efforts. As European refugees awaited passage to the United States after World War II, for example, they were shown models of farms in Iowa to demonstrate the bounty that awaited them. And while Cold War animosities limited contact between the United States and the Soviet Union, in 1955 a group of Soviet farm experts spent a month touring the Midwest to learn about improved farm efficiency and the natural abundance of the corn and wheat belts. They were followed in 1959 by Nikita Khrushchev's trip to Iowa in order to see the "real America," where he was met by indifferent Iowans who had already grown accustomed to the parade of foreign visitors to their farms.[43] Understanding the reach of the Cold War therefore requires us to look beyond traditional diplomatic sources to uncover these histories. The early history of the IFYE does this by uncovering US farmers as protagonists in international relations that played out in the natural environment around the world.

Peter Simons is Visiting Assistant Professor of History at Hamilton College in New York. His work examines the interplay of the natural environment and international relations. He is currently completing a manuscript, *Global Heartland*, which traces the roots of Cold War diplomacy to the international networks of food production, development and distribution created by farmers in the United States.

Appendix: Preparing for Farm Life Abroad

In the summer of 1952, Marvel LaBrie of South Dakota also traveled to Europe as an IFYE delegate to Belgium.[44] Like Joann Campbell, she received minimal preparation for her time abroad. Her French language records provided more entertainment than instruction, and the other orientation materials mailed to her with information on local and US history, foreign policy and the US agricultural bureaucracy seemed secondary to practical details such as arranging for inoculations and applying for a passport. Having finished the self-directed study, LaBrie and the other delegates traveled to Washington, DC for an experience more celebratory than instructional, with tours of the monuments and visits to officials from the Department of Agriculture, Agricultural Extension and the Department of State. In the course of these meetings, delegates would learn about the types of questions they might encounter about the United States, such as why Americans have homes for the aged or why there is no significant ideological difference between major parties. But rather than receiving scripted answers, delegates were instructed to not answer defensively or be pushed to make embarrassing admissions. At no point did they receive training in agricultural methods or briefings on scientific agriculture that they could bring abroad. However, this minimal amount of preparation was not an oversight; rather, it reflected the confidence of IFYE sponsors that membership of the 4-H and its ideals of clear thinking, loyalty, service and better living would ensure that the delegates would successfully carry out the program's goals. It further showed how sincerely they believed that the rural family values at the heart of 4-H and the IFYE were enough to fight communism and prevent another world war.

Notes

1. Harry Gilroy, "Crossing the Atlantic on a Floating Campus," *New York Times*, 29 June 1952, 13.
2. Sam Lebovic, "From War Junk to Educational Exchange: The World War II Origins of the Fulbright Program and the Foundations of American Cultural Globalism, 1945–1950," *Diplomatic History* 37(2) (2013): 280–312.
3. Randall E. Stross, *The Stubborn Earth: American Agriculturalists on Chinese Soil, 1898–1937* (Berkeley, CA: University of California Press, 1986); Nick Cullather, *The Hungry World: America's Cold War Battle against Poverty in Asia* (Cambridge, MA: Harvard University Press, 2010).
4. See, for example, Joseph Helfert Papers, Wisconsin Historical Society (hereinafter WHS), Madison, WI.
5. Robert G. Lewis (Wisconsin State Director), 31 May 31, 1949, box 6, folder 9, Farmers Educational and Cooperative Union of America, Wisconsin Division, WHS.
6. Quoted in Elizabeth Borgwardt, *A New Deal for the World: America's Vision for Human Rights* (Cambridge, MA: Harvard University Press, 2005), 116.
7. Bruce E. Field, *Harvest of Dissent: The National Farmers Union and the Early Cold War* (Lawrence, KS: University Press of Kansas, 1998), 65.
8. The details of Campbell's experience with IFYE are detailed in Joann Campbell, *Joann Campbell's Letters from Finland: An Ohio Girl's Experiences as a Delegate of the International Farm Youth Exchange*, Paul F. Erwin (ed.) (Cincinnati, OH: Creative Writers and Publishers, 1967).
9. Campbell, *Letters*, 301.
10. National 4-H Club Foundation and the Cooperative Extension Service, *The International Farm Youth Exchange: A People-to-People Program*, 1958.

11. Elizabeth S. Colclough, "Peace Corps Prelude," *Travel*, July 1961, 54.
12. US Department of State, *International Educational Exchange Program 1948–1958*, Publication 6710, International Information and Cultural Series 60 (Washington, DC: GPO, November 1958); Paul R. Conroy, "On Giving a Good Account of Ourselves," *Antioch Review* 18 (1958): 411–19.
13. Campbell, *Letters*, 70.
14. "Plan of Action for International Farm Youth Exchange Project, 1948," 1947, National Agricultural Library (hereinafter NAL), Beltsville, MD.
15. Dick Taylor, "A Missouri Farm Boy in Switzerland," in Dan Tabler (ed.), *4-H Stories from the Heart* (Bloomington, IN: iUniverse, 2011), 73–75; Laurel K. Sabrosky, *Information Which Might Give a Few Clues as to Effectiveness of American International Farm Youth Exchange Delegates Abroad (Europe)*, IFYE Evaluation Report No. 4 (Washington, DC: Federal Extension Service, September 1954).
16. Campbell, *Letters*, 83.
17. Ibid., 98, 128.
18. Ibid., 206.
19. Ibid., 110, 118.
20. Anna Marie Boyd, "An Analysis of the Role of the International Farm Youth Exchange Program in Cross-Cultural Communication," MA thesis (Pullman, WA: Washington State University, 1971), 24; "Whiteside County Taking Lead in Exchange Program," *Sterling Daily Gazette*, 22 February 1951, 2.
21. Meta Marie Keller, "International Farm Youth Exchange to Help Understanding," *Sterling Daily Gazette*, 22 February 1951, 2; "14 Young Envoys Back from Europe," *New York Times*, 5 October 1948, 28.
22. Haru Matsukata, "Our Youngest Ambassadors," *Saturday Evening Post*, 19 February 1955, 36.
23. 4-H Collection, University of Minnesota Archives, Minneapolis, MN.
24. Laurel K. Sabrosky, *An Evaluation of the Special Indian Section of the International Farm Youth Exchange Project in Pickaway County, Ohio, in 1953*, IFYE Evaluation Report No. 3 (Washington, DC: Federal Extension Service, February 1954).
25. Boyd, "Analysis of IFYE," 20.
26. Sabrosky, *Evaluation of the Special Indian Section*, 3; US Department of State, *Preparation for Tomorrow: A German Boy's Year in America*, Department of State Publication 4138 (Washington, DC: GPO, 1951).
27. Chuck Walk, "Argentine Farmer in N. Iowa," *Mason City Globe Gazette*, 20 May 1960.
28. US Department of State, *Preparation for Tomorrow*, 40.
29. Robert Heumann, *Report of Mr. Robert Heumann* (Washington, DC, December 1950), NAL, 1.
30. "President Sees Asians," *New York Times*, 31 October 1954, 69.
31. Roy E. Hranicky and Louis Belle White, *The Five H's: Hand, Heart, Head, Health ... and Holland* (Orange Grove, TX, 1950), 8.
32. Taylor, "Missouri Farm Boy in Switzerland," 75.
33. Sabrosky, *Evaluation of the Special Indian Section*, 4.
34. Ibid., 17.

35. Ibid., 6.
36. [Mrs. D.] Alexander, "Peace in Kansas," *American Magazine*, April 1955, 18.
37. Calvert W. Jones, "Exploring the Microfoundations of International Community: Toward a Theory of Enlightened Nationalism," *International Studies Quarterly* 58 (2014): 682–705.
38. Reminiscences written by IFYE alumni commonly connect their IFYE experience to subsequent work for USAID, Alliance for Project and other development programs. See, for example, Doris Imhof Johnson, *Philippine Experiences of a Kansas Farm Girl* (Bloomington, IN: Trafford, 2012).
39. Campbell, *Letters*, 24.
40. Amrys O. Williams, "Cultivating Modern America: 4-H Clubs and Rural Development in the Twentieth Century," Ph.D. dissertation (Madison, WI: University of Wisconsin, 2012), 207–8.
41. Campbell acknowledged that IFYE opened the door to subsequent technical assistance [25]; early finance reports show scores of local groups who sponsored individual delegates, but also corporations such as International Harvester and Allis Chalmers that financed the national organization, US Extension Service, *Sources of Funds: 1950 International Farm Youth Exchange* (Washington, DC, 1950), NAL.
42. "31 Young Farmers Leave for Europe," *New York Times*, 23 June 1949, 9.
43. Richard Orr, "Coon Rapids Calm," *Chicago Daily Tribune*, 23 September 1959, 2.
44. Marvel M. LaBrie, *This was My Europe* (Bowling Green, OH: Republican Press, 1953).

References

Borgwardt, Elizabeth. *A New Deal for the World: America's Vision for Human Rights* (Cambridge, MA: Harvard University Press, 2005).

Boyd, Anna Marie. "An Analysis of the Role of the International Farm Youth Exchange Program in Cross-Cultural Communication," MA thesis (Pullman, WA: Washington State University, 1971).

Campbell, Joann. *Joann Campbell's Letters from Finland: An Ohio Girl's Experiences as a Delegate of the International Farm Youth Exchange*, Paul F. Erwin (ed.) (Cincinnati, OH: Creative Writers and Publishers, 1967).

Cullather, Nick. *The Hungry World: America's Cold War Battle against Poverty in Asia* (Cambridge, MA: Harvard University Press, 2010).

Field, Bruce E. *Harvest of Dissent: The National Farmers Union and the Early Cold War* (Lawrence, KS: University Press of Kansas, 1998).

Hranicky. Roy E. and Louis Belle White. *The Five H's: Hand, Heart, Head, Health … and Holland* (Orange Grove, TX, 1950).

Johnson, Doris Imhof. *Philippine Experiences of a Kansas Farm Girl* (Bloomington, IN: Trafford, 2012).

Jones, Calvert W. "Exploring the Microfoundations of International Community: Toward a Theory of Enlightened Nationalism," *International Studies Quarterly* 58 (2014): 682–705.

Lebovic, Sam. "From War Junk to Educational Exchange: The World War II Origins of the Fulbright Program and the Foundations of American Cultural Globalism, 1945–1950," *Diplomatic History* 37(2) (2013): 280–312.
Stross, Randall E. *The Stubborn Earth: American Agriculturalists on Chinese Soil, 1898–1937* (Berkeley, CA: University of California Press, 1986).
Taylor, Dick. "A Missouri Farm Boy in Switzerland," in Dan Tabler (ed.), *4-H Stories from the Heart* (Bloomington, IN: iUniverse, 2011), 73–76.
Williams, Amrys O. "Cultivating Modern America: 4-H Clubs and Rural Development in the Twentieth Century," Ph.D. dissertation (Madison, WI: University of Wisconsin, 2012).

12

THIRD WORLD STUDENTS AT SOVIET UNIVERSITIES IN THE BREZHNEV PERIOD

Julie Hessler

Introduction

Cultural connections between the Soviet Union and the Third World have attracted attention in a number of works recently, perhaps most notably Tobias Rupprecht's excellent new book.[1] Among other topics, Rupprecht highlights how educational aid strengthened Soviet relations with Third World countries. Students from the Third World formed a large and growing contingent at Soviet institutions of higher education from the 1960s to the 1980s, and, in contrast to the typical Western view of the Soviet Union as a dreary, technologically backward and politically repressive place, many Asian, African, Latin American and Middle Eastern students came away impressed by the USSR's free university education, generous stipends and unlimited hot showers. In interviews with Rupprecht, Latin American alumni of Soviet educational institutions again and again described their studies in the USSR as the "best time of their life."[2]

The purpose of this chapter is to examine some of the institutional means by which Soviet universities and institutes accommodated international students. With the influx of students from the Third World, Soviet *vuzy* (a helpful shorthand for institutions of higher education) had to develop techniques to provide for these students' special academic needs. Soviet officials wanted their country's universities and institutes to be perceived as world-class educational institutions, particularly in the technical fields, but they faced some serious challenges when it came to educating international students from the Third World. Some of these challenges will be familiar to educators at Western universities today. To take the most obvious, Third World students' Russian language skills ranged from limited to nonexistent at the outset of their studies, and their secondary schooling frequently fell short of normal admissions standards. Institutional support systems mitigated these problems in a distinctively socialist way by establishing collective responsibility for each student's academic success.

Soviet officials had a second major goal for international education, namely the inculcation of socialist values and political sympathy for the USSR. Interestingly, Rupprecht's interview subjects denied that they had been subject to any political pressures, and Soviet educational recruitment materials featured vociferous disclaimers of Western allegations that Soviet universities trained "foreign revolutionaries" or sought to influence the students' political views.[3] Yet educators spoke openly of this objective in institutional settings, just as Americans did with respect to the Fulbright exchange. Scholars have long noted the importance of *vospitanie*—best understood in this context as a mix of character education, ideology and civics—to Soviet higher education more generally as a concomitant of universities' role in training future leaders.[4] Cultivating socialist or progressive leadership was no less central to the Soviet educational mission vis-à-vis international students, but of course these students arrived with preconceptions and experiences that differed from those of the Soviet mainstream. Educators accordingly developed special techniques for influencing foreign students' characters and political outlooks into "committed internationalists and true friends of the USSR."[5]

The chronological focus of the chapter is 1965 to 1980, a time of institutional stability and ever-increasing global demand for Soviet higher education.[6] By and large, the mechanisms for coping with, and influencing, international students had been developed earlier, during the early 1960s. The first wave of students from the Third World had contributed to political ferment on Soviet campuses,[7] but international student unrest appears to have dissipated in the more quiescent atmosphere of the Brezhnev years. By focusing on a period of stability and growth, this chapter highlights successful aspects of the Soviet system of educating international students. Many of the sources for the chapter come from Soviet educational institutions in what is now Belarus, but the dynamics observed there were reflected all around the former Soviet Union.

Educating Foreign Students: Some Basics

Foreign students were admitted to the Soviet Union to study through an entirely separate admissions process from Soviet students. Their numbers were determined primarily by bilateral treaties on cultural cooperation between the home governments and the USSR, though additional students, mostly from the Third World, were sponsored by Soviet public organizations.[8] According to archival data compiled by Constantin Katsakioris, the number of international students from Africa, Asia, the Middle East and Latin America in the Soviet Union rose very rapidly during the Brezhnev years, from roughly 17,000 in the 1966–67 academic year to nearly 53,000 in 1979–80.[9] Within this total, the number from individual countries could fluctuate substantially on a year-to-year basis. The Democratic Republic of Vietnam was an extreme case in the 1950s and 1960s, with numbers oscillating from fourteen to 243 to zero to 1,067 between 1958 and 1961, but other countries had variable numbers as well, most often in connection with the rise and fall of left-leaning political regimes.[10] Far from all countries of origin were socialist, though; notably large contingents in the 1970s came from the socialist countries of Mongolia, Vietnam, Cuba and the People's Democratic Republic of Yemen, to be sure, but also from non-socialist India, Nigeria, Ghana, Mexico, Colombia, Syria, Jordan and Lebanon.[11]

Students from the Third World, though not from Eastern Europe, spent their first year in a preparatory faculty, which had the dual purpose of providing a crash course in Russian and bringing the students up to speed in the sciences. The overwhelming majority of Asian, African, Latin American and Middle Eastern students came to the Soviet Union to study scientific or technical subjects, above all medicine and engineering, but Soviet educators felt that their background in those fields suffered by comparison with graduates of Soviet secondary schools.[12] Preparatory programs thus offered biology, chemistry and physics courses geared at an advanced high school level, with textbooks (rarely sufficient in number) available in English, French, Spanish, Arabic, Vietnamese and Russian.[13] Oral instruction was ordinarily in Russian in these courses, but science instructors in the preparatory faculty often had a foreign-language background as well and coordinated closely with Russian language instructors.

Students' performance in the preparatory courses determined their placement for the remainder of their studies. At Belorussian State University (BGU), only a small percentage of graduates of the preparatory faculty was assigned to stay for the regular five-year university program.[14] In part, this reflected the fact that most Soviet *vuzy* were not capable of mounting a preparatory program, so the major universities and institutes that did have preparatory facilities were expected to train students for the much larger number of institutions that did not. Students with the best grades were assigned to the top-ranking *vuzy*, which is to say the "universities" (broad-based research and teaching institutions with strength in humanities as well as scientific subjects; in the whole USSR, there were fifty-one of these in 1970 and sixty-eight in 1982)[15] and the most prestigious institutes (more specialized *vuzy*, predominantly in engineering, applied science and economics). Students with the lowest grades in the preparatory courses were not assigned to institutions of higher education at all, but were funneled into specialized vocational schools, called technicums or *proftekhuchilishcha*, for training in various skilled trades.

Yet even within the cohort of top students designated for a university education, there was considerable movement between the preparatory course and the main faculty. BGU received international students for its core academic programs from several other institutions in the late 1960s and 1970s, including the Belorussian and Leningrad Polytechnical Institutes, the Azerbaijan Oil and Chemistry Institute, the Moscow Auto-Roads Institute, and Kiev, Leningrad, Voronezh and Moscow State Universities.[16] These assignments were made by the USSR Ministry of Higher and Specialized Secondary Education (Minvuz), with little to no input from the universities and institutes themselves.[17] University-level administrators would have liked to influence the number of foreign students allocated to them, as well as their fields of study and countries of origin, but petitions on these subjects were routinely ignored by Minvuz officials in Moscow. Thus, in 1969, the rector of BGU protested that he had "repeatedly" requested that "no more than twenty-five foreign students" be assigned to BGU's main faculties on the grounds that the university was not equipped to handle them. This request, however, ran counter to the political thinking in Moscow, which favored expanding international education for foreign policy reasons. In practice, BGU had been getting between forty and eighty new foreign students a year, not including the preparatory faculty, with 125 planned for the following academic year.[18]

With regard to the country of origin, the main desire of administrators was to limit the number of distinct national contingents. These contingents, organized into so-called *zemliachestva* (national student associations), served as a key intermediary between the individual students and the university, and administrators, teachers and Komsomol activists found it easier to deal with larger cohorts from a smaller number of countries than with numerous tiny contingents of one to three students each (a situation that frequently prevailed). Another preference was for more Eastern Europeans as against foreign students from the Third World. In the Belorussian context, this desire reflected the increasing importance of cross-border ties in the late Soviet period;[19] students from Eastern Europe, whose numbers increased exponentially in the 1970s,[20] spoke Russian, had excellent academic preparation and were already acculturated to Soviet-style socialism.[21] They did not even need *zemliachestva*, as virtually all of the Eastern European students in the USSR were members of their countries' Communist youth organizations or Communist Parties, and institutional interactions with them could run through "fraternal" Party or Komsomol channels instead of the less reliable *zemliachestva*.

Education and *Vospitanie*: Overlapping Responsibilities, Interwoven Objectives

Many different councils, offices and individuals were charged with the integration of international students into Soviet life. Each republic and major city had a council for relations with foreign students. Likewise, the Komsomol had such a council at the university and municipal levels as well as a "sector" of the oblast, republican and central committees. Universities and institutes themselves had a number of overlapping councils and assemblies dedicated to international students. To give the example of the Belorussian Polytechnical Institute, foreign and Soviet student representatives, along with faculty, formed a "Friendship Council," which met four times a year, while faculty, staff, administration and an official liaison from the university Komsomol committee constituted a "Council for Work with International Students," chaired by the rector (the equivalent of a university president). Administrators also convened an assembly of all the *zemliachestvo* presidents once a month and held a general assembly of all foreign students once a semester.[22] How enthusiastically students took to these forums depended on the institution; the Central Committee of the Komsomol in Moscow certainly received reports from some *vuzy* that "the Friendship Council lacks authority and inspires little interest."[23] Be that as it may, institutional councils and assemblies afforded an opportunity for public input and discussion of issues involving international students in addition to top-down policy transmission.

The day-to-day administration of international student affairs at the *vuz* level was handled by the dean's office for work with international students, known as the Interdekanat. The Interdekanat's functions were similar to those of international student offices at American universities; the Interdekanat coordinated activities for international students both on and off campus and provided various kinds of support. At the same time, the Interdekanat kept tabs on the foreign students. Individual files monitored each student's academic progress, political views, attitude toward the Soviet Union and comportment, with up-to-date academic transcripts but also an array of testimonies from office staff, teachers, and Soviet classmates and roommates. Upon graduation, the Interdekanat drew on the student's file to produce a 1–2-page "attestation" of the student's character, performance and professional qualifications, seemingly to be used as a confidential reference when the graduate applied for jobs.[24]

Attestations exemplified the Soviet Union's dual goals for international education by giving equal weight to academic assessment and character evaluation. At the Belorussian Polytechnical Institute (BPI), for which dozens of attestations from the mid 1970s are preserved, attestations began with basic biographical information (year of birth, home country and town, social class of parents, whether the student was married or single) and indicated whether the student had come to the USSR through a governmental exchange program or through one of the public organization's scholarships. The attestation then identified the student's major (at BPI, this was typically a highly specialized technical subject, such as "technology of machine building, metal-cutting stations, and instruments") and turned to an assessment of the student's academic performance and intellectual potential. This meant listing the cumulative grade point average on the Soviet five-point scale, but also commenting on whether the student's grades were uniform across subjects or much stronger in one area than others, and evaluating the student's capacity for research. Students always had one or more internships as part of their course of study, and the attestation described their performance in a production setting. All of these assessments shaped the recommendations at the end of the attestation for the kinds of work positions appropriate to the student's background, as well as the student's aptitude for continuing studies at a graduate level. The underlying assumption of these documents was that a graduate would find work in his or her specialty.[25]

The attestations devoted roughly equal space to students' personal characteristics and attitudes. Was the student hot-tempered or calm? Sociable or reserved? Hardworking or undisciplined? These attributes, which indicated how the student might contribute to a collective and thus had obvious relevance to the workplace, were among the most frequently mentioned, but less value-laden personality traits, such as the fact that a student liked to tell jokes, appeared occasionally as well. Attestations also commented on students' participation in civic life at the institute. If the student had taken on any leadership roles, that was always noted, as was evidence of a student's authority among fellow students. Students were cited for their willingness to participate in ideological activities, such as volunteer Saturday work projects (*subbotniki*) or public presentations at schools and international friendship evenings. On the negative side, violations of dormitory rules and incidents of disorderly conduct were registered. Students' attitudes toward Soviet life and state policies, especially in the international arena, and their openness to friendship with Soviet students rounded out the picture.

The BPI attestations generally presented a clear-headed portrait of the institute's graduates. Academic merit, character and pro-Soviet politics did not always coincide in these documents; a student described as a "model of good behavior in the dorms" might also be glossed as "arrogant and hot-tempered"; an outstanding researcher might show zero interest in civic or social life; and a talented student might have "relations with girls of questionable behavior."[26] If such negative characteristics appear as fixed personality traits in postgraduation attestations, the centrality of *vospitanie* to Soviet educational philosophy meant that this was not the operative assumption during the educational process. Educators hoped to intervene in the development of students' personalities as well as political outlooks. In the effort to mold students' characters, the Interdekanat was not expected to play the leading role. That task fell to teachers, especially from the Russian language department and from the preparatory faculty, as well as to Soviet students assigned to foreign students as roommates or study group leaders. Their efforts to mold the hearts, minds and even personalities of international students intertwined sociability, acculturation and intellectual exchange with monitoring, correction and attempts at political persuasion. Inevitably, some foreign students chafed at these interventions. As a student expelled for political reasons from People's Friendship University in Moscow put it, "the senior instructors walk around the dormitory asking you what you think of such-and-such a student."[27] Such criticisms notwithstanding, Soviet educators construed this kind of interaction in a positive light. In fact, for many instructors, it was a mandatory part of the job, subject to critical evaluation during contract renewal reviews on a par with teaching, scholarship and service.[28]

Clear evidence of the role of instructional faculty in what was called *vospitatel'naia rabota* with foreign students comes from the minutes of department meetings in the BGU preparatory faculty. Every instructor in the preparatory faculty was assigned as a *kurator* ("curator") of one or more *zemliachestvo*, and faculty meetings regularly discussed their work in this capacity. Some of these discussions were devoted to the special challenges of working with one or another national group, e.g. why the Afghans were so far behind in their studies (especially an issue in 1979–80!) or why the Arabs and Algerians were especially resistant to *vospitanie*.[29] Other discussions focused on the curators' duties and exchanged techniques for shaping student attitudes. All curators were expected to hold orientation sessions with their national contingents at the start of the academic year to discuss appropriate behavior in the dormitories, study skills, time management and other aspects of university life. In addition, curators were expected to pay regular visits to the dormitories so as to become better acquainted with the students in their contingent and to carry out what was called "individual work" — one-on-one conversations aimed at influencing students' political views. Curators sometimes had to spend part or all of their winter, spring and summer breaks with the students in their *zemliachestva*, accompanying them to university-sponsored ski camps, sports bases and work sites, or arranging field trips in Minsk. They had to show up to celebrations of the students' national holidays, providing help with arrangements when necessary. Once again, how energetically instructors carried out these duties came in for evaluation at the time of a performance review.[30]

Up to a point, faculty members were held responsible for the success of their students. If an international student (and still more a whole study group or *zemliachestvo*) was struggling academically, instructors were obliged to hold extra classes to bring them up to speed.[31] Collective responsibility for each student was, in fact, a distinctive feature of Soviet higher education. All students at Soviet *vuzy* were assigned to a study group in the major field upon matriculation. In the preparatory faculty, study groups frequently coincided with national contingents, in part for linguistic reasons and in part because the different national contingents often arrived at different times, whether before or as much as six weeks after the beginning of the academic year.[32] In the main faculties, though, international students were integrated into study groups with their Soviet counterparts. The collectivist ethos dictated that the whole study group (typically six to eight students) shared responsibility for the academic performance of each of its members. Like teachers, study groups were thus expected to work with struggling students so that every member of the group would achieve passing grades. This was likewise true of *zemliachestva*, at least in the eyes of administration, with the difference that each *zemliachestvo* and, more particularly, its elected president had to answer for members' behavior as well as their academic success.

The principle of collective responsibility illustrates how *vospitanie* was interwoven with academic and professional training in Soviet higher education. Collective activities, such as sharing lecture notes and studying together, were structured into the educational experience, thereby socializing students into a core socialist value. It seems likely that this was genuinely helpful for international students, especially in their first year or two in the program; they gained a ready-made circle of acquaintances and stood to benefit academically from collaboration with native Russian speakers. Collective responsibility also dovetailed with the official rationale for international education, which centered on developing countries' societal need for highly qualified specialists rather than students' individual self-fulfillment. This rationale was also a one-way street. Although Soviet students exercised their "internationalist duty" when working with foreign students, the exposure to other cultures that they thereby gained barely figured in Soviet conceptions of international education. Soviet students' relationship to Asian, African and Latin American students was modeled on the imagined relationship between the USSR and the foreign students' home countries; that is, Soviet students were expected to embody in a personal way a paternalistic relationship of "sincere friendship" and "disinterested aid."

Vospitanie in the sense of ideological education had its curricular niche in the social sciences. Through the mid 1960s, international students were exempt from social science requirements, and the home governments occasionally insisted on barring their students from these classes as a condition of educational exchange. Vietnamese students, for example, were not permitted to take Marxism-Leninism, political economy or even the general introduction to the Soviet Union and its history offered in many preparatory faculties. Their exemption rankled; at a number of campuses, social science instructors were told to devote extra hours to "individual work" with the Vietnamese students, and occasionally the students were drawn into Marxism-Leninism "study circles," led by social science instructors, that were virtually indistinguishable from a formal class.[33] At the People's Friendship University, instructors found that Indian students (also subject to a prohibition in the 1960s) were afraid to attend lecture courses in the social sciences lest someone from the embassy scrutinize a photograph of the class, but could be persuaded to attend seminars.[34] Kiev State University worked a lecture cycle on Marxism-Leninism and the history of the Communist Party of the Soviet Union (CPSU) into its geology courses, and was planning to expand this practice to other science departments.[35] In May 1965, after two years of discussion in the Ministry of Higher Education, the need to activate social science departments in the political education and *vospitanie* of foreign students was the centerpiece of a joint CPSU Central Committee/Council of Ministers decree.[36] Foreign students lost their exemption from the "History of the CPSU" sequence, which Tobias Rupprecht's otherwise nostalgic interview subjects remember as "really doctrinaire,"[37] and by the late 1960s, even Vietnamese students had to sit through Marxism-Leninism and political economy, though they usually kept their political views to themselves.[38]

Perhaps because of students' tepid response to the standard social science offerings, educators developed a number of more attractive means of integrating politics into foreign students' education. These included standing seminars on "The Soviet Union and New Africa" and "Latin America," which took place across the USSR. Led by area specialists and social science professors, these seminars relied on a curriculum and discussion questions developed centrally at Minvuz. International students, particularly if they were on the left, reportedly enjoyed the opportunity to discuss the current politics of their continent in a relatively freewheeling setting.[39] The seminars also sponsored essay competitions for student research on the continents in question, which encouraged projects in the Soviet social scientific mold. Winning essays in the first annual competition sponsored by the Africa seminar included three essays by African students as well as nine by Soviet students, with titles along the lines of "Objective possibilities of non-capitalist development of African countries."[40]

Both under the aegis of the standing seminars and more generally, essay competitions were among educators' favorite vehicles for enticing international students into social science programs. Outstanding students in any major could be encouraged to research an aspect of their home country, but in the process they were obliged to work under the supervision of a social science instructor and to frame their research problems with the instructor's guidance, often in relation to a competition or conference theme. The best essays were then showcased in university-wide conferences of student social scientific research, with a chance of further selection to participate in a conference at the republican or even all-Union level. At BGU, considerable effort was put into attracting international student participation in these competitions and conferences during the late 1960s and 1970s. For example, in 1969, in connection with the Lenin centenary, higher education officials specifically chose the conference theme "V. I. Lenin—leader of working people of the whole world" so as to encourage international student participation, and the BGU administrators were gratified with international students' response. Five international students' papers, on such topics as "Lenin and the revolution in Vietnam" and "V. I. Lenin on the role of the people in history," were selected as part of the BGU delegation to the Belorussian republican conference of student scientific research.[41] This Olympiad format, so successful in the math and science context, was perceived by administrators as a powerful motivational device for the social sciences. Not incidentally, it married traditional academic skills of research, writing and analysis, as well as originality, to the Soviet ideological program.

Conclusion

By the 1970s, work with international students was integrated into the academic structure and governance of Soviet universities and institutes to an impressive degree. Faculty, staff, administration and the Soviet student body all recognized the special needs of international students from developing countries, and the "internationalist duty" to assist them was translated into programmatic and pedagogical accommodations, the mandatory inclusion of international students in various campus councils and activities, and a lot of campus discussion. The fact that this discussion was organized from above and was framed in terms of "tasks" of "academic, ideological-political, and *vospitatel'naia* work," not to mention the fact that university administrators might have preferred not to deal with Third World students at all, did not negate the successes of Soviet educational institutions in promoting international students' academic progress and integration into campus life.

Academic instruction was clearly intertwined with character formation and ideology at Soviet *vuzy*. This did not distinguish educational goals for foreign students from the overarching mission of Soviet higher education, but international students' backgrounds, language constraints and divergent academic requirements caused educators to come up with distinctive techniques for shaping students' personalities and worldviews.

Julie Hessler is Associate Professor of History at University of Oregon. She is the author of *A Social History of Soviet Trade: Trade Policy, Retail*

Practices, and Consumption, 1917–1953 (Princeton University Press, 2004) and, with Robert O. Paxton, *Europe in the Twentieth Century*, 5ᵗʰ edn (Cengage, 2010). Her current research focuses on Soviet cultural engagement with developing countries in Asia, Africa, Latin America and the Middle East. Her research to date has focused on educational exchanges involving Third World students at Soviet universities, and the development of social scientific expertise on the Third World at Soviet universities and research institutes.

Notes

1. Tobias Rupprecht, *Soviet Internationalism after Stalin: Interaction and Exchange between the USSR and Latin America during the Cold War* (Cambridge: Cambridge University Press, 2015); David C. Engerman, "The Second World's Third World," *Kritika: Explorations in Russian and Eurasian History* 12(1) (2011): 183–211; Maxim Matusevich, *No Easy Row for a Russian Hoe: Ideology and Pragmatism in Nigerian-Soviet Relations, 1960–1991* (Trenton: Africa World Press, 2003).
2. Rupprecht, *Soviet Internationalism*, 227.
3. Ibid., 209. For critical allegations, see Aclan Sayilgan, *Education of Foreign Revolutionaries in the USSR: Comintern Schools to Lumumba University* (Ankara: Baylan Press, 1973). For a refutation, see Dmitri Bilibin, *Foreign Students in the USSR* (Moscow: Novosti, 1984), 21, 72; Nikita Khrushchev, 17 November 1960 speech, *Pravda*, 18 November 1960, p. 1.
4. George Avis (ed.), *The Making of the Soviet Citizen: Character Formation and Civic Training in Soviet Education* (London: Croom Helm, 1987).
5. Variations of this phrase appear in several places, e.g. Russian State Archive for Social-Political History (RGASPI), 3ʳᵈ repository (the Komsomol, or VLKSM) (henceforth RGASPI/VLKSM), f. 1, op. 39, d. 233, ll. 13–14.
6. Constantin Katsakioris, "Soviet Lessons for Arab Modernization: Soviet Educational Aid to Arab Countries after 1956," *Journal of Modern European History* 8(1) (2010): 85–106.
7. Julie Hessler, "Death of an African Student in Moscow: Race, Politics, and the Third World," *Cahiers du Monde russe* 47(1) (2006): 33–64.
8. Dmitri Bilibin, *Foreign Students in the USSR* (Moscow: Novosti, 1984), 6–10.
9. Katsakioris, "Soviet Lessons," 96.
10. RGASPI/VLKSM, f. 1, op. 46, d. 407s, l. 8. In 1966 alone, Cambodia, Algeria, Ceylon, Zambia, Morocco, Niger, Rwanda and Guinea discontinued sending students to the USSR; see Natalia Tsvetkova, "International Education During the Cold War: Soviet Social Transformation and American Social Reproduction," *Comparative Education Review* 52(2) (2008): 199–217, at 212; Rupprecht, *Soviet Internationalism*, 196; Katsakioris, "Soviet Lessons," 95.
11. Katsakioris, "Soviet Lessons," 95.
12. Bilibin, *Foreign Students*, 19.

13. List of languages from Kiev State University, RGASPI/VLKSM, f. 1, op. 39, d. 387, l. 140.
14. National Archive of the Republic of Belarus (henceforth NARB), f. 1445 (Komitet Molodezhnykh Organizatsii, henceforth KMO), op. 1, d. 31, l. 1.
15. *Narodnoe obrazovanie, nauka i kul'tura v SSSR. Statisticheskii sbornik x* (Moscow: Statistika, 1971), 158; Bilibin, *Foreign Students*, 25.
16. NARB f. 205, op. 8, d. 1025, l. 19 (data from 1968).
17. Rupprecht, *Soviet Internationalism*, 198–204, as well as RGASPI/VLKSM, f. 1, op. 46, d. 294, ll. 102–11; op. 39, d. 233, l. 3.
18. NARB f. 205 (BGU), op. 8, d. 1025, ll. 38–39.
19. NARB f. 1445 (KMO), op. 1, d. 31, l. 16.
20. L.D. Vasil'eva, citing Polish sources, listed figures of 340 Polish students in the USSR in 1972, rising to 2,300 in 1975: L.D. Vasil'eva, *Sovetsko-pol'skoe sotrudnichestvo v oblasti nauki i vysshego obrazovaniia, 1945–1975* (Kiev: Naukova dumka, 1981), 55.
21. State Archive of the Russian Federation (henceforth GARF) f. 9606 (Minvuz USSR), op. 1, d. 1532, l. 4 (report from Kiev GU).
22. NARB f. 1220 (Minvuz BSSR), op. 2, d. 139, ll. 2–10.
23. RGASPI /VLKSM, f. 1, op. 39, d. 280, l. 54.
24. Exactly which employer might use these references is unclear. International students' visas expired upon graduation, and relatively few were able to stay on to work in the USSR. An obvious target was Soviet-run projects in the home country. For a series of attestations from the Belorussian Polytechnical Institute, see NARB f. 1220 (Minvuz BSSR), op. 2, d. 885.
25. Ibid., ll. 20–21, 23–24.
26. Ibid., 20–21, 23–24, 126.
27. Hessler, "Death of an African Student," 59–60.
28. NARB f. 205 (BGU), op. 8, d. 2136 (1979–80 academic year), e.g. 51–52. *Vospitatel'naia rabota* was one of six categories in which instructors were evaluated, along with scholarship, teaching, other pedagogical work, efforts to raise their qualifications and civic activity/service.
29. Ibid., ll. 3, 12–13, 83.
30. Ibid., 77–83, 109–11.
31. Ibid., 14.
32. NARB f. 205 (BGU), op. 8, d. 320, l. 79.
33. NARB f. 205 (BGU), op. 8, d. 320, ll. 96–97; see also RGASPI/VLKSM, f. 1, op. 39, d. 231, ll. 16–24.
34. Indian students were likewise prohibited by their government from taking social science courses in the early 1960s. GARF f. 9606 (Minvuz SSSR), op. 1, d. 1532, l. 80.
35. GARF f. 9606 (Minvuz SSSR), op. 1, d. 1532, ll. 4–6 (stenogram of an October 1963 conference at Minvuz on strengthening the role of social science departments in the *ideino-vospitatel'naia rabota* with foreign students); ibid., op. 2, d. 135, ll. 63–73.
36. Cited in NARB f. 205 (BGU), op. 8, d. 320, ll. 96–97; also referenced in RGASPI/VLKSM f. 1, op. 39, d. 233, l. 7.
37. Rupprecht, *Soviet Internationalism*, 209.

38. RGASPI/VLKSM f. 1, op. 39, d. 281b, ll. 15–21; d. 284, l. 10; op. 39, d. 134, l. 11 says that the Vietnamese government began allowing Vietnamese students to take Soviet social science courses in 1967.
39. RGASPI/VLKSM f. 1, op. 39, d. 394, l. 144; d. 395, l. 21; d. 399 (on Latin American standing seminar); d. 400 (on African seminar).
40. Ibid., d. 400, ll. 26–27.
41. NARB f. 205, op. 8, d. 1025, ll. 3–9.

References

Avis, George (ed.). *The Making of the Soviet Citizen: Character Formation and Civic Training in Soviet Education* (London: Croom Helm, 1987).
Bilibin, Dmitri. *Foreign Students in the USSR* (Moscow: Novosti, 1984).
Engerman, David C. "The Second World's Third World," *Kritika: Explorations in Russian and Eurasian History* 12(1) (2011): 183–211.
Hessler, Julie. "Death of an African Student in Moscow: Race, Politics, and the Third World," *Cahiers du Monde russe* 47(1) (2006): 33–64.
Katsakioris, Constantin. "Soviet Lessons for Arab Modernization: Soviet Educational Aid to Arab Countries after 1956," *Journal of Modern European History* 8(1) (2010): 85–106.
Matusevich, Maxim. *No Easy Row for a Russian Hoe: Ideology and Pragmatism in Nigerian-Soviet Relations, 1960–1991* (Trenton, NJ: Africa World Press, 2003).
Narodnoe obrazovanie, nauka i kul'tura v SSSR. Statisticheskii sbornik (Moscow: Statistika, 1971).
Rupprecht, Tobias. *Soviet Internationalism after Stalin: Interaction and Exchange between the USSR and Latin America during the Cold War* (Cambridge: Cambridge University Press, 2015).
Sayilgan, Aclan. *Education of Foreign Revolutionaries in the USSR: Comintern Schools to Lumumba University* (Ankara: Baylan Press, 1973).
Tsvetkova, Natalia. "International Education During the Cold War: Soviet Social Transformation and American Social Reproduction," *Comparative Education Review* 52(2) (2008): 199–217.
Vasil'eva, L.D. *Sovetsko-pol'skoe sotrudnichestvo v oblasti nauki i vysshego obrazovaniia, 1945–1975* (Kiev: Naukova dumka, 1981).

 13

US EXCHANGE PROGRAMS WITH AFRICA DURING THE CIVIL RIGHTS ERA

Hannah Higgin

Introduction

The creation of the Bureau of Educational and Cultural Exchange (CU) in 1959 as part of the American Department of State was concurrent, not coincidentally, with African decolonization and the rapid, pursuant proliferation of African students in the United States in the late 1950s and early 1960s. Though the onset of the Cold War led the US government to increase its support for foreigners studying and training in America, it took over a decade before a distinct bureau carried out Washington's scholarship programs.[1] Similarly, though the Cold War brought greater American attention to Africa than had existed before, Washington's involvement in the region increased as more nations became independent or moved toward independence. This process began in 1957 with Ghana and reached a crescendo in 1960—the Year of Africa—in which seventeen nations became independent.

Washington's approach to Africa was pragmatic. Cold War exigencies led the US government to combine idealism and notions of global responsibility related to faith in American exceptionalism with more traditional concerns about economic and strategic self-interest. As a result, the US government avoided long-term commitments, cost, risk and responsibilities whenever possible, preferring to leave Africa to its allies. Washington was easily distracted when crises emerged elsewhere and its relations with Africa were primarily shaped by incidents outside Africa, especially those related to domestic affairs and Cold War events.[2] As an ambassador who served in Zambia in the mid 1960s half-joked, "only Antarctica was less important."[3] Many government insiders had parallel views of the CU, characterizing it as the "slum area of US foreign policy," the "pasture for old horses" and "the graveyard of incompetents."[4]

Concerns over potential power vacuums in decolonized Africa heightened fears in the American foreign policy establishment that the continent constituted a new theater ripe for Cold War conflict. This, combined with Kennedy's genuine interest in Africa, elevated the importance of the long-neglected region.[5] Independence also transformed exchangees into "multipliers" who would contribute "to the development and progress of [their] country and as ... potential leaders in its international and domestic activities."[6]

The transformation of Africans—by no means new to America— into multipliers elevated the importance of scholarship programs. Washington feared losing Africans seeking a university education to the Soviet Bloc, which was also looking to win influence in independent Africa. Moscow pointedly renamed People's Friendship University, founded in 1960, Lumumba University in early 1961 after the Congolese independence leader.[7] By 1962, Lumumba University provided scholarships and what the US Ambassador to Guinea at the time called "intensive indoctrination" to 3,000 students from Africa.[8] However, Africans, facing poor conditions and racist hostilities, began defecting from the Soviet Bloc in 1962.[9] The experiences of one Kenyan student encapsulated this tug-of-war. After a year at Harvard, he defected to the Soviet Union and, finding it worse, returned to Harvard, graduating in 1962.[10]

The issue of winning the allegiance of African youth played a vital role in the official extension of Washington's concern beyond students sponsored by the US government. In 1961, President Kennedy told his Secretary of State that students—not least Africans and Asians— could not leave America "disappointed any longer."[11] Through the end of the decade, the government continued to identify American race relations as African trainees' biggest concern.[12] "Probably every African visiting the United States," as a 1960 pamphlet on hosting African students put it, "encounter[ed] discrimination in one form or another."[13] In 1960, a total of 1,165 African students studied at US colleges and universities—nearly four times more than the number that had done so a decade earlier.[14] By early 1967, approximately 9,000 African students studied in America.[15] Once Africans became multipliers, discrimination perpetrated against one had the potential to reverberate exponentially.

Becoming Multipliers

In 1950, when 410 Africans studied in America at over 300 colleges,[16] only six black Kenyans had ever received a higher education at all. Though Britain was relatively less hostile than other metropoles toward American influence, black Africans from British colonies seeking an American education met staunch resistance from colonial officials through the 1950s. Communism provided a tidy justification. It was preferable, a 1949 editorial in the influential *East Africa Standard* declared, for "a few Africans to be deprived of education than to risk that some of them would 'return to spread evil doctrines and unrest among ignorant elements in the population.'"[17]

The few native Kenyans who did manage to study in America in the early 1950s circumvented the traditional route in doing so, including R. Mugo Gatheru, born the son of tribal leaders and squatters on settler land in 1925. Though he secured the sponsorship of a respected black sociologist to study in America, colonial officials denied his visa request. It was only by moving to India and then to London over the course of years that he was finally able to secure an American student visa.

In late September 1952, the "shadow of the Mau Mau" that preceded British decolonization in Kenya coalesced with American anticommunist fears. Gatheru was then an undergraduate at Lincoln University, where other notable British Africans, including Azikiwe and Nkrumah, the first Presidents of Nigeria and Ghana, studied before him in 1930 and 1935, respectively. The Justice Department claimed they had confidential information that made Gatheru deportable. His American supporters linked the charges against him to McCarthyism; Gatheru assumed that his problems stemmed from the British Colonial Office. With Kenya in "the midst of a bloody civil war," deportation would do more than cut short an education. As a Kikuyu, "the most talked about people in Africa," thanks to headlines about those who led the Mau Mau uprising, Gatheru was sure that he would "be thrown into a concentration camp immediately" if he returned to Kenya before the end of the crisis.[18]

By the end of 1952, Gatheru's case was national news.[19] NAACP chief counsel and Lincoln alumnus Thurgood Marshall—who successfully argued *Brown v. Board* before the Supreme Court shortly after Gatheru's interrogation—enquired on Gatheru's behalf at the Justice Department.[20] The NAACP maintained their interest in the case, with the organization's head discussing the suit with Attorney General Brownell, against whom the suit was lodged in 1954. Shortly thereafter Brownell famously expressed his view that *Plessy v. Ferguson* was wrongly decided in his *amicus curiae* at the re-argument of *Brown v. Board*.[21]

Brownell's office did not agree to drop its attempts to strip Gatheru of his visa until summer 1957.[22] Circumstance, rather than five years of fighting, likely won the day: the decision coincided with Ghanaian independence. On the condition that he dropped his suit, Gatheru continued his education and spent his career as a professor of African and Middle-Eastern History at Sacramento State College.[23]

Indicative of the growing importance of Africa by 1960, President Eisenhower—who did not continue Truman's tradition of meeting groups of foreign trainees in America supported by the American aid apparatus—personally met with and feted the man that the White House deemed the government's aid agency's 50,000th visitor program trainee. Not coincidentally, given that trainees arrived in groups and were therefore not assigned a particular number, the selected trainee whose meeting with the President received wide press coverage was a resident of the African country to which Washington pinned its highest hopes. Mr Akinremi Akapo, a forty-eight-year-old senior social development officer from Lagos, Nigeria, was on a six-month program in community development at the University of California's Institute of International Studies.[24] Unlike Eisenhower, Kennedy valued and personally courted black African favor. Kennedy revived Truman's tradition, hosting a dozen foreign students from eleven different countries on the White House lawn in late 1962. Alluding to the many opportunities and successes that lay before them, Kennedy mentioned that Nkrumah had studied at Lincoln.[25]

In 1961, when all foreign student welfare first fell under the CU's purview, at least 2,500 African students studied in the United States.[26] A 1961 survey revealed that African students "expected to find racial discrimination in the South, and did, but many were shocked to find it in the northern states as well."[27] Such realities threatened to betray Washington's carefully honed narrative that racial discrimination was relegated primarily to the South.

One case of discrimination in the north in 1962 had serious potential national security implications. The eldest son of Nigeria's then-Governor General Nnamdi Azikiwe, Chukwuma threatened to sue the city of Cambridge and the State of Massachusetts over alleged police discrimination and mistreatment. Over the course of the following weeks, State Department officials endeavored to gather the whole story and to convince Chukwuma not to file suit, while preventing the matter from becoming public.[28]

Though the officer in charge on the night of Chukwuma's arrest admitted overzealousness by the arresting officers, he balked at the accusation of racist motives. It was 2 am, they were pursuing a black rapist and Chukwuma was slow to explain himself or produce identification. Regardless of motivation, if the incident and its northern locale became public, it would "immeasurably compound [the] problem," according to the American Ambassador in Nigeria: racial discrimination was "hard enough [to] explain" to disgusted foreign and domestic observers when it occurred the South, where segregation was still the law.[29]

Concern over a potential international backlash was serious enough for National Security Advisor McGeorge Bundy to weigh in. The former Harvard dean discounted racial discrimination as the cause of any mistreatment. He echoed Harvard officials, suggesting that if the State Department had to weigh in, it could cite the "ancient and honored tradition" of "bad relations between the Cambridge police and the students of Harvard," which had "nothing to do with race, creed or color." Undermining this argument, however, was the fact that all agreed that "police treatment [of Chukwuma was] courteous" only after he produced his student identification. Chukwuma, who reported having defended "himself against violent assault by [a] policeman" in Cambridge "several months" earlier, believed that police action against him was racially motivated.[30]

The State Department and Governor General Azikiwe quietly settled the matter, to mutual benefit. Like those at the State Department, Azikiwe hoped the incident would "not receive publicity." News of the incident reached Azikiwe while he was quelling discontent in his home region, also the home of the first American-style university in Africa, which had just opened and was supported by Washington.[31] Further, the interuniversity African Scholarship Program of American Universities (ASPAU), which sought to meet urgent African needs for undergraduate training, founded by Harvard's David Henry in 1959—the same year that Chukwuma started there—in cooperation with the Nigerian government, was partially funded by Washington. By 1962, the ASPAU linked twenty-four African countries with 213 American universities.[32] Azikiwe expressed "warm appreciation" of the State Department's effort in the early summer of 1962, and reminded his son that he was a guest in America. Admonishing Chukwuma "not to do anything that would mar good relationships between [the] US and Nigeria," Azikiwe advised his son to "look at [the] incident in perspective of all [the] hospitality and advantages which he has received from [the] American people."[33] By 1967, the ASPAU brought 1,300 Africans from thirty-three nations to the United States and sent them to 232 universities.[34] The widespread perception that American racism was primarily a problem relegated to the American South, though weakened by northern urban unrest in the later 1960s, persisted.

American Racism: Not So Black and White

Regardless of where in the country Africans were, their presence in America highlighted the paradox that perceptions of "blackness" in American racial constructs went beyond skin color. Though African visitors often faced discrimination similar to that experienced by black Americans, foreign passports could elicit superior treatment.[35] On a summer tour of America, an undergraduate from 1959 to 1961 at Macalester University in St. Paul, Minnesota, the Ghanaian Kofi Annan—Secretary General of the United Nations from 1997 to 2006— informed a barber who refused to "cut niggers' hair," "I'm not a nigger. I'm from Africa." It worked; the barber cut his hair. Annan, like many educated West Africans—who saw their struggle for independence as against the British, not "whites"—"tended to look on the racial problems of the United States more with scholarly curiosity than personal anger."[36] To Annan, and apparently to the bigoted barber he encountered, he was African, not black.

The relationship between Black American and African students was not an easy one either. The American press widely reported that a 1961 survey found that 63 percent of African students had trouble getting along with black Americans, with 38 percent reporting they had no black American friends. These students commonly suggested that black Americans caused this divide.[37] Africans noted that black Americans were unfriendly and deemed themselves superior to Africans by virtue of coming from "civilization" rather than "the jungle." Likewise, some black Africans identified with black Americans, while others discriminated against them, affording lowly status to the "descendants of slaves."

Many African students attended historically black universities before, during and after the 1960s. Lincoln University—the alma mater of Nkrumah, Azikiwe and Gatheru, as well as Thurgood Marshall and Langston Hughes—was one such institution. Between 1954 and 1962, 120 African students from fourteen countries studied there. In 1962, 15 percent of Lincoln's 400 students were foreign, coming predominantly from Africa and the West Indies.[38] With longstanding ties to Africa, Lincoln also served as an orientation center for Washington-supported students.³⁹ Many Washington policymakers believed that Lincoln, located in Oxford, Pennsylvania, was "ideal" for orienting Africans to America because of its non-urban environment and because, some assumed, it would be easier for African students "to make their initial adjustments to academic routine in a negro men's school where they did not have the added burden of adjusting to a multitude of daily inter-racial situations."⁴⁰ When students were deemed sufficiently accustomed to American culture and its educational system and were "ready to move into the American academic community," they were, the deputy director of the CU's Africa programs explained, sent on to other colleges across the United States.⁴¹ The notion that surrounding African exchangees with dark-skinned peers would ease adjustment reveals a major misunderstanding of cultural divides and constructs surrounding race.

A 1964 CU report acknowledged that the reality of Africans studying at an all-black university were "considerably more obscure." Reports of isolation on campus and in the wider community pervaded the thirty-six interviews on which the report was based. Those interviewed spoke about the lack of initiative that black Americans took "to establish relationships with the Africans," a "quite active dislike" of Africans and a "cultural bar" that divided the two groups into "two different worlds." American classmates reportedly only invited "very few" of their African classmates—different in culture, language and understanding of race—home during vacations.⁴²

Invitations to stay in the homes of Americans in segregated and nonsegregated communities alike, initially championed by Eisenhower in his People-to-People initiative, were believed to help deepen intercultural understanding. Homestays proved very effective in the cases of two future African luminaries who studied at predominantly white institutions in the 1960s. Kofi Annan was pleased by the generosity of some white Americans, including that of his friend Susan Linnee and her parents. One evening, when Linnee's parents were away from their home in a Minneapolis suburb, a neighbor saw Annan and reported a strange black man to the police. Upon learning what happened, the Linnees pointedly invited Annan and his roommate to dinner and, when they "showed up in their jalopy, a pink Studebaker, Susan's parents stepped out onto the porch so all neighbors could see them greeting Annan in the waning daylight."⁴³ Kenyan Wangari Muta Maathai, winner of a 2004 Nobel Peace Prize and part of the African Airlift of 1960, recounted being "impressed by [the] generosity" of American families to the African students at Mount St. Scholastica College in segregated Atchison, Kansas. During college breaks she had a "second home" with the family of her lifelong friend Florence Conrad Salisbury, a white girl from Wichita. She reported never "being homesick or lonely," even "at a time when there was so much conflict between the races in the United States."

Maathai nevertheless saw racial violence on TV and took an interest in the Civil Rights Movement. She noted in her memoir: "An African had to go to America to understand slavery and its impact on black people ... It is in America that words such as 'black,' 'white,' 'Negro,' 'mulatto,' 'skin color,' 'segregation,' 'discrimination,' and 'the ghetto' take on lives on their own." She often wondered why black Americans were treated as harshly as she had "witnessed in Kenya as the British attempted to crush the Mau Mau movement." Britain was a colonial power, but America was supposed to be "the land of the free and the home of the brave."[44]

African Exchangees and American Civil Rights

In 1963, the national press covered the first black student to be accepted to Mercer University, a previously all-white Baptist institution in Macon, Georgia.[45] Ghanaian Sam Oni's acceptance to Mercer was no accident: the quiet machinations of liberal alumni and, even more discreetly, University President Rufus C. Harris, led to his admission.[46] Seeking to avoid anything remotely resembling the bloody battle to desegregate the University of Alabama, Mercer admitted Oni not as a Negro, but as a foreign student. This, according to an editorial in the *Christian Index*, published by the powerful Georgia Baptist Convention, would not signify a change in "conditions ... but a slight change [of] hearts." Cold War concerns were also cited.[47] Recent events exacerbated the already-common clash between segregationist beliefs and the Cold War imperative of fostering ties with Africans. Just one week before reporting on Oni, the *New York Times* reported that students from Ghana and Guinea withdrew from Soviet Bloc universities because of discrimination.[48]

Oni knew that many were against his admission. He was well read on everything from Emmett Till's murder to Rosa Parks' refusal to yield her seat, to the admission of Autherine Lucy and James Meredith to the University of Alabama in 1956 and the University of Mississippi in 1962, respectively. He also knew that three months before he arrived at Mercer, segregationists murdered Civil Rights activist and NAACP Field Secretary Medgar Evers. All these events were reported in African newspapers.[49] Though he knew he "was going to be the first black face on campus," Oni later recalled it was "quite another thing to actually have the experience."[50]

Despite a special committee's recommendation that "Mercer University consider all applicants for admission based on qualifications, without regard to race, color of skin, creed or origin," committee members remained deeply concerned about thwarting any further integration. Though two black locals also started as students in 1963, of the 2,000 students at Mercer, Oni was the only black student who lived on campus.

The others were "carefully screened" to make sure they did not "represent any organization or any concerted drive for the integration of the university."[51] As a foreigner, the committee assumed that Oni had too few local connections to agitate for further integration. However, the committee did not know—though the missionary alumni who championed Oni's acceptance did—that Oni was dismissed from secondary school for organizing a two-day student protest against the imperial exam system and the dearth of African teachers. The committee members had more prosaic concerns: the integration of bathrooms and cafeterias. They also advised that the dean discourage Oni from having visitors in the dorm, lest he befriend local blacks.

Not surprisingly, Oni faced discrimination. Though he later played down the seriousness of his day-to-day alienation, he found one incident "very jarring, very harrowing, and very stressing." The pastor of the church located on campus sought out the very religious student, speaking to him in his dorm room. "I've come to let you know," the pastor stated frankly, "that you won't be welcome to worship in my church on Sunday."[52]

Oni instead worshipped a bus ride away. "We are very honored today to have among us a young man who came to us through our own missionary efforts," the pastor remarked before being interrupted by a belligerent parishioner. "I'm not going to sit here and watch you destroy this church by bringing niggers into this congregation," the man proclaimed, rising to his feet, soon to be joined by others. The matter, called to a vote, was finally settled after multiple counts, with a clear majority favoring Oni's membership.[53] The so-called "quiet desegregation" of Vineville Baptist Church made national headlines.[54]

Oni was not alone in his challenge to find a church despite missionary ties. A Congolese student at Berea College in Kentucky was turned away from the Baptist church nearest the campus. Dejected, he told the college president that everyone in his tribe knew where he was and was deeply interested in what happened to him. "We have all been converted to Christianity by Southern Baptist missionaries," he continued. "If I write home that the son of a chief has been turned away from a Southern Baptist church, I can't answer for the lives of the missionaries."[55] Similarly, though American Nazarene missionaries were active in southern Africa, Swazi Peace Corps training staffers in Louisiana at the end of the 1960s were turned away from the local Nazarene church.[56]

After three years of living with the "nonsense of segregation," Oni returned to the national news. In 1966, ushers forcibly removed him from the church on Mercer's campus and handed him to the police. When he returned the following week, a false bomb threat led to an evacuation. That day, he told reporters he "made his point" and would not try again.[57] The congregation, which swelled by a hundred parishioners during the controversy, clarified their point by firing the pastor and his assistants who preached integration.[58] The discrimination that Oni faced, though not as pervasive as that faced by local blacks, remained bad enough that when he graduated he "vowed never to step foot on ... Southern soil again."[59]

Conclusion

Washington recognized that foreign students would learn about American racial disparities and discrimination when studying in the United States, and that nonwhites would likely grapple with inequalities. Racial realities posed a clear threat to keeping and winning Cold War allies. Nevertheless, the predominantly one-way flow of exchange with Africa boomed during the 1960s, including that backed by direct government support. As more African students arrived with the rapid decolonization of the early 1960s, Washington extended its oversight beyond those with government sponsorship to all foreign students. Such support, however, was weak and traditional problems of racial discrimination persisted. Ultimately, as with America's wider Africa policy and CU programs in general, the handling of African students in the United States by Washington was pragmatic and piecemeal.

White Americans puzzled over why black Africans and black Americans did not necessarily mesh, while also extending Africans a "foreigner privilege" not afforded to black Americans. Though important relations existed between black Americans and Africans, such ties were far from universal.[60] Race was a construct, mutable. Ultimately, experiences of African exchangees in America during the height of the Civil Rights Movement reaffirmed the persistence of the so-called

"Negro problem" famously pinpointed by Gunnar Myrdal. It remained a specifically American dilemma.

Hannah Higgin earned her Ph.D. from the University of Cambridge in 2015. She teaches American history and the history of Western civilization at Blair Academy. Three of her articles appear in *Scribner's Dictionary of American History, Supplement: America in the World, 1776 to the Present* (Charles Scribner's Sons, 2015). She has received numerous research grants, from the Harry S. Truman Presidential Library, the Dwight D. Eisenhower Foundation, the John F. Kennedy Presidential Library and Museum, and the Lyndon Baines Johnson Foundation, among others. She is currently working on a monograph based on her dissertation, *Disseminating American Ideals in Africa, 1949–1969*.

Notes

1. J. Manuel Espinosa, *Landmark Events in the History of CU: 1938 to 1973* (Washington, DC: CU, 1973); Randolph Wieck, *Ignorance Abroad* (Westport, CT: Praeger, 1992), 124.
2. Waldemar Nielsen, *The Great Powers & Africa* (New York: Council on Foreign Relations, 1969), 231–33.
3. John Seiler, *US Foreign Policy toward Southern Africa* (Johannesburg: Southern African Institute of International Affairs, 1973), 1.
4. Wieck, *Ignorance*, 1.
5. Philip Muehlenbeck, *Betting on the Africans* (Oxford: Oxford University Press, 2013); Thomas Noer, "New Frontiers and Old Priorities in Africa," in Thomas Patterson (ed.), *Kennedy's Quest for Victory* (New York: Oxford University Press, 1989).
6. *The Agency for International Development During the Administration of Lyndon B Johnson, Volume I*, p. 628, folder Part III, Chapters XIV thru XVII, Administrative History, box 1, Lyndon B. Johnson Library (henceforth LBJL).
7. Jason Parker, "'Made-in-America Revolutions'? The 'Black University' and the American Role in the Decolonization of the Black Atlantic," *Journal of American History* 96(3) (2009): 743; Muehlenbeck, *Betting*, 77.
8. William Attwood, *The Reds and the Blacks* (London: Hutchinson & Co, 1967), 102.
9. Hannah Higgin, "Disseminating American Ideals in Africa, 1949–1969," Ph.D. dissertation (Cambridge: University of Cambridge, 2014), 224.
10. Robert Stephens, *Kenyan Student Airlifts to America, 1959–1961* (Nairobi: East African Education Publishers Ltd, 2013), 19.
11. John Kennedy, "Memorandum to the Secretary of State" (8 August 1961); Dean Rusk, "Foreign Students in the United States" (2 September 1961),

folder NSAM 66 Foreign Students in the United States, NSF box 133, John F. Kennedy Library (henceforth JFKL).
12. Brendan Jones, "Job Program Aids African Students," *New York Times*, 26 February 1967.
13. *African Students in the United States: A Guide for the Sponsors of Student Exchange Programs with Africa*, Committee on Educational Interchange Policy (December 1960), 15, folder Scholarships 1958–1960, Educational and Cultural Exchange, 1954–1961, State Department, James William Fulbright Papers, box 14, University of Arkansas.
14. "Educational and Cultural Exchange with Africa," *African Studies Bulletin* 4 (2) (1961): 1, folder EDX2 Africa: Educational and Cultural Exchange with Africa: The Program of the Department of State, 1961, CU, box 337, University of Arkansas.
15. Seth Spaulding and Michael Flack, *The World's Students in the United States* (New York: Praeger, 1976), 491.
16. "Bias Here Shocks African Students," *New York Times*, March 19, 1950.
17. R. Mugo Gatheru, *Child of Two Worlds* (London: Routledge & Kegan Paul, 1964), 119.
18. Ibid., xi, 161, 172–73, 177, 179.
19. "Student from Kenya Faces Ouster by US," *New York Times*, 5 December 1952.
20. Mary Dudziak, "Working toward Democracy: Thurgood Marshall and the Constitution of Kenya," *Duke Law Journal* 56 (3) (2006): 730.
21. James Meriwether, "African Americans and the Mau Mau Rebellion," *Journal of American Ethnic History* 17(4) (1998): 70–71; Gatheru, *Child*, xi; Herbert Brownell, "Eisenhower's Civil Rights Program: A Personal Assessment," *Presidential Studies Quarterly* 21(2) (1991), 236–37.
22. Gatheru, *Child*, 182–83.
23. Evan Mwangi, "A Tribute to Mugo Gatheru," *Daily Nation* (Nairobi), 11 December 2011.
24. "Personal Data on the 50,000th ICA Participant—Akinremi Akapo," (22 January 1960) in folder Africa, White House Office, Office for the Special Assistant for National Security Affairs, Operations Coordinating Board Series, Subject Subseries, box 1, Dwight D. Eisenhower Library.
25. "12 Foreign Students Greeted by Kennedy," *New York Times*, 5 December 1962; G. Mennen Williams, "Letter to President Kennedy," 11 May 1961, folder White House, Corresp w/, Papers of G. Mennen Williams, box 7, University of Michigan.
26. "African Students: A Self-Portrait," *Milwaukee Journal*, 17 December 1961.
27. "African Students in US Harassed But Serious," *Milwaukee Sentinel*, 7 December 1961.
28. "Chukwuma Azikiwe" (8 June 1962), 1, folder Nigeria, General, Azikiwe Case 5/24/62- 6/30/62, National Security Files, Countries, box 144, JFKL.
29. Joseph Palmer II, "Telegram to Secretary of State," Lagos (22 May 1962), folder Nigeria, General, Azikiwe Case 5/24/62- 6/30/62, NSF, Countries, box 144, JFKL.

30. McGeorge Bundy, "Memorandum for G. Mennen Williams" (24 May 1962); Dean Rusk, "Telegram to US Embassy in Lagos," Department of State (May 1962); "Chukwuma Azikiwe" (8 June 1962), 3; Joseph Palmer II, "Telegram to Secretary of State," Lagos (22 May 1962), folder Nigeria, General, Azikiwe Case 5/24/62- 6/30/62, NSF, Countries, box 144, JFKL.
31. Joseph Palmer II, "Telegram to Secretary of State," Lagos (22 May 1962; 31 May 1962; and 1 June 1962), folder Nigeria, General, Azikiwe Case 5/24/62- 6/30/62, NSF, Countries, box 144, JFKL; "University of Nigeria, Nsukka"; Nnamdi Azikiwe, "Heroes and Heroines of New Africa," *Nigerian-American Quarterly*, United States Information Service (February–March 1961), folder 119, box 194, University of Nigeria Program, Michigan State University.
32. "Straight-A Africans," *Time*, 21 December 1962.
33. "Telegram from Lagos to Secretary of State," 21 June 1962, folder Nigeria, General, Azikiwe Case 5/24/62- 6/30/62, NSF, Countries, box 144, JFKL.
34. *Proposed Economic Assistance Programs FY 1967* (March 1966), folder Miscellaneous Loose Material, Office Files of Bill Moyers, box 80, LBJL.
35. "Africans Find Negroes Cool," *Milwaukee Journal*, 6 December 1961.
36. Stanley Meisler, *Kofi Annan* (Hoboken, NJ: John Wiley & Sons, 2008), 20.
37. "African Students in US Harassed But Serious"; "Africans Find Negroes Cool"; "African Students: A Self-Portrait"; "African Students Hit US Lack of Negro Tolerance," *Modesto Bee*, 7 December 1961.
38. "Lincoln U Maintains Leadership Tradition," *African Students' Outlook on America*, United States Information Service, Accra (November 1962), A, folder Centers, Africa, 1954–1991, RG 306 United States Information Agency, A1 (1066) Historical Subject Collection, box 209, National Archives, College Park, Md.
39. Higgin, "Disseminating," 248.
40. John Seiler, *Southern African Students in the United States*, CU (18 September 1964), 52–53, folder Sieler, John: Southern African Students in the United States, 1964, CU box 326, University of Arkansas.
41. Ambassador William B Jones Oral History (24 June 2010), Foreign Affairs Oral History Project, Association for Diplomatic Study and Training.
42. Seiler, *Southern*, 52–54.
43. Meisler, *Kofi Annan*, 20.
44. Wangari Muta Maathai, *Unbowed* (London: William Heinemann, 2007), 78–79, 84–86; "Compare US with Africa," *Atchison Daily Globe*, 26 October 1960.
45. Claude Sitton, "University in South May Admit African as a 'Foreign' Student," *New York Times*, 22 February 1963; "Ghanaian Applies in Georgia," *New York Times*, 23 February 1963; "Georgia College to Desegregate," *New York Times*, 19 April 1963.
46. Claude Sitton, "University in South"; *Fifth Annual Report of the United States Advisory Commission on International Educational and Cultural Affairs, July 1, 1966–June 30, 1967*, Washington, DC, folder Fifth Annual Report (2 of 4), CU, box 190, University of Arkansas; Will D. Campbell, *The Stem of Jesse* (Macon, GA: Mercer University Press, 2005), 80; Andrew Manis, *Macon Black and White* (Macon, GA: Mercer University Press, 2004), 222–32.

47. Claude Sitton, "University in South".
48. "Ghanaian Applies"; "African Students to Leave Bulgaria," *New York Times*, 15 February 1963.
49. Campbell, *Stem*, 79, 81.
50. Sam Oni Oral History (22 April 2009), Mercer University.
51. "Georgia College"; "3 Negroes Accepted by Georgia College," *New York Times*, 8 September 1963; "Mercer U. in Georgia Accepts 3 Negroes," *New York Times*, 17 September 1963; Campbell, *Stem*, 83–85.
52. Oni Oral History.
53. Ibid.; Manis, *Macon*, 227–28.
54. "Georgia Church Integrates by Accepting a Ghanaian," *New York Times*, 23 September 1963.
55. William Sloane Coffin, *Once to Every Man* (New York: Athenaeum, 1977), 145.
56. Chris Matthews, interview by author, 1 August 2012, NBC Studio (Washington, DC).
57. "Segregated Macon Church Evacuated in Bomb Threat," *New York Times*, 3 October 1966.
58. Manis, *Macon*, 230.
59. Oni Oral History
60. Paul Gilroy, *The Black Atlantic. Modernity and Double Consciousness* (Cambridge, MA: Harvard University Press, 1993); Brenda Gayle Plummer, *In Search of Power* (Cambridge: Cambridge University Press, 2013).

References

Attwood, William. *The Reds and the Blacks* (London: Hutchinson & Co, 1967).
Coffin, William Sloane. *Once to Every Man* (New York: Athenaeum, 1977).
Espinosa, J. Manuel. *Landmark Events in the History of CU: 1938 to 1973* (Washington, DC: CU, 1973).
Gatheru, R. Mugo. *Child of Two Worlds* (London: Routledge & Kegan Paul, 1964).
Gilroy, Paul. *The Black Atlantic: Modernity and Double Consciousness* (Cambridge, MA: Harvard University Press, 1993).
Jones, Brendan. "Job Program Aids African Students," *New York Times*, 26 February 1967.
Higgin, Hannah. "Disseminating American Ideals in Africa, 1949–1969," Ph.D. dissertation (Cambridge: University of Cambridge, 2014).
Maathai, Wangari Muta. *Unbowed* (London: William Heinemann, 2007).
Meisler, Stanley. *Kofi Annan* (Hoboken, NJ: John Wiley & Sons, 2008).
Meriwether, James. "African Americans and the Mau Mau Rebellion," *Journal of American Ethnic History* 17(4) (1998): 70–71.
Muehlenbeck, Philip. *Betting on the Africans* (Oxford: Oxford University Press, 2013).
Mwangi, Evan. "A Tribute to Mugo Gatheru," *Daily Nation* (Nairobi), 11 December 2011.

Nielsen, Waldemar. *The Great Powers & Africa* (New York: Council on Foreign Relations, 1969).
Noer, Thomas. "New Frontiers and Old Priorities in Africa," in Thomas Patterson (ed.), *Kennedy's Quest for Victory* (New York: Oxford University Press, 1989), pp. 253–83.
Parker, Jason. "'Made-in-America Revolutions'? The 'Black University' and the American Role in the Decolonization of the Black Atlantic," *Journal of American History* 96(3) (2009): 727–50.
Plummer, Brenda Gayle. *In Search of Power* (Cambridge: Cambridge University Press, 2013).
Seiler, John. *US Foreign Policy toward Southern Africa* (Johannesburg: Southern African Institute of International Affairs, 1973).
Sitton, Claude. "University in South May Admit African as a 'Foreign' Student," *New York Times*, 22 February 1963
Spaulding, Seth, and Michael Flack. *The World's Students in the United States* (New York: Praeger, 1976).
Stephens, Robert. *Kenyan Student Airlifts to America, 1959–1961* (Nairobi: East African Education Publishers Ltd, 2013).
Wieck, Randolph. *Ignorance Abroad* (Westport, CT: Praeger, 1992).

 14

Working on/Working with the Soviet Bloc
IREX, Scholarly Exchanges and Détente

Justine Faure

Introduction

In 1971, Allen H. Kassof, Executive Director of the International Research and Exchanges Board (IREX), expressed satisfaction that by working not only "on the USSR" but also "with the USSR," his organization had successfully detached scholarly exchanges with the Soviet Bloc from the earlier "Know the Enemy" approach.[1]

This collaborative style was one of the trademarks of IREX, a non-governmental organization jointly sponsored by the American Council of Learned Societies (ACLS) and the Social Science Research Council founded in 1968 and responsible for overseeing nearly 90 percent of academic exchanges with the USSR in the 1970s.[2] This quasi-monopoly stemmed from three factors. First, IREX was essentially the only American operator that managed programs with all Soviet Bloc countries (the USSR, Poland, Hungary, Romania, Czechoslovakia, Bulgaria and Yugoslavia, as well as the German Democratic Republic after 1975). Second, IREX offered extended study tours, usually of one year, which meant a large volume of exchanges (at that time exchanges were counted in "man-months"). Finally, IREX, thanks to its more innovative approach, between 1968 and 1973 gradually centralized most humanities and social sciences exchanges with the Soviet Bloc. It became the manager of programs overseen by the Inter-University Committee on Travel Grants (IUCTG, created in 1956), such as the Senior Scholars Exchange Program, the Graduate Students and Young Faculty Exchange Program (1958), the East European Graduate Students and Scholars Exchange (1962), and the Exchange of Language Teachers with the Soviet Union (1963). It was also given the responsibility for research exchanges between the ACLS and the Soviet Academy of Sciences (created in 1962). Finally, the Ford Foundation transferred to IREX the Soviet and Eastern European branch of its Foreign Area Fellowship Program (FAFP, created in 1952), its Fellowship Program in the social sciences (1957) and its Management Education Program (1970). Uniting governmental and non-governmental programs under IREX required a thoroughly redesigned approach and the development of innovative mechanisms that could take advantage of Détente by increasing collaboration between researchers on both sides of the Iron Curtain. One of the most important characteristics of IREX's approach was to transform the aforementioned programs from one-way fellowships into reciprocal exchanges.

This chapter offers a "bottom-up history" of scholarly exchanges by following the major figures of IREX, both administrators and researchers, as closely as possible and by exploring how the spirit of the programs and the concrete aspects of the exchanges shaped transnational scientific networks and joint research projects while enhancing the circulation of knowledge and practices between East and West. It first describes IREX and its specific practices for managing academic exchanges, and then analyzes the case of the extensive Hungarian-American exchanges that IREX supported to demonstrate the extent to which exchanges with the Soviet Bloc successfully generated powerful transnational scientific collaborations.

IREX Programs: Mechanisms and Objectives

IREX was created to promote high-level research on the Soviet Bloc by focusing exclusively on advanced graduate students and faculty, and financing only research sojourns, as opposed to lecture tours and teaching.[3] Candidates had to meet rigorous standards, involving a detailed application that retraced their personal and scientific backgrounds. They were also asked to present a several-page research proposal and list their in-country scholarly contacts, as well as every course they had taken related to their specialty. They were also required to provide a language assessment and three letters of recommendation from academics who were able to evaluate their research proposals. Shortlisted candidates were interviewed by top American specialists on the Soviet Bloc and took a highly rigorous language-screening exam. Many researchers reported that they had never undergone such a thorough evaluation process, and selection committees were provided with clear instructions to base their decisions on scholarly excellence. This attitude clashed with that of the IUCTG, whose leaders envisaged that American exchange scholars, in addition to conducting their research, would act as ambassadors of the American Way of Life. According to this view, fellows were originally meant to be "American students steeped in the American tradition, since one of the purposes of the program is to send the best representatives of American culture to the Soviet Union."[4] Although this criterion was subsequently abandoned, the selection committees were asked to verify that future fellows could defend the United States against communist criticism by answering questions such as "why are the capitalist war-mongering peoples of the US surrounding the peace-loving socialist peoples with bases?", "why do only the sons and daughters of the rich have the right to a college education in the US?" and "how could twenty-six million Americans vote for Goldwater?" In order to prevent any risk of KGB blackmail, selection committees were also asked to evaluate the candidates' "sexual maturity," with the proviso that "it may be necessary to be blunt."[5]

This elitist perspective was embraced by the IREX top management[6] and yielded a relatively modest number of acceptances. In the 1970s, an average of seventy American grants for individual IREX programs in the USSR were made, with thirty-five awarded for Eastern Europe. This also created occasional friction with the State Department, which favored a more people-to-people approach to increase contacts between American and communist societies. However, these divergences did not prevent the federal government from funding IREX, via the State Department and later via the United States Information and Communications Agency (USICA) and the National Endowment for the Humanities (NEH). These agencies thus contributed significantly to the 1979 US$3 million IREX budget: the USICA contributed 39.2 percent, the NEH 21.7 percent and the Ford Foundation 13.6 percent.

The second IREX objective was to contribute to the "emergence of a transnational community of researchers." The organization paid particular attention to Soviet Bloc scholars and although it had no voice in their selection because they were chosen by their own governments, it did create two innovative grant programs to match American and Soviet Bloc researchers with similar research fields. These programs—Ad Hoc Grants to Promote New Exchanges (Ad Hoc Grants) and Grants for Collaborative Projects (CoPro)—were intended to facilitate contact between researchers seeking innovative research opportunities and to finance joint projects such as publications and conferences. The final phase of the collective aspect of IREX programs was a cluster of bilateral Commissions on the Humanities and Social Sciences between the ACLS and the Soviet (1975), Hungarian (1977), East German (1981) and Polish (1981) Academies of Sciences, a group operated by IREX. The goal of these commissions was to create collaborative scientific projects typically spanning three years both by centralizing existing initiatives as well as supporting new projects. Joint research projects made it possible to exceed the comparatively small volume of individual exchanges: in 1973–74, 300 researchers participated in individual exchanges and 250 others in joint programs, and by 1976–77, these figures had risen to 327 and nearly 1,100, respectively.

The third goal of IREX was to encourage American social science research on the Soviet Bloc, a goal that Allen Kassof supported as a sociologist who was particularly keen for American research to cover a broad range of topics related to the Soviet Bloc. Next, IREX maintained especially close contacts with the Ford Foundation, which, like other large philanthropic foundations, attributed great importance to the social sciences. Further, although some Soviet Bloc countries did experience a social science renaissance—such as sociology in Poland—the relatively small number of American researchers were unfortunately less able to take advantage of these opportunities. Kassof methodically employed several strategies to increase the proportion of social science candidates. The first, rather obvious, strategy was to ask selection committees to favor social science applicants, particularly sociologists, economists and anthropologists. This favorable treatment became apparent in both individual and joint programs, which saw increases in the numbers of Ad Hoc and CoPro Grants awarded to social science projects: from 1969 to 1972, 50 percent of the American researchers sent to the USSR were historians, 34 percent were language and literature scholars, and only 9 percent were social scientists. From 1976 to 1978, the figures were respectively 44 percent, 29 percent and 21 percent. However, social science doctoral students and researchers—the potential pool of candidates—were scarce, because historians, linguists and literary scholars had traditionally dominated Slavic Studies. IREX responded by transforming Foreign Area Fellowship Program (FAFP) grants to encourage social science-focused Slavic Studies. Labeled "Preparatory Fellowships," these new grants were primarily reserved for young American social science researchers (with an emphasis on political science, anthropology, law, sociology and economics), non-specialists of the Soviet Bloc to whom IREX offered a one-year grant to increase their linguistic and academic skills in the United States. This preparatory year was succeeded by a second IREX grant that supported a year of field research, 118 of which were awarded between 1972 and 1979.

These efforts to augment the number of social science exchanges were also motivated by political considerations. Kassof felt that these kind of exchanges fostered greater openness by importing alternative ideas and critical perspectives behind the Iron Curtain. He described himself in interviews as a cold warrior, referring in several archival documents to the "contamination" and "happy corruption"[7] that Americans could bring to communist societies by practicing open scholarship behind the Iron Curtain. IREX strongly encouraged proposals that explored sensitive subjects, but the selection committee tended to reject candidates who could not also show that they were prepared for the complications that they might face.[8] After they were selected, IREX asked them to draft versions of their proposals modified for the communist authorities or even to create alternate topics in the event that they were compelled to reorient their research after arriving in-country. The historian John Micgiel is a case in point: in 1982, he left for an exchange to Poland, which was in a state of siege, nominally to pursue an inoffensive subject, although in reality he was working on the repression of anticommunist resistance during the latter half of the 1940s.[9] Finally, researchers confronted one troubling question after returning: what should they do with the findings of their research if they ran counter to the regime's positions? Should they be published at the risk of never returning to the country, heavily amended or even left unpublished? The anthropologist Katherine Verdery won an IREX grant in 1973 and later referred to this as "the most depressing aspect" of her experience in Romania.[10] She recently explained the paucity of books by American anthropologists who traveled to Romania in the 1970s by their desire to limit the visibility of their research by focusing on articles, which were considered more confidential and less detailed.[11]

Clearly, IREX leaders were acutely aware of the political significance of the exchanges and their role in the Cold War and in American public diplomacy.[12] However, they opposed instrumentalizing the exchanges for purposes other than the specific imperatives of academic research. From the outset, IREX made it clear that the two basic principles of its activities were "to insulate intellectual exchange from the exigencies of international politics, and to establish its independence from any sources of influence other than those devoted to the advancement of knowledge."[13] This attitude prompted Kassof to decline to suspend IREX programs after the brutal repression of the Prague Spring in 1968. He remained similarly circumspect about the usefulness of linking exchanges behind the Iron Curtain to human rights questions.

An additional unique feature of IREX programs was the organization's management of relations with communist authorities, particularly with the network of Academies of Sciences, where the most serious research was conducted in the Soviet Bloc, as opposed to the universities. IREX leaders made frequent visits to strengthen their ties to Soviet Bloc leaders and also sponsored regular visits by in-country partners to the United States that often included a tour of large university campuses. This was characteristic of the innovative approach implemented by IREX: when the Fulbright Program was launched in the USSR (1973–74), a United States Information Agency (USIA) official explained that his Soviet counterparts were unhappy about the oversight of the exchanges, particularly because American officials so infrequently visited Moscow and did not speak Russian. The author linked this attitude to the fact that the Soviets had become accustomed to the attentive treatment of IREX.[14] This red-carpet treatment undoubtedly helped maintain relationships that Kassof often characterized as "business-like," although he was also a very tough negotiator who forcefully conducted—and won—negotiations with communist authorities when he felt that local practices threatened the scientific integrity of the exchanges. In one dramatic episode in 1973, IREX suspended its Hungary programs following the expulsion of one of its fellows, the Hungarian-American historian István Deák.[15]

In addition to this type of decisive action, IREX could pressure Soviet Bloc partners in the name of reciprocity, the core concept of most exchange programs and an important pressure point in negotiations with communist governments, which were eager to maintain the exchanges. Moscow clearly encouraged scientific exchanges with the West during the Détente years. The USSR and its allies saw them as a useful instrument for professionalizing their diplomatic apparatus and for training experts who specialized in the West, as well as for sending KGB members to the United States and acquiring knowledge about Western scientific and technological progress (in the case of IREX, the majority of the scholars from the Soviet Bloc were engineers and physicists).[16] Thus, when an American nominee was rejected, IREX could threaten to reject an incoming nomination and often did so. However, reciprocity could also be a double-edged sword: in 1976, after the Ford Foundation reduced IREX funding because of a shift in policy toward American social problems (it reduced its contribution from US$1.2 million in 1974–75 to US$500,000 in 1978–79), IREX was forced to reduce its programs in Eastern Europe at the precise moment when local governments were prepared to ease oversight and increase the number of exchanges.

The two principal goals of the IREX programs were to advance American scientific knowledge, particularly in the social sciences, and to increase East–West transnational cooperation. The question is whether the organization successfully achieved these goals.

Scientific Mobility, Collaborative Research and Cultural Circulation

Clearly, not every IREX initiative was uniformly successful. Certain participants in individual programs abandoned Slavic Studies without making any meaningful contribution to what was known about the Soviet Bloc. Others, despite their best efforts, collided with local bureaucracy and were unable to satisfactorily conduct their research. Some Ad Hoc Grants, and even some CoPro Grants, revealed themselves to be, in the terminology of IREX, "fishing expeditions" that amounted to a form of academic tourism instead of leading to joint research projects. Finally, some joint projects were simply just disappointing. For example, IREX had invested great hopes in a Conference on Romanian–American Cooperation in the Social Sciences that was organized in 1972 in Sterling Forest, New York. The conference was meant to assemble American and Romanian researchers in demography, economics, political science, psychology and sociology as a way of generating research proposals. Ultimately, one of the few concrete results of this project, beyond ensuring that the Romanians became more hospitable to Americans coming to Romania, was a multilingual glossary of sociological terms, edited for the Americans by John Mogey of Boston University. Several years later, in 1979, plans to establish a bilateral commission with Romania based on the Soviet and Hungarian models were abandoned after encountering difficulties with the Ceauşescu regime. The case of Romania illustrates that East–West scholarly relations, despite the favorable environment of Détente, never became completely normalized and remained at the mercy of sudden reversals at the hands of Soviet Bloc officials.

However, despite these occasional difficulties or failures, IREX programs often resulted in true scholarly cooperation and solid transnational networks. The most striking example of these successful initiatives was a series of exchanges between American and Hungarian historians that enjoyed significant financial support from IREX because the agency saw it as a successful model of collaborative research. In the 1970s, this support resulted in the approval of several individual grants for tenured researchers and their doctoral students, complemented by numerous Ad Hoc and CoPro Grants. The Institute on East Central Europe (IECE) at Columbia University, which was directed by the historian István Deák from 1968 to 1979, represented the heart of this Hungarian-American network. One of the few research centers in the United States focused on Eastern Europe at the time, the Institute was generously supported by the Ford Foundation, which certified it as a "national resource center for the study of East Central Europe," and by the federal government, which selected it as an NDEA Language and Area Center.[17]

The Institute of History of the Hungarian Academy of Sciences (in particular its deputy director, György Ránki, and the historians Iván Berend and Péter Hanák) was one of the closest Soviet Bloc partners of the Institute. Ránki and Berend were former Ford Foundation fellows, while Ránki and Hanák had participated in a conference organized by Indiana University in April 1966 on the subject of nationalities under the Habsburg Empire. The conference established the foundation for close, amicable cooperation between American and Central European specialists.[18] These contacts were made easier by the fact that the majority of the Americans were Hungarian exiles. They were also members of the same generation as their Hungarian colleagues (Peter Sugar, who taught at the University of Washington, was born in Budapest in 1919, Hanák in 1921, Deák in 1926, and Ránki and Berend in 1930) and many also shared having survived the Holocaust.

Relations between the IECE and the Institute of History led to the appointment of historians to the Hungarian Visiting Lectureship at Columbia, which was established in 1973 with Hungarian government support. Hanák, Ránki and Berend were also well known at the IECE, where they lectured or conducted seminars. Their presence was an undeniable asset for American researchers, because they helped future IREX scholars present their research projects as precisely and realistically as possible based on their Hungarian colleagues' advice. In one instance, the political scientist Charles Gati was applying to IREX for a sensitive research project in 1975—"Populism and Revolutionary Transformation in Hungary, 1935–1948"—and met with Ránki in New York, who suggested the best libraries in Hungary to work in (in particular the Parliament Library), as well as Iván Berend, Rector of Karl Marx University, who also offered assistance.[19]

Support from local researchers was a boon to IREX fellows behind the Iron Curtain. Ties to the Institute of History were especially helpful, and Ránki ensured that every IREX scholar in Hungary had a research assistant. American researchers also benefited from his political connections. He obtained interviews for Charles Gati with István Bibó,

Ferenc Donát (Rákosi's former chief of staff) and Zoltán Vas, a former Politburo member who gave him access to the 2,000 pages of his unpublished autobiography. Ránki's influence also helped Gati to become the first Westerner to gain access to the archives at the Institute of Party History in 1976.[20] Several American historians, including István Deák and Steven Vardy, published articles in the Institute's journal, *Történelmi Szemle*, which also published critical reviews of Western books.

IREX scholars' reports about their experiences in Hungary are replete with praise for local contacts and uniformly characterized their research tours as successes. This positive evaluation was typical of IREX-sponsored exchanges, as revealed by another survey conducted in 1975 of 358 American IREX fellows who participated in exchanges between 1969 and 1974.[21] In response to the question "overall, how would you rate your experience abroad?", 50 percent said the experience was outstanding, 40 percent rated it very good and only 3 percent rated it fair or poor. Nearly 50 percent of IREX fellows also said that they completed roughly the expected amount, while another 30 percent said they actually got more work done than expected.

For their part, American historians went to considerable lengths to open the doors to the scientific and academic dimensions of their universities to their Hungarian colleagues. Significantly, Iván Berend entitled one of the chapters of his autobiography "In the International Community of Historians; Friends All Over the World."[22] Deák's efforts on behalf of these scholars were remarkable. He did everything possible to promote the presence of the Eastern European researchers visiting his institute. His final report on the Ad Hoc Grant that he received in 1969 to fund a lecture tour for the Hungarian historian Domokos Kosáry is an excellent example—Deák had written eighty letters to universities and scientific institutions to announce the historian's visit, resulting in twenty positive responses and ultimately in a dozen lectures across the United States.[23] He also wrote critical reviews of a number of Hungarian studies published by journals ranging from the *American Historical Review* and the *Political Science Quarterly* to the *Slavic Review*. Deák also helped a number of Hungarian historians publish their work.[24] His commitment to his native country, which was mirrored among other researchers from the region, including Peter Sugar, Piotr Wandycz, Anna Cienciala and Stephen Fisher-Galati, provides significant evidence of the key role as cultural mediators between East and West played by exiles. These activities in turn fueled broader processes of cultural circulation and interchange between the United States and Eastern Europe. The case of Hungary is not an exception: in the late 1960s, the historian Charles Jelavich estimated that approximately

60 percent of the researchers specializing in East European Studies in the United States were either exiles or the children of emigrés, which can be explained by the poor quality of the teaching of the region's languages.[25]

The involvement of IREX in Hungarian-American networks reached a kind of zenith in the ACLS-Hungarian Academy of Sciences Commission on the Humanities and Humanitics Aspects of the Social Sciences. Established in 1977, this partnership first became operative in 1979, and its first initiatives came from historians. In January and July 1980, István Deák, Carl Schorske (Princeton), György Ránki, Péter Hanák and several other researchers met several times in New York and Budapest to create a History subcommittee. Their first collective research project was "Ethnicity, Social Class, and Cultural Change in Hungary and the United States: A Study in Comparative History," which resulted in a conference in 1982 that was followed by a second project, "Intellectuals and the Left."

This opening to the world of Western research among Hungarian historians produced a gradual drift from nationalist and Marxist historiography, particularly regarding the Austro-Hungarian period. Iván Berend recalls that they distanced themselves from an unreflective critique of the Empire in which imperial Austria had "colonized and exploited" a rebellious Hungary and "blocked Hungary's road to modernization," replacing this view with a more positive interpretation of the empire's achievements that underscored the economic benefits that Hungary had derived from its association with Vienna. Again according to Berend, this move away from Marxist thought (which nevertheless continued to influence these historians) resulted in a perspective that held culture to be independent of the economy, that valued external influences and that adopted a more complex view of modernization that did not reflexively condemn foreign investments as simple manifestations of capitalist imperialism.[26] There was a significant political dimension to the integration of Hungarians into the international historical community. Indeed, as Iván Berend remarked, their visibility provided them with a certain degree of political protection, because the regime hesitated to move against individuals with extensive Western networks.[27]

Conclusion

To conclude, the study of IREX programs provides a highly relevant vantage point from which to observe and understand the Cold War.

IREX activities during the 1970s demonstrate the extent to which Détente was not an illusion but a reality, at least at the level of academic exchanges. Exchanges between the United States and the Soviet Bloc flourished over a ten-year period, resulting in a highly interactive, dynamic environment in which IREX played a key role. IREX also reveals that a transnational approach casts a new light on the history of East–West confrontation. On the other side of the Iron Curtain, individuals, knowledge and practices were able to circulate. Although in the context of the Cold War a powerful political dimension accompanied this circulation, it facilitated sustained interaction and connection across the East–West divide. The resulting contacts in turn enabled meaningful academic encounters and networks, while also transcending the logic of confrontation. The history of IREX also represents an intriguing example of a fully functional public-private network in the midst of the Cold War. As a non-governmental organization rooted in the academic world but financed by the federal government and the Ford Foundation, IREX was at the heart of sometimes harmonious, sometimes conflictual cooperation between its different funding sources. Ultimately, because of the repercussions of scholars' mobility on the construction of new knowledge, IREX served as a key player in Soviet and Eastern European Studies, and the history of the organization helps us understand how these fields evolved during the Cold War.

Justine Faure is Associate Professor at Strasbourg University and former Fulbright Fellow (2010). Her research interests focused on the history of the Cold War and US Diplomacy toward Eastern Europe. In 2004 she published her Ph.D. on American-Czechoslovak relationships: *L'ami américain. La Tchécoslovaquie au cœur de la diplomatique américaine, 1943–1968* (Tallandier), which was translated into Czech: *Americký přítel. Československo ve hře americké diplomacie 1943–1968* (Nakladatelsvtí Lidové Noviny, 2005). She is about to publish in French her new book on Slavic Studies and East-West Scholarly Exchanges, which focuses mainly on IUCTG and IREX programs.

Appendix: Allen H. Kassof

Born in New York in 1930, Allen Kassof developed an interest in the study of the Soviet Union in the early 1950s in the context of McCarthyism, which motivated him "to develop an objective knowledge" about the USSR. He attended the Harvard Graduate School, completing an A.M.

in International and Regional Studies (Soviet Studies) followed by a doctorate in sociology on "The Soviet Youth Program: Socialization in a Totalitarian Society." He also held the position of Research Assistant at the Russian Research Center, where he helped analyze interviews with Soviet exiles who were part of the Harvard Project on the Soviet Social System. He received research funding from the Ford Foundation through the Foreign Area Fellowship Program (FAFP) and from the IUCTG (a one-month grant to travel to Russia in 1956). He completed his doctorate in 1960 and accepted a position in 1961 as Assistant Professor at Princeton University. He published several books and articles on Soviet society during the 1960s, notably *The Soviet Youth Program: Regimentation and Rebellion* (Cambridge: Harvard University Press, 1965) and the seminal essay "The Administered Society: Totalitarianism without Terror" (*World Politics*, 1964/4, 558–575), which introduced the influential concept of "administered society" to deconstruct the nature of totalitarianism in an evolving Soviet Union. He was chosen as the Executive Director of IREX in 1968 because, in addition to his academic status and involvement in the IUCTG, he was well known to the Ford Foundation, one of the major funding sources for the IUCTG and subsequently for IREX. The foundation had partly financed his hiring by Princeton in 1961 through a grant from its International and Training Research Program. Between 1968 and 1973, he worked part-time at IREX and part-time at Princeton, eventually resigning from the university to focus entirely on administration until his retirement in 1992.

Notes

1. Rockefeller Archive Center (henceforth RAC), Social Science Research Council Records (henceforth SSRC), Accession 1, Series 1, Subseries 24, box 256, folder 1504: Joint Committee on Slavic Studies Annual Meeting, 19 February 1971.
2. *The Raised Curtain: Report to the Twentieth Century Fund Task Force on Soviet-American Scholarly and Cultural Exchanges* (New York: Twentieth Century Fund, 1977), 72–73.
3. The IREX archives were deposited at the Library of Congress by Allen Kassof. Their inventory was made in 2010 upon my request. I also met Allen Kassof in August 2010. See Justine Faure, *Études slaves, sciences sociales et Guerre froide: Production et circulations des savoirs entre les États-Unis et l'Europe de l'Est (1943–1979)*, habilitation à diriger des recherches, Université Paris-I Panthéon Sorbonne, 2015.
4. Library of Congress (henceforth LOC), Manuscript Division, IREX Records, box 329, folder "IUC: Policy Meeting—February, 1958": IUCTG meeting, 22 February 1958.

5. Columbia Rare Book and Manuscript Library, Records of the IUCTG, Box 1, folder 15 "Participant Selection 1963–1965": Interview Manual, confidential, December 1964.
6. RAC, Ford Foundation Archives, roll 3011: Allen Kassof to Ivo Lederer, 22 February 1973.
7. RAC, SSRC Records, Accession 2, Series 1, Subseries 59, box 203, folder 2286: meeting with SSRC, 6 September 1969 and an unpublished document written by Allen Kassof, 14 July 1992.
8. LOC, IREX Records, box 210, folder "Selection Comm. 1972–1973": Memorandum to Selection Committee, East European Exchange Program, 1972–73.
9. John Micgiel, interview with author, New York, September 2010.
10. LOC, IREX Records, box 112, folder 14: Final Report, 1974.
11. Katherine Verdery, "An Anthropologist in Communist Romania 1973–1989," *Problems of Post-Communism* 4 (2013): 35–42 (at 37).
12. See, for example, *IREX Annual Report, 1975–1976*, 4: "It is pointless to insist there should be no connection between East-West academic exchanges and diplomatic interests."
13. *IREX Annual Report, 1968–1969*, 2.
14. William James, "A Promising Future: The Fulbright Program with the USSR," *Annals of the American Academy of Political and Social Science* 491 (1987): 118–25.
15. For more on this subject, see Deák's account: "Scandal in Budapest," *New York Review of Books*, 19 October 2006.
16. Sergeï Zhuk, paper for the 2015 Convention of the Association for Slavic, East-European and Eurasian Studies: "The KGB People, Soviet Americanists and Soviet-American Academic Exchanges, 1958–1985."
17. The NDEA (National Defense Education Act), signed in 1958 after the Soviet Union successfully launched Sputnik I, was designed to foster US education in science, mathematics and foreign languages.
18. Charles Jelavich and R.J.R., "The Conference," *Austrian History Yearbook* 3(1) (1967): 1–7.
19. LOC, IREX Records, box 140, folder 3: Addendum to Research Proposal.
20. Ibid.: Final Report, 20 September 1977.
21. RAC, SSRC Records, R.G. 2, Series 1, Sub-Series 59, box 204, folder 2295: Kadushin Report.
22. Iván Berend, *History in My Life: A Memoire of Three Eras* (Budapest: Central European University Press, 2009), 107–18.
23. LOC, IREX Records, box 121, folder 12.
24. For example, Ránki and Berend contributed to the volume edited by Sylva Sinanian, István Deák and Peter Ludz, *Eastern Europe in the 1970s* (New York: Praeger, 1972). In 1974, they published their book *Economic Development in East Central Europe in the 19th and 20th Centuries* with Columbia University Press, which was translated from Hungarian.
25. Charles Jelavich (ed.), *Language and Area Studies: East Central and Southeastern Europe. A Survey* (Chicago, IL: University of Chicago Press, 1969), 21.

26. Berend, *History*, "Experiencing and Writing History: A Special Friend, Books and Debates," 119–54.
27. Berend, *History*, 93.

References

Berend, Iván. *History in My Life: A Memoire of Three Eras* (Budapest: Central European University Press, 2009).
Faure, Justine. *Études slaves, sciences sociales et Guerre froide: Production et circulations des savoirs entre les États-Unis et l'Europe de l'Est (1943–1979)*, habilitation à diriger des recherches, Université Paris-I Panthéon Sorbonne, 2015.
Jelavich, Charles (ed.). *Language and Area Studies: East Central and Southeastern Europe: A Survey* (Chicago, IL: University of Chicago Press, 1969).
Sinanian, Sylva, István Deák and Peter Ludz (eds). *Eastern Europe in the 1970s* (New York: Praeger, 1972).
Verdery, Katherine. "An Anthropologist in Communist Romania, 1973–1989," *Problems of Post-Communism* 4 (2013): 35–42.

PART IV

THE GLOBALIZATION MOMENT

NEW GEOGRAPHY AND NEW CHALLENGES

 15

AMERICAN FOUNDATIONS AND THE CHALLENGE OF FUNDING INTERNATIONAL FELLOWSHIP AND EXCHANGE PROGRAMS SINCE 1970

Patricia L. Rosenfield

Introduction

International fellowship and exchange programs have featured in the portfolios of American philanthropic foundations since the early twentieth century. Such programs reflect the commitment of foundations to strengthening human capital as an integral component of building new fields of knowledge and action or strengthening existing ones. Grants to individuals continue to expand the expertise of American and overseas scholars and practitioners, and promote cross-national and cross-disciplinary collaboration.

Up until 1969, individual grants programs were often managed internally by foundation staff. Grants were made directly to successful applicants in the United States or overseas. Grants for larger fellowship or exchange programs with more administrative responsibilities were made to universities or through "intermediary" institutions, such as the Social Science Research Council (SSRC), the American Council of Learned Societies (ACLS) and the Institute of International Education (IIE).

Following World War I, the Rockefeller Foundation (RF) and Carnegie Corporation of New York (CCNY) supported, along with other fellowships and exchanges, foundation-sponsored international travel and study grants both for Americans and overseas scholars and practitioners.[1] From 1928 to 1968, CCNY provided travel and study grants for individuals from across the British Empire to visit the United States and Canada, for exploration of new approaches in educational curriculum, museum or library development.[2]

When Henry Ford II decided to enlarge the scope of the Ford Foundation (FF) to make it an international foundation in 1949, he established a committee to review the options. One of the committee's recommendations, accepted by the board of trustees in 1950, was to "support activities ... to enable individuals more fully to realize their intellectual, civic, and spiritual potentialities."[3] Like RF and CCNY, these activities included fellowships, exchanges and travel and study grants, many made directly to individuals and managed internally by foundation staff. By 1961, Ford was championing the value of these programs: "the exchange students and scholars represent the vital arteries of the international activities of the academic community."[4]

Until 1969, these programs were constrained only by foundation priorities and/or limited financial and staff resources. The Great Depression, Joseph McCarthy's communist witch hunts and the Cold War did not deter foundations' support of fellowships and exchanges. Starting in 1969, however, major challenges resulted from the American domestic political process: the Tax Reform Act of 1969 and, more than three decades later, the US Department of Treasury's regulations on international grant-making in the wake of the 11 September 2001 (popularly known as 9/11) terrorist attacks. Another challenge has recently emerged from foundations' increased attention to quantitative evaluation based on business metrics, including rates of return, performance standards and expected outcomes. These measures favor grants with short-term, narrowly calibrated results, whereas the impacts of fellowships are often revealed in the long run and are usually multifaceted, affecting the individual, the institution, the field and, at times, public opinion and policymaking.

This chapter examines the impact of these external and self-imposed challenges on foundation support for international fellowship and exchange programs in the late twentieth and into the twenty-first centuries. The examples are drawn primarily from archival research on two of the foundations with a commitment to international fellowships and exchanges, the FF and CCNY.[5] The archival material is complemented by interviews with current practitioners. The chapter concludes with reflections on the future of foundation support for international fellowship and exchange programs.

The Impetus for the 1969 Tax Reform Act

Concerns about foundation abuses have featured in congressional hearings since the early 1900s. They became prominent in the 1950s, when congressional investigations focused on self-dealing, lack of transparency and inadequate accounting and reporting. The 1969 Tax Reform Act, the culmination of these concerns, resulted in a new overall regulatory framework for private foundations that included "limitations on grants to individuals 'for travel, study, or similar purposes.'"[6]

The FF and its President in 1968, McGeorge Bundy, are often assigned responsibility for some of the unexpectedly harsh restrictions on foundation activity related to political campaigns and grants to individuals. The FF was flagged for its fellowships to eight staff members of Senator Robert F. Kennedy following his assassination on 5 June 1968. The members of the House Ways and Means Committee, which led the investigations of foundations, considered these grants to be politically charged and reeking of favoritism. They linked them to Bundy, who from 1961 to 1966 served as National Security Advisor to Presidents John F. Kennedy and Lyndon B. Johnson, respectively, and was viewed as part of the elite Eastern Establishment.[7] Nonetheless, the record shows that the individuals who received support were, in fact, associated with ongoing FF grants. The rationale for travel and study support was as credible for them as for any other FF grants.[8]

The individuals did not just receive a check in the mail; each submitted a detailed proposal. Approved in July 1968, they were supported under a Foundation-Administered Project drawing on resources appropriated by the Foundation's board for "quick, though relatively small actions, to meet critical situations in the nation."[9] As the grantees completed their work, they reported on the results. Foundation staff had followed proper procedures. However, Bundy further indicated that "there were two or three miscalculations." Staff believed that the shock caused by Robert Kennedy's assassination would lead people to want to help the distraught grantees.[10] Instead, the intense congressional questioning spawned misunderstandings by ordinary citizens and journalists. A February 1969 newspaper article, for example, misquoted the purpose of the grants to Kennedy's advisors, claiming, for example, that one staff member was on "a honeymoon trip around the world."[11]

The abuses, whether real or perceived, resulted in congressionally mandated limitations on foundation grants to individuals:

> The Act imposes sanctions upon the making of grants to individuals by private foundations unless the grantees are chosen in open competition or on some other objective and nondiscriminatory basis, in accordance with procedures approved in advance by the Internal Revenue Service ... Except where the procedures or standards set forth are followed, the Act requires that any grant by a private foundation be directed toward

the production of a specific product (a book, paper, or other study, or a scientific development or useful process), the achievement of a specific objective, or the improvement or enhancement of a literary, artistic, musical, scientific, teaching, or other similar capacity, talent, or skill.[12]

The foundations lost their traditional flexibility in the internal management of individual grants. From this period onward, they have had to assess whether the benefits of exercising this lever for social change are worth the additional administrative costs.

The Impact of the 1969 Tax Reform Act on Foundation Programs

The FF and CCNY reflected the spectrum of foundation reactions to the Act. The Ford leadership recognized that it was not as constraining as it might have been and continued to support internally run fellowships and exchanges, whereas CCNY ended support for such programs.

In his 1972 oral history, Bundy presented a relatively optimistic assessment of the impact, commenting that, despite the greatly increased complexity of the rules and legal costs, as well as the new tax on income, "the bill is more good than bad."[13] The FF's 1976 review of individual grants reinforced Bundy's comments about increased procedural and administrative burdens related to foundation-directed fellowships. The authors noted that these procedures "were far more proscriptive toward grants to individuals than ... toward grants to organizations."[14] To receive Internal Revenue Service (IRS) approval for awarding individual grants, FF had to create new procedures that led to heavier administrative burdens.

The FF would continue to accept direct fellowship applications from individuals or nominations from a nonprofit institution, an outside expert or an expert Foundation staff member. On every nomination except the institutional nomination, staff needed to ask for written peer reviews from at least two experts. When a staff member made the nomination, a senior member of the FF was also required to submit a written evaluation. Moreover, the FF had to provide information on how it would supervise individuals and the reporting process. As with other grants, these procedures also needed to explain how funds would be recovered if the grant was not finished or if staff suspected misuse of funds.

With the extensive review and reporting requirements, costs per Foundation-administered fellowship must have increased. Yet, in the six years following the Act's passage, the added costs neither impeded the FF's development of individual grants programs nor prevented the support of future fellowship programs. In fact, staff noted in the review that "the IRS-approved procedures have provided useful guidelines for equitable treatment of individuals and appropriate safeguards against arbitrary or casual grant-making."[15]

In the Fiscal Year (FY) 1975, for example, individual fellowships accounted for approximately 6.4 percent of the grants awarded; there were 1,206 new international individual fellowships managed internally at the Foundation, for a "record" total of US$11.6 million.[16] Between 1950 and 1976, the Foundation had granted directly about US$225 million to individuals. Even with 1975 budget declines in all programs, internally managed individual grants were around 6.1 percent of all grants for a total of US$7.8 million. The 1976 staff review, however, noted that the numbers were reduced primarily as a consequence of the Education and Research Division's decision "to turn over several large fellowship programs to outside agencies ... [awarding] 560 minority fellowships that a year earlier would have been made directly by the foundation as grants to individuals." Clearly, that division did not want to take on the additional administrative burdens, and so chose to support its fellowship programs through other agencies. In addition, international individual grants fell from 1,309 to 1,206, although the international offices in New York and overseas remained "the heaviest user of grants to individuals."[17]

In 1976, a separate FF review of the accomplishments and challenges of an internally managed fellowship program focused on minority participation in foreign field research. Recognizing the increased Foundation-wide administrative burden, FF staff members questioned whether they should use an intermediary for administrative efficiency or continue with internal administration. However, they also noted the "tangible and intangible benefits [that] may accrue to fellows who receive an award directly administered by the Ford Foundation."[18] In the end, they decided that the benefits to awardees and staff outweighed the costs and continued to manage the program internally.

Alan Pifer, President of CCNY from 1967 to 1982, reacted more negatively than Bundy to the passage of the Tax Reform Act.[19] The Corporation's long tradition of internally managed travel and study grants was one of the casualties. In the mid-1960s, as CCNY's overseas program focused increasingly on Africa, staff directed travel and study grants toward leaders of African higher education institutions. Soon thereafter, concurrent with the 1968 House Ways and Means Committee hearings, the Corporation decided to end such direct support. Anticipating the restrictions and increased costs, the Corporation no longer ran international individual exchanges or fellowship programs. Instead, grants for these programs were provided to the African-American Institute. As a result, Corporation staff met fewer of those individuals, losing close contact with a wide range of new scholars and leaders.

With the exception of individual grants to write books, which followed procedures similar to those of the FF, CCNY did not revive an internally managed fellowship program until Vartan Gregorian became President in 1997. Gregorian's rationale echoed that of earlier Corporation leaders, including founder Andrew Carnegie:

> It is scholarship—deep, thoughtful, incisive research, thinking and analysis—that has the capacity to reintegrate and reconnect the disparate, ever-multiplying strands of knowledge, to bring *meaning* to information and to forge wisdom upon the anvil of changing times ... These were among the reasons that one of my priorities ... was to reestablish the Corporation's historic support for individual scholarship for the first time in more than thirty years.[20]

The guidelines for the Carnegie Scholars Program ultimately approved by the IRS had to describe persuasively the relationship of the new program to existing grant programs and its procedures: nomination by external individuals; review by at least two other individuals; final review and recommendation by an external expert committee; and final decisions by the trustees. Regular reporting, recordkeeping and assessment processes were also included.

Rik Treiber, former CCNY Associate Corporate Secretary and Director, Grants Management, was responsible for the administrative monitoring of the new program's implementation. He noted that one of the major impacts of the Tax Reform Act was that most foundations did not develop such programs.[21] Instead, they funded them through organizations such as the IIE, the SSRC and the ACLS; this approach meant that foundations could reduce their direct administrative support, but it also resulted in distancing the program officer from the fellowship holder, phasing out a relationship that was often beneficial to both. The Corporation in the 1990s and 2000s also funded program-specific individual grants through these intermediary organizations. In 2015, however, it launched a new foundation-directed individual fellowship program, the Andrew Carnegie Fellows Program. This initiative reinforces the strategic value of the Corporation running its own program, especially when it is cross-programmatic and staff seek to benefit from closer contact with the individual fellows.[22]

Voluntary Guidelines: A Rapid Federal Response to 11 September 2001

Following the terrorist attacks in the United States on 11 September 2001, Executive Order 13224, issued by President George W. Bush and authorized by the 1977 International Emergency Economic Powers Act, placed an even greater burden on all foundations and their support for internally managed international fellowship and exchange programs. One of its particularly onerous provisions required that each potential grantee must be checked against a "blacklist of individuals and organizations suspected of terrorism, materially aiding terrorism, or associating with terrorists."[23] Originally, only twenty-seven names designated by the Treasury Department, in consultation with the State Department, were on that list; by 2016, there were 951 pages, with many thousands of names (including multiple versions of the same name).[24] Even more than the Tax Reform Act, this Executive Order, made "without the check of Congressional deliberation,"[25] complicated the work of foundations and other NGOs that support international activities, including fellowships and exchanges. The Treasury Department, for example, lists nineteen different name search approaches.[26]

Further concern about foundations' inadvertently financing terrorists led the US Department of the Treasury to issue in 2002 "Anti-terrorist Financing Guidelines: Voluntary Best Practices for US-Based Charities." These guidelines were voluntary only in title. Although they stated that "nonadherence to these Guidelines … does not constitute a violation of existing U. S. Law," they also noted that "conversely, adherence to these Guidelines does not excuse any person (individual or entity) from compliance with any local, state, or federal law or regulation, nor does it release any person from or constitute a legal defense against any civil or criminal liability for violating any such law or regulation." In other words, supporting someone on the designated list could subject a foundation (or any institution) to criminal charges or fines.[27] As Teresa Odendahl has elaborated:

> The Treasury Guidelines specifically advise international funders to gather information on potential grantee groups, their employees, subcontracting organizations, and vendors, as well as to check the lists … "The charity should run the names through public databases…" All of this furor is also based on questionable "evidence" that charities are a *significant* source of funding for terrorist activities.[28]

In 2005, Odendahl and her team interviewed ten foundation representatives about the Guidelines' impact on grantmaking. Many found the Guidelines unwieldy and costly to follow. They needed to check regularly: "some do it daily, others weekly or monthly. In implementing the new list checking systems, the price tag varied from being negligible for some grantmakers to as high as US$500,000 for one or two other notable foundations."[29] Some foundations checked all grantees. As one unidentified senior staff member told Odendahl, "anytime a name gets entered into our database ... it gets checked ... you put in almost any name and come up with a partial match. When this happens, program staff members check to verify that the person is not the same as the one listed."[30] Such protection is only feasible for foundations with sufficient administrative resources. For example, in 2004, CCNY refocused the Carnegie Scholars program on "Islam and the Modern World" in order to promote scholarly attention to this critical topic. Even though the program only changed its focus and all of the IRS-approved procedures remained the same, CCNY needed to submit a new request to the IRS both to revise the program focus and to indicate explicitly how it would follow the new Guidelines.[31] This necessitated new, time-consuming obligations, especially since many potential grantees, although US citizens or permanent residents (a requirement of the program), were foreign-born.

Treiber explained that "you need to check the names against lists from very different agencies with different lists and with different activities and different databases. Even if you don't see the name you're not necessarily free of the penalties for freezing the assets. The name may be added to the list later. This means that only a handful of institutions are able to keep track of organizations not on the lists. At Carnegie Corporation, we compared the names with the names and birth dates. Another serious problem is with false positives."[32] The Corporation's current Associate Corporate Secretary and Director, Grants Management, Nicole Howe Buggs, reiterated that the Guidelines can be "a deterrent for smaller foundations ... You need to have experienced staff and be able to participate in appropriate grantmaker networks, working with legal departments and lawyers. It is costly."[33]

Organizations that want to work in the Middle East must also follow another set of guidelines from the Treasury Department's Office of Foreign Asset Control (OFAC). OFAC is responsible for identifying countries, organizations and individuals against whom there are sanctions prohibiting American financial dealings. It uses a complicated formula to determine the acceptability of working with certain organizations or individuals in countries under US sanctions, such as Iran or Syria. Foundations need to obtain licenses or certification for such activities. At the time of writing, special exemptions are required, for example, to invite someone from one of these countries to participate in an international meeting.

Two other perspectives indicate different possibilities for handling the voluntary guidelines. The Open Society Foundation (OSF) maintains a legal department to assist its program staff. Thus, Martha Loerke, Director of OSF's Scholarship Programs, found that the guidelines were not "blocking us too much." She added: "It seems to be a fairly quick process for our legal department to run our candidates' names through."[34] When working in countries where there are sanctions, the OSF has received OFAC licenses.

On the other hand, smaller foundations are unable to tackle legal obligations of this magnitude. If they want to fund scholarships and exchange programs, they turn to intermediaries with those capabilities. IIE, as indicated earlier, has often assumed this role. Daniela Kaisth, then Vice-President for External Affairs and IIE Initiatives, commented that "we do not hear so much about OFAC/IRS issues being difficult to navigate and inhibiting international exchange programs. Perhaps this is because the work of the Institute is to remove the administrative burden to foundations managing such initiatives themselves."[35]

In addition to the legitimate concerns about the time-consuming nature of list-checking, the resources expended in consulting lawyers and the embarrassing situations that develop with false positives, there are also ethical questions that deserve attention. Odendahl notes that "America's foundations [have come] dangerously close to acting as the enforcement or police arm of the lists and even more troubling, passing it on to their grantees."[36] She has questioned whether these obligations chip away at the social contract between grantee and grantor. She has also commented that "the 'culture of compliance' ... seems at odds with the potentially independent, idealistic, progressive nature of much international funding."[37] Although serious concern about terrorism is warranted, foundations face an ethical dilemma in considering if the voluntary guidelines and OFAC licenses undermine philanthropy's core values.

The Impact of Quantitative Evaluation

Foundations have long tempered their enthusiasm for international fellowships and exchanges with concerns about their impact. As early as 1952, the Presidents of CCNY, RF and FF were questioning the outcomes of these programs. Together, they supported a study undertaken jointly by the SSRC and the IIE to address questions including "how do these fellowships contribute to international understanding as well as understanding of the United States? Are these fellowships more effective for people who are younger or for those more mature? They were also concerned about the educational benefits of such exchanges."[38] Although the study results persuaded these presidents to continue with individual grants, the questions are amplified in the current era by the invigorated focus on quantitative evaluation measures drawn from the for-profit sector, including performance standards, expected outcomes, rates of return and maximizing short-run impact.

Individual fellowship and exchange programs often cannot be assessed by quantitative impact measures beyond completion of the fellowship or production of a book. Moreover, even qualitative benefits of fellowship and exchange programs are hard to predict or assess — strengthening a field of knowledge, contributing to policymaking, informing public opinion or improving international cooperation and understanding.[39] The aforementioned review of the FF's minority participation Fellowship Program led to continued Foundation management of the grant on the basis of intangible benefits to the grantee. The Carnegie Scholars program was justified in part based on its potential (but not necessarily explicit) contribution to new foundation strategies.

Howe Buggs indicated that CCNY was defining performance standards that would make sense given differing timeframes, goals and objectives.[40] Loerke indicated that the OSF recognizes "the long-term nature of scholarship programs. Our accountability rests as much on the integrity of our process as it does on the actual outcome of individual grants in achieving the overall mission of the foundation."[41] Loerke also noted that for programs working with nontraditional applicants from marginalized situations, "evaluation ... begins at the beginning — with recruitment and selection." They are still exploring ways of understanding the long-term benefits to fellowship grantees. Nonetheless, the OSF leadership continues to support grants to individuals.

IIE staff members have a broad perspective on foundations' support for a wide range of individual grants programs.[42] Their sense is that "few major international fellowship programs ... have really invested in evaluation measurement."[43] Despite the difficulties in obtaining quantitative measures of effectiveness and impact, the IIE mentioned three new fellowship programs, including the Gates Cambridge Scholarship program starting in 2000, the MasterCard Foundation Scholars Program in 2006 and Schwarzman Scholars in 2016. Nevertheless, the IIE team identified developments that could adversely affect such support:

We are also seeing new trends, themes, and models emerge that may impact foundation investment in fellowships. These include ... more short-term fellowships; more fellowships focused on very specific issue areas or skills development, such as for journalists in Africa; the concept of "affirmative obligation," in which fellowship recipients are asked to consider paying back their fellowship at some point so that others may have the opportunity; and the addition of non-academic aspects of fellowships, such as internships, volunteering, service learning, etc. [44]

Conclusion

Two differing conclusions emerge from this review of the impact of Congressional legislation, federal regulations and foundation-imposed measurement constraints on philanthropic support for individual international fellowships. The larger foundations that can afford to address the legal, programmatic and grants management obligations are continuing to internally fund individual grants. However, smaller foundations with more limited staff and financial assets are shying away from doing so. Comments from the IIE team prompt further concerns that the types of programs being funded, such as short-term exchanges, are in direct response to regulatory and evaluation procedures rather than strategic opportunities.

The official regulations described above have transformed the nature of individual grant programs. These initial findings, however, would benefit from a series of empirical studies that examine the historical and contemporary rationale and scope of foundation support for internally managed fellowship and exchange programs. Such research could provide guidance going forward for those foundations eager to support individuals, but wary of the programmatic challenges. This would enable foundations to return fellowships and exchanges to what CCNY President John Gardner described in 1961 as their "honored place in enlightened philanthropic programs."[45]

Patricia L. Rosenfield is Senior Fellow at the Rockefeller Archive Center (RAC), Sleepy Hollow, New York. From 2013 to 2015, she directed the RAC's Ford Foundation History Project as part of her responsibilities connecting practitioners and scholars of philanthropy. The project's overview publication, *The Ford Foundation: Constant Themes, Historical Variations, 1936–2001*, was coauthored with Rachel Wimpee and is available at http://rockarch.org/publications/ford/overview. In 2014, PublicAffairs published Rosenfield's *A World of Giving: Carnegie*

Corporation of New York—A Century of International Grantmaking. She previously directed the Corporation's Carnegie Scholars Program and its program on Strengthening Human Resources in Developing Countries.

Notes

I am grateful for the insights of: Nicole Howe Buggs, CCNY; Daniela Kaisth, formerly Institute of International Education; Martha Loerke, Open Society Foundations; Rik Treiber, Peter G. Peterson Foundation and formerly CCNY; and my RAC colleagues, Jack Meyers, James Allen Smith, Laura Miller, Tom Rosenbaum, Barbara Shubinski, Rachel Wimpee and Marissa Vassari. Dr Miller's expert editing and reading of the draft chapter are deeply appreciated, as are Dr Wimpee's special review efforts. The opinions expressed in this chapter are solely the responsibility of the author and do not reflect policy of the RAC, the FF or the author's previous employer, the CCNY. The author is responsible for errors of fact or interpretation.

1. Akira Iriye, *Cultural Internationalism and World Order* (Baltimore, MD: Johns Hopkins University Press, 1997), 100; *100 Years: The Rockefeller Foundation*, "Education, International Education Board", Rockefeller100.org, Rockefeller Archive Center (henceforth RAC), retrieved 1 December 2014 from http://rockefeller100.org/exhibits/show/education/international-education-board.
2. Patricia L. Rosenfield, *A World of Giving: Carnegie Corporation of New York—A Century of International Philanthropy* (New York: PublicAffairs, 2014), 96.
3. Gaither Study Committee, *Report of the Study for the Ford Foundation on Policy and Program* (New York: Ford Foundation, 1949), 79; Patricia L. Rosenfield and Rachel Wimpee, *The Ford Foundation: Constant Themes, Historical Variations, 1936–2001*, RAC, 2015, retrieved 2 April 2017 from http://rockarch.org/publications/ford/overview/FordFoundationHistory1936-2001.pdf.
4. Anon., "Why Foreign Students: Need for New Look at Educational Exchange," 1, 15 September 1961, Report 001366, Ford Foundation Records (henceforth FFR), Catalogued Report (FA739), RAC.
5. The research also draws on the author's experience directing CCNY's Carnegie Scholars Program, 1999–2011.
6. Thomas A. Troyer, "The 1969 Private Foundation Law: Historical Perspective on its Origins and Underpinnings," *Exempt Organization Tax Review* 27(1) (2000), 60; James Allen Smith, "The Foundation Center: 50 Years on," in M. Nauffts (ed.), *Philanthropy in the 21st Century* (New York: Foundation Center, 2006), 1–12; David D. Hammack and Helmut K. Anheier, *A Versatile American Institution: The Changing Ideals and Realities of Philanthropic Foundations* (Washington, DC: Brookings Institution Press, 2013), 83–84; Dennis P. McIlnay, "Philanthropy at Fifty: Four Moments in Time," *Foundation News and Commentary* 39(5) (1998).

7. John F. Kennedy Presidential Library and Museum, "Biographical Profiles: McGeorge Bundy," retrieved 2 April 2017 from http://www.jfklibrary.org/Research/Research-Aids/Ready-Reference/Biographies-and-Profiles/McGeorge-Bundy.aspx.
8. Ford Foundation, "Travel and Study Awards for members of the staff of the late Senator Robert F. Kennedy," Request for Grant Action, 10 July 1968, FFR, Grants, Grant 689-0762, Reel 5634, RAC.
9. Ibid.
10. McGeorge Bundy, Ford Foundation Oral History Project, interviewer, Charles T. Morrissey, 11 February 1972, 16, FFR, RAC.
11. Philip Warden, "Ford Grants Aid Travel of Congressmen," *Chicago Tribune Press Service*, 21 February 1969, retrieved 2 April 2017 from http://archives.chicagotribune.com/1969/02/21/page/71/article/ford-grants-aid-travels-of-congressmen.
12. United States Congress Joint Committee on Internal Revenue Taxation, General Explanation of the Tax Reform Act of 1969, H.R. 13270, 91st Congress, Public Law 91-172, Washington, US Govt. Printing Office, 1970, 50, retrieved 2 April 2017 from https://archive.org/details/generalexplanati00jcs1670.
13. McGeorge Bundy, Oral History Project, 20.
14. Ford Foundation, "Grants to Individuals: New Light on an Old Subject," March 1976, Report 004046, FFR, Catalogued Reports (FA739), RAC, 7.
15. Ibid., 10.
16. Ibid., Appendix F-1.
17. Ibid., 15–16.
18. Pearl T. Robinson memo to Robert H. Edwards, "The Middle East and Africa Field Research Fellowship Program for Afro-Americans," 7 July 1975, Report 009022, FFR, Catalogued Reports (FA739), RAC.
19. Alan Pifer, "Foundations and the Unity of Charitable Organizations," in *Philanthropy in an Age of Transition: The Essays of Alan Pifer* (New York: Foundation Center, 1984), 52–53, originally published in CCNY, *Annual Report 1969*, CCNY Records. Pifer called for a commission to address concerns about the Act. John D. Rockefeller III established the Commission on Private Philanthropy and Public Needs, on which Pifer served. Its 1975 report helped limit the most damaging parts of the Act: see Olivier Zunz, *Philanthropy in America: A History* (Princeton, NJ: Princeton University Press, 2011), 226–32; and Eleanor L. Brilliant, *Private Charity and Public Inquiry: A History of the Filer and Peterson Commissions* (Bloomington, IN: Indiana University Press, 2000), 87-98.
20. Vartan Gregorian, "Foreword," in *Carnegie Scholars Program: A Five-Year Review 2000–2004* (New York: Carnegie Corporation of New York, 2005), vii.
21. Rik Treiber, interview with author, 19 August 2014.
22. This new program supports individual research in the social sciences and humanities on urgent contemporary issues: retrieved 2 April 2017 from https://www.carnegie.org/interactives/acfellows/#!
23. Teresa J. Odendahl, "Foundations and Their Role in Antiterrorism Enforcement: Findings from a Recent Study and Implications for the

Future," 9 June 2005, talk at the Foundation Center, Washington DC, Center for Public & Nonprofit Leadership, Georgetown University, Washington, DC, 2, retrieved 2 April 2017 from http://cnpl.georgetown.edu/doc_pool/odendahl060905.pdf.

24. Retrieved 2 April 2017 from http://www.treasury.gov/resource-center/sanctions/SDN-List/Pages/default.aspx.
25. Odendahl, "Foundations," 1. See also Mark Sidel, "Counter-terrorism and the Enabling Legal and Political Environment for Civil Society: A Comparative Analysis of 'War on Terror' States," *International Journal of Not-for-Profit Law* 10(3) (2008), 749, retrieved 2 April 2017 from http://www.icnl.org/research/journal/vol10iss3/vol10iss3.pdf.
26. US Department of the Treasury, Resource Center, Specially Designated Nationals List, retrieved 2 April 2017 from https://www.treasury.gov/resource-center/sanctions/SDN-List/Pages/default.aspx.
27. US Department of the Treasury, Anti-terrorist Financing Guidelines: Voluntary Best Practices for US-Based Charities, December 2005, 1, retrieved 2 April 2017 from http://www.treasury.gov/resource-center/terrorist-illicit-finance/Documents/guidelines_charities.pdf.
28. Odendahl, "Foundations," 2, emphasis in original.
29. Ibid., 5.
30. Ibid., 7.
31. Vartan Gregorian, "Foreword," *Carnegie Scholars Program: a five-year review of scholarship on Islam 2005—2009* (New York: Carnegie Corporation of New York, 2010), vii.
32. Treiber, interview.
33. Nicole Howe Buggs, interview with author, 2 December 2014.
34. Martha Loerke, interview with author, 3 December 2014.
35. Daniela Kaisth, interview with author, 4 December 2014. Kaisth retired from IIE in mid-2015.
36. Odendahl, "Foundations," 6.
37. Ibid., 10.
38. Rosenfield, *World of Giving*, 176–78; Social Science Research Council, Evaluation of the experience of foreign students who are studying or have studied in the USA, FFR, Grants, Grant 0520091, Reel 0403, RAC; Rockefeller Foundation Records, Social Science Research Council Cross-Cultural Education, RG1.1, Series 200, Box 59, Folder 704, 2 April 1952, RAC.
39. For an overview of FF fellowship and exchange grant evaluation efforts since 1954, see Ford Foundation History Project, "Ford Foundation Fellowship Program Evaluations: A Review of Recommended Next Steps," May 2014, RAC.
40. Buggs, interview.
41. Loerke, interview.
42. Kaisth, summarized comments received from her colleagues, 4 December 2014.
43. However, the FF has made a major investment in a ten-year evaluation of its largest grant ever, the $355 million International Fellows

Program. Retrieved 2 April 2017 from http://www.iie.org/Programs/Ford-Foundation-IFP.
44. Kaisth, interview.
45. John Gardner, President, CCNY, *Annual Report 1961*, 15, CCNY Records, Rare Book and Manuscript Library, Columbia University Libraries.

References

Brilliant, Eleanor L. *Private Charity and Public Inquiry: A History of the Filer and Peterson Commissions* (Bloomington, IN: Indiana University Press, 2000).
Gaither Study Committee. *Report of the Study for the Ford Foundation on Policy and Program* (New York: Ford Foundation, 1949).
Gregorian, Vartan. "Foreword," in Carnegie Corporation of New York, *Carnegie Scholars Program: A Five-Year Review 2000–2004* (New York: Carnegie Corporation of New York, 2005), vii–viii.
Hammack, David D., and Helmut K. Anheier. *A Versatile American Institution: The Changing Ideals and Realities of Philanthropic Foundations* (Washington, DC: Brookings Institution Press, 2013).
Iriye, Akira. *Cultural Internationalism and World Order* (Baltimore, MD: Johns Hopkins University Press, 1997).
Pifer, Alan. "Foundations and the Unity of Charitable Organizations," in A. Pifer, *Philanthropy in an Age of Transition: The Essays of Alan Pifer* (New York: Foundation Center, 1984), 52–53.
Rosenfield, Patricia L. *A World of Giving: Carnegie Corporation of New York—A Century of International Philanthropy* (New York: PublicAffairs, 2014).
Sidel, Mark. "Counter-terrorism and the Enabling Legal and Political Environment for Civil Society: A Comparative Analysis of 'War on Terror' States," *International Journal of Not-for-Profit Law* 10(3) (2008), retrieved 2 April 2017 from http://www.icnl.org/research/journal/vol10iss3/vol10iss3.pdf.
Smith, James Allen. "The Foundation Center: 50 Years on," in M. Nauffts (ed.), *Philanthropy in the 21st Century* (New York: Foundation Center, 2006), 1–12.
Troyer, Thomas A. "The 1969 Private Foundation Law: Historical Perspective on its Origins and Underpinnings," *Exempt Organization Tax Review* 27(1) (2000): 52–65.
Zunz, Olivier. *Philanthropy in America: A History* (Princeton, NJ: Princeton University Press, 2011).

 16

GLOBAL NETWORKS, SOFT POWER AND THE US MILITARY
Carol Atkinson

Introduction

This chapter describes the international programs at the US military's war and staff colleges. The US military has welcomed foreign military personnel (soldiers and defense-related civilians) into its professional military schools since the late 1800s. At first, the foreign students were only observers, but later they attended as full-fledged participants. Today, the foreign students are required to accomplish the same work as their US counterparts. The incorporation of foreign military personnel into the student bodies of the war and staff colleges was initially controversial, but the military programs have proven their worth both from the perspective of the foreign governments who have sent their soldiers for training in the United States and from the perspective of the US military. For the United States, the programs help to build knowledge about US society and US culture, as well as support for US foreign policies. For the US military, the programs build understanding and trust necessary for effective cooperation and interoperability with US forces.

The US military has many different types of educational programs that host foreign participants; however, the US military's war and staff colleges are particularly noteworthy because these are the elite professional military institutions of the United States. Their graduates, both US and foreign, are the rising leaders in their militaries and in their defense establishments. The foreign governments that send their soldiers to study at US war and staff colleges send their brightest and most capable personnel. In turn, the foreign (and US) graduates of US war and staff colleges rise through the ranks to become multinational force commanders, chiefs of their services or their defense establishments, and even sometimes heads of state. Thus, unlike many other types of exchange programs for high school or university students, the military programs host military and government personnel who have, or will likely have, a direct and significant impact on the domestic and foreign policies of their home countries. The military programs are designed to accomplish three specific goals: (1) to increase understanding and defense cooperation between the United States and foreign countries; (2) to support combined operations and interoperability between US forces and other nations' militaries; and (3) to increase the ability of participating nations to instill and maintain democratic institutions and practices within their militaries and governments.[1]

The chapter begins by placing military educational exchanges within the overall context of US security cooperation. It provides information on US military exchange programs, including their goals and funding sources. The next section of the chapter then looks specifically at the exchange programs at some of the US military's war and staff colleges. Finally, it examines how the military programs have contributed to US national security by building and maintaining a US-centric global military network that extends US soft power into some of the highest levels of governance around the world.

US Security Cooperation and Military Educational Exchanges

Military educational exchange programs have long been a part of US security cooperation. Soldiers and defense-related civilians from around the world have been invited to participate in numerous US military technical training and professional education programs for over one hundred years. On an annual basis, the US military currently hosts over 60,000 foreign participants in numerous US training and education courses across the United States, in NATO schools and as part of regional combatant command initiatives throughout the world. In fiscal year 2013 alone, approximately 64,000 students from 152 countries participated in US-sponsored military training under numerous security cooperation initiatives.[2]

The purposes and funding of these courses are quite varied. Foreign governments can purchase slots for their personnel at US professional military schools (such as the war and staff colleges) as well as other types of courses, such as technical training associated with the equipment that they purchase from the United States. In fiscal year 2013, foreign governments spent more than US$447 million to send their personnel to US military schools.[3] The US government also provides grant funding for foreign military personnel and defense-related civilians whose governments cannot afford to send them to US education and training courses. The US Department of State funds the US government's premier military educational grant program, called International Military Education and Training (IMET), as well as funding training related to improving the ability of African countries to support peacekeeping operations, and training that strengthens the ability of Central and South American countries to combat international drug trafficking.[4] In fiscal year 2013, the Department of State spent US$106.4 million on funding the IMET program,[5] which supports attendance at a variety of courses from short one-week training courses to the education programs at US professional military schools that last about one year. Highlighting the importance of the professional military schools to US security cooperation, approximately 50 percent of IMET funding is allocated for grants to foreign personnel to participate in the educational programs at the US war and staff colleges.[6]

In addition to these State Department-funded opportunities, the US Department of Defense funds five regional centers (such as the George C. Marshall European Center for Security Studies in Germany) as well as a variety of other types of professional military education courses, including cadet exchanges at the military academies, and courses supporting a variety of operational missions such as antiterrorism, landmine awareness and clearance, disaster response, humanitarian assistance, drug interdiction and law enforcement, and pilot training.[7] According to senior US military commanders, IMET courses are "enormously" beneficial for both for the foreign personnel who attend in terms of their personal professional development and for the US military in terms of improving interoperability with US forces.[8]

US War and Staff College Programs

The military educational programs at the US war and staff colleges are one among many opportunities that the US Department of Defense opens to foreign military participation. However, the war and staff college programs are one of the most effective in terms of building US influence abroad for a variety of reasons, which are described below.[9] These reasons also help us to identify specific characteristics of the exchange experience at the war and staff colleges that make these types of programs effective in fostering goodwill toward the United States, and increasing understanding between the foreign participants and US citizens—all important in building US influence abroad. In terms of operational effectiveness, the military's programs are instrumental in building a US-centric network of military and national defense professionals who know one another, share common operational concepts and have established varying levels of mutual understanding and trust.

The first reason why military programs have been effective in accomplishing their objectives is that the participants live in local US communities and interact on a daily basis with US people. Living in a local US community results in a more authentic experience, whereby the participant can see and evaluate positives and negatives firsthand rather than relying on mass media or other secondary sources of information.

Second, the schools are longer in duration than most of the other types of training and education courses offered by the US government. At the war and staff colleges, the foreign participants attend the school's ten to eleven-month course along with their US counterparts, yet their stay is longer because the schools also have orientation programs for the foreign officers (and their families) prior to the beginning of the formal course. Some of the foreign officers may also attend a US Department of Defense English language course in preparation for their program if they need to improve or refresh their English language skills. Thus, most of the participants spend at least an entire year in the United States.

Third, the educational programs are specifically designed to build social and professional networks between US officers and their foreign counterparts. Integration and socialization into the US military community are not left to chance, but are an explicit goal with specific activities designed to help accomplish them. Unlike educational exchanges at civilian universities, socialization and community building are not collateral effects that might or might not happen when people are in the same room together for a class. The military schools have designed curriculum, sponsorship programs, field trips and specific educational environments in order to build a sense of community amongst the students.

Fourth, the participants are the rising elite leaders within their militaries. At the staff colleges, the students are midcareer officers: the majority are majors and lieutenant commanders with about twelve years of experience as an officer. At the war colleges, the students are senior officers. The majority are colonels and captains (the equivalent naval rank) with about twenty years of experience in their militaries.

Thus, they are likely to hold influential positions within their home governments or multinational organizations in the future.

Fifth, the programs host participants from a wide range of countries. There is usually only one person from a particular country at any one college. This is important in terms of building cross-cultural relationships because a participant cannot socially retreat into a group of compatriots from his or her home country. This is unlike civilian exchange programs at US universities that host large cohorts of students from the same country where the exchange participants may be much more culturally isolated because they choose to live, study and socialize with other exchange students from their home country.

Sixth, the military officers are encouraged to bring their families with them and the majority do so. The family is a "force multiplier" that opens up even more social and cultural opportunities for the foreign officers, such as involvement in children's schooling and children's sports teams, and providing motivation to go on family trips. Children and spouses help to involve the officer in a wider array of activities than if the officer was alone. The family also helps to soften the effects of culture shock by being a trusted environment within which to share the challenges and successes of living in a foreign country.

In the United States, each of the four military services (the Army, the Navy, the Marine Corps and the Air Force) has its own war college and its own staff college devoted to educating the US officer corps. At the national level, the Department of Defense also runs several schools in the Washington, DC area that are focused on national-level decision-making, the integration of the military capabilities of all of the services, and the fostering of inter-agency cooperation between the military and relevant agencies of the US government. All of these elite professional military schools have exchange programs. The following section briefly describes the programs at the National Defense University, US Army war and staff colleges, and US Navy schools.

US National Defense University

The National Defense University (NDU) at Fort McNair in Washington, DC contains the most elite of the US military's professional schools. The goal of these schools is to educate personnel, both military and civilian, already identified as national defense leaders. The focus is on joint ("joint" means two or more different military services) planning and operations, as opposed to doctrine and command issues specific to any individual military service. The International Fellows Program at NDU began in 1984 with six international fellows. As of May 2017, there have been over 1,800 international graduates representing approximately 130 countries.[10] The 2015 student bodies at the NDU's three main schools included 102 international fellows representing sixty-four different countries. As of February 2015, forty-nine international fellows had been inducted into NDU's International Fellows Hall of Fame.[11] In order to receive this honor, an international graduate must "have attained through merit the highest positions in their nation's armed forces, service component, or government, or ... have held an equivalent position in a multinational organization."[12] Admiral José Santiago Valdés Álvarez is a good example: a 1995 graduate of the Industrial College of the Armed Forces, he had a long military career, including service as Chief of the General Staff of the Mexican Navy and became the first Mexican officer to be inducted into NDU's Hall of Fame in 2014. In reflecting upon his time at NDU, Admiral Valdés observed: "NDU gave me the opportunity to learn more about American citizens, showed me the real American culture, [enhanced my] strategic thinking and global vision, and showed me the importance of having long-term views of economic, political, social, and military issues. It helped us work with American organizations and in strengthening relations between Mexico and the United States."[13]

US Army Schools

The US Army's Command and General Staff College (CGSC) at Fort Leavenworth, Kansas, has the oldest exchange program of any of the military schools. According to historian John Reichley, the first foreign participant was a Swiss officer who came to study at Leavenworth in 1894, but he did not finish the course. The first foreign officers, two lieutenants from the Mexican Army, graduated in 1908. A Puerto Rican officer graduated in 1910 and then two Cuban officers in 1912.[14] Since then, the presence of foreign officers has continued to grow. The class of 2015 had a total of 1,100 graduates, including sixty-nine foreign officers.[15] As of May 2014, more than 7,500 foreign defense-related personnel (mostly military officers) had graduated.[16] Much like the participants in the other military schools, the influence of CGSC graduates extends worldwide. More than half of the foreign graduates have earned the rank of general officer and 256 officers from seventy different countries have become chief of their military, commander of a multinational force, or head of state.[17] Notably, as of April 2014, twenty-eight foreign graduates of CGSC had become heads of state.[18] One of the most renowned of these graduates is the former President of Indonesia, Susilo Bambang Yudhoyono: he was the first popularly elected President of Indonesia, serving in that capacity from 2004 until 2014, and he is widely credited with improving prosperity, stability and democratic accountability in Indonesia. Before becoming a politician, Yudhoyono was a career soldier, retiring as a general officer from the Indonesian military in 2000. He is a 1991 graduate of the US Army Command and General Staff College and was inducted into the CGSC Hall of Fame in 2005. In a speech during his induction ceremony, he described his experience as follows:

> "and as with the other inductees, I would not have been sent here without the friendship of the United States, a mutual friendship that proudly continues today. It is a vital friendship, for these educational exchanges allow us to learn about each other, and from one another as soldiers, as nations, as citizens of the world. I learned from my peers here that honor and duty crosses national boundaries. We learned from each other the value of democracy, of human rights, as well as the importance of sovereignty. We learned from each other how to move forward in this tenuous obstacle course called nation-building. That immeasurable experience was strengthened by the friendships made during my stay. Friendships, between nations as well as individuals, are what relieve us in times of crisis."[19]

In 2015, Yudhoyono pushed for an Indonesian scholarship program that would fund the attendance of a second Indonesian officer annually at CGSC (the first officer is funded through IMET), another clear indicator of the value to his home government of the CGSC experience.

The US Army's War College at Carlisle Barracks, Pennsylvania, has a curriculum focusing on how to use landpower at the strategic and global levels.[20] Its International Fellows Program began in 1977 and the first international students graduated in the summer of 1978. The Army War College currently has the largest number of foreign military personnel in its international program, both in absolute numbers and in percentages. The class that graduated in the summer of 2015 had 387 officers, of whom there were seventy-nine international officers from seventy-three countries (about 20 percent of the student body).[21] As of May 2014, 1,380 international fellows had graduated; of these, 594 (43 percent) had obtained the rank of general officer, and forty-eight had achieved the highest-ranking position in their military, an equivalent position in a multinational organization, or become head of state.[22] Of note, in 2014, Major General Kristin Lund of Norway, a 2007 graduate of the US Army War College, became the first female Force Commander of a United Nations (UN) peacekeeping force (see appendix).[23]

US Navy Schools

The US Naval War College is located in Newport, Rhode Island. Unlike the other US military services' war and staff colleges, the US Navy did not integrate international officers into its main programs until quite recently, but developed separate programs for them, and some of this separation still remains. At the senior level, US personnel attend the College of Naval Warfare and the international students attend the Naval Command College. The senior-level international program began in 1956 and as of May 2017, 2,148 foreign officers representing 91 countries had graduated; of these, about 50 percent had achieved flag rank (the naval equivalent of general officer), and 194 had become heads of their navies. International alumni include two heads of state, three defense chiefs, numerous ambassadors, legislators and other high-ranking government officials.[24] Although the international students are integrated with their US counterparts in the classroom, the programs retain some differences. For example, the international students are not eligible for advanced degrees and do not receive formal grades.[25] A comparable separation of programs remains at the intermediate level, with US personnel attending the College of Naval Command and Staff and international students attending the Naval Staff College. The intermediate-level program began in 1972 and as of May 2017, there have been over 2,300 international alumni, representing 134 countries; of these, 327 had become flag officers (the naval equivalent of general officer) and 136 had become head of their military service.[26]

The naval programs, despite their different organization, have similar impacts to the schools of the other services. The comments of Rear Admiral Emil Eftimov, a 2005 graduate of the Naval Command College, illustrate the importance of field trips and experiential learning. Admiral Eftimov, from the Bulgarian Navy, remarked:

> "for me, the US Naval War College offered not only a good defense education, but a mix of personality infusions, learning of regional defense models, and different methods of strategic applications. My learning of how the US system of defense and government works brought all of us closer together for a better understanding of the US system, and of one another. The NCC field trips to Coca Cola and Boeing Corporations, for example, were unforgettable visuals on how a free enterprise works; their history and leadership-management styles, business development, how they employ people, and how does private industry intertwine with the defense sectors. These visits helped me to think differently ... And these forays bonded one even closer to their classmates from several different

countries; we'd discuss, compare, and discern the industrial sites mode of operando as a total group."[27]

US Military Soft Power: Extending US Influence Abroad

The ostensible purpose of most education programs is classroom learning; students enroll in order to learn information that will be useful in their current and future jobs. However, as many of the chapters in this book show, international scholarship and exchange programs also help the host country to build its soft power through participants' social and cultural experiences. In general, a country's international influence is strengthened when people in other parts of the world have a positive perception of it; they like what its government and people stand for, and they wish to emulate those desirable characteristics. Joseph Nye has labeled this type of persuasive influence "soft power."[28]

Most international scholarship programs help the host country accrue some measure of soft power because participants often have a positive experience during their time abroad, or at least regard the time abroad with nostalgia. In this respect, military officers are similar to most participants the world over: they come away from their time abroad with increased understanding and affinity for their host country, their host institution, and the people who invited them into their homes and lives. They have good memories and tell their friends back home about their travels, their studies and the people they met. If they held stereotypes about their host nation, they would have confronted them; and, in the process, they might help to dispel prejudices that others might have. The exchange participants can now navigate the culture and language of their host country much more easily.[29]

While the international programs at US military professional schools share some similarities with other types of scholarship programs, there are some differences. For example, the educational environment at the US military's war and staff colleges is specifically designed to build social cohesion and a positive experience. Each student is assigned to a small seminar group of twelve to sixteen students that generally includes two international officers, each from a different region of the world. This group remains together throughout the day for a five-month period. Different instructors teach different subjects but the students always remain together in the same room, which is unlike the civilian university practice of having students mix with a different group of students in a different classroom for each class. The military students, unlike university students, have a "home-base" or core group that they get to know very well as a function of their primary school activity: going to classes. The military's seminar groups also participate in intramural sports, social events and group planning exercises together. Each foreign military officer is also assigned at least one sponsor, who helps the officer navigate US society and also invites the officer and his family to social gatherings and holiday celebrations with the sponsor's family. This intensive social integration in the military schools is key to building trust, cooperation and familiarity amongst the officers from different countries. These types of activities and organizational structures are how the military schools have explicitly designed social environments that help the students build cross-cultural understanding and a global network of professionals, some of whom know each other very well.

Most of the international officers at US war and staff colleges, as well as their spouses and children, enjoy their time in the United States and come away with fond memories of it. In many instances, the friendships that they formed will last throughout their careers and into retirement. The majority of the participants try to keep in contact with their fellow classmates (both US and international) and with the people, both military and civilian, who were their hosts and sponsors.[30] The US war and staff colleges also have active international alumni associations that help their graduates to stay in touch—for example, by hosting continuing education seminars as well as reunions abroad and in the United States. With the advent of Facebook (in 2004) and Twitter (in 2006), keeping in touch is much easier, with Facebook alumni webpages and Twitter updates through which the schools keep in touch with US and international alumni. As an example, at the National Defense University, all alumni receive a free lifetime Google-based email account with the @ndualumni.org extension. NDU also maintains an easy-to-use webpage where alumni can click on a link and update fellow alumni about their important life events, such as promotions and new jobs.

Conclusion

Academic research on how the military is used as an instrument of foreign policy rarely examines how the US military seeks to improve interoperability and extend its influence through military exchange programs. As a consequence, it neglects how soft power is built by military institutions, and, in particular, by the US military. Political science is replete with analyses of how the United States uses its military hard power assets coercively: to attack an enemy, to defend against an attack, to deter military buildups, to counter new weapon systems, to threaten adversaries and the like. However, the US military has also been successful in building its soft power by actively engaging militaries around the world through a variety of programs, of which the international programs at US war and staff colleges are one of the most important.

The programs at the US war and staff colleges are unique, important and worthy of scholarly attention because they help to build soft power amongst one of the most important and influential groups of people for a country's domestic and foreign policies: current and future military leaders. The programs host participants from autocratic countries as well as from democratic countries. These officers are not just ordinary citizens, but wield both the weapons of war and political power. The ideas that they take away from their time in the United States reach into the highest levels of military and political decision-making around the world. As one example, I have shown in previous analyses that countries that participate in the exchange programs at the US war and staff colleges are two times more likely to successfully transition away from authoritarianism and 8 percent more likely to improve their human rights practices.[31]

The construction of soft power is an explicit goal of the international exchange and scholarship programs at the US military's war and staff colleges, and the faculty and staff at these schools work hard to build it. Through their efforts and those of the US and international alumni, the US military has been able to strengthen military-to-military ties, build partner relationships, improve interoperability with US allies, and increase goodwill toward the United States and its citizens.

Carol Atkinson is author of *Military Soft Power: Public Diplomacy through Military Educational Exchanges*. This book examines how the US military extends its influence or "soft power" worldwide through the professional and social networks developed by US and foreign military officers at the US military's elite schools, its war and staff colleges. She is a 1984 graduate of the US Air Force Academy and holds a Ph.D. in Political Science from Duke University. She was both a student and instructor at the US Air Force's staff college. She retired as a lieutenant colonel from the military in 2005 and subsequently taught international relations at several US universities. She was also an exchange student herself in 2013 as a Fulbright Scholar at the G.S. Rakovski National Defense College in Sofia, Bulgaria.

Appendix: Kristin Lund

On 17 February 2015, Major General Kristin Lund of Norway became the first female graduate of the U.S Army War College to be inducted into the college's International Hall of Fame. A 2007 graduate of the War College, General Lund was recognized for her service as commander of the United Nations Peacekeeping Force in Cyprus (UNFICYP) since August 2014, as well as her pioneering role for military women. She is the first woman to command a UN peacekeeping force, the first female Army officer to be promoted to the rank of Major General in Norway and the first international woman to attend the US Army War College.[32] She began her military career by enlisting in Norway's Home Guard Youth in 1976. She later attended the Officer's Candidate School for the Army Logistics Branch and officially joined the Army in 1979.[33] She has had a distinguished career, with deployments in 1986 to Lebanon with the UN Interim Force, in 1991 to the Middle East for the US-led Operation Desert Storm; in 1992–93 to Bosnia with a UN Protection Force and later NATO-led forces; and in 2003–04 to Afghanistan with the International Security Assistance Force.[34] In her remarks to War College students, she described her experience at the Army War College as "truly an academic and cultural experience for life" and noted, "the network that you can establish ... is priceless. There are so many occasions when I have met fellow graduates from the Army War College and on all those occasions our joint experience in this institution has provided a very good starting point for cooperation."[35]

Notes

1. US Department of Defense and US Department of State, *Foreign Military Training, Fiscal Years 2013 and 2014, Joint Report to Congress, Volume I*, II-1–II-2.
2. Ibid., ii.
3. Ibid., II-1.
4. Ibid., II-1–II-2.
5. US Department of State, *Congressional Budget Justification, Foreign Assistance*, Summary Tables, Fiscal Year 2014, 3, retrieved 2 April 2017 from http://www.state.gov/documents/organization/208292.pdf.
6. US Government Accountability Office (GAO), "International Military Education and Training, Agencies Should Emphasize Human Rights Training and Improve Evaluations," October 2011, 12, retrieved 2 April 2017 from http://www.gao.gov/new.items/d12123.pdf.

7. US Department of Defense and US Department of State, *Foreign Military Training*, II-3–II-7.
8. General (retired) David Petraeus, interview with author, 29 March 2016.
9. For detailed analysis and empirical assessment of these factors, see Carol Atkinson, *Military Soft Power: Public Diplomacy through Military Educational Exchange Programs* (Lanham, MD: Rowman & Littlefield, 2014).
10. US National Defense University (NDU), "NDU International Alumni Program," International Student Management Office, retrieved 2 May 2017 from http://ismo.ndu.edu/Alumni/AlumniProgram.aspx.
11. Simone K. Bak, "Latvian Foreign Minister Inducted into International Fellows Hall of Fame," *ISMO News Stories*, 5 February 2015, retrieved 2 April 2017 from http://ismo.ndu.edu/News/tabid/8824/Article/572204/latvian-foreign-minister-inducted-into-international-fellows-hall-of-fame.aspx.
12. US National Defense University (NDU), "International Fellows Hall of Fame Program," International Student Management Office, retrieved 2 April 2017 from http://ismo.ndu.edu/Alumni/InternationalHallofFameProgram.aspx.
13. US National Defense University (NDU), "NDU Inducts Two International Alumni into Hall of Fame," National Defense University, press release, 8 September 2014, retrieved 2 April 2017 from http://www.ndu.edu/News/PressReleases/tabid/6464/Article/572612/ndu-inducts-two-international-alumni-into-hall-of-fame.aspx.
14. John Reichley, *International Officers: A Century of Participation at the United States Army Command and General Staff College* (Fort Leavenworth: US Army Command and General Staff College, 1994).
15. Command and General Staff College Foundation, 2015, "CGSC Class of 2015 Graduates June 12," news release posted on 16 June 2015, retrieved 2 April 2017 from http://www.cgscfoundation.org/cgsc-class-of-2015-graduates-june-12.
16. "Three to Be Inducted into Fort LV's International Hall of Fame," *Leavenworth Times*, 24 April 2014, retrieved 2 April 2017 from http://www.leavenworthtimes.com/article/20140424/News/140429558.
17. "International Hall of Fame Welcomes 3," *Leavenworth Times*, 8 May 2014, retrieved 2 April 2017 from http://www.ftleavenworthlamp.com/article/20140508/News/140509370.
18. "Three to Be Inducted into Fort LV's International Hall of Fame."
19. Susilo Bambang Yudhoyono, "International Hall of Fame Award," speech presented at the International Hall of Fame Award Ceremony, Fort Leavenworth, Kansas, 12 September 2005, *DISAM Journal* 28(1) (2005): 96–97.
20. "About the US Army War College," US Army War College, retrieved 2 April 2017 from http://www.carlisle.army.mil/overview.htm.
21. "CSA Honors Army War College Class of 2015: Intellectual, Strategic, Necessary," *Army War College Community Banner*, 5 June 2015, retrieved 2 April 2017 from http://www.carlisle.army.mil/banner/archiveDisplay.cfm?articleMonth=6&articleYear=2015.

22. "International USAWC Alumni Return to Carlisle," *Army War College Community Torch*, Spring 2014 (faculty edition), 23.
23. Ibid., 22.
24. US Naval War College, *Naval Command College*, retrieved 1 May 2017 from https://www.usnwc.edu/Departments---Colleges/International-Programs/Naval-Command-College.aspx.
25. Ibid.
26. US Naval War College, *Naval Staff College*, retrieved 1 May 2017 from https://www.usnwc.edu/Departments—-Colleges/International-Programs/Naval-Staff-College.aspx.
27. Interview by David F. Manning, transcribed in *Global Arms of Seapower: The Newport Connection* (Lawrence, KS: Minuteman Press, 2014), 263.
28. Joseph S. Nye, Jr., "Get Smart: Combining Hard and Soft Power," *Foreign Affairs* 88(4) (2009), 161.
29. For in depth analysis, see Atkinson, *Military Soft Power*.
30. Ibid.
31. Ibid.
32. "Norwegian Maj Gen Kristin Lund joins International Hall of Fame," *Army War College Banner*, 17 February 2015, retrieved 26 March 2016 from http://www.carlisle.army.mil/banner/archiveDisplay.cfm?articleMonth=2&articleYear=2015.
33. Interview by David F. Manning, transcribed in *Global Arms of Strategic Balance* (Lawrence, KS: Minuteman Press, 2012), 97.
34. "First UN female force commander takes reins in Cyprus," *UN News Centre*, 11 August 2014, retrieved 26 March 2016 from http://www.un.org/apps/news/story.asp?NewsID=48462#.VvceQWQrJuU.
35. As quoted in "Norwegian Maj Gen Kristin Lund joins International Hall of Fame."

References

Atkinson, Carol. *Military Soft Power: Public Diplomacy through Military Educational Exchange Programs* (Lanham, MD: Rowman & Littlefield, 2014).

Manning, David F. *Global Arms of Seapower: The Newport Connection* (Lawrence, KS: Minuteman Press, 2014).

Manning, David F. *Global Arms of Strategic Balance* (Lawrence, KS: Minuteman Press, 2012).

Nye, Joseph S., Jr. "Get Smart: Combining Hard and Soft Power," *Foreign Affairs* 88(4) (2009): 160–163.

Reichley, John. *International Officers: A Century of Participation at the United States Army Command and General Staff College* (Fort Leavenworth, KS: US Army Command and General Staff College, 1994).

 17

AMERICAN FULBRIGHTERS IN CHINA (1979–2014)
Guangqiu Xu

Introduction

In 1979, the Chinese leaders realized that China had to open its educational system to developments in the outside world in order to help the Chinese learn Western science and technology to attain China's Four Modernizations in science and technology, industry, agriculture and defense. The year 1979 saw China opening its doors to foreigners, especially teachers from the West, and since then, a number of American Fulbrighters have been invited to teach and do research every year.

Have American Fulbrighters had an ideological impact on Chinese campuses? If so, how? What are Beijing's reactions to Fulbrighters' influence in Chinese universities? What are the implications of the Chinese government policy toward Western ideology? This chapter begins with a general overview of the China Fulbright Programs, then focuses on the impact of the Americans on the Chinese in the past thirty-five years and finally discusses the implications of the impact of American Fulbrighters on China.[1]

The Ideological Impact of American Fulbrighters in China

In the fall of 1979, the Beijing government formally requested American assistance in the recruitment and support of about twenty specialists in English language teaching over a three-year period. The Council for International Exchange of Scholars (CIES), a private agency cooperating with the US government in the administration of Fulbright scholar grants for advanced research and university teaching, selected four Teaching English as a Second Language (TESL) specialists and assigned them to Beijing University in March 1980. For the first time, Americans returned to the Chinese classroom since 1949. Today the China Fulbright programs are one of the largest in the world, consisting of three parts: American lecturers and research scholars in China, American graduate students in China, and Chinese visiting research scholars and graduate students in the United States. Currently, each year approximately ten to twenty US lecturers, five to ten US research scholars, and fifty to seventy American graduate students and recent graduates are in China, while approximately one hundred Chinese visiting research scholars, professional associates, foreign language teaching assistants and Ph.D./MA candidates in American Studies are in the United States each year.[2]

American professors not only help Chinese carry out higher education reforms, but have also influenced the Chinese with Western values and ideology. Their ideological impact on the Chinese students can be seen in several areas.

First, American Fulbrighters in China help Chinese students understand better American political and economic systems as well as American society. Since the Fulbright exchange programs were developed to urge Americans to take responsibility for creating a constructive image of Americans, the Fulbright programs in China have become a tool of American public diplomacy. Most Chinese students were ignorant about the United States when China opened its doors to Western society. They lacked basic knowledge of American political and legal systems, federalism, the Constitution, the structure of the American welfare state, working and living conditions, and the social reality of a multiracial, multiethnic society. Under the influence of powerful official propaganda, many Chinese students still had negative perceptions of American culture and society. Their stereotype of Americans was of a hedonistic, violence-prone and restless people who indulged themselves in all their desires and neglected their family responsibilities. They thought Americans were haunted by the specter of unemployment and enjoyed no social security; students had heard plenty about the genocide of the Native Americans and discrimination against black people, and they identified American women's liberation with divorce and sexual license.

There are many examples of these attitudes. Priscilla Oaks, teaching at Beijing University between 1981 and 1982, was asked such questions as: "What is the Bible?" "Does the police or the army guard your foreign hotels?" "You say you live in a house that has more than one room; why aren't your children living with you?" After a discussion of an American movie that had been widely shown in China, a student insisted that there was still slavery in the United States. When Oaks protested, the student argued: "your newspapers aren't allowed to print the truth about such things."[3]

As one Chinese student wrote to Mary Louis Buley-Meissener, who taught American literature at Beijing Teachers College: *"The Godfather* is a great American novel because it exposes the dark side of American society ... Irwin Shaw's *Rich Man, Poor Man* is important because it helps us see how people behave in a capitalist society. They are crazy, hypocritical, and obsessed with money."[4] Charlotte Furth, who taught at Beijing University, commented: "For thirty years of Cold War abroad and ten years of the Cultural Revolution at home, they have studied almost nothing about American history or culture."[5]

Although most Chinese students are ignorant of (and biased against) Americans, they are eager to learn and are fully capable of absorbing virtually all ideas that American professors provided in the classroom. The American teachers note the Chinese students' eagerness and enthusiasm for learning, despite the problems involved in attending classes taught in English and in a very different teaching style. The Chinese enthusiasm impressed the Americans, and some American professors reported that their students were the best they had ever encountered.

As Anthony G. Trimarchi remarked, "the Chinese are not interested in any strong anti-American views of America. They had their stomachs filled with this before. Now they are interested in a less biased approach."[6] William Whiteside, teaching at Beijing University for the academic year of 1982–83, noted that the students' "view of Americans is not that of the purveyors of anti-American propaganda."[7] Bruce Ronda spent the 1984–85 academic year as a Fulbright lecturer in American Studies at the Shanghai International Studies University: "I found my students to be much more generous defenders of American values and behavior than I, although they did confess that at first they were suspicious of the intentions of the US government in sending an American professor to teach American studies."[8] John Scherting, teaching American Studies at Nanjing University from 1987 to 1988, concluded: "I like to think that some of my classroom activities provided the Chinese with a better understanding of why Americans are the way they are."[9]

Second, American Fulbrighters help to create an environment of academic freedom in their classrooms. This helps Chinese students question their own values and political system. Eugenia Kaledin, teaching "Themes in American Life: Individualism and Dissent" in

1986, received this in a final paper by a third-year student at Beijing University: "Marxists believe that the masses shape history ... Yet when the whole world is sleeping dead, a human being cries out and wakes it up; at that moment he creates history."[10] The student argued that both the heroes and the masses were shaping history, challenging the Marxist opinion that the masses, and only the masses, were historical subjects. Theodore Samuel Gup of the Chinese Academy of Social Science Graduate Institute of Journalism commented: "If there are others who come with the notion that all Chinese students have been so thoroughly indoctrinated that they are incapable of critical examination of their own system, then they are in for a surprise. After a while, I began to wonder who had been indoctrinated by whom."[11]

Some Fulbrighters even believed that they played an important role as confidants or counselors to their Chinese students and fellow teachers. This role manifested itself in discussions about sensitive political issues. Some American professors proved "safe" friends with whom Chinese students could share personal or political opinions that could not be shared with other Chinese. "American professors," according to Hong Yu, "could usually be trusted to listen to the Chinese students' opinions without sharing this information with others. They acted as important and trusted confidants, holding the information they shared within their apartments."[12] Teaching at the Zhongshan University, Kent Morrison said: "once they got to know me, they 'opened up,' not only with their own stories, but their own assessments and explanations of the system in which they live."[13] In such an environment of academic freedom, Chinese students began to reject blind acceptance of customs and tradition, and to question and challenge the official ideology, criticizing their own political and economic systems. The Chinese started to criticize not only their own political system, but also Marxism as a whole. Some Chinese students became dissatisfied with their own country and began to demand democracy.

Third, American professors helped the Chinese students absorb Western values and ideology. American Fulbright professors helped the Chinese students better understand some political concepts. When Anthony Trimarchi taught "the History and Development of American Political Thought," he tried to focus on the theme of liberty and equality. By the end of the semester, he claimed that "this course was the most enjoyable one which I taught. Moreover, it had a profound impact on the students."[14] When teaching philosophy at Beijing Foreign Studies University in 1987, James Grant observed that students responded particularly well to the discussions on Western political theory. They were examining the evolution of the democratic idea in America at the very time of the student demonstrations for increased democracy in 1987, and so the classes were particularly interested. Grant wrote that "all of them agreed that people in China have no real understanding of what democracy means, and they thus felt privileged to be able to get a deeper understanding of the idea."[15]

When David Marshall was teaching at Nanjing University during the 1986–87 academic year, he tried to help his students understand the concept of freedom. They first thought that freedom meant the state of being free. After extensive discussion, they found that freedom also meant political liberty: freedom of speech, freedom of the press and so on. "The political analogy was not missed by any of the students," said Marshall.[16]

Craig Calhoun, teaching at the Beijing Foreign Studies University during the spring of 1989, pointed out that "in the late 1980s, democracy may have been a more vital topic of discussion at Beijing University than at the University of California."[17] When Leo Chang taught political science at Beijing University, he tried to introduce a number of different theories about international politics to the students, who were familiar only with Marxist views of international politics. By the end of the semester, "a surprising number of the students in the class were open to Morgenthau's approach to international politics."[18] When James Grant taught philosophy at Beijing Foreign Studies University in 1986, he tried to help his students learn about liberal social theory. After "breaking virgin ground with the students' minds, he could see a lot of intellectual growth." "[T]he students are very interested to learn about liberal social theory," he said.[19]

Finally, American professors use the method of comparison to help Chinese students compare Western political and economic systems with their Chinese counterparts. When Thad Barnowe taught business administration at Zhongshan University, he tried to make comparisons, teaching that both China and the United States were facing some basic and common problems in achieving their results. Barnowe presented facts about the management problems American organizations faced and solutions to those problems, and he told the Chinese students that the success of American enterprises resulted not only from their management techniques but also from their treatment of employees and policies of social responsibility. He concluded that China needed to learn not only the technologies of the West but also its economic systems.[20]

While teaching at Fudan University, Bruce Wilson tried to make "the comparison of Chinese and Western theories one of the running themes of the seminar."[21] Teaching American history at Beijing University,

Bruce Stave wrote: "I tried to stimulate conversation by asking for comparison of the American and Chinese Revolution ... This led to a good discussion of the three concepts and how they applied or didn't apply to the American as well as Chinese society."[22]

In brief, the Chinese students, taught by Americans in the politically sensitive disciplines of the social sciences and humanities, began to develop positive perspectives on the United States and to understand some political concepts. American lecturers saw their political and ideological impact on the Chinese students. Bruce Ronda stated that if China continues to rely on Americans to offer interdisciplinary courses in American Studies, "the result may be a kind of cultural imperialism."[23]

American ideological and political influences on the Chinese campus can also be seen from the surveys that reveal the spread of Western ideas and values. A survey conducted in 1983 of university students in Shanghai suggests that university students began to oppose blind acceptance of the Communist Party's ideology as early as 1983.[24] Another survey conducted with 300 undergraduates at Shanghai University in early 1985 found that 20 percent of them believed that China should learn Western concepts of democracy and freedom, and 33.5 percent believed that China should advocate individualism.[25] As Cuo Yushi, Vice-President of East China Teacher's University, warned: "Many students, especially those studying liberal arts subjects, are interested in Western theories rather than Marxism-Leninism."[26]

A large-scale survey on the condition of ideological and political work at Beijing University was conducted in 1986 by the Municipal Party Committee, the Youth League and the Municipal Education Union. Thirty thousand questionnaires were sent to students. Most students believed that the demonstrations had promoted democratization.[27] This survey suggested a crisis in ideology among the university students in Beijing. In 1986, another survey was conducted of the university students in Beijing. It revealed that "the influx of Western ideas and culture on the campus ha[d] influenced greatly students bedazzled by the appearance of democracy in the West. The bourgeois liberalism had taken a strong hold on college students."[28]

In 1988, a survey was conducted among students at eighteen Shanghai universities, with the support of the Shanghai Education Commission. This survey showed that contemporary Western ethics were widespread and that traditional values had declined.[29] As one writer commented, all kinds of currents in Western philosophy became very popular on the Chinese campuses. The most famous philosophers were "Sartre, Nietzsche, Maslow, and Adler," and their ideas about the infinite potential of human beings and individual freedom of choice had a profound impact on theoretical thinking.[30]

Interviews that I conducted at several universities in China also indicated that Americans played a significant role in introducing Western ideology to Chinese students, who learned about Western ideas and values while taking courses taught by Americans.[31] As Liang Xiaofan, an undergraduate student in the history department at Zhongshan University, said, "after the semester, we learned a lot of new political concepts and ideas which changed our opinions of our political and economic systems."[32]

The Official Reaction to Western Values and Ideas

When China opened its doors to the West after Mao's death in 1976, its primary intention was to use Western scientific technological expertise for China's modernization goals. China needed Western teachers in the natural sciences and technology to help the Chinese understand recent scientific and technological developments in order to enable it to catch up with the economic achievements of Western countries. In addition, because China was carrying out social experimentation and being reintegrated into the global economy, it urgently needed scholars who could understand Western society and culture as well as Western social science techniques in such areas as economics, law and management.

The Chinese leaders, however, wanted their students to reject the "dross" of Western ideology while absorbing useful techniques. In 1979, Jiang Nanxiang, then Chinese Minister of Education, said that Chinese universities should follow the line of socialism and should not transmit ideologies and values from the West.[33] Deng Xiaoping, the paramount leader in China, in his 1982 speech at the Twelfth Congress of the Communist Party, stated that China should "resist corrosion by decadent ideas from abroad, and never permit the bourgeois way of life to spread in our country."[34] The Chinese leaders were aware of the risk of "cultural contamination" from the West, but they seemed confident in the ability of their students to absorb Western techniques but reject Western ideology. Beijing requested that Washington send American professors to China, but wanted them to bring only technological knowledge, not their ideology and cultural values.

In these circumstances, not all American scholars received support and cooperation from their host universities. Donald J. Lewis, teaching law in 1984–85 at Nankai University in Tianjin, said: "I was perceived more as a threat than a benefit to the Nankai Law program."[35] During the second nationwide Anti-spiritual Pollution Campaign in 1986, Hugh G. Casey Jr., teaching law at Wuhan University, was asked by a university official to "tell students that demonstrations were not the way for progress of China."[36]

Some universities even went so far as to prohibit Chinese students from communicating with Fulbrighters because they were afraid of the penetration of Western ideas into campus. For example, Siegfried G. Karsten taught economics in the Department of International Economy at Jilin University (1986–87). He complained that "the most serious problem arose with students being advised not to communicate with me outside the classroom and not to tell me anything."[37] Americans' reports reveal that under the pretext of concerns over their safety, some universities prevented American professors from contacting students outside the classroom.

It is not surprising that after the Tiananmen Incident of June 1989, the Chinese government immediately suspended the China Fulbright program. Delivering his speech before a national higher education meeting in July 1989, Li Tieying, commissioner of the State Education Commission, connected bourgeois liberalism with some courses in the social sciences and humanities, which, he asserted, uncritically introduced bourgeois social theories. He implied that American social science and humanities professors were responsible for the flood of bourgeois ideas into Chinese universities.[38] Chinese social sciences and humanities were once again subject to tight control; Chinese professors and graduate students had to strive hard for their professional survival and for that of their departments.

Subsequently, official attacks on the US educational exchange policy toward China began. On 24 August 1989, the official *Renmin Ribao* (*People's Daily*) published an editorial welcoming the early-returning students to China, criticizing the 1989 student demonstrators for understanding little of China's "essence" and claiming that bourgeois liberal ideology from the American-led West had poured into Chinese universities in recent years to fill an ideological vacuum created by the lack of study of Marxist-Leninist thought.[39]

The Beijing government saw the far-reaching Western influence on Chinese university campuses in the 1980s as a clear consequence of conscious cultural imperialism and an effort to bring about "peaceful evolution." The official media put the concept of "peaceful evolution" into the historical context of US policy in the 1950s, saying that the push for peaceful evolution began with John Foster Dulles, Secretary of State in the 1950s, but had escalated since 1979. Some official articles claimed that the US government had used some specific strategies for "peaceful evolution," such as the donation of academic books and journals, the promotion of academic exchanges and international scholarly conferences, and the sending of teachers and students to China.[40]

The official attack on the US educational exchange policy toward China has not stopped the infiltration of Western ideas and values into Chinese campuses since 1989. Twenty-five years later, in 2015, China's education authorities still pledged to redouble efforts to limit the use of foreign textbooks in universities to stem the infiltration of "Western values." The pledge is the latest step in President Xi Jinping's ideological campaign, which has already enveloped the media and the internet and is being expanded to tertiary campuses. Education Minister Yuan Guiren urged the institutions in January 2015 to exert tighter control over the use of imported textbooks "that spread Western values." Universities are urged to keep classrooms clear of remarks that "defame the rule of the Communist Party, smear socialism or violate the constitution and laws." Teachers must also not grumble in class to avoid "passing on negative emotions to their students," Yuan reportedly said. Universities in China are told to step up propaganda and teaching of Marxism and Chinese socialism to ensure that such values "get into the students' heads." The institutes would be assessed on their use of set textbooks on Marxism.[41]

A number of sources contributed to the spread of Western ideology on the Chinese campus: the generally relaxed political climate on the campuses; the growing contact with Western teachers and students; and the ineffectiveness of political-ideological education at the universities. No doubt, American Fulbright lecturers were one of the sources, especially in cities such as Beijing and Shanghai, although they formed only a small proportion of the large number of Western teachers, including British, Canadian, French, German and other American professors, who were teaching in China during the 2000s.[42]

The study of Beijing's reaction to Western values spreading among Chinese students helps cast light on the influence of Westerners, because scholars differ as to the impact of imported ideas on Chinese society. Some believe that the Westerners who worked in China had great influence. For example, after studying sixteen Western advisors in China from 1620 to 1960, Jonathan Spence concluded that "if their wider goals were not realized, the Western advisers nevertheless left their imprint firmly on Chinese society by compelling some form of confrontation with the most advanced levels of Western technique."[43] Other scholars argue that Westerners in China had no impact on the Chinese. After studying foreign teachers in China from 1979 to 1989, Edgar Porter wrote: "I can also attest that no foreigner lives long in China without realizing that he or she makes little or no impact on the Chinese people without permission to do so from those same people."[44]

Conclusion

The case of the Fulbrighters in China does indicate that Westerners have an impact on the Chinese and so help transform Chinese society. After the Opium War of 1839–42, some Chinese national leaders advocated learning from the West because they realized that China was militarily weak and could not withstand invasion by the powerful Western countries. The Chinese had to study Western mathematics, science and languages to strengthen China against the West. When the Western powers posed a threat to China in the latter half of the nineteenth century, the Chinese government started to invite Western educators—advisors, administrators and teachers—to China to import Western science, technology and other applicable knowledge. After the downfall of the last Chinese emperor in 1912 national leaders invited Westerners to introduce Western technology to promote modernization. Thus, from the mid nineteenth century to the mid twentieth century, thousands of Western teachers taught in Chinese universities, and their influence continued until 1949.

The Westerners, however, brought to the Chinese not only Western technology but also Western ideology. Many Chinese believed that acceptance of Western ideology meant submission to the Westerners. To Chinese leaders, Western ideology posed a threat to the hierarchical and authoritarian political system in China. They therefore tried to reject the ideology while adopting Western technology in order to maintain traditional Confucian virtue. After the Chinese Communists took over mainland China, few Western teachers were allowed to teach in China between 1949 and 1979. When American professors returned to Chinese campuses after 1979, the Chinese students expected not only Western knowledge and methods for handling the practical problems of China, but also Western ideas and values. Having no sense of selectivity or critical perspective when they came into contact with Western ideas, cultures, practices and institutions, the Chinese students were willing to absorb whatever they saw as useful. Today, Chinese leaders are facing the same problems as the previous governments have since the nineteenth century, and the influx of American professors of social science and humanities seems to have aggravated political and cultural contradictions within China.

To speed up China's Four Modernizations drive, the Beijing government opened China's doors to the West in the late 1970s for the first time since 1949. The China Fulbright Programs helped let the Chinese students understand US society, its foreign policies and its political and economic system, creating a positive image of the United States in China and having a political and ideological impact on many Chinese students. That unavoidable side-effect of inviting American lecturers to China was especially significant on the campuses. Today, the Beijing government is in a dilemma: how can it solve the problem of reconciling the demand for Western teachers with the rejection of Western ideology?

Guangqiu Xu is a lecturing professor of history of Jinan University and a visiting professor of Xi'an International Studies University in China. He is the author of four books, one of which, *Congress and the US-China Relationship, 1949–1979* (The University of Akron Press, 2007), won the 2008 Best Adult Book Award from the Chinese American Librarians Association. He has also published more than thirty articles. He received the US National Endowment for the Humanities Grant in 2006, the Fulbright-Hays Award in 2009 and the Fulbright Scholarship Award in 2012. He was US Fulbright Visiting Professor at the National University of Singapore between 2012 and 2013.

Notes

1. For a comprehensive study of the Fulbright China Program from 1979 to 1989, see Guangqiu Xu, "The Ideological and Political Impact of US Fulbrighters on the Chinese Students, 1979–1989," *Asian Affairs* 26(3) (1999): 139–57.
2. For a study of the significance of the Chinese visiting research scholars under the China Fulbright Programs, see Zhongguo Fubulaite Xueyouhui Lunwenji (A collection of the Chinese Fulbright alumni's articles) (Beijing: Zhongguo renmin daxue chubanshe, 2014), edited by the Chinese Fulbright Alumni.
3. Priscilla Oaks to CIES, 1982, Box 153, Council for International Exchange of Scholars Records (henceforth CIES), Special Collection Division, University of Arkansas Libraries at Fayetteville.
4. Mary Louis Buley-Meissener, "Teaching American Literature in China: Learning How Students Read and Respond," *English Education* (October 1990): 192–99.
5. Charlotte Furth to CIES, 1982, Box 153, CIES.
6. Anthony G. Trimarchi to CIES, 1981, Box 153, CIES.

7. William B. Whiteside to CIES, 1983, Box 153, CIES.
8. Bruce Ronda, "American Studies in China: Experiences and Reflections," *China Exchange News* 13(3) (1985): 10–12.
9. John Scherting to CIES, 1988, Box 155, CIES.
10. Eugenia Kaledin to CIES, 1986, Box 154, CIES.
11. Theodore Samuel Gup to CIES, 1986, Box 154, CIES.
12. Hong Yu, interview with author, Fudan University, 27 August 1986.
13. Kent Morrison to CIES, 1984, Box 154, CIES.
14. Anthony G. Trimarchi to CIES, 1981, Box 153, CIES.
15. James Grant to CIES, 1986, Box 155, CIES.
16. David F. Marshall to CIES, 1987, Box 155, CIES.
17. Craig Calhoun, *Neither Gods nor Emperors: Students and the Struggle for Democracy in China* (Berkeley, CA: University of California Press, 1994), 244–57.
18. Morgenthau is the author of the book *Politics among Nations*, which was used by Dr Chang during his teaching at Beijing University. See Leo Chang to CIES, 1985, Box 154, CIES.
19. James Grant to CIES, 1986, Box 155, CIES.
20. Thad Barnowe to CIES, 1983, Box 153, CIES.
21. Bruce Wilson, "Thoughts on Teaching at Fudan University," *China Exchange News* 13(3) (1985): 13–15.
22. Bruce Stave, "Teaching and Learning in the People's Republic of China," *China Exchange News* 13(3) (1985): 5–8.
23. Ronda, "American Studies."
24. Geng Xiao and Zhu Yuejing, "Dangdai qingnian zhuiqiude 'lixiang xingxiang' yu daode bangyang jiaoyu" ("The Ideal Image Contemporary Youth Pursue and Education of Moral Model"), *Shanghai qingshaonian yanjiu* (*Study of the Youth in Shanghai*) 3 (1984): 6–7.
25. "Students Stress Independence," *Beijing Review*, 22 April 1985, 27.
26. "Young Intellectuals Do Not Pay Attention to Marxism-Leninism," *Wenhui bao*, 20 July 1985, 2.
27. Wang Sunyu et al., "Daxuesheng zhong dangde jainshe gongzuo chutan" ("An Initial Study of Party Construction Work among University Students"), in Beijing Municipal Party Committee Research Office (ed.), *Xinshiqi daxuesheng sixiang zhengzhi jiaoyu yanjiu* (*A Study of Ideological and Political Education among University Students in the New Era*) (Beijing: Beijing Normal University Press, 1988), 67–78.
28. Yang Jingyun, Li gongyi et al., "Guanyu daxuesheng chengzhang daolu wentide tansuo" ("A Study of the Problems of the Development of University Students"), in *Xinshiqi daxuesheng sixiang zhengzhi jiaoyu yanjiu*, 59–65.
29. Zhao Yicheng, "Jiazhide chongtu" ("Conflict of Values"), *Weidinggao*, 25 April 1988, 29–31.
30. Li Shaojun, "Gerenzhuyi zhi chao" ("The Trend of Individualism"), *Hainan jishi* (*Chronicle of Hainan*) 5 (May 1989): 18–27.
31. Interviews with the author: Liang Xiaofan, Zhongshan University, 4 July 1986; Yang Dong, Beijing University, 10 August 1986; Hong Yu, Fudan

University, 27 August 1986; Song Yao, Xian International Studies University, 1 June 2012; Wang Nan, Jinan University, 10 July 2013, Deng Wu, East China Normal University, 10 June 2014.
32. Liang Xiaofan, interview with the author, Zhongshan University, 4 July 1986.
33. "College Education: Socialist Orientation Reiterated," *Beijing Review*, 27 April 1979, 8–9.
34. *Xinhua News Agency*, 1 September 1982.
35. Donald J. Lewis to CIES, 1985, Box 154, CIES.
36. Hugh G. Casey Jr. to CIES, 1987, Box 155, CIES.
37. Siegfried G. Karsten to CIES, 1987, Box 155, CIES.
38. *Zhongguo jiaoyu bao (China's Education Newspaper)*, 30 August 1989, 6.
39. *Renmin ribao (People's Daily)*, 24 August 1989.
40. Sun Renjian and Bai Zhongkao, "Xifang zhexue sichao shentao gaoxiao sixiang jiaoyu" ("Western Ideology Penetrated into Political Education of Universities"), *Jiangsu gaojiao (Jaingsu Higher Education)* 4 (1990): 7–9; Guo Xiaocong, "Cong Xifang sichau dui daxuesheng de yingxiang fansi gaoxiao sixiang zhengzhi gongzuo" (To Re-examine the Political Ideological Work in Universities with Regard to the Western Influence among University Students), *Caojiao tansuo (Higher Education Study, Guangzhou)* 1 (1990): 34–39.
41. Andrea Chen and Zhuang Pinghui, "Chinese Universities Ordered to Ban Textbooks that Promote Western Values," *South China Post*, 27 September 2015, retrieved 2 April 2017 from http://www.scmp.com/news/china/article/1695524/chinese-universities-instructed-ban-textbooks-promote-western-values?page=all.
42. According to F.A. Kretschmer, an American teacher at the Beijing Institute of Tourism from 1986 to 1992, the Chinese government employed about 30,000 foreign nationals as teachers, advisors and specialists throughout China during that time. See F.A. Kretschmer, *An American Teacher in China: Coping with Cultures* (Westport, CT: Bergin & Garvey, 1994), 1. See also Ruth Hayhoe, "A Comparative Analysis of Chinese-Western Academic Exchange," *Comparative Education* 20(1) (1984): 39–56.
43. Jonathan Spence, *To Change China: Western Advisers in China, 1620–1960* (Boston, MA: Little, Brown, 1969), 291.
44. Edgar Porter, *Foreign Teachers in China: Old Problems for a New Generation, 1979–1989* (New York: Greenwood Press, 1990), 92.

References

Buley-Meissener, Mary Louis. "Teaching American Literature in China: Learning How Students Read and Respond," *English Education* (October 1990): 192–99.
Calhoun, Craig. *Neither Gods nor Emperors: Students and the Struggle for Democracy in China* (Berkeley, CA: University of California Press, 1994).

Hayhoe, Ruth. "A Comparative Analysis of Chinese-Western Academic Exchange," *Comparative Education* 20(1) (1984): 39–56.
Kretschmer, F.A. *An American Teacher in China: Coping with Cultures* (Westport, CT: Bergin & Garvey, 1994).
Porter, Edgar. *Foreign Teachers in China: Old Problems for a New Generation, 1979-1989*. (New York: Greenwood Press, 1990).
Spence, Jonathan. *To Change China: Western Advisers in China, 1620–1960* (Boston, MA: Little, Brown, 1969).
Wang, Sunyu et al. "Daxuesheng zhong dangde jainshe gongzuo chutan" ("An Initial Study of Party Construction Work among University Students"), in Beijing Municipal Party Committee Research Office (ed.), *Xinshiqi daxuesheng sixiang zhengzhi jiaoyu yanjiu* (*A Study of Ideological and Political Education among University Students in the New Era*) (Beijing: Beijing Normal University Press, 1988), 67–78.
Xu, Guangqiu. "The Ideological and Political Impact of US Fulbrighters on the Chinese Students, 1979–1989," *Asian Affairs* 26(3) (1999): 139–59.
Zhongguo Fubulaite Xueyouhui Lunwenji. (A collection of the Chinese Fulbright alumni's articles). Beijing: Zhongguo renmin daxue chubanshe, 2014. Edited by the Chinese Fulbright Alumni.

 18

IMPORTING BARBARIAN KNOWLEDGE
The JET Program and the Development of Cultural Internationalism in Japan (1987–2014)

Jesse Sargent

Introduction

This chapter proposes an examination of a program developed independently by a non-Western nation: the "Japan Exchange and Teaching Program" founded in 1987. This investigation is particularly important because it not only highlights unique methods of accomplishing the intended "exchange" aimed at by such programs, but also reveals remarkable cultural and historical consistencies in the Japanese approach to exchange. It encourages us to see such exchange programs not as a unique modern phenomenon, but instead as a particular instantiation of consistent cultural inclinations visible from a long-term perspective, which might provoke new reflections on Western cases.

Reflecting on premodern Japan, singular cultural tension between isolation and exchange persistently appears throughout the *longue durée* of Japanese history. Geographically isolated at the eastern reaches of Eurasia, it was not until the seventh century that Japanese sovereigns were able to establish regular foreign contacts.[1] The Japanese state then imported Chinese models for the calendar, written language, architecture and urban infrastructure. Human exchange facilitated such developments, with Buddhist monks and Confucian scholars from abroad often achieving high positions in the Japanese government. Over time, external exchanges increased and decreased in line with the strength or relative weakness of domestic authority: strong centralized control increased exchange, while a weak center permitted chaotic, destructive competitive scrambles. The early modern Tokugawa Shogunate tightly controlled opportunities for exchange while centralizing its own power, during the two-century-long policy of *Sakoku*, or literally "chained country."[2]

This policy was forcefully ended by the arrival of the United States' "Black Ships" in 1853 and the overwhelming technical superiority that they demonstrated. In response, a newly founded Meiji government embarked on a path of modernization that would allow them to use such "barbarian methods to control the barbarian."[3] The new state contracted with foreign governments, bringing in over 3,000 Western advisors or "educators," both scientific and military, from Prussia and France, Britain and the United States to train their bureaucrats and soldiers.[4] Following their slogan of *fukoku kyouhei*,[5] the Japanese were able to build a rich economy and a strong military through the knowledge transmitted via this exchange. Yet echoing *Sakoku* attitudes from the proceeding centuries, Western knowledge and influence was considered politically volatile for the general public, and therefore the Meiji government kept this training and exposure to foreign ideas tightly controlled within the elite governing class. The grand twentieth-century expansion enabled by this controlled exchange ended in defeat during World War II at the hands of the US government.

Postwar Recovery and *Kokusaika* Consciousness

In defeat, Japan's relationship with the external world was largely severed once more. While Americans provided security and guidance in reform, the Japanese were preoccupied with the internal concerns of economic reconstruction and demilitarization. The "Yoshida doctrine" of the transformative 32nd Prime Minister Shigeru Yoshida proclaimed that Japan would concentrate its full resources on re-creating a "rich country," while relinquishing all management of international affairs to the United States. This strategic approach stimulated what would become known as East Asia's greatest "economic miracle" of the twentieth century. Western learning (languages, sciences, etc.) would still be largely confined to the elite classes, while the populace was fully employed in manufacturing and service industries at large state-supported corporate conglomerates called *zaibatsu*.[6] Over the next two decades, Japan would not only recover from its postwar recession but would also initiate a total revolution in Japanese economic and consumer society. The middle class broadened significantly; annual pay raises for workers averaged 15 percent throughout the 1960s, as the proportion of white-collar workers doubled.[7] Popular, domestically manufactured consumer goods like televisions, washing machines and refrigerators became common fixtures in Japanese households, critical indicators of the "good life" of the West. Kimono sales plummeted in favor of Western clothes; rice consumption sank relative to "Western" commodities such as meats, wheat, sugar, eggs and milk. The education system was expanded and reformed, centralized and standardized across all primary and secondary levels.[8] Coordinating with the American occupiers forced the addition of foreign language teaching as part of this general curriculum. Thus, public consciousness regarding foreign commodities (both material and intellectual) began to spread rapidly.

However, the internal focus on this recovery meant that Japan did not develop a national understanding or relationship with the international environment. The advantageous monetary exchange terms of the Bretton Woods system meant that Japan could simply ship its high-quality manufactured goods abroad without deeper cultural or intellectual engagement. This same monetary dynamic reinforced the general populace's isolation by making it unaffordable for regular Japanese citizens to travel abroad. By the 1970s, however, the Nixon decoupling of the gold standard for the dollar in 1971 and the 1973 OPEC oil crisis had demonstrated the dependence of Japanese fortunes on favorable international conditions.[9] Throughout the 1970s and early 1980s, a strong, revitalized Japanese state frustrated Western nations by regularly intervening in international currency markets to preserve an artificially low yen. These same Japanese elites continued to tour the world, buying up expensive properties and infrastructure, basking in their position as "number one."[10] *Nihonjinron*, or "theories of Japanese culture," attempted to distill the unique ethnic characteristics in which their economic success stood rooted.[11] Prideful insensitivity to international diversity characterized virtually all upper echelons of society, epitomized by Prime Minster Yasuhiro Nakasone, who in 1986 proclaimed that Japan's key to success was its "purity" and "homogeneity", in contrast with an America "burdened" by blacks and Hispanics, who lowered the average level of education and intelligence.[12] Complaints in both America and Europe rapidly grew that Japan was a closed, self-interested and chauvinistic society that refused to engage in creating a "level playing field."

Responding to both these internal and external pressures, Prime Minister Nakasone's government initiated a grand educational reform to open Japan to new levels of international exchange: to "prepare Japan for global leadership by remaking Japan into an international state" under the term *kokusaika*, or "internationalization."[13] The reforms would respond to foreign criticism by embracing an active, independent role for Japan in the international space and opening itself to foreign influence and training, while introducing the general populace through public support and education to both "international understanding" and communication with people of different nationalities. This would not only satisfy international critics, but would also respond to rising demand at the local level within Japan for opportunities to "internationalize." Japanese ministries scrambled to design new action plans in response to Nakasone's grand strategy. One concrete proposal to meet these goals was submitted by a midlevel bureaucrat, Mr Nose Kuniyuni, in the Ministry of Home Affairs.[14] He suggested that Japan could again engage in a national-scale importation of skilled foreigners for domestic training, distributing them throughout the country using the new standardized, centralized education system. Thus, the Japan Exchange and Teaching (JET) Program was born.

The Japan Exchange and Teaching Program

Structure

In 1986, the Ministry of Foreign Affairs immediately seized on the idea of the JET Program as a diplomatic tool, to be presented as a "gift" in May of that year to the American delegation and US President Ronald Reagan on behalf of Prime Minister Nakasone and the Japanese people at an international summit in Tokyo. This "great experiment" would hire young, college-educated foreigners at great expense to the Japanese government and would integrate these public employees into school systems and government offices across all levels of the country. Two positions would be created: the Coordinator for International Relations (CIR) would work out of prefectural and city offices to promote *kokusaika* in local civil society, while Assistant Language Teachers (ALTs) would teach foreign languages in tandem with career Japanese teachers in junior high school and high school English courses.[15] Resources from the Japanese national ministries would support the effort; the Ministry of Education would produce a new English curriculum for paired "team-teaching" between Japanese Teachers of English (JTEs) and ALTs; the Ministry of Home Affairs would coordinate with local governments and provide a budget for regional "development" through internationalization; and the Ministry of Foreign Affairs and its foreign consulates would take charge of recruiting and promoting the image of the program abroad. On 31 July 1987, thirty-five CIRs and 813 ALTs from the United States, the United Kingdom, New Zealand

and Australia arrived in Tokyo to much fanfare as the first JET Program participants.[16]

Yet this well-intentioned program was rife with problems from the start. Japan's famously insular bureaucratic ministries minded their own interests, eschewing cooperation. It became clear that the actual management of the massive new program required the formation of a dedicated body to serve its needs while coordinating between multiple ministries and agencies in ways they could not (or would not) themselves. In addition, the scale and penetration of the program complicated this management from the centralized, top-down perspective that the government in Tokyo usually employed. Thus, during the second year of the program's operation in 1987, the Council of Local Authorities for International Relations (CLAIR) was founded, housed as an administrative office within the Ministry of Home Affairs.[17] With personnel drawn from multiple ministries, local prefectural and city offices, combined with former foreigner English teacher advice, CLAIR essentially gave advice *to* local authorities *from* local authorities, in a context where most had little idea about how to use a relatively untrained foreign worker dropped into their office from above. As the JET Program expanded, CLAIR's mandate for promoting *kokusaika* also increased. Manuals and training booklets for program participants were developed.[18] Local *kokusaika* departments were established in each of the prefectural government offices, networked together by CLAIR. Private *kokusaika* associations and town governments furthermore appealed to CLAIR for advice on connecting internationally for economic or cultural exchange.[19] This structure represented a shift in traditional central government programs by explicitly devolving the management of local *kokusaika* processes to the local authorities themselves; instead, CLAIR simply provided a supporting or coordinating role.

The program itself remained the major responsibility of CLAIR, and, despite some early challenges, it soon took hold. In two years the program's membership more than doubled to 1,987 participants. Canadians and Irish joined the ranks, and in 1989 French and German citizens arrived to teach their respective languages. By 1994, the program had again doubled to 4,135 participants from 11 eleven countries, and by 2002, it peaked at 6,273 participants from 40 forty countries.[20] New positions for Sports Exchange Advisors (SEAs) were created, and the JET Alumni Association (JETAA) was founded to maintain a relationship with former JET participants, being run out of the overseas consulates of the Ministry of Foreign Affairs. In the 2000s, elementary school positions were opened for JET participants, as private English

-teaching companies rushed to compete for skyrocketing demand in at all levels of schooling. Today over 900 local government organizations host participants directly contracted by the local authority, rather than through the central government or CLAIR.[21] With virtually every local school district maintaining at least one dedicated participant, the JET Program has become synonymous with standardized English education in Japan.

Criticism

Flooding local school districts with these upper-class, college-educated foreigners did not necessarily mean that teachers and Boards of Education understood how to use them properly, even with the intense support of CLAIR. One negative result of the decentralized flexibility built into the JET Program was a considerable level of confusion over their intended purpose on a daily basis.[22] Indeed, some teachers even rejected the "imposition" of these foreign "ambassadors" all together. The presence of English native speakers in the classroom immediately drew attention to the poor command of spoken English that many JTEs themselves possessed, having been trained in the language largely by intensive written grammar, syntax and translation exercises in previous decades.[23] This "pressure" of a mandate from above to transform JTEs' teaching methodologies according to a nebulous goal of *kokusaika*, while at the same time being undercut by an ALT native-speaker with little to no teaching experience, caused a great deal of friction between the two groups. Employed ALTs would often be left in staff rooms, simply to wait until a certain passage needed to be read or a "native English" listening test needed to be administered.[24] ALTs frequently saw this as an intentional slight and distanced themselves further from school activities, thus confirming the pre-conceptions of many JTEs regarding the lack of training, dedication and responsibility in their ALT counterparts.

Beyond these binary classroom interactions, the JET Program must be viewed as a major aspect of a wholesale reform of the education system itself in which traditional test-oriented data cramming would be ideally replaced by critical thought and logical exposition.[25] JET participants, in their aforementioned capacity as "cultural ambassadors," were supposed to train students in the "Western" techniques students lacked as part of new *kokusaika* education. Yet, as the JET Program (still) requires no specific evidence of philosophic or pedagogical skills from its applicants, many participants have been confused by the expectation that they could impart such "innately understood" techniques to a Japanese student. Worse still, even if an ALT comes prepared with a degree in pedagogy, the Japanese education system has not transformed the evaluation measures used for high school and college entrance exams to reflect their goal of imparting "international" communication skills. Instead, students are still tested on technical grammar and vocabulary, which leads many JTEs to accuse the Ministry of Education of using "the rhetoric of values without acting upon them."[26] Since the primary responsibility of JTEs is still preparing their students to pass such entrance exams, this dissonance leads to a certain "schizophrenia" in classroom activities. The inability to resist ministry directives merely shifts the local rejection onto the ALTs themselves, as some conservative teachers "perceive the ALT ... and their methods ... as a virus that could potentially harm the intellectual development of students."[27]

Ideology

Of greatest concern are the ideological grounds of the JET Program, which reinforce a certain type of cultural essentialism and preferential bias. Indeed, while the program proclaims to its support for "internationalization" and "foreign language" training, in reality these seem instead to mean homogenized "Americanization" and "English language training" in practice . Thus, in 2014, 55.1% percent of JET participants were from the United States, and 87.2% percent hailed from the program's six major anglophone countries (the United States, the United Kingdom, US, UK, Australia, New Zealand, Canada, and Ireland).[28]

Despite their inclusion in the program during its third year in operation, French and German participants still stand at 0.4 and 0.3% percent respectively. Furthermore, within this narrow anglophone bias, some reports have surfaced regarding "white preference" and racial prejudice against "minority" JET participants, to the point where a JTE had reportedly asked an African-American ALT: "Can you speak standard English?"[29] White native speakers are alleged to use "pure" and "authentic" English, coupled with "perfect, innate knowledge of the language and culture," which automatically equips them to be the best and most natural teachers of English, and therefore, "international understanding."

The corresponding cultural essentialization occurs in domestic self-definitions as well, which is reflected through native conceptions of "self" and "other."[30] While Nakasone and the other education reformers of 1980s Japan wanted to appropriate best practices from abroad, they also hoped to project their nationalist promotion of Japan into the international space more effectively. Echoing an old discourse of *nihonjinron*, the educational curriculum suggests that through intensive training in English, a Japanese national might best understand how to most effectively communicate his "Japaneseness" to the international sphere. Japanese students read English lessons about *rakugo* performance art, the Hiroshima bombing of 1945, or the uniqueness of Japanese language. Students are expected to "communicate" and explain to their ALT "foreigners" about these "Japanesenesses." The entire rhetoric of *kokusaika* explicitly focuses on reified differences and a diametrical opposition between the Japanese and international spheres. Furthermore, this discourse homogenizes Japan internally to an extreme extent, overlooking the racial diversity that Japanese nationalists are eager to ignore. More than two million Chinese and Korean nationals live and work in Japan, yet Chinese and Korean were not added as target languages until a decade after the Program's inception, and these nationals still represented only 3% percent of total participants in 2014.[31] Japan's diverse minorities like Ainu, Korean-descendant Japanese, or second- generation Japanese who have returned from abroad (e.g. Brazil) are completely ignored from in this narrative. According to this homogenized *nihon–kokusaika* dichotomy, a bilingual English-Japanese-speaking child is a wonder to be praised, while a bilingual Portuguese-Japanese child deserves no recognition. Essentially, the Japanese approach engages in a rather rampant combination of cultural relativism and cultural absolutism: both "Japanese" and "foreign" spheres are portrayed as totally internally homogeneous, while in comparison with each other they remain totally dissimilar.

In the same vein, the Japanese government uses this promotion of *nihonjinron* in English to educate JET participants about a carefully crafted and stylized image of Japan, predicated upon the idea that these temporary teachers will eventually return back to their home countries. In a way, the JET Program functions like a "reverse Peace Corps" by bringing foreigners into the country, actively imparting "Japaneseness" to them and seeding them throughout the international world. Joji Hisaeda, Director of the Second Cultural Affairs Division at the Ministry of Foreign Affairs, expresses the idea most clearly:

> From the viewpoint of the Ministry of Foreign Affairs, it is significant as part of Japan's national security policy that these youths go back to their respective countries in the future and become sympathizers for Japan. In the case of the United States and France, for instance, they often get criticized by many countries for promoting their own independent international policies. All the same, they will carry through with these policies because these nations have sufficient national strength … In

Japan's case, the nation is far from possessing such strength to carry out policies in defiance of world opinion. Therefore, highly deliberate, even artificial efforts are required to create sympathizers for Japan as part of national security policy. From this point of view, we consider the JET Program is an extremely important and at the same time effective policy instrument.[32]

The explicit connection between national security and creating "sympathizers" through the JET Program highlights the original foreign pressures which that triggered the Program's proposal in the mid -1980s. The JETAA Alumni Association remains an important soft power international network then, which Japan's foreign consulates monitor and fund with taxpayer money. Japanese multinational corporations or universities consistently hold job fairs and post offers through these networks, hoping to gain access to foreign resources with training in "Japaneseness." Many alumni have returned home to study Japan-related topics with a level of preparation that is "something we could only have dreamed of ten years ago."[33] Rather than "internationalizing Japan," perhaps the JET Program's true end can be found in "Japanifying the International."

Conclusion

The importance of the *longue durée* perspective with which this chapter begins lies in recognizing the remarkable consistency in strategy that Japan displays in its relations with the "foreign." Historically suspicious of domestic disorder sown by uneven foreign exchanges, Japan displays a preference for establishing a strong central authority to tightly control any international influences and turn them to that authority's own advantage. The JET Program's most recent turn toward decentralization and the delegation of decision-making power to local authorities should not distract us from the fact that the Japanese government, ministries, and CLAIR shape the demand into an internal market which that must approach the international through the intermediation of the national. This intermediation allows the national authorities to control the ideological grounds of the exchange: instilling a patriotic, essentialized, and homogenized image of Japan for its own people and the foreigners with whom they communicate. They are also able to control who the desirable partners for this exchange are, limiting it as far as possible to selective sections of the globe's "White Anglo-Saxon Protestant Nations." Conflicts over these ideological grounds continue to this day.[34]

Nevertheless, in its nearly thirty years of operation, the JET Program has undergone massive transformations and improvements. The difficult initial years bequeathed lessons to new generations of participants, and the program has slowly adapted. Over 90 percent of program participants now say they would "recommend" or "strongly recommend" the program to a friend. Early contract terminations have fallen below 1 percent. The program has now been expanded fully into elementary schools, with government mandates following slowly in the wake of optional expansions. The Japanese government cannot "reprogram" its people overnight; the grassroots implementation of guided policies from above allows each local authority to navigate its particular context as it tries to introduce Japan to the "other." The question is not whether Japanese people as "X" can learn about foreign-ness as "Y," but whether they can collaborate to produce "XY" and not just "X+Y." Tajino asks "what would you expect from a performance by two musicians, such as a pianist and a singer, at the same concert? Would you expect two separate solo performances? Or would you prefer to hear them playing a harmonious duet?"[35] The answer to this question for Japan is still in the process of being negotiated at all levels of society through instruments like the JET Program. The Japanese approach demonstrates many unique qualities: exchange as importation rather than exportation, slowly encouraging local transformation processes with support and rhetoric while avoiding iron-clad mandates and regulations at the outset, and instead codifying the best local practices after public acceptance. But what is important to note in the context of a *longue durée* perspective is that we should also not be surprised at the Japanese tendency to mix international importation of knowledge and expertise with attempts to use this knowledge in the maintenance of a strong national identity and ideology. Indeed, this could almost be expected from a nation who used those first imported Chinese characters to write a voluminous mythology about the divine origins of their people.[36] The real question is: is this a tendency purely Japanese, or is it not present in any nation? Perhaps it is simply endemic to the nature of exchange with the "other."

Jesse Sargent is a Ph.D. candidate in the Department of International History at the Graduate Institute of International and Development Studies, Geneva. From 2006 until to 2010, he worked as an Assistant Language Teacher on the JET Program in Nakagawa Village, Nagano, where he was a regular contributor to Prefectural AJET publications. During his ongoing research on the cross-cultural conversion techniques of early modern Jesuit missionaries in Asia, he has been an associate at Harvard University's Program on US–Japan Relations, and currently works as a visiting researcher at the Centro de História d'Aquém e d'Além-Mar, Universidade Nova de Lisboa, Portugal.

Appendix: The JET Alumni Association

The JET Alumni Association (JETAA) was created in 1989 on the recommendation of Scott Olinger, a former JET turned CLAIR Program Coordinator, who convinced his office that a formal organization was needed to assist JET participants making the transition back home. As of 2016, the JETAA has 23,000 registered members (out of a total of 53,000 former grantees) in 52 fifty-two regional sections across 17 seventeen countries, most numerous in the United States, Australia and New Zealand. While the activities of each regional sections vary significantly according to the size and resources of local membership, most JETAA chapters organize events such as festivals, concerts, or conferences to promote Japanese culture, while furthermore also assisting former JETs in leveraging using their Japanese experiences to find employment or graduate studies funding after their return. JETAA chapters are designed to work in close coordination with their local Japanese consulate or embassy as nonprofit organizations, yielding important results. In strong constrast with the program's outset, virtually all aspects of the international recruitment process—advertisement, selection, and pre-departure orientation—are now managed primarily by local JETAA chapters with support from their respective consulates. An alumni magazine, *JET Streams*, essay contests, alumni directories, and other activities have been generously funded by CLAIR to continue developing an international community of returned JET alumni, including a recent consensus-building Global Forum held in Tokyo on the thirtieth anniversary of the program's foundation. Thus, while the alumni themselves have certainly benefited as members, the Japanese government itself has also recognized the powerful gains granted by supporting an international JETAA network.

Notes

1. Charles Holcombe, *The Genesis of East Asia, 221 B.C.–A.D. 907* (Honolulu, HI: University of Hawaii Press, 2001).
2. Japanese: 鎖国; In reality, exchange continued illicitly at the local level. See Ronald P. Toby, *State and Diplomacy in Early Modern Japan: Asia in the*

Development of the Tokugawa Bakufu (Princeton, NJ: Princeton University Press, 1984).
3. W.G. Beasley, *Japan Encounters the Barbarian: Japanese Travelers in America and Europe* (New Haven, CT: Yale University Press, 1995), 16.
4. David McConnell calls this a "remarkable precedent to the JET Program." David L. McConnell, "Japan's Image Problem and the Soft Power Solution: The JET Program as Cultural Diplomacy," in Kasushi Watanabe and David L. McConnell (eds), *Soft Power Superpowers: Cultural and National Assets of Japan and the United States*, (London: M.E. Sharpe, 2008), 18–36, here 20.
5. Japanese: 富国強兵; literally, "Rich Country, Strong Army."
6. Japanese: 財閥; literally "Asset clans."
7. Peter Duus, "Showa-Eera Japan and Beyond: From Imperial Japan to Japan Inc.," in Victoria Lynn Bestor et al. (eds), *Routledge Handbook of Japanese Society and Culture* (New York: Routledge, 2011).
8. Yuko Goto Butler, "Foreign Language Education at Elementary Schools in Japan: Searching for Solutions Amidst Growing Diversification," *Current Issues in Language Planning* 8(/2) (2007): 129–147 (130). See also Duus, "Show-era," 23.
9. Duss, "Showa-era," 25.
10. Ezra Vogel, *Japan as Number One: Lessons for America* (Cambridge, MA: Harvard University Press, 1979).
11. Japanese: 日本人論; literally "Arguments on the Sun-origin people." David L. McConnell, *Importing Diversity: Inside Japan's JET Program* (Berkeley, CA: University of California Press, 2000), 15.
12. Susan Chira, "Nakasone Apologies for Comments that Offended US Minorities," *New York Times*, 27 September 1986, retrieved 5 April 2017 from http://www.nytimes.com/1986/09/27/world/nakasone-apologizes-for-comments-that-offended-us-minorities.html.
13. Japanese: 国際化; literally "Taking the form of that on the limits of the country." Roger Goodman, "The concept of Kokusaika and Japanese educational reform," *Globalization, Societies and Education* 5(1) (2007): 71–87; Roger Goodman, "Japanese education and education reform," in Victoria Lynn Bestor et al. (eds), *Routledge Handbook of Japanese Society and Culture* (New York: Routledge, 2011); McConnell, *Importing*, 17.
14. David L. McConnell, "Education for Global Integration in Japan: A Case Study of the JET Program," *Human Organization* 55(4) (1996): 446–57 (447).
15. Akira Tajino and Yasuko Tajino, "Native and Non-native: What Can They Offer? Lessons from Team-Teaching in Japan," *ELT Journal* 54(/1) (2000): 3–11. Tajino cites government manuals which that define team-teaching's purpose: "to develop students' abilities to understand a foreign language and express themselves in it, to foster a positive attitude toward communicating in it, and to heighten interest in language and culture, deepening international understanding" (4).
16. Japanese officials lavishly praised these "cultural ambassadors." As one claimed: "It is my honest wish that through mixing with local people you

will play your part as a stone in protecting the castle of peace." (McConnell, *Importing*, 64).
17. Retrieved 5 April 2017 from http://www.clair.or.jp/e/index.html.
18. See the 2014 versions: 自治体国際化協会 (Council of Local Authorities on International Relations), *The ALT Handbook* (Tokyo: CLAIR, 2013), retrieved 5 April 2017 from http://www.jetprogramme.org/documents/pubs/alt_2013.pdf; 自治体国際化協会 (Council of Local Authorities on International Relations), *General Information Handbook* (Tokyo: CLAIR, 2014), retrieved 5 April 2017 from http://www.jetprogramme.org/documents/pubs/gih2014_e.pdf.
19. For example, CLAIR still runs an internet board for various such private associations and local governments that might advertise their interest in a particular international connection. See, for example: http://www.clair.or.jp/e/exchange/shimai/kibou.html.
20. Public information retrieved 5 April 2017 from http://www.jetprogramme.org/e/introduction/history.html.
21. CLAIR, *General Information Handbook*, pp 191–193.
22. McConnell, *Importing*, 32.
23. Anthony Crooks, "Professional Development and the JET Program: Insights and Solutions Based on the Sendai City Program," *JALT Journal* 23(/1) (2001): 31–46 (32).
24. Tajino, "Native and Non-native," 5.
25. Goodman, "Japanese Education," 52–53.
26. Crooks, "Professional Development," 37.
27. Ryuko Kubota, "The Impact of Globalization on Language Teaching in Japan," in David Block and Deborah Cameron (eds), *Globalization and Language Teaching* (London: Routledge, 2002), 26.
28. Detailed statistics on the 2014 JET Program participants can be found online; retrieved 5 April 2017 from http://www.jetprogramme.org/documents/stats/2014_jet_stats_e.pdf.
29. Kubota, "Impact," 21–22.
30. The important conceptual division of *uchi* (内; "inside") and *soto* (外; "outside") are is both implicit and explicit in social groups and Japanese language. Japanese are part of the "in" group, which must explain itself to the "out" group by appropriating outer norms. We should not be surprised that the word for "foreigner" keeps this division clear: *gaikokujin*, 外国人, literally "outside-country-person").
31. In fact, seventh-7th grade English lessons drive home the idea that a Japanese "Koji" and his friend "Bin," a Chinese, do not speak each other's respective languages and, instead, when together, "They speak English."
32. Quoted in McConnell, *Importing*, 266.
33. Ibid., 258–260.
34. See the ongoing debate between the international press and Japanese national ministries: Michael Fitzpatrick, "Japan's Divided Education Strategy," *New York Times*, 12 October 2014, retrieved 5 April 2017 from http://www.nytimes.com/2014/10/13/world/asia/japans-divided-education-strategy.html; MEXT, "Statement by Minister of Education, Culture,

Sports, Science and Technology of Japan on the 12 October *New York Times* article 'Japan's Divided Education Strategy,'" retrieved 17 November 2014 from http://www.mext.go.jp/english/topics/1353287.htm.
35. Tajino, "Native and Non-native," 6.
36. *See* 日本書紀 or "The Chronicles of Japan." For an early translation, see William George Aston, *Nihongi: Chronicles of Japan from the Earliest Times to 697 AD* (London: Japan Society of London, 1896).

References

Aston, William George. *Nihongi: Chronicles of Japan from the Earliest Times to 697 AD* (London: Japan Society of London, 1896).
Beasley, W.G. *Japan Encounters the Barbarian: Japanese Travelers in America and Europe* (New Haven, CT & London: Yale University Press, 1995),
Butler, Yuko Goto. "Foreign Language Education at Elementary Schools in Japan: Searching for Solutions Amidst Growing Diversification," *Current Issues in Language Planning* 8(/2) (2007): 129–147.
Chira, Susan. "Nakasone Apologies for Comments that Offended US Minorities," *New York Times*, 27 September 1986, retrieved 5 April 2017 from http://www.nytimes.com/1986/09/27/world/nakasone-apologizes-for-comments-that-offended-us-minorities.html.
Crooks, Anthony. "Professional Development and the JET Program: Insights and Solutions Based on the Sendai City Program," *JALT Journal* 23(/1) (2001): 31–46.
自治体国際化協会 (Council of Local Authorities on International Relations). *The ALT Handbook* (Tokyo: CLAIR, 2013)
———. *General Information Handbook* (Tokyo: CLAIR, 2014)
Duus, Peter. "Showa-era Japan and beyond: from Imperial Japan to Japan Inc.," in Victoria Lynn Bestor et al. (eds), *Routledge Handbook of Japanese Society and Culture* (New York: Routledge, 2011), 13–28.
Fitzpatrick, Michael. "Japan's Divided Education Strategy," *New York Times*, 12 October 2014, retrieved 5 April 2017 from http://www.nytimes.com/2014/10/13/world/asia/japans-divided-education-strategy.html.
Goodman, Roger. "The Concept of Kokusaika and Japanese Educational Reform," *Globalization, Societies and Education* 5(/1) (2007): 71–87.
———. "Japanese Education and Education Reform," in Victoria Lynn Bestor, et al. (eds), *Routledge Handbook of Japanese Society and Culture*, ed. Victoria Lynn Bestor, et al. (New York: Routledge, 2011), 52–62.
Holcombe, Charles. *The Genesis of East Asia, 221 B.C.-–A.D. 907* (Honolulu, HI: University of Hawaii Press, 2001).
Kubota, Ryuko. "The Impact of Globalization on Language Teaching in Japan," in David Block and Deborah Cameron (eds), *Globalization and Language Teaching*, (London: Routledge, 2002), 13–28.
McConnell, David L. "Education for Global Integration in Japan: A Case Study of the JET Program," *Human Organization* 55(/4) (1996): 446–457.

———. McConnell, David L. *Importing Diversity: Inside Japan's JET Program* (Berkeley, CA: University of California Press, 2000).

———. "Japan's Image Problem and the Soft Power Solution: The JET Program as Cultural Diplomacy," in Kasushi Watanabe and David L. McConnell (eds), *Soft Power Superpowers: Cultural and National Assets of Japan and the United States* (London: M.E. Sharpe, 2008), pp. 18–36.

———. "Education for Global Integration in Japan: A Case Study of the JET Program," *Human Organization* 55/4 (1996): 446–457.

Tajino, Akira and Yasuko Tajino. "Native and Non-native: What Can They Offer? Lessons from Team-Teaching in Japan," *ELT Journal* 54(/1) (2000): 3–11.

Toby, Ronald P. *State and Diplomacy in Early Modern Japan: Asia in the Development of the Tokugawa Bakufu* (Princeton, NJ: Princeton University Press, 1984).

Vogel, Ezra. *Japan as Number One: Lessons for America* (Cambridge, MA: Harvard University Press, 1979).

19

NEW ACTORS OF THE POST-COLD WAR WORLD (EUROPE, CHINA AND INDIA)
Toward a Genuine Globalization of Scholarship Programs
Ludovic Tournès

Introduction

The global geography of scholarship programs established during the Cold War has undergone profound changes since the 1980s. This period not only witnessed the end of the Soviet Union, which had attracted large numbers of students from communist countries and from the Global South, but it also saw the relative retreat of the United States, even if the post-9/11 period has seen the beginnings of a new rise in this respect. Above all, this period has also seen the emergence of new actors that have asserted their ambitions through programs that, although very different, all reveal a desire to play a larger role in the circulation of knowledge at an international level and to become important sites of intellectual and economic activity. This will be examined through three successive case studies: the European Union (EU) and its Erasmus program, China and the development of a global network of Confucius Institutes, and the many-sided and ambitious policy of India when it comes to scholarship programs. These three actors, whose emergence has been both recent and very rapid, have clearly shaped a new geography of scholarship programs that will undoubtedly be reinforced in the coming decades. In this new global landscape, the Euro-American world is slowly losing its centrality, even though it remains a major player.

Erasmus: Academic, Economic or Political Program?

Launched in 1987, the Erasmus program rose in the space of one generation to become the largest scholarship program in history, funding three million students and 350,000 university teachers and administrators between 1987 and 2013,[1] and even—according to the European Commission—creating a legacy of one million babies born to "Erasmus couples."[2] It was also, without a doubt, the first truly multilateral program. Indeed, while programs like those of the Rockefeller Foundation and the Fulbright organization claimed to have a multilateral character, this was in part fictitious since these programs were in fact more like a collection of bilateral programs centered on the United States. This is not the case for the Erasmus program, in which any Member State can send scholarship holders to (or receive them from) any other Member State.

The name adopted by the program speaks volumes about its ambition: although it is an acronym for European Action Scheme for the Mobility of University Students, it is also, of course, a reference to Erasmus of Rotterdam. Erasmus was both one of the most important figures of the Renaissance and the embodiment of the main features of that transformative period in European history: the ambition to embrace all fields of human knowledge, the cosmopolitanism of the "Republic of Letters" and the central position that Europe acquired in the world from the Age of Discoveries onward. Moreover, the Latin sound of the acronym is also a subliminal reference to the fact that Latin had been the continent's international language and the most tangible manifestation of its unity during that period, even if this "Europe" was only that of the educated elites. Be that as it may, the ambition symbolized by this name was never expressed in such terms by the European officials who devised the program, as if the unity of Europe, its common identity and its international influence were taboo subjects in the history of the European project because of the reticence of Member States to abandon their sovereignty. Instead, other objectives were emphasized at the moment of the program's creation. It was said to have two main goals: fostering economic cooperation and development through the promotion of student mobility, with the aim of creating a single market; and promoting the global influence of European higher education through the establishment of multiple international partnerships.

While European cooperation in higher education had its origins in meetings between the education ministers of the various members of the European Economic Community (EEC) during the 1970s, the key date in the creation of the Erasmus program was 1986 with the signing of the Single European Act. This Act signaled the determination of the EEC's Member States to deepen the integration process, the years following the oil crises of 1973 and 1979 having seen a rise in euroscepticism owing to the inability of European countries to formulate a common response to the economic crisis. The Single European Act created the conditions for almost completely removing the obstacles to the free circulation of persons and goods throughout the continent, which came into effect with the signing of the Maastricht Treaty in 1992. Clearly, the creation and expansion of the Erasmus program were inseparable from the pursuit of European integration in multiple other fields, not least in air transport, with the deregulation of that sector in 1997, and in the financial sector, with the creation of the euro in 2002, two developments that greatly facilitated the circulation of the program's participants around the continent. Another major factor in the development of the program was the collapse of the Communist Bloc. Even though Erasmus was launched two years before the fall of the Berlin Wall, the considerable expansion of the program during the 1990s and 2000s would not have been possible without the enlargement of the EU that followed the collapse of the people's democracies, with sixteen new members joining the EU between 1995 and 2013.

This key fact largely explains the program's impressive statistics: during the first year of its existence, in 1987, 3,244 students from eleven countries received a scholarship; by 2013, this number had reached 270,000, plus 52,000 teachers and administrators from thirty-three countries. The milestone of one million scholarships was reached in 2002, fifteen years after the program began; the two-millionth scholarship was granted just six years later in 2008; and the three-millionth in 2013. By the year 2020, the European Commission hopes to have reached a total of five million participants. The massive scale of the Erasmus program is something that makes it unique when compared to the majority of scholarship programs created since the end of the nineteenth century. Most of these programs have been on a modest scale, counting their scholarship holders in tens or in hundreds each year, and while some of them were larger (like the Fulbright program), the Erasmus program operates on an unprecedented scale. Whether this program can be considered to have truly democratized international mobility is a matter of debate, particularly considering the modest sums offered as scholarships, which make mobility difficult for students from poorer backgrounds. What is certain, however, is that Erasmus marks the beginning of a new era in the history of scholarship programs when compared to the comparatively elitist and restricted programs of previous periods.

This feature is largely due to the program's stated objective of promoting economic competitiveness in Europe.

In fact, not only is the Erasmus program more than simply an academic scholarship program, but, from the 1990s onward, it has also been increasingly integrated into the economic strategy of the EU. There are two main reasons for this. The first is that educational policy was historically the prerogative of the Member States, which, ever since the European project began, have been very reticent to delegate responsibility in this area to the European Commission. As a result, the Erasmus program was not able, at least in its early stages, to present itself as an educational program, for fear of offending national governments unwilling to relinquish their sovereignty. The second reason is that the international economic climate has become increasingly difficult since the 1990s, particularly as a result of the financial crises of 1997 and 2008. These new circumstances have driven Europe into developing an increasingly ambitious policy for overcoming the convulsions of the global economy and meeting the challenge of competition from other countries, particularly in Asia. In fact, from 2007 onward, the link between student mobility and labor market integration has become increasingly important, and the concept of "employability" is now omnipresent in the documents of the European Commission relating to the Erasmus program. This has become a major component of the "Europe 2020 strategy for growth and jobs"[3] designed to combat unemployment across the continent. Mobility is now considered by the program's organizers to increase students' employability by allowing them to develop not only their skills in their own fields of study but also their linguistic skills and, through international experience, their ability to adapt to different contexts. Since 2007, a growing proportion of Erasmus students have been working in businesses rather than studying at universities: between 2007 and 2013, 210,000 students spent all or part of their time abroad in a company, and 30 percent of them were offered a position at the end this period.[4] A total of 21 percent of Erasmus scholarship holders were involved in such a scheme in 2013, a figure that has been increasing steadily since 2007.[5] It would not be an exaggeration, therefore, to state that the Erasmus program is increasingly becoming an instrument of economic policy.

Nevertheless, the program's academic side remains essential, all the more so since it is not limited to the promotion of academic mobility within Europe, but also seeks to increase European higher education's global influence. From this perspective, it is worth underlining the fact that what is considered to be *the* Erasmus program is in reality a whole range of programs targeting different groups and directed toward different geographic regions. This characteristic is not entirely new in the history of scholarship programs: the Fulbright Program, to take just one example, has taken a wide variety of forms over the course of its history, whether in terms of the duration of scholarships or the groups at which they were targeted (students, teachers, researchers, etc.). Yet this fact is particularly important when it comes to understanding the dual logic of the Erasmus program: encouraging mobility within Europe and promoting Europe around the world. Indeed, the Erasmus programs are organized according to three concentric circles, corresponding to three geographic regions of increasing size. The first circle is made up of the members of the EU and the handful of other countries that, over the years, have come to take part in the program (Iceland, Liechtenstein, Norway, Switzerland and Turkey). These countries are participants in the program of student mobility in Europe. The second circle was created in 1990 when the Tempus program was founded: this program was a direct consequence of the fall of the Berlin Wall and sought to participate in the restructuring ("modernization" in the language of the European Commission)[6] of the higher education systems of the former people's democracies, as well as those of states created by the breakup of the Soviet Union and of others around the Mediterranean (Algeria, Egypt, Israel, Jordan and Morocco). The Tempus program was in reality a program of development aid, through which Europe intended to position itself as the provider of expertise in the field of higher education to the aforementioned countries by supporting exchanges of students and researchers as well as transnational partnerships between institutions collaborating on the project. The creation of this program should also be interpreted as a European response to American activism in Eastern Europe after 1989, particularly through private foundations such as the Soros Foundation, which aimed to re-educate the elites of former Communist states through the reconstruction of local education systems along American lines.[7] Between 2007 and 2013, almost 700 European institutions and 900 non-European institutions were involved in the Tempus program.[8] Finally, the third geographic circle encompasses almost the whole planet: it was established in 2004 with the creation of the Erasmus Mundus program, which aimed to open up European higher education institutions to the world and to create international partnerships, both to contribute to the influence of European higher education and to attract the greatest minds from all over the world to Europe. Since it began, the program has sought not only to strengthen existing links with Europe's traditional partners, like the United States, but also to create or reinforce links with other partners such as Russia, Ukraine, China, India, and Brazil. The Jean Monnet program should also be included in this third circle. This program aims to promote the study of Europe both in EU Member States and in all the aforementioned circles through the creation of Jean Monnet chairs for reputed researchers, as well as through the promotion of transnational partnerships.

In sum, the Erasmus program is as much a global program as it is a European one. It is also as much a political program as it is an academic and economic one, since it is one of the many signs of the EU's diplomatic strategy to advance European integration without stepping on the toes of its Member States, which jealously guard their prerogatives. This strategy includes promoting Europe on the international stage in the field of higher education and knowledge, a field in which the individual Member States possess their own strong and longstanding traditions. The European Commission has been able to draw upon these traditions in order to affirm Europe's place in the higher education landscape of the post-Cold War world. This strategy has largely been a successful one, though it is questionable whether it has really contributed to promote the European model as a whole throughout the world and to counterbalance the negative effects of recent crises on Europe's international image (the Greek bankruptcy, the migration crisis and Brexit).

China and the Confucius Institute: Back to National Power Politics

China is another major actor in the post-Cold War academic landscape. Its expansion in this field is more recent, since it dates back to the 2000s. The year 2004 saw the creation of the Confucius Institute, which is part of China's ambitious strategy to assert its "soft power"—this expression coined by the American political scientist Joseph Nye was actually used by the head of state Hu Jintao in 2007 during his speech to the Congress of the Communist Party of China.[9] By creating the Confucius Institute, the Chinese government was explicitly drawing inspiration from older historical examples such as the Alliance française and the British Council,[10] the objective of which was to promote a national culture, particularly through the spread of the language. Similarly, the central objective of the international network of Confucius Institutes is to promote the teaching of Chinese around the world. The overall project is led by a government agency called the Office of Chinese Language Council International (frequently referred to as Hanban), the objective of which is to implement an ambitious "Overseas Chinese education plan" with a handsome grant from the government.[11] The ambition of the Institute is vast—it intends to develop a network of institutes throughout the world with multiple functions: "[1/] promotional centers discovering, exploring and expanding the demand for Chinese education in the countries where they are located; [2/] teaching centers ...; [3/] research centers improving strategies and methods for learning Chinese according to practical situations in that specific country or region; [4/] training centers providing support to various Chinese learning institutions with instructors and techniques; [5/] and test centers taking on the responsibility of promoting various Chinese language proficiency tests."[12] In reality, all these functions can be summed up as one single goal: promoting the Chinese language and above all making the Confucius Institute the "central base"[13] for all activities linked to Chinese language learning in the countries concerned. The Chinese government thus intends to become the sole purveyor of Chinese teaching in the world and thus to control the entire chain, from the selection of textbooks to the choice of teachers and subjects taught. In accordance with this centralizing idea and with the help of a very significant budget, the government negotiates with local higher education institutions to set up institutes within their walls. These institutes fall into two categories: Confucius Institutes and Confucius Classrooms. The institutes are formal organizations, usually hosted by a higher education institution; the classrooms are less formal structures involving the provision of classes, notably in secondary schools.

The results of this ambitious policy were soon felt: by 2006, there were already 122 structures (institutes and classrooms) in the world, including forty-four in twenty-one different countries in Europe, forty-three in seventeen different countries in Asia, twenty-five in three different counties in the Americas (of which seventeen are in the United States) and four in two countries in Oceania.[14] By 2015, this figure had risen to 500 institutes and 1,000 classrooms in 135 countries, catering to a total of 1.9 million students,[15] for which the Chinese government had selected 44,000 teachers, Chinese as well as local, to teach in the institutes. The geographic spread was as follows: 167 institutes in forty European countries, 158 in nineteen countries in the Americas, 111 in thirty-three Asian countries, forty-six in thirty-two African countries and eighteen in three countries in Oceania.[16] This expansion is impressive: in just ten years China has managed to build an international network almost as large as that of the Alliance française, which has existed for over a century and was a pioneer in the field of language diplomacy.[17]

In order to implement this ambitious strategy in as short a time as possible and to impose its own standards in terms of Chinese teaching, the Chinese government sent its own teachers and institute administrators abroad. Unlike the Alliance française and the British Council, which leave a large degree of autonomy to local branches, the whole project is directed from Beijing. In 2006, the government sent more than 1,000 teachers to over eighty countries to staff the institutes and classrooms.[18] In 2015, this number had risen to 3,700.[19] Moreover, a policy of scholarships was put in place very early in order to allow local students and teachers to attend the institutes that had been set up in their countries, and subsequently to become teachers in the newly created classrooms. In 2015, 43,000 local teachers were trained in the institutes; of this figure, 1,146 teachers from sixty countries were granted scholarships to study at institutes in China itself.[20] Such a two-stage strategy had already been employed by the Rockefeller Foundation in the 1920s in its policy of training nurses: this policy involved, on the one hand, giving modest scholarships to nurses to acquire basic training in their future profession in their own countries while, on the other hand, selecting a small elite cadre to be sent to American nursing schools to receive more rigorous training in order to become the future directors of European nursing schools. The objective of the Chinese government through its scholarship policy is clearly identical: it seeks to train those destined to manage local institutes and coordinate Chinese teaching in key countries, according to the principles decreed by the Chinese government. This is the case, for example, in Thailand: in 2006, Hanban signed an agreement with the Thai government in order to develop Chinese teaching in that country. For this purpose, 100 scholarships were granted to Thai students to study in China before returning to their own country to take up teaching positions in schools.[21]

Moreover, Hanban has also set up a major scholarship program aimed at foreign students and researchers wanting to study Chinese in China. All levels of study are included in this policy. In 2015, there were over 8,700 undergraduate and graduate students who went to China, a rise of 12 percent on the previous year.[22] In general, these scholarships are of a duration of one or two university semesters for undergraduate students and of one or two years for master's level students. Again, the program is global, but particular attention is given to neighboring countries: in 2015 Hanban thus created "Chinese language teachers training classes" for students from Southeast Asia in twelve Chinese universities, which enabled almost 400 students from neighboring countries to study in China on scholarships.[23] Hanban also set up the "Confucius China studies program" for students wishing to undertake a doctorate on questions related to Chinese language or culture: between 2005 and 2015, 260 student scholarship-holders went to study in China; in 2015 alone, there were 112, a rise of 50 percent on the previous year. Finally, they also created a scholarship program for researchers: in 2015, forty-three academics from twenty-one countries were funded to conduct research in China.[24] This voluntarist policy seems to have borne fruit: Hanban estimates that, between 2005 and 2015, 3,000 students who had gone to study in China subsequently became Chinese teachers on their return to their home countries.[25] In addition, like all major scholarship programs, Hanban has created a "Global Alumni Association of Confucius Institutes" in order to maintain links with former students of the institutes and to promote the teaching of Chinese.

The centralizing and authoritarian policy of the Chinese government soon attracted criticism. A number of universities have denounced the pressure exercised by Hanban during the negotiations that led to the creation of local institutes: in exchange for a generous grant, Hanban was said to have demanded the right to oversee teaching content and to have obtained an assurance that sensitive political issues (such as the question of Tibet and the 1989 Tiananmen Square protests) would not be mentioned within the institutes.[26] Without access to first-hand documents on the subject (notably the contracts between the Chinese government and the universities in question, which are not made public), it is difficult to judge for certain. Yet the fact remains that several universities have closed their institutes in the wake of protests from the academic body. In October 2013, Marshall Sahlins, the renowned anthropologist at the University of Chicago, published a very critical article on the Confucius Institutes.[27] A few months later, in June 2014, the American Association of University Professors published a report criticizing the Confucius Institutes,[28] describing them as propaganda establishments and calling on universities to reconsider their associations with Hanban unless they could renegotiate their contracts to have more freedom in the design of courses and the recruitment of teachers. In the wake of these controversies, some universities decided to close their institutes (the University of Chicago and Penn State University). In 2015, one European institution, Stockholm University, did the same.[29] It is difficult to say whether this is a trend that will continue or is merely just a few isolated incidents. But, looking at the Hanban statistics, this episode seems to have done little harm to the spread of the institutes; in 2013, before the controversy broke out, there were ninety Institutes in the United States, while in 2015, there were 109.[30] But behind this figure, what is the reality on the ground? Have other institutes closed down in the United States or elsewhere in the world? Only a detailed analysis would allow this question to be answered. What is certain is that the impressive growth of the Confucius Institutes shows that China is now a global power in the field of academic scholarship programs. While these are above all related to the teaching of Chinese, universities in China have also developed an ambitious policy of international relations, which suggests that programs in other fields will also expand rapidly over the coming years.

India: Developing South–South Exchanges

India is another interesting case of the emergence of a new actor in the post-Cold War landscape of scholarship programs. While the Chinese scholarship policy is centered on language teaching and is entirely controlled by the government, India has seen the rise of a range of scholarship programs since the 1990s in a diverse range of fields, sponsored both by the government and by private actors.

The government is obviously a key actor in this process, managing dozens of scholarship programs through its various ministries and agencies. Its policy regarding scholarships is able to rely on a very large network of higher education institutions (undoubtedly the largest in the world) made up of 343 universities and 17,000 colleges.[31] One of the most important bodies in this field is the Indian Council for Cultural Relations (ICCR), a government agency that, though founded in 1950, has expanded its activities since the beginning of the 2000s as part of the Indian government's ambitious policy of soft power.[32] Scholarship programs, a large number of which are managed by the ICCR, are incontestably part of this policy: after the fall of the Taliban following the American-led operation in Afghanistan in 2001, India became one of the most important partners in the reconstruction of the country; in 2005, a program was created to allow Afghan students to study in India. In the same vein, a program dedicated to allowing African students to study in India was strengthened in 2008. In 2016, the Indian Council of Cultural Relations was managing at least twenty scholarship programs aimed at foreign students. These programs are open to students from all around the world, although, broadly speaking, the countries of Asia are favored. This is the case, for example, for the General Scholarship Scheme, which is essentially concerned with countries of Africa and Asia, but also includes Russia and some countries of the Americas (Trinidad and Tobago). It is also the case for the Technical Cooperation Scheme of the Colombo Plan. The SAARC Fellowship Scheme, meanwhile, is reserved for citizens of the member states of the South Asian Association for Regional Cooperation (SAARC) created in 1985. Another program is reserved for African students, while numerous others are bilateral and targeted at students from the following countries: Kenya, Sri Lanka, Mauritius, Bhutan, the Maldives, Afghanistan, Mongolia, Nepal and Bangladesh.[33] Western countries are far less well represented: there is a program for students from Commonwealth countries, while another, the Cultural Exchange Program, is open to sixty-eight countries in Asia, Africa and Europe, but does not include the United States. In total, one can estimate that over 3,000 scholarships are offered each year by the various programs of the ICCR, the vast majority aimed at the countries of Southeast Asia and Africa: the General Scholarship Scheme, for instance, offers 500 scholarships per year,[34] while the Afghan program offers 1,000 and the African program 900.[35] The bilateral programs offer a few dozen scholarships annually (around forty for Sri Lanka, for example). To this must be added the specific programs for the Indian diaspora, spread across around sixty countries.[36] This policy of scholarships largely directed toward Asia, and in which Europe and the Americas have a secondary position, bears witness to the fact that the center of gravity in the global landscape of scholarship programs is beginning to shift: while Western countries still play a central role, in the coming decades the emergence of new actors will clearly bring about major changes in the geography of international academic exchanges, which represents an important market.

Other Indian ministries also manage scholarship programs. The Ministry of Science and Technology, for example, has numerous programs allowing students of neighboring countries to come to work in Indian research laboratories. Within the Ministry of External Affairs, meanwhile, the Technical and Economic Cooperation Program was created in 1964, an ambitious program of bilateral cooperation with a number of partner countries, which is testament to India's determined involvement in the movement of nonaligned countries since the 1950s. Indeed, the aim of the program is to compete with the programs of development aid created since the 1950s by the great powers (the United States and Russia, as well as Great Britain, France and Germany) and by international organizations (the United Nations Development Program, the International Labor Organization and the World Bank) by using its status as a country of the South to present itself as more capable of understanding the issues of developing countries and therefore better placed to provide them with the expertise they require, as an alternative to the modernization programs pursued by Western institutions that do not always meet local needs. The Technical and Economic

Cooperation Program is presented as follows: "161 countries in Asia, Africa, East Europe, Latin America, The Caribbean as well as Pacific and small island countries are invited to share in the Indian developmental experience acquired over six decades of India's existence as a free nation. As a result of different activities in this program, there is now a visible and growing awareness among other countries about the competences of India as a provider of know-how and expertise as well as training opportunities, consultancy services and feasibility studies."[37] As part of this program, the Indian government offers scholarships to citizens of neighboring countries, following a similar logic to that of the Marshall Plan of 1948–52, as these scholarships enable recipients to go to India for training in different fields before returning to their own countries to put their newly acquired knowledge into practice. The program is aimed at economic actors who can follow training courses in fields such as management, engineering or banking. But it also includes a military section, undoubtedly aimed at the training of officers of the armed forces of neighboring countries, the instability of which is a source of concern for the Indian government.

Government agencies are not the only providers of scholarships. Private actors have been involved too, particularly the great industrialists who, since the late nineteenth century, have habitually created foundations. In this field, India has a tradition as old as that of the United States, and Indian foundations have played a similar role in the development of higher education and research to that played by the Rockefeller and Carnegie Foundations in the United States in the early twentieth century. The Tata industrial dynasty is a characteristic example, but is certainly not the only one. The founder of this dynasty, Jamsetji Tata (1839–1904), made his fortune in business and then in metallurgy, and laid the foundations of an industrial empire that has continued to thrive under his successors to this day. A nationalist and supporter of Indian independence, he put part of his fortune toward the creation of an Indian elite capable of taking over the running of the country; with this goal in mind, supporting Indian higher education institutions and granting scholarships for young Indians to go and study in the best universities of the West were already among his objectives in the late nineteenth century. In 1892, he created his first foundation, the J.N Tata Endowment for Higher Education, which granted scholarships for study at British universities, notably Cambridge. His successor Ratan Tata created the Ratan Tata Foundation, which, as well as financing higher education institutions, carried on the tradition of scholarships, sending numerous students to the London School of Economics from the 1920s onward.[38] One can also mention the creation of the Lady Tata Memorial Trust in 1932 by Dorabji Tata in memory of his wife, who had died of leukemia the previous year. This foundation was devoted to supporting medical research into this disease and, from the start (and still today), offered individual scholarships to Indian and foreign researchers developing research projects in Indian laboratories. The list goes on and on: like all the great industrial dynasties, the Tatas created a labyrinthine network of foundations dedicated to specific activities, each offering its own scholarships. It seems that this policy accelerated during the 1990s and 2000s. There are several indications of this acceleration, notably the creation in 2000 of a Fellowship Program administered by the Ratan Tata Trust and the creation in 2006 of the Tata Innovation Fellowships, financed by the Trust but administered by the Ministry of Science and Technology.[39] The creation of scholarship programs is also a means of establishing or continuing collaborations with world-renowned higher education institutions. In 1997, for example, the Sir Ratan Tata Post-doctoral Fellowship program was created with the London School of Economics, supporting research on Southeast Asia; similarly, the Tata Center was founded at the Massachusetts Institute of Technology in 2012, followed by its sister institution, the Indian Institute of Technology in Bombay in 2014, in order to develop joint Indian-American research projects.[40] Since the beginning of the twentieth century, the scholarship policy of the Tata dynasty thus seems to have shifted from sending Indians to English universities to training Indians at Indian universities to matching elite institutions in Europe and America on an equal basis in joint programs.

The key conclusion that can be drawn from this rapid and nonexhaustive sketch of Indian scholarship programs is that India now has all the attributes to be considered a major scientific power, and scholarships are now one of the tools being used both to bring students and researchers from all over the world to India and to allow Indians to work internationally. From this point of view, India has no cause to be envious of traditional scientific powers like the United States and European countries. Moreover, it is important to note that these scholarship programs map out a system of scientific flows on a global scale, in which Western countries play a secondary role behind Asia and Africa. While this could be interpreted as a sign that India is a regional rather than a global power, it above all demonstrates that South–South academic exchanges have been expanding massively since the end of the Cold War and that India plays an important — indeed, central — role in this.

Conclusion

From the three examples described here emerge both a major historical continuity and a major rupture in the history of scholarship programs in the politics of state power. The continuity concerns the role of scholarship programs in state power politics. Whether in the twenty-first century or at the end of the nineteenth century, these programs have always been tools used for promoting international influence. They are, and always have been, tools of power politics, albeit soft power. The proof of the permanence of their role is that a new political structure like the EU has made an exchange program one of the pillars and symbols of its global strategy. The rupture concerns the global geography of scholarship programs: essentially centered on three countries at the end of the nineteenth century (Great Britain, Germany and France), they were joined by the United States from the 1920s, a country that became dominant in the 1930s and even more so after 1945. Since the end of the Cold War, this map has shifted: on the one hand, Europe has incontestably made a comeback in the global competition for scientific talent, even if it still remains far behind the United States; on the other hand, and above all, non-Western actors have emerged, of which China and India are two examples. These two countries are increasingly present in the international market of scholarship programs, and their strategy is not limited to integrating into networks dominated by the major Western institutions of higher education; it also consists of creating their own networks and, notably, in developing South–South partnerships. At the beginning of the twenty-first century, we are witnessing a genuine globalization of scholarship programs, the growth of transnational circulations in the Western world being paralleled by the same phenomenon in the global South. Even though Europe and America remain central in the landscape of scholarship programs, it is clear that Asia is now playing a growing role.

Notes

1. "Erasmus. Facts, Figures and Trends. The European Union Support for Students and Staff exchanges and University Cooperation in 2012–2013," retrieved 8 April 2017 from http://ec.europa.eu/dgs/education_culture/repository/education/library/statistics/ay-12-13/facts-figures_en.pdf. See also the website of the European Commission, especially at https://ec.europa.eu/education/ and http://ec.europa.eu/programmes/erasmus-plus.

2. Press release, 22 September 2014, retrieved 8 April 2017 from http://europa.eu/rapid/press-release_IP-14-1025_fr.htm.
3. "Erasmus. Erasmus. Facts, Figures and Trends," 5.
4. Ibid., 5–6.
5. Ibid., 9–10.
6. Ibid., 26.
7. See Tereza Pospíšilová, "Transnational Philanthropy and Nationalism: The Early Years of Central Europan University," *Monde(s): Histoire, espaces, relations* 6 (2014): 126–46.
8. "Erasmus. Erasmus. Facts, Figures and Trends," 29.
9. Stéphanie Balme, "L'impuissance paradoxale du 'soft power' de la Chine post-Mao," *CERISCOPE Puissance* (2013), retrieved 8 April 2017 from http://ceriscope.sciences-po.fr/puissance/content/part4/l-impuissance-du-soft-power-chinois. See also Anja Lahtinen, "China's Soft Power: Challenges of Confucianism and Confucius Institutes," *Journal of Comparative Asian Development* 14(2) (2015): 200–26.
10. *The Office of Chinese Language Council International Annual Report* (2006), 011/part 2. The annual reports of the Confucius Institute since its creation are available online at http://www.hanban.edu.cn/report.
11. Ibid., 007/part 2.
12. Ibid.
13. Ibid.
14. See the complete list of countries in *The Office of Chinese Language Council International Annual Report* (2006), 047.
15. *The Office of Chinese Language Council International Annual Report* (2015), 3.
16. Ibid., 66; see the detailed table at 66–73.
17. François Chaubet, *La politique culturelle française et la diplomatie de la langue: L'Alliance française (1883–1940)* (Paris: l'Harmattan, 2006).
18. *The Office of Chinese Language Council International Annual Report* (2006), 019/part 2.
19. *The Office of Chinese Language Council International Annual Report* (2015), 21.
20. *Ibid.*
21. *The Office of Chinese Language Council International Annual Report* (2006), 031/part 6.
22. *The Office of Chinese Language Council International Annual Report* (2015), 37.
23. Ibid., 22.
24. Ibid., 29.
25. Ibid., 37.
26. See "Is Stanford Collaborating with Chinese Propaganda? Just Asking," *Forbes*, 5 October 2014, retrieved 8 April 2017 from http://www.forbes.com/sites/eamonnfingleton/2014/10/05/is-stanford-collaborating-with-chinas-espionage-program/#3e9cca13795f.
27. Marshall Sahlins, "Confucius Institutes Censor Political Discussions and Restrain the Free Exchange of Ideas: Why, Then, Do American Universities Sponsor Them?" *The Nation*, 30 October 2013, retrieved 8 April 2017 from https://www.thenation.com/article/china-u.

28. American Association of University Professors, "On Partnership with Foreign Governments: The Case of Confucius Institutes," June 2014, retrieved 8 April 2017 from https://www.aaup.org/report/confucius-institutes.
29. "China's Confucius Institutes and the Soft War," *The Diplomat*, 8 July 2015, retrieved 8 April 2017 from http://thediplomat.com/2015/07/chinas-confucius-institutes-and-the-soft-war.
30. *The Office of Chinese Language Council International Annual Report* (2015), 72.
31. "Study in India," retrieved 8 April 2017 from http://www.archive.india.gov.in/overseas/study_india/studyinindia.php.
32. Sudha Ramachandran, "India's Soft Power Potential," *The Diplomat*, 29 May 2015, retrieved 8 April 2017 from http://thediplomat.com/2015/05/indias-soft-power-potential. See also Aakriti Tandon, "The Modi Government and India's Projection of its Soft Power," *The Round Table*, 29 February 2016, retrieved 8 April 2017 from http://www.commonwealthroundtable.co.uk/commonwealth/the-modi-government-and-indias-projection-of-its-soft-power.
33. Indian Council for Cultural Relations, "Many Other Schemes," retrieved 8 April 2017 from http://www.iccr.gov.in/content/many-other-schemes.
34. "Indian Government Scholarships for Asia, Africa and Latin America," retrieved 8 April 2017 from http://www.studyandscholarships.com/2013/12/indian-government-general-scholarships-scheme.html; "Study in India," retrieved 8 April 2017 from http://www.archive.india.gov.in/overseas/study_india/studyinindia.php?id=10.
35. "Indian Government ICCR Scholarship for 900 African undergraduate/postgraduate students 2017/2018," retrieved 8 April 2017 from http://www.afterschoolafrica.com/11492/indian-government-iccr-scholarship.
36. "Scholarship Programmes for Diaspora Children," Ministry of External Affairs, retrieved 8 April 2017 from https://www.mea.gov.in/spdc.htm.
37. "Indian Technical and Cooperation Programme," Ministry of External Affairs, retrieved 8 April 2017 from http://itec.mea.gov.in/?1320?000.
38. See Marie Scot, *La London School of Economics and Political Science (1895–2010): Internationalisation universitaire et circulation des savoirs* (Paris: PUF, 2011), 52–54.
39. Ministry of Science and Technology of India, Department of Biotechnology, *Annual Report (2014–15)*, 19, retrieved 8 April 2017 from http://www.dbtindia.nic.in/annual-report.
40. "Mission," Tata Center, retrieved 8 April 2017 from https://tatacenter.mit.edu/mission.

References

Balme, Stéphanie. "L'impuissance paradoxale du 'soft power' de la Chine post-Mao," *CERISCOPE Puissance* (2013), retrieved 8 April 2017 from http://ceriscope.sciences-po.fr/puissance/content/part4/l-impuissance-du-soft-power-chinois.

Chaubet, François. *La politique culturelle française et la diplomatie de la langue: L'Alliance française (1883–1940)* (Paris: l'Harmattan, 2006).

Lahtinen, Anja. "China's Soft Power: Challenges of Confucianism and Confucius Institutes," *Journal of Comparative Asian Development* 14(2) (2015): 200–26.

Pospíšilová, Tereza. "Transnational Philanthropy and Nationalism: The Early Years of Central European University," *Monde(s): Histoire, espaces, relations* 6 (2014): 126–46.

Scot, Marie. *La London School of Economics and Political Science (1895–2010): Internationalisation universitaire et circulation des savoirs* (Paris: PUF, 2011).

Conclusion

150 Years of Scholarship Programs
Old Trends and New Prospects in the Global Landscape
Giles Scott-Smith and Ludovic Tournès

In the Introduction we summarized the current state of the art in the historical study of scholarship programs, providing a set of four periodizations and a framework for analysis for future research. By framing the field of study as scholarships instead of exchanges, we point out that the activity is in some shape or form an award to the participant—they have to request or apply to go abroad, and they are granted or awarded the means to do so. This is distinct from the more neutral-sounding use of "exchange," since it emphasizes that there is some form of intent behind the programs: they are created for identifiable groups, for particular purposes and by a definable organization. The nineteen chapters in the book illustrate the breadth and depth of types of scholarships that have been run and continue to be run since the late nineteenth century. From this body of case studies, a number of important conclusions can be drawn.

First, scholarship programs are not solely the domain of academia. Scholarships are a vital element to the academic world, providing the means for scholar mobility, the interchange of ideas and intellectual products, and processes of "internationalization" more broadly (all key features of the current EU-run research funding environment, for instance). Yet, as the chapters demonstrate, other fields of activity—the military, postcolonial development, agriculture, sports and medicine—have invested heavily in the belief that skills and training can be enhanced through the mobility of expertise. This emphasizes once again how scholarships are a transversal topic of research, at the crossroads of several fields of history, and for this reason up to now have not been treated as a single, legitimate research terrain in their own right.

Second, the long-term perspective adopted in the book has brought to light some permanent features in the history of scholarship programs. Scholarship programs are often used as an additional way to pursue power politics through different means, since many were conceived as instruments of "soft power" and "nation branding." This is a constant feature, which was present in the efforts of France at the end of the nineteenth century to promote the French language and attract foreign students, through the policies of Germany, the United States, Britain and the Soviet Union, up to the present-day promotion of the Chinese language by the Confucius Institutes, the "European idea" by the EU and technical development by India. But this national power politics has also delivered major results for the worldwide circulation of knowledge, even if these same programs have also tended to reinforce the imbalance between center and periphery in the global systems of power. During the nineteenth century, scholarship networks were used deliberately to confirm the centrality of European powers, and during the Cold War they were used for the same purposes by the superpowers. At the same time, they have been pivotal for generating and facilitating international scientific cooperation. As has been demonstrated by recent research on philanthropic programs, awarding scholarships is a cheaper way to promote the circulation of knowledge than large investments in equipment and institutions (although these kinds of investments have often been combined).

The third element concerns the tension that exists between two principles: on the one hand, the unilateral principle of promoting a national/imperial model by using scholarships to establish an "intellectual metropole" around which and through which scholarly networks function; and on the other hand, the principle of reciprocity and exchange, which emerged in the 1910s with the creation of the first bilateral academic programs, the global programs of philanthropies such as the Rockefeller Foundation, and internationalist programs such as those of the League of Nations Health Organization. The strength of internationalist thought during the interwar period marks an important stage in the history of scholarship programs because it emphasized the concept of *exchange*. However, this did not undermine unilateral interests, and throughout the twentieth century the two trends have awkwardly coexisted, sometimes in the same program. A significant example is the Fulbright Program, which was meant to both promote the American economic and political model abroad and "internationalize" American society at home. The results of this global program are only now coming into focus through a new wave of archival-based research. Scholarships have continued to oscillate between these two poles of promotion and exchange.

Alongside these recognizable trends are also notable examples of evolution and change. One aspect in particular concerns the geographic circuits of exchange. From the late nineteenth century onward, the transnational circulations through organized programs have become increasingly global in scope. Beginning with the original inter-European or inter-imperial systems centered on Europe, from the 1910s the United States rapidly matched and then moved beyond the Europeans as a new site of intellectual exchange. After 1945, the Soviet Union took on an expansive role as the self-declared center of the communist and underdeveloped world, and in this way the Cold War was a vital stage in the globalization of scholarship programs. At the same time, the programs of the UN system also contributed to the globalization of scholarships, although many of them reproduced the unilateral model by bringing grantees from the Global South to learn the recipes of development and modernization from experts in the North. Since the 1990s, new centers of intellectual exchange with explicit political goals have been developed by China, India and the European Union (EU). Within Europe itself, Britain, Germany and France have held on to their status as major destinations, but other countries have also emerged (for example, Spain, one of the most popular destinations among Erasmus students), and the EU's expansion during the 1990s and 2000s has further diversified the continent's geography of scholarships.

Another evolving aspect concerns the number of people involved in scholarship programs. As already noted in the Introduction, while in the 1880s there were annually only a few hundred participants worldwide, by 2000 there were 1.8 million students studying in a country other than their own. Even this is a conservative figure, since it does not include those involved in military, technical assistance, health and other specialist programs, and there are signs that the numbers of people circulating through programs is likely to increase in the future. Education, especially higher education, is a profitable market, and the concept of the "knowledge economy" is now central for the national, regional and global economic strategies of countries and organizations. Governments, private institutions and international organizations will continue to send their members abroad to learn new knowledge and skills, and by the same token will try to attract those with the desired expertise to their higher education institutions, laboratories or companies. This is a telling detail of the resilience of scholarships and organized exchange and the ongoing appeal of personal intercultural experience, since it could be expected that their usefulness would fade in an era of increasing digital communications and virtual technologies. The fact that the opposite has been occurring instead points to other factors beyond merely technology as being more decisive: the postcolonial turn in global power relations, causing a shift in wealth from West to East; the related rise in nationalist discourses of actors who previously had not invested in promoting their ideological and/or cultural worldview; and the fact that technology has not fundamentally shifted the driving forces behind the scholarship experience: "while digital technology and the opportunities for progress and access it provides are not doubted, the experiential values of international education remain at the heart of individuals' aspirations to learn and grow. Technology is a tool as important as people make it."[1]

The third important novelty in the history of scholarship programs seems to have been introduced by the Erasmus program, the principles and organization of which are profoundly different from the majority of other scholarships. Erasmus is used as an additional component of the EU's economic strategy coordinated by the European Commission, and it is employed "internally" as a means to strengthen ties between European countries and to develop a sense of belonging to a common entity called Europe, especially among the youth. The EU therefore employs novel principles that differ both from the traditional power politics that have guided the scholarship policies of nation-states and from the internationalism introduced by international organizations and philanthropies in the 1910s. Whether this starts a new trend in the history of scholarship programs will have to be assessed in future research.

Looking ahead, what factors will affect the future development of scholarships at the global level? One factor to watch will be both the policies and continuing appeal of the United States as a center of global learning. Public diplomacy in the United States has always been a site of contestation between competing interest groups, with the role of the state in promoting American culture and society abroad generating opposition from those who want it left wholly to the private sector. Negative perceptions of the United States among global publics have also dented American assumptions of predominance, with the Vietnam War and the War on Terror being pivotal moments.[2] The number of international students studying in the United States almost doubled in the 2005–16 period, from 564,000 to just over one million.[3] Yet the numbers of Americans studying abroad has stagnated. In 2005 a Senate commission recommended aiming for one million Americans abroad by 2017, and the lack of "global literacy" among American students was recognized as a "national liability" and a serious deficiency for "the defense of United States interests, [and] the effective management of global issues." President Obama called for "100,000 strong in the Americas" as part of an effort to send more US students to Latin America. Despite these concerns, the global figure remains at around 300,000.[4] As the chapters by Lonnie R. Johnson and Patricia L. Rosenfield have demonstrated, the structural pillars of the growth of the United States as a powerhouse of intellectual exchange in the twentieth century have been undermined by market mechanisms and a polarizing political culture. This does not mean that the United States is departing from the scene or that its wide appeal as a scholarship destination is disappearing (far from it, as the figures above testify), since its structural advantages (in terms of intellectual centers of excellence, training and technological development) will continue. However, it *does* mean that the infrastructure on which the United States built its leading position in the past is changing radically, and also quite rapidly, with uncertain long-term consequences for the position of the United States in global knowledge networks. But even this needs to be clarified, since while US academic scholarships may be declining in importance in a global context, the importance of its military training programs remain unparalleled in importance for many of its allies. The diversity of types of scholarship programs prevents a simple set of conclusions being drawn.

Nevertheless, signs of what the shifting position of the United States may mean can be found in recent think-tank reports covering international education. The OECD projects a total international student population of eight million by 2025, and the US share of that figure will inevitably decline (it was a mere 16 percent in 2012). The shift in wealth and higher education investment can be seen in the types of international students at American colleges and universities: Chinese students represented 31.5 percent of the total in 2015–16, but they are increasingly undergraduates looking for a prestigious US destination, while graduate students are actually staying at home due to the greatly improved quality and facilities of their own national institutions. The rise of middle classes in many emerging economies is translating into new circuits of regional exchange that no longer necessarily involve the United States as a global hub, as has occurred in Latin America and the Asia-Pacific.[5] China, with over 300 universities of its own, hosted 328,000 international students in 2012, a trend fueled by the low cost of living, multiple scholarship opportunities and the chance to experience the society of a rising global power at first hand. As one report has wisely put it, "this is a wake-up call to any university that might rest on their laurels expecting students to flock to them based upon previous assumptions."[6]

Of course, predicting future trends places one at the mercy of unexpected political developments, security concerns and erratic economic shifts, but the outlines for a twenty-first-century geography of global scholarship mobility are already coming into focus. The trends identified from the previous century will continue to shape the scholarship landscape, with unilateral, nationalist, power political interests coexisting with more globalized, transnational, market-orientated impulses. As this book has shown in detail, the history of scholarships since the late nineteenth century is one of both change and continuity. Nevertheless, it may be that the consolidated impact of global power shifts and regional economic developments since the 1990s will have dramatic influences on this field of activity, bringing volatility to the scholarship market and more uncertainty for those centers of interchange that benefited from the "long twentieth century" of Euro-American dominance.

Notes

1. Elizabeth Shepherd, "Megatrends: Predicting the Future of International Education," *IIE Networker* (Fall 2013), 13.
2. See Giles Scott-Smith, "Soft Power in an Era of US Decline," in Inderjeet Parmar and Michael Cox (eds), *Soft Power and US Foreign Policy: Theoretical, Historical and Contemporary Perspectives* (London: Routledge, 2010), 165–81; Hallvard Notaker, Giles Scott-Smith, and David Snyder (eds), *Reasserting America in the 1970s: US Public Diplomacy and the Rebuilding of America's Image Abroad* (New York: Berghahn Books, 2016); Kathy Fitzpatrick, *The Future of US Public Diplomacy: An Uncertain Fate* (Leiden: Brill, 2009).
3. See the Institute of International Education website at http://www.iie.org/Services/Project-Atlas/United-States/International-Students-In-US#.WK739rF7Hq0, retrieved 21 February 2017.
4. "Title V—Study Abroad," *Congressional Record*, V. 153, Pt. 7, 18 April 2007 to 26 April 2007, 9640; "International Education: What Place in US Public Diplomacy?" United States Institute of Peace, 14 November 2016, retrieved 8 April 2017 from http://www.usip.org/events/international-education-what-place-us-diplomacy; "Mexico's Higher Education Sector Eyeing Expansion," *ICEF Monitor*, 23 July 2013, retrieved 8 April 2017 from http://monitor.icef.com/2013/07/mexicos-higher-education-sector-eyeing-expansion.
5. "Four Trends that are Shaping the Future of Global Student Mobility," *ICEF Monitor*, 2 September 2015, retrieved 8 April 2017 from http://monitor.icef.com/2015/09/four-trends-that-are-shaping-the-future-of-global-student-mobility.
6. *Megatrends: Predicting the Future of International Education*, British Council, November 2013, 12.

References

Fitzpatrick, Kathy. *The Future of US Public Diplomacy: An Uncertain Fate* (Leiden: Brill, 2009).
Notaker, Hallvard, Giles Scott-Smith, and David Snyder (eds). *Reasserting America in the 1970s: US Public Diplomacy and the Rebuilding of America's Image Abroad* (New York: Berghahn Books, 2016).
Scott-Smith, Giles. "Soft Power in an Era of US Decline," in Inderjeet Parmar and Michael Cox (eds), *Soft Power and US Foreign Policy: Theoretical, Historical and Contemporary Perspectives* (London: Routledge, 2010), 165–81.

Selected Bibliography

Research on scholarship programs is an emerging field characterized by a small number of general studies and a focus on a handful of (predominantly US) programs. This reflects both the number and size of US programs created since the 1920s and the availability of archives. The organization of this bibliography into "US Programs" and "Non-US Programs" is thus a reflection of the state of the art in the field rather than a scientific choice. Researchers will find additional references in the introduction and chapters of this book. This bibliography does not claim to be comprehensive; it represents an overview of the most relevant works in the view of the editors.

General Studies on Scholarship Programs and Academic Mobility

Ackers, Louise. "Scientific Migration within the EU," *Innovation: The European Journal of Social Science Research* 18 (2005): 275–76.

Blumenthal, Peggy, Craufurd Goodwin, Alan Smith and Ulrich Teichler. *Academic Mobility in a Changing World: Regional and Global Trends* (London: Jessica Kingsley, 1996).

Frank, David John, and John W. Meyer. "Worldwide Expansion and Change in the University," in Georg Krücken, Anna Kosmützky and Mark Torka (eds), *Towards a Multiversity? Universities between Global Trends and National Traditions* (New York: Transaction Publishers, 2007), 19–44.

Gürüz, K. *Higher Education and International Student Mobility in the Global Knowledge Economy* (Albany, NY: State University of New York Press, 2008).

Holloway, Sarah, and Jöns Heike. "Geographies of Education and Learning," *Transactions of the Institute of British Geographers* 37 (2012): 482–88.

Jöns, Heike. "Brain Circulation and Transnational Knowledge Networks: Studying Long-term Effects of Academic Mobility to Germany, 1954–2000," *Global Networks* 9 (2009): 315–38.

Karady, Victor. "Student Mobility and Western Universities: Patterns of Unequal Exchange in the European Academic Market (1880–1939)," in C. Charle, J. Schriewer and P. Wagner (eds), *Transnational Intellectual Networks: Forms of Academic Knowledge and the Search for Cultural Identities* (Frankfurt am Main: Campus, 2004), 361–400.

Kévonian, Dzovinar, and Guillaume Tronchet (eds). *La Babel étudiante. La Cité internationale universitaire de Paris (1920–1950)* (Rennes: Presses universitaires de Rennes, 2013).

Meyer, Jean-Baptiste, David Kaplan and Jorge Charum. "Nomadisme des scientifiques et nouvelles géopolitiques du savoir," *Revue internationale des sciences sociales* 168 (2001): 314–54.
Twonmbly, Susan, Mark Salisbury, Shannon Tumanut and Paul Klute. "Study Abroad in a New Global Century: Renewing the Purpose, Refining the Purpose," *ASHE Higher Education Report* 38 (2012).
Wilson, Iain. *Manufacturing Sympathy? Exchange Programmes and Political Influence* (London: Palgrave Macmillan, 2014).

US Programs

General Books and Articles

Arndt, Richard T. *The First Resort of Kings: American Cultural Diplomacy in the Twentieth Century* (Washington, DC: Potomac Books, 2005).
Atkinson, Carol. "Does Soft Power Matter? A Comparative Analysis of Student Exchange Programs 1980–2006," *Foreign Policy Analysis* 6 (2010): 1–22.
———. *Military Soft Power: Public Diplomacy through Military Educational Exchange Programs* (Lanham, MD: Rowman & Littlefield, 2014).
Brewster Smith, M. "Evaluation of Exchange of Persons," *International Social Science Bulletin* 7 (1955): 387–97.
Bu, Liping. *Making the World Like Us: Education, Cultural Expansion, and the American Century* (New York: Praeger, 2003).
Byrnes, Robert F. *Soviet-American Academic Exchanges 1958–1975* (Bloomington, IN: Indiana University Press, 1976).
Espinosa, J.M. *Inter-American Beginnings of US Cultural Diplomacy, 1936–1948* (Washington, DC: Department of State, 1976).
Kassof, Allen. "Scholarly Exchanges and the Collapse of Communism," *Soviet and Post-Soviet Review* 22 (1995): 263–74.
Kramer, Paul. "Is the World Our Campus? International Students and US Global Power in the Long Twentieth Century," *Diplomatic History* 5 (2009): 775–806.
Lane-Toomey, Cara K., and Shannon R. Lane. "US Students Study Abroad in the Middle East/North Africa: Factors Influencing Growing Numbers," *Journal of Studies in International Education* 17(4) (2013): 308–31.
Loayza, Matt. "'A Curative and Creative Force': The Exchange of Persons Program and Eisenhower's Inter-American Policies, 1953–1961," *Diplomatic History* 37(5) (2013): 946–70.
Miller, H. "US Government Programs of International Exchange: 1952," *Educational Record* 34 (1953): 313–326.
Ninkovich, Frank A. *The Diplomacy of Ideas: US Foreign Policy and Cultural Relations 1938–1950* (Cambridge: Cambridge University Press, 1981).
Richmond, Y. *US-Soviet Cultural Exchanges 1958–1986: Who Wins?* (Boulder, CO: Westview Press, 1987).
———. *Cultural Exchange and the Cold War: Raising the Iron Curtain* (University Park, PA: Pennsylvania State University Press, 2003).

Riegel, O. "Residual Effects of Exchange of Persons," *Public Opinion Quarterly* 17(3) (1953): 319–27.
Scott-Smith, Giles. "The Ties that Bind: Dutch-American Relations, US Public Diplomacy, and the Promotion of American Studies since WW II," *The Hague Journal of Diplomacy* 2 (2007): 283–305.
——. "Mapping the Undefinable: Some Thoughts on the Relevance of Exchange Programs within International Relations Theory," *Annals of the American Academy of Political and Social Science* 616 (2008): 173–95.
——. "Exchange Programs and Public Diplomacy," in N. Snow and P. Taylor (eds), *The Routledge Handbook of Public Diplomacy* (London: Routledge, 2008), 50–56.
——. "Searching for the Successor Generations: Exchange Programs, Networks of Influence, and US Foreign Policy towards Western Europe in the 1980s," in Ken Osgood and Brian Etheridge (eds), *The United States and Public Diplomacy: New Directions in Cultural and International History* (Leiden: Brill, 2010), 345–70.
——. "Cultural Exchange and the Corporate Sector: Moving beyond Statist Public Diplomacy?" *Austrian Journal of Political Science* 3 (2011): 301–13.
——. "The Heineken Factor? Using Exchanges to Extend the Reach of US Soft Power," *American Diplomacy* (June 2011), retrieved 8 April 2017 from http://www.unc.edu/depts/diplomat/item/2011/0104/comm/scottsmith_heineken.html.
Walton, Whitney. "Internationalism and the Junior Year Abroad: American Students in France in the 1920s and 1930s," *Diplomatic History* 29 (2005): 255–78.
Wilson, E., and F. Bonila. "Evaluating Exchange of Persons Programs," *Public Opinion Quarterly* 19 (1955): 20–30.

The US State Department's Foreign Leader/International Visitor Program

Elder, R. *The Foreign Leader Program: Operations in the United States* (Washington, DC: Brookings Institution, 1961).
Jachec, Nancy. "Transatlantic Cultural Politics in the Late 1950s: The Leaders and Specialists Program," *Art History* 26 (2003): 533–55.
Kellermann, Henry J. *Cultural Relations as an Instrument of US Foreign Policy: The Educational Exchange Program between the United States and Germany, 1945–1954* (Washington, DC: Department of State, 1978).
Scott-Smith, Giles. "Her Rather Ambitious Washington Program: Margaret Thatcher's International Visitor Program Visit to the United States in 1967," *Contemporary British History* 17 (2003): 65–86.
——. "Searching for the Successor Generation: Public Diplomacy, the US Embassy's International Visitor Program and the Labour Party in the 1980s," *British Journal of Politics and International Relations* 8 (2006): 214–37.
——. "The US State Department's Foreign Leader Program in France during the Early Cold War," *Revue Française d'Etudes Américaines* 107 (2006): 47–60.
——. "The Export of an American Concept of Leadership: The World as seen through the US Department of State's Foreign Leader Program," in

H. Krabbendam and W. Verhoeven (eds), *Who's the Boss? Leadership and Democratic Culture in America* (Amsterdam: Free University Press, 2007), 177–86.

——. *Networks of Empire: The US State Department's Foreign Leader Program in the Netherlands, France and Britain, 1950–1970* (Brussels: Peter Lang, 2008).

——. "Mutual Interests? US Public Diplomacy in the 1980s and Nicolas Sarkozy's First Trip to the United States," *Journal of Transatlantic Studies* 9 (2011): 326–41.

——. "Still Exchanging? The History, Relevance, and Effect of International Exchange Programs," *e-International Relations* (September 2012).

The Fulbright Program

Annals of the American Academy of Political and Social Science 491 (1987), special issue on the Fulbright Program.

Arndt, Richard T., and David Lee Rubin (eds). *The Fulbright Difference, 1948–1992: Studies on Cultural Diplomacy and the Fulbright Experience* (New Brunswick, NJ: Transaction Publishers, 1993).

Bowman, John E. "Educating American Undergraduates Abroad: The Development of Study Abroad Programs by American Colleges and Universities," Council on International Educational Exchange, Occasional Papers 24 (1987).

Byrnes, Robert F. *Soviet-American Academic Exchanges, 1958–1975* (Bloomington, IN: Indiana University Press, 1976).

Commission franco-américaine d'échanges universitaires (ed.). *Dix années d'échanges Fulbright, 1949–1959* (Paris, 1960).

Dawes, N. *Two-Way Street: The Indo-American Fulbright Program, 1950–1960* (New Delhi: Asia Publishing House, 1962).

Delgado Gomez-Escalonilla, Lorenzo. *Westerly Wind: The Fulbright Program in Spain* (Madrid: LID Editorial Empresarial, 2009).

Dudden, Arthur Power, and Russell R. Dynes (eds). *The Fulbright Experience, 1946–1986: Encounters and Transformations* (New Brunswick, NJ: Transaction Publishers, 1987).

Garner, Alice, and Diane Kirby. "'Never a Machine for Propaganda?' The Australian-American Fulbright Program and Australia's Cold War," *Australian Historical Studies* 44 (2013): 117–33.

Groennings, Sven. "The Fulbright Program in the Global Knowledge Economy: The Nation's Neglected Comparative Advantage," *Journal of Studies in International Education* 1(1) (1997): 95–105.

Johnson, Walter, and Francis J. Colligan. *The Fulbright Program: A History* (Chicago, IL: Chicago University Press, 1965).

Lebovic, Sam. "From War Junk to Educational Exchange: The World War II Origins of the Fulbright Program and the Foundations of American Cultural Globalism, 1945–1950," *Diplomatic History* 37(2) (2013): 280–312.

Mendelsohn, Harold, and Frank. E. Orenstein. "A Survey of Fulbright Award Recipients: Cross-cultural Education and its Impacts," *Public Opinion Quarterly* 19 (1955): 401–7.

Mohanty, Sachidananda. *In Search of Wonder: Understanding Cultural Exchange: Fulbright Program in India* (New Delhi: Vision Books, 1997).
Rupp, J. "American Studies and the Fulbright Program: A Plea for Repoliticizing," in H. Krabbendam and J. Verheul (eds), *Through the Cultural Looking Glass: American Studies in Transcultural Perspective* (Amsterdam: Free University Press, 1999), 32–52.
——. "The Fulbright Program, or the Surplus Value of Officially Organized Academic Exchange," *Journal of Studies in International Education* 3 (1999): 59–82.
Salamone, Frank A. *The Fulbright Experience in Benin* (Williamsburg, VA: Department of Anthropology, College of William and Mary, 1994).
Scott-Smith, Giles. "The Fulbright Program in the Netherlands: An Example of Science Diplomacy," in Jeroen van Dongen (ed.), *Cold War Science and the Transatlantic Circulation of Knowledge* (Leiden: Brill, 2015), 128–54.
Sussman, Leonard R. *The Culture of Freedom: The Small World of Fulbright Scholars* (Savage, MD: Rowman & Littlefield, 1992).
Xu, Guangqiu. "The Ideological and Political Impact of US Fulbrighters on Chinese Students: 1979–1989," *Asian Affairs* 26 (1999): 139–57.

The Rockefeller Foundation

Assmus, Alexi. "The Creation of Postdoctoral Fellowships and the Siting of American Scientific Research," *Minerva* 31(2) (1993): 151–83.
Beilke, Jayne R. "The Politics of Opportunity: Philanthropic Fellowship Programs, Out-of State Aid and Black Higher Education in the South," *History of Higher Education Annual* 17 (1997): 50–71.
Bullock, Mary Brown. "A Case Study of Transnational Flows of Chinese Medical Professionals: China Medical Board and Rockefeller Foundation Fellows," in Mary Brown Bullock and Bridie Andrews (eds), *Medical Transitions in Twentieth-Century China* (Bloomington, IN: Indiana University Press, 2014), 285–96.
Coben, Stanley. "Foundation Officials and Fellowships: Innovation in the Patronage of Science," *Minerva* 14(2) (1976): 225–40.
Fleck, Christian. "Long-Term Consequences of Short-Term Fellowships," in Giuliana Gemelli (ed.), *The Unacceptables: American Foundations and Refugee Scholars between the Two World Wars and after* (Brussels: Peter Lang, 2000), 51–81.
Tournès, Ludovic. "Le réseau des boursiers Rockefeller et la recomposition des savoirs biomédicaux en France (1920–1970)," *French Historical Studies* 29(1) (2006): 77–107.
——. "La fondation Rockefeller et la naissance de l'universalisme philanthropique américain," *Critique Internationale* 35 (2007): 173–97.
——. *Sciences de l'homme et politique: les fondations philanthropiques américaines en France au XXe siècle* (Paris: Editions des classiques Garnier, 2011).

The Ford Foundation

Berghahn, Volker. *America and the Intellectual Cold Wars in Europe* (Oxford: Oxford University Press, 2001).

Czernecki, Igor. "An Intellectual Offensive: The Ford Foundation and the Destalinization of the Polish Social Sciences," *Cold War History* 13(3) (2013): 289–310.

Stensrud, Ingeborg. "'Soft Power' Deployed: Ford Foundation's Fellowship Programs in Communist Eastern Europe in the 1950s and 1960s," *Monde(s): Histoire, espaces, relations* 6(2) (special issue on Transnational Philanthropies) (2014): 111–28.

Non-US Programs

Rhodes

Kenny, Anthony J.P. (ed.). *The History of the Rhodes Trust 1902–1999* (Oxford: Oxford University Press, 2001).

Rotberg, Robert I. *The Founder: Cecil Rhodes and the Pursuit of Power* (Oxford: Oxford University Press, 1988).

Schaeper, Thomas J., and Kathleen Schaeper. *Rhodes Scholars: Oxford and the Creation of an American Elite* (Oxford: Berghahn Books, 2010).

Ziegler, Philip. *Legacy: Cecil Rhodes, the Rhodes Trust and the Rhodes Scholarships* (New Haven, CT: Yale University Press, 2008).

Erasmus

Ballatore, Magali. *Erasmus et la mobilité des jeunes européens* (Paris: PUF, 2010).

Corradi, Sofia. *Student Mobility in Higher Education. Erasmus and Erasmus Plus*, Laboratory of Lifelong Learning, Department of Education and Training, Roma Tre State University, 2015, retrieved 8 April 2017 from http://www.sofiacorradi.eu/uploads/7/8/4/2/78425292/erasmus_ingl_web.pdf.

Erlich, Valérie. *Les mobilités étudiantes* (Paris: La Documentation française, 2012).

Herrmann, R.K., and M.B. Brewer. "Identities and Institutions: Becoming European in the E.U.," in Richard K. Herrmann, Thomas Risse and Marilynn B. Brewer (eds), *Transnational Identities: Becoming European in the EU* (Lanham, MD: Rowman & Littlefield, 2004), 1–22.

Jallade, Jean-Pierre, Jean Gordon and Noëlle Lebeau. *Student Mobility within the European Union: A Statistical Analysis* (European Institute of Education and Social Policy, 1996).

Latour, Marion. *La mobilité des étudiants en Europe, les 25 ans du programme Erasmus*, (Sèvres: Centre de ressources et d'ingénierie documentaire, 2012).

Maiworm, Friedhelm, and Ulrich Teichler. *Study Abroad and Early Career: Experiences of Former ERASMUS Students*, Higher Education Policy Series 35, ERASMUS Monograph No. 21 (London: Jessica Kingsley, 1996).

Oborune, Karina. "Becoming More European after Erasmus? The Impact of the Erasmus Programme on Political and Cultural Identity," *Epiphany: Journal of Transdisciplinary Studies* 6(1) (2013): 182–202.
Papatsiba, Vassiliki. *Des étudiants européens. Erasmus et l'aventure de l'altérité* (Berne: Peter Lang, 2003).
——. "Student Mobility in Europe: An Academic, Cultural and Mental Journey? Some Conceptual Reflections and Empirical Findings," *International Perspectives on Higher Education Research* 3 (2005): 29–65.
——. "Making Higher Education More European through Student Mobility? Revisiting EU Initiatives in the Context of the Bologna Process," *Comparative Education* 42 (2006): 93–111.

Other Programs

Ahn, Song-ee. "Exchange Studies as Actor-Networks: Following Korean Exchange Students in Swedish Higher Education," *Journal of Research in International Education* 10 (2011): 46–57.
Alamgir, Alena K. "Recalcitrant Women: Internationalism and the Redefinition of Welfare Limits in the Czechoslovak-Vietnamese Labor Exchange Program," *Slavic Review* 73 (2014): 133–55.
Bergerson, Andrew Stuart. "In the Shadows of the Towers: An Ethnography of a German-Israeli Student Exchange Program," *New German Critique* 71 (1997): 141–76.
Brown, Lorraine and Gurhan Aktas. "Turkish University Students' Hopes and Fears about Travel to the West," *Journal of Research in International Education* 11 (2012): 3–18.
Daly, Amanda J. "Determinants of Participating in Australian University Student Exchange Programs," *Journal of Research in International Education* 10 (2011): 58–70.
Daly, Amanda J., and Michele C. Barker. "Australian and New Zealand University Students Participation in International Exchange Programs," *Journal of Studies in International Education* 9 (2005): 26–41.
Garneau, Stéphanie. "Les expériences migratoires différenciées d'étudiants français: De l'institutionanlisation des mobilités étudiantes à la circulations des élites professionnelles?" *Revue européenne des migrations internationales* 23 (2007): 139–61.
Impekoven, Holger. *Die Alexander von Humboldt-Stiftung und das Ausländerstudium in Deutschland 1925–1945: Von der 'geräuschlosen Propaganda' zur Ausbildung der 'geistigen Wehr' des 'Neuen Europa'* (Bonn: Bonn University Press, 2013).
Jöns, Heike, Elizabeth Mavroudi and Michael Hefferman. "Mobilising the Elective Diaspora: US-German Academic Exchanges since 1945," *Transactions: Institute of British Geographers* 40 (2015): 113–27.
Katsakioris, Constantin. "Transferts Est-Sud: Echanges éducatifs et formation de cadres africains en Union soviétique pendant les années soixante," *Outre-Mers. Revue d'histoire* 95(354–55) (Special issue on USSR and the South) (2007): 83–106.

———. "Soviet Lessons for Arab Modernization: Soviet Educational Aid towards Arab Countries after 1956," *Journal of Modern European History* 8(1) (2010): 85–105.

———. "The Soviet-South Encounter: Tensions in the Friendship with the Afro-Asian Partners, 1945–1965," in Patryk Babiracki and Kenyon Zimmer (eds), *Cold War Crossings: International Travel and Exchange across the Soviet Bloc, 1940s–1960s* (Arlington, TX: Texas University Press, 2014), 134–65.

Pietsch, Tamson. *Empire of Scholars: Universities, Networks and the British Academic World, 1850–1939* (Manchester: Manchester University Press, 2013).

Scott-Smith, Giles. "Mending the 'Unhinged Alliance' in the 1970s: Transatlantic Relations, Public Diplomacy, and the Origins of the European Union Visitors Program," *Diplomacy and Statecraft* 16 (2005): 749–78.

Yu, Priscilla C. "Taiwan's International Exchange Program: A Study in Cultural Diplomacy," *Asian Affairs* 12 (1985): 23–45.

Unpublished Works

Alrutz, L. "The Foreign Leader Exchange Program and Africa South of the Sahara," MA thesis (Washington, DC: American University, 1968).

Bu, L. "Foreign Students and the Emergence of Modern International Education in the United States, 1910–1970," Ph.D. dissertation (Pittsburgh, PA: Carnegie Mellon University, 1995).

Duggan, S. "The Politics of US-German Educational Exchange: Perspectives of German Decision-Makers," Ph.D. dissertation (Stanford, CA: Stanford University, 1988).

Halpern, S. "The Institute of International Education: A History," Ph.D. dissertation (New York: Columbia University, 1969).

Higgin, H. "Disseminating American Ideals in Africa, 1949–1969," Ph.D. dissertation (Cambridge: University of Cambridge, 2014).

Johnston, H.W. "United States Public Affairs Activities in Germany, 1945–1955," Ph.D. dissertation (New York: Columbia University, 1956).

Ketzel, C. "Exchange of Persons and American Foreign Policy: The Foreign Leader Program of the Department of State," Ph.D. dissertation (Berkeley, CA: University of California, 1955).

Kim, Y.H. "Public Diplomacy and Cultural Communication: The International Visitor Program," Ph.D. dissertation (Los Angeles, CA: University of Southern California, 1990).

König, T. "Das Fulbright in Wien: Wissenschaftspolitik und Sozialwissenschaften am 'versunkenen Kontinent,'" Ph.D. dissertation (Vienna: University of Vienna, 2008).

Konta, C. "Waging Public Diplomacy: The United States and the Yugoslav Experiment 1950–1972," Ph.D. dissertation (Trieste: University of Trieste, 2016).

Mahin, D. "History of the US Department of State's International Visitor Program," draft manuscript for the History Project, Bureau of Educational and Cultural Affairs, US Department of State, 1973.

Mikhailova, L. "The History of CIEE: Council of International Educational Exchange and its Role in International Education Development, 1947–2002," Ph.D. dissertation (Minneapolis, MN: University of Minnesota, 2003).

Mueller Norton, S. "The United States Department of State International Visitor Program: A Conceptual Framework for Evaluation," Ph.D. dissertation (Medford, MA: Tufts University, 1977).

Schmidt, O. "Civil Empire by Cooptation: German-American Exchange Programs as Cultural Diplomacy, 1945–61," Ph.D. dissertation (Cambridge, MA: Harvard University, 1999).

 Web Resources

This section provides a selection of resources for professors and students for use in undergraduate or graduate research seminars. It does not provide information on archives (this can be found in the chapter notes, where other web resources are also listed).

Historical Documents

Cecil Rhodes' will:
http://files.rhodesscholarshiptrust.com/governancedocs/WillandCodicils.pdf
Other documents on the Rhodes Trust:
http://www.rhodeshouse.ox.ac.uk/rhodes-trust/key-governance-documents
Fulbright Amendment to the Surplus Property Act of 1944 (Public Law 584, 1946):
   https://babel.hathitrust.org/cgi/pt?id=mdp.39015030796620;view=1up; seq=43
United States Informational and Educational Exchange Act, 1948 (Smith-Mundt Act):
   http://www.state.gov/documents/organization/177574.pdf
Mutual Educational and Cultural Exchange Act, 1961 (Fulbright-Hays Act):
   https://www2.ed.gov/about/offices/list/ope/iegps/fulbrighthaysact.pdf

Maps and Statistics

Humboldt Stiftung scholarship program (since 1953): statistics
https://www.humboldt-foundation.de/web/statistics.html
UNESCO Institute for Statistics, Global Flow of Tertiary-Level Students:
http://http://uis.unesco.org/en/uis-student-flow
Statistics and reports on the Erasmus program since 2004:
http://ec.europa.eu/education/tools/statistics_en.htm

Annual Reports

Rockefeller Foundation (since 1914):
https://www.rockefellerfoundation.org/about-us/governance-reports/annual-reports

Ford Foundation (since 1951):
https://www.fordfoundation.org/library/?filter=Annual%20Report
Fulbright Program (since 2004):
https://eca.state.gov/fulbright/about-fulbright/j-william-fulbright-foreign-scholarship-board-ffsb/ffsb-reports
Institute of International Education (since 1919)
https://www.iie.org/en/Why-IIE/Annual-Report

Directories of Scholars

Commonwealth Fund Harkness Fellowships:
1925–97:
http://www.commonwealthfund.org/grants-and-fellowships/fellowships/harkness-fellowships/harkness-fellowship-alumni
Since 1997:
http://www.commonwealthfund.org/grants-and-fellowships/fellowships/harkness-fellowships/harkness-fellows#/sort=@fdate63677%20descending
Fulbright Scholar Directory:
1948–98: http://libinfo.uark.edu/SpecialCollections/FulbrightDirectories
2006–10: http://www.cies.org/fulbright-scholar-list-archive
Since 2010: http://www.cies.org/fulbright-scholars
John Simon Guggenheim Foundation:
http://www.gf.org/fellows/all-fellows
Rhodes Scholars: complete list, 1903–2014:
http://www.rhodeshouse.ox.ac.uk/about/rhodes-scholars/rhodes-scholars-complete-list

Reports and Other Documents

Bonnet, Annick. *La mobilité étudiante Erasmus,* report for the Agence Europe Education Formation France, 2012:
http://www.agence-erasmus.fr/docs/mobilite-Erasmus-CIEP.pdf
Rotem, Ari, Michael A. Zinovieff and Alexandre Goubarev. "A Framework for Evaluating the United Nations Fellowship Programs," *Human Resources for Health* 8 (2010):
http://human-resources-health.biomedcentral.com/articles/10.1186/1478-4491-8-7

Institutional Homepages of Key Scholarship Programs

Congress-Bundestag Youth Exchange (Germany):
http://www.usagermanyscholarship.org/
Ford Foundation International Fellowships Program, 2001–13 (United States):
http://fordifp.net/Home.aspx

Confucius Institutes scholarships (China):
http://english.hanban.org/jxjen.htm
EU Visitors Program:
http://europa.eu/euvp/en
International Visitor Leadership Program (United States):
https://eca.state.gov/ivlp
JET Programme (Japan):
http://jetprogramme.org/en/
NATO Defense College Fellowship Program:
http://www.ndc.nato.int/research/research.php?icode=4
Technical and Economic Cooperation Program (India):
http://itec.mea.gov.in/?1320?000
UNESCO:
http://www.unesco.org/new/en/fellowships/programmes
United Nations Department of Economic and Social Affairs:
https://esa.un.org/techcoop/fellowships
World Health Organization:
http://www.who.int/hrh/education/fellowships/en

 Index

African Scholarship Program of American Universities (ASPAU), 220
Alliance française, 52, 310, 312
American Council of Learned Societies (ACLS), 231, 234, 247, 252
Annan, Kofi, 221, 222
Association of Universities of the British Commonwealth (AUBC), 65, 66, 68, 70, 71, 72, 74, 75
Atlantic Charter, 158
Autour du Monde Scholarship Program, 13, 54
Azikiwe, Chukwuma, 219–220

Barroso, Jose Manuel, 19
Bartholdy, Albrecht Mendelssohn, 119
Beard, Mary, 135
Belorussian Polytechnical Institute (BPI), 207–208
Belorussian State University (BGU), 204–205, 209, 211, 212
Blair, Tony, 3
Board of Foreign Scholarships, 176, 177, 178
British Council, 68–69, 70, 71, 73, 74, 75, 310, 312
Bundy, McGeorge, 220, 249, 250
Bush, George W., 181
Butler, Harold, 158

Canada Council, 72
Carballo de Mendoza, Fresia, 166
Carnegie Corporation of New York (CCNY), 11, 247–257

Carnegie Endowment for International Peace, 13
China Foundation for the Promotion of Education and Culture, 15
Cilento, Ralph, 159–160
Clavin, Patricia, 5
Clinton, Willam Jefferson ("Bill"), 35, 180, 181
Cold War, 9–10, 15–17, 137, 159, 173–175, 180, 189, 241, 318, 324
Commission for the Prevention of Tuberculosis in France, 128
Commission for the Relief in Belgium Educational Foundation, 15
Commonwealth Fellowships (Harkness), 76
Commonwealth Relations Office (CRO), 67, 69, 74
Commonwealth Scholarship and Fellowship Plan (CFSP), 65, 75
Commonwealth University Interchange Scheme (CUIS), 12, 65–75
Confucius Institutes, 18, 310–314
Congress-Bundestag Youth Exchange Program (CBYX), 12, 79–88
Council for International Exchange of Scholars (CIES), 276
Crowell, Elisabeth, 128–130, 131, 134, 136
Cull, Nicholas J., 3

David-Weill, David, 58
Davis, William M., 55
Day, Edmund E., 118
Deák, István, 238, 239, 240

Deutsch de la Meurthe, Emile, 58
Deutsche Forschungsgemeinschaft, 121
Diehl, Charles, 55
Dulles, John Foster, 283

Eagleburger, Lawrence, 82
Einaudi, Luigi, 119
Eisenhower, Dwight D., 195, 219, 222
Embree, Edwin, 129, 136
Erasmus Program, 18, 306–310, 325
Exhibition scholarships, 37

Falnes, Oscar J., 145
Fehling, August Wilhelm, 113, 114, 117, 118, 119, 120, 121
Fleck, Christian, 117
Flügge, Eva, 116, 118, 122
Fondation pour une Entraide Intellectuelle Européenne, 16
Food and Agriculture Organization (FAO), 140, 147
Ford Foundation, 190, 232, 248, 249–251, 255
Foreign Leader Program, 3, 15, 174
French-Serbian Academic Exchange Agreement, (1916) 60–61
Fulbright Program, 3, 9, 15, 16, 17, 18, 67, 173–183, 236, 276–286
Fulbright, J. William, 3, 173, 179

Gallois, Henry, 164
Gates Cambridge Scholarship Program, 256
Gatheru, R. Mugo, 218
Glass, Philip, 3
Globalization, 17–19, 324
Gordon-Walker, Patrick, 67
Gregorian, Vartan, 252
Guggenheim, Murry, 58

Hamm-Brücher, Hildegard, 82, 86, 89
Harnack, Arvin R., 116
Hawke, Bob, 35
Heiser, Victor, 143
Hetherington, Sir Hector, 66–68, 75–76

Huizinga, Johan, 119
Humboldt Stiftung, 12

Imperial networks, 10–12
Indian Council for Cultural Relations (ICCR), 314–315
Information and Educational Exchange Act (Smith–Mundt), 174, 176
Institute of International Education (IIE), 11, 15, 57, 247, 251, 255, 256, 257
Institute on East Central Europe, Columbia University (IECE), 238
Interdekanat, 207
International Farm Youth Exchange (IFYE), 188–197
International Institute for Labor Studies (IILS), 165
International Institute of Intellectual Cooperation (IIIC), 57
International Labor Organization, 14, 156–165, 315
International League of Red Cross Societies, 135, 136
International Military Education and Training (IMET), 264
International Olympic Committee (IOC), 99, 105
Internationalism, 12–15, 57, 164
Inter-University Committee on Travel Grants (IUCTG), 231, 233
IREX Program, 16, 231–241

Japan Exchange and Teaching Program (JET), 290–299
Johnson, Lyndon B., 179, 249
Junta para Ampliacion de estudios e investigaciones scientificas (1907), 55

Kahn, Albert, 13, 54
Kassof, Allen H., 231, 234, 235, 241–242
Kenya Distributive and Commercial Workers' Union, 164

Kennedy, John F., 217, 219, 249
Kennedy, Robert, 249
Keynes, John Maynard, 189
Khrushchev, Nikita, 197
Kohl, Helmut, 82, 87
Komsomol, 206
Kuczynski, Jürgen, 118

Lady Tata Memorial Trust, 317
Laura Spelman Rockefeller Memorial, 101, 113–121, 127–137
League of Nations, 14, 145, 158
League of Nations Health Organization, 144
Lee Hysan Foundation, 40–41
Lincoln University, 219, 221–222
Loerke, Martha, 255, 256
Lund, Kristin, 268, 273

Maathai, Wangari Muta, 222
Manile General Hospital, 131
Manley, Norman, 35
Marciniak, Bronislaw, 183–184
Marjolin, Robert, 1
Marshall Plan, 10, 189, 316
MasterCard Foundation Scholars Program, 256
Mercer University, 223–225
Merkel, Angela, 88
Monod, Jacques, 3
Morse, David, 159, 161
Mutual Educational and Cultural Exchange Act (Fulbright–Hays), 178–179
Myrdal, Gunnar, 3, 226

Nakasone, Yasuhiro, 292–293, 296
Nanxiang, Jiang, 282
National Association for the Advancement of Colored People (NAACP), 218–219
National Defense University (US), 266–267, 271
National Endowment for the Humanities, (NEH) 233
Nkrumah, Kwame, 219

North Atlantic Treaty Organization (NATO), 80, 84, 263
Notgemeinschaft der Deutschen Wissenschaft, 115, 116, 121

Office national des universités et écoles françaises (ONUEF), 54–56, 57, 59
Office of Chinese Language Council International (Hanban), 310–314
Office of Foreign Asset Control (Treasury Dept), 254–255
Oni, Sam, 223–225
Open Society Foundation (OSF), 255, 256
Organisation for Economic Cooperation and Development (OECD), 326
Oxford Summer Meetings, 53

Peking Union Medical College, 131
People's Friendship (Lumumba) University, 16, 211, 217
People to People Program, 222
Pifer, Alan, 251
Predöhl, Andreas, 116

Ránki, György, 238–239, 240
Ratan Tata Foundation, 316, 317
Reagan, Ronald, 80, 83, 87, 180, 293
Rhodes, Cecil John, 33–34, 35, 36, 38
Rhodes Scholarships, 2, 3, 11, 33–49
Rhodes Trust, 38, 41, 115
Rockefeller, John D., 58, 101, 103, 158
Rockefeller Foundation, 1, 11, 13, 101, 158, 248, 255, 312, 316
Rockefeller Foundation International Health Board, 143
Rockefeller Foundation Fellowship Program, 14, 16, 113–121, 127–137, 140–151
Romanian University Office (1923), 57
Roosevelt, Franklin D., 189

Rostow, Walt W., 3
Rusk, Dean, 3
Ruml, Beardsley, 113, 115, 121

De Sa, Derek John, 46–47
Sahhad, Wasim, 35
Sawyer, Wilbur A., 145
Schmidt, Helmut, 81
Schmidt-Ott, Friedrich, 114–115
Scholarships (definition), 2–3
Schwartzman Scholars, 256
September 11, 2001 (9/11), 17, 181–182, 248, 253, 325
Servan-Schreiber, Jean–Jacques, 3
Shouyi, Dong, 108
Social Science Research Council, 11, 247, 252, 255
Solana, Javier, 3
Soni, K.K., 164, 165
Stipetic, Katarina, 137–138
'Successor generation', 80–81, 88

Tata Endowment for Higher Education, 316
Technical and Economic Cooperation Programme (India), 4, 316
Thatcher, Margaret, 3
Thomas, Albert, 158
Tiananmen Square protests, 18, 283, 313
Treiber, Rik, 252, 254
Truman, Harry S., 174, 219
Turner, John, 35

United Nations, Division of Social Affairs, 159
United Nations, Expanded Program of Technical Assistance, 156, 160
United Nations Development Program, 315

United Nations Educational, Scientific and Cultural Organization (UNESCO), 14, 140, 147, 161
United Nations International Children's Emergency Fund (UNICEF), 140, 147
United Nations Relief and Rehabilitation Administration (UNRRA), 14, 16, 140, 141, 142, 144, 145, 146, 147, 148, 150, 159
United States Agency for International Development (USAID), 196
United States Information Agency (USIA), 174, 175, 179, 180, 181, 191, 233, 236
Universities Bureau of the British Empire (1912), 55, 65, 66
US Army Command and General Staff College (CGSC), 267–268
US Naval War College, 269

Vincent, George E., 129
Vossler, Otto, 116

Weidenfeld, Werner, 86
Wilson, Woodrow, 56
World Alliance of YMCAs, 13
World Bank, 315
World Health Organization (WHO), 14, 136, 140, 141, 142, 144, 145, 147, 148, 149, 150, 151

Xiaoping, Deng, 18, 282

Yoshida, Shigeru, 291
Young Men's Christian Association (YMCA), 13, 16, 97–106
Youth Leadership Initiatives, 182
Yudhoyono, Susilo Bambang, 268

www.ingramcontent.com/pod-product-compliance
Lightning Source LLC
Chambersburg PA
CBHW072045110526
44590CB00018B/3038